# WELFARE REFORM AND SOCIAL INVESTMENT POLICY IN EUROPE AND EAST ASIA

# Also available in the
# Research in Comparative and Global Social Policy series

### Welfare, Populism and Welfare Chauvinism
By **Bent Greve**

*"This important book sets out to tackle the welfare–populism nexus and convincingly shows that the new divisions in our societies instigate welfare chauvinism."*
**Steffen Mau**, Humboldt University of Berlin

PB £26.99 ISBN 9781447350446
HB £75.00 ISBN 9781447350439
168 pages December 2020

### Minimum Income Standards and Reference Budgets
International and Comparative Policy Perspectives
Edited by **Christopher Deeming**

*"The volume offers a rich, historically and culturally grounded international menu of perspectives on an important social policy approach, with lessons for both research and policy at a time of growing economic insecurity."*
**Baroness Ruth Lister**, Loughborough University

HB £75.00 ISBN 9781447352952
272 pages May 2020

### Local Policies and the European Social Fund
Employment Policies Across Europe
By **Katharina Zimmermann**

*"Moving beyond the methodological nationalism that has characterised most of the existing literature, this innovative study offers a fresh perspective on the variegated influence of European integration on social policy."*
**Daniel Clegg**, University of Edinburgh

HB £75.00 ISBN 9781447346517
224 pages October 2019

### The Moral Economy of Activation
Ideas, Politics and Policies
By **Magnus Paulsen Hansen**

*"In this well researched and theoretically sophisticated book, Magnus Hansen sheds new and important light on the moral economy of activation."*
**Daniel Béland**, McGill University

HB £75.00 ISBN 9781447349969
250 pages September 2019

For more information about the series visit
**bristoluniversitypress.co.uk/**
**research-in-comparative-and-global-social-policy**

# WELFARE REFORM AND SOCIAL INVESTMENT POLICY IN EUROPE AND EAST ASIA

## International Lessons and Policy Implications

Edited by
Young Jun Choi, Timo Fleckenstein
and Soohyun Christine Lee

First published in Great Britain in 2021 by

Policy Press, an imprint of
Bristol University Press
University of Bristol
1-9 Old Park Hill
Bristol
BS2 8BB
UK
t: +44 (0)117 954 5940
e: bup-info@bristol.ac.uk

Details of international sales and distribution partners are available at
policy.bristoluniversitypress.co.uk

British Library Cataloguing in Publication Data
A catalogue record for this book is available from the British Library

ISBN 978-1-4473-5273-0 hardcover
ISBN 978-1-4473-5276-1 ePub
ISBN 978-1-4473-5275-4 ePdf

Cover design: Andrew Corbett

Bristol University Press and Policy Press use environmentally responsible
print partners.

Printed in Great Britain by CPI Group (UK) Ltd, Croydon, CR0 4YY

FSC
www.fsc.org
MIX
Paper from
responsible sources
FSC® C013604

# Contents

# List of figures and tables

## Figures

## Tables

# Notes on contributors

**Mi Young An** is a Professor in the Department of Public Administration at Kookmin University, South Korea. Her main research focuses on family, gender, division of paid and unpaid work, income inequality, social policy and comparative studies. Her works have appeared in *Social Policy & Administration* and *Social Policy & Society* among others. Email: myan@kookmin.ac.kr

**Ga Woon Ban** is the Head of Centre for Social Policy at Korea Research Institute for Vocational Education & Training. His research interests are social policy and innovation of human capital, skills and labour market and international comparative study of adult competencies. Email: gwban@krivet.re.kr

**Hyejin Choi** is Associate Research Fellow in the Institute for Health and Social Affairs. Her research examines the care policy in Korea and other European countries with a particular focus on vulnerable and disadvantaged populations. Her work appeared in the INQUIRY. Email: choihj@kihasa.re.kr

**Young Jun Choi** is a Professor in the Department of Public Administration, Yonsei University. His research interests include aging and public policy, social investment policy, comparative welfare states and comparative methods. His research has been published in international journals including *Journal of European Social Policy*, *International Journal of Social Welfare*, *Ageing and Society* and *Government and Opposition*. Email: sspyjc@yonsei.ac.kr

**Niccolo Durazzi** is Lecturer in Political Economy of Social Policy at the University of Edinburgh. His research examines the transition to the knowledge economy of Western European and East Asian advanced capitalist democracies with a particular focus on labour market, education and training policy. His work appeared, among others, in the *Journal of European Public Policy*, *Socio-Economic Review* and *Politics & Society*. Email: niccolo.durazzi@ed.ac.uk

**Sonia Exley** is an Associate Professor in the Department of Social Policy at the London School of Economics and Political Science. Sonia's specialist area of research is education policy. She has a particular interest in the marketisation and privatisation of education systems across the world and the implications that such developments may have for disadvantaged groups. Sonia is Deputy Editor of the *Journal of Education Policy* and her work has been published in a range of journals including *Comparative Education* and the *Journal of Social Policy*. Email: s.exley@lse.ac.uk

**Timo Fleckenstein** is an Associate Professor in the Department of Social Policy at the London School of Economics and Political Science. His research focuses on labour market, family and education policies with a particular interest in the comparison of Europe and East Asia. Timo's work has been published in *World Politics*, *Comparative Political Studies* and *Journal of European Social Policy*, among others. Email: t.fleckenstein@lse.ac.uk

**Ijin Hong** is an Associate Professor at the School of Government, Sun Yat-sen University, P.R. China. She majored in Sociology and Political Institutions (La Sapienza University in Rome) and in Social Welfare (Yonsei University, Seoul). Her work has been published in several journals such as *Social Policy and Administration*, *Journal of Comparative Policy Analysis*, *Political Quarterly*, *Stato e Mercato* and *Korean Journal of Social Policy*. In 2017, she joined the East Asian Social Policy Network (EASP) as a member of the organising committee. Email: hongyzh5@mail.sysu.edu.cn

**Yun Young Kim** is an Assistant Professor in the Department of Social Welfare at the Jeonbuk National University, South Korea. After achieving his PhD from the University of Bristol, he worked for Korea Institute for Health and Social Affairs. His research interests are comparative social policy, social services, public policy and macro quantitative methods. His research has been published in *Policy & Society*, *Sustainability*, *Disaster Prevention and Management*, *Korean Comparative Government Review* and *Healthcare*. Email: yun2050@jbnu.ac.kr

**Jieun Lee** was recently awarded her PhD by the Department of Social Policy and Social Work at the University of York, UK. Before undertaking her PhD, she worked for the National Pension Research Institute in South Korea. Her research interests lie in pensions, family policy, social investment, poverty and inequality in comparative perspective. Currently, she is based in Stuttgart, Germany and is working as an independent researcher. Email: jieunlee0213@gmail.com

**Jooha Lee** is a Professor in the Department of Public Administration, Dongguk University, South Korea. His main research interests are comparative social policy, welfare politics, governance and policy implementation. He is co-author of *The Korean State and Social Policy* and his work has been published in international journals, including *Policy Sciences*, *Voluntas*, *Policy Studies*, *International Review of Administrative Sciences*, *Journal of Democracy* and *International Journal of Social Welfare*. Email: leejooha@dongguk.edu

**Soohyun Christine Lee** is Korea Foundation Senior Lecturer (Associate Professor) in Korean & East Asian Political Economy in the Department of European and International Studies, King's College London. Dr Lee's research interests lie in the comparative political economy of welfare states with a regional focus on East Asia and Europe. Looking at how countries in the two different regions address the common challenges to the welfare state, her research investigates under what conditions successful welfare state reform can be achieved. Her work has been published in *World Politics*, *Comparative Political Studies*, *Politics & Society* and *Journal of Contemporary Asia*, among others. Email: soohyun.lee@kcl.ac.uk

**Sung-Hee Lee** is a Lecturer in Sociology at the University of Derby. Sung-Hee is keen to influence and subsequently change working women's care experiences, particularly where there are enduring and pervasive cultural gender ideologies, discriminatory assumptions and social injustices, not only in the practice of informal care but also in the workplace. She is currently commencing a research project investigating the childcare policy development in East Asia and assessing the impact on working mothers' work–life balance. Her international publication record is reflected in *Social Policy & Society*, *Social Politics* and *Asian Journal of Women's Studies*, including other collaborative governmental research projects working with Korea Institute for Health and Social Affairs, Korea Women's Development Institute and the City of Seoul. Email: S.Lee@derby.ac.uk

**Samuel Mohun Himmelweit** is a Research Officer in the Department of Social Policy at the London School of Economics. He is also undertaking a PhD in the same department. His research interests focus on family and labour-market policy in comparative perspective and on the role of ideas in welfare state development and change. His PhD examines the role that ideas played in recent work–family policy change in Germany and the UK. Email: s.f.mohun-himmelweit@lse.ac.uk

**Jaehyoung Park** is a Director of Social Welfare Policy Division, Ministry of Economy and Finance, South Korea. He is also undertaking a PhD in the Department of Social Policy at the London School of Economics. His research interests focus on social investment policy such as active labour market policies and work–family policies in comparative perspective. His PhD examines the effectiveness and determinants of social investment policy in OECD countries by using quantitative and qualitative methods. Email: arahanta@korea.kr

# Acknowledgements

This book started out as a collaborative research project with support from the British Academy's International Partnership and Mobility Programme, which allowed us to bring together enthusiastic colleagues based in the UK and South Korea to study the opportunities and limits of social investment reforms in Europe and East Asia. Through workshops in Seoul and Leeds, and presenting our research at the International Sociological Association's World Congress in Toronto, the collaboration and exchange of ideas grew, including feedback from peers. The research was facilitated by additional support from the Korea Foundation's Policy-Oriented Research Programme, the Academy of Korean Studies' Laboratory Programme for Korean Studies (AKS-2018-LAB-1250002) and the National Research Foundation of Korea (2017S1A2A2041808). Timo Fleckenstein and Soohyun Christine Lee also thank Yonsei University's Institute for State Governance Studies for hosting them when they visited Seoul.

# Preface from the series editors

*Heejung Chung (University of Kent, UK)*
*Alexandra Kaasch (University of Bielefeld, Germany)*
*Stefan Kühner (Lingnan University, Hong Kong)*

In a world that is rapidly changing, increasingly connected and uncertain, there is a need to develop a shared applied policy analysis of welfare regimes around the globe. Research in Comparative and Global Social Policy is a series of books that addresses broad questions around how nation states and transnational policy actors manage globally shared challenges. This book series includes a wide array of contributions, which discuss comparative social policy history, development and reform within a broad international context. It invites innovative research by leading experts on all world regions and global social policy actors and aims to fulfil the objectives: to encourages cross-disciplinary approaches that develop theoretical frameworks reaching across individual world regions and global actors; to provide evidence-based good practice examples that cross the bridge between academic research and practice; and not least, to provide a platform in which a wide range of innovative methodological approaches – whether national case studies, larger-N comparative studies, or global social policy studies – can be introduced to aid the evaluation, design and implementation of future social policies.

This book edited by Timo Fleckenstein, Soohyun Lee and Young Jun Choi provides an exemplary case of cross-national comparative studies. It brings together leading experts from across two world regions, Europe and East Asia, to discuss social investment strategies – currently one of the most influential policy approaches around the world. The contributions critically discuss to what extent social investment can (or possibly cannot) tackle some of the key challenges faced by contemporary welfare states – namely greater social inequality and the decline in social mobility. By inviting a number of authors tackle the same social issue using different country cases (rather than just examining cases side by side) this volume is able not only to deepen our understanding of varieties of social investment strategies, but also discusses how some of the drawbacks connected to social investment may be overcome. The contributions tell us that, despite remarkable differences, at the level of the problems associated with social investment measures, the countries studied also show significant similarities. Furthermore, the case studies of East Asian countries provide important lessons for benchmarking or cautionary tales for more established Western welfare states as well as the emerging welfare geography in the Global South.

As the editors note, although historically regarded as latecomers into welfare state development, East Asian countries now act as front-runners in terms of the fast paced reforms they have undertaken especially in the social investment policy areas such as family, education and labour market policies. These countries were also among the first to face some of the key challenges of welfare states, such as low fertility and an ageing society. Just as the East attempted to gain policy lessons from the West in the early stages of its social development, maybe it ought to be the West's turn this time to actively engage in policy diffusion.

Overall, through providing a rich collection of evidence, this volume provides both academics and policy makers with a better understanding of the socio-economic and socio-political conditions for the success and failures of social investment policies in tackling issues of inequalities and social risks. We hope that it will fill a vital gap in providing policy evidence for global challenges from a cross-regional perspective that can be of benefit for a wide range of countries around the world.

# Introduction: social investments and welfare reform in Europe and East Asia

*Timo Fleckenstein, Soohyun Christine Lee and Young Jun Choi*

## Why social investment?

Across the Organisation for Economic Co-operation and Development (OECD) world, social investment policies are expanding, which Hemerijck (2015) describes as a 'quiet paradigm revolution'. Nordic countries are widely considered the pioneers in social investment policies – with Sweden having already embarked on progressive policies during the post-war era and thus presenting the longest track record of remarkable social investments (Morel et al, 2012). Much attention has been paid to Sweden's ambitious, active labour market policies, which are aimed at upskilling workers, and the country's employment-oriented family policies (most notably childcare provisions, but also parental leave schemes helping with work–family reconciliation), which promote mothers' participation in the labour market. In addition to its extensive childcare provisions, the country's comprehensive education and healthcare systems have earned Sweden recognition as a 'social service state' (Huber and Stephens, 2001).

While Nordic countries remain the frontrunners, with the greatest financial commitment to social investment policies (Kuitto, 2016), we observe that latecomers from not only Continental Europe and the Anglo-Saxon world, but also East Asia, have made considerable efforts to catch up with the Northern European pioneers. The rise of social investments, especially the expansion of employment-oriented family policy (Lewis et al, 2008; Ferragina and Seeleib-Kaiser, 2015), presents an important dimension of the recent transformation of advanced welfare capitalism, which, despite the prominence of retrenchment, cannot be reduced to welfare state regress. For instance, Germany, which has a long legacy of promoting traditional families, made considerable efforts to expand its childcare provisions (including childcare for those under three years of age), in addition to introducing an earnings-related parental leave scheme that largely resembles the Swedish leave policy. The United Kingdom has also seen a remarkable rise of early childhood education and care, where the government had previously rejected any responsibility for the family because it was considered a 'private matter' into which the state had no right to intervene. Childcare policies are also prominently featured in East Asia, even though Japan and South Korea, with their strong Confucian legacies, have had a rather long history of traditional approaches to family that strongly resemble the historical Continental European experience rooted in Catholicism. Yet Japan and Korea have embarked on childcare expansion, with the former as the pioneer in the region. Though starting later, Korea has 'overtaken' its neighbour, with a more ambitious childcare strategy. Successive governments have incrementally expanded the care provisions, and it is now available free of charge to all children of pre-school age (Fleckenstein and Lee, 2014, 2017).

Family policy is a key domain of the social investment approach, and it illustrates numerous weaknesses in the welfare settlements of the Golden Age, where social policies were, by and large, geared toward the male-breadwinner model (Lewis, 1992; Orloff, 1993; Daly and Rake, 2003). This is particularly true for the social insurance-heavy welfare states of Continental Europe, but also for the less generous Anglo-Saxon and East Asian countries. This focus on 'compensating', which is primarily concerned with wage replacement to protect the income of the male breadwinner in the event of ill-health, unemployment or old age, is widely seen as increasingly inadequate in post-industrial societies.

Bonoli (2005) introduces the notion of 'new social risks', which he describes in a later work as 'situations in which individuals experience welfare losses and which have arisen as a result of the socio-economic transformations that have taken place over the past three to four decades and are generally subsumed under the heading of post-industrialisation' (Bonoli, 2007: 498). Like the works of earlier feminist critics, the new social risk literature (see also Esping-Andersen, 1999; Taylor-Gooby, 2004) critically moves the focus beyond income protection. Work–family reconciliation for parents with young children, especially for single parents, is identified as a key challenge in post-industrial societies, which have not only seen an increase in women's desire to work in line with their rising educational attainment, but also an increased pressure for households to have two earners in the face of rising costs of living. The challenge of work–family reconciliation is not restricted to parents, but also affects people with frail, elderly family members, a situation that has become much more common with rising life expectancy. This includes the fast-growing number of 'super-elderly' people, who are 85 years of age or older and have a high likelihood of needing elder care. Work–family conflict indicates the need for de-familialisation measures (Esping-Andersen, 1999) that reduce the reliance on families, which are increasingly struggling in post-industrial societies. Accordingly, while childcare provisions are the most prominently discussed measures, elder care provisions are also of great importance.

In addition to work–family reconciliation issues, Bonoli raises the problem of low and obsolete skills as a new social risk in post-industrial societies. Certainly, the presence of low-skilled workers is by no means new, but in the past these workers were predominantly employed in manufacturing industries, where they benefitted from collective bargaining, which provided them with decent wages and job protection. In post-industrial societies, low-skilled workers are primarily found in much more vulnerable service-sector jobs (such as retail, cleaning and hospitality), which do not provide remuneration or working conditions that comparable to those of the manufacturing jobs of the past. In other words, having low or obsolete skills – the latter also associated with structural and technological change – involves a much greater risk of social exclusion than in the industrial era. Increased insider–outsider polarisation in post-industrial societies, particularly the rising number of workers at the periphery of the labour market, has been described as 'dualisation'. Critically, not only does labour market dualisation entail poor renumeration and working conditions for outsiders, it also means less social protection, especially in social insurance-heavy welfare states built around the assumption of standard employment. Moreover, private welfare contributes to the dualisation of social protection, because those in precarious employment do not normally have access to generous occupational benefits, such as corporate pensions (Emmenegger et al, 2012). Insufficient social insurance coverage has become a major concern in the face of greater employment instability and polarisation in post-industrial labour markets, which are characterised by a decline in the standard employment that defined the industrial age for which the welfare state was initially built (Bonoli, 2005; Durazzi et al, 2018).

The rise of new social risks associated with post-industrialisation, combined with welfare state retrenchment in social protection, has translated into greater social inequality across the developed world. In wider policy circles, the OECD's publication *Growing Unequal* (2008) has received considerable attention – among other reasons because the OECD is not normally associated with social policy advocacy. In this report, the OECD acknowledges that greater economic prosperity has benefitted the rich more than the poor, and that the middle classes have also fallen behind in many countries. Changes in the labour market have been identified as the most important driver of increasing social inequality, with low-skilled workers especially struggling. Obviously, it can be concluded from the OECD findings that we cannot rely on 'trickle-down' mechanisms to create more inclusive societies; instead, government policy is the key to ensuring that all parts of society benefit from economic success (see also Atkinson, 2015).

Importantly, the emergence of greater social inequality is associated with a decline in social mobility. Social mobility is by no means a new topic in the social policy literature. Many studies have illustrated the strong relationship between earnings and labour market status for parents and their children, both in Western and East Asian countries (see, for instance, Tyree and Treas, 1974; Biblarz et al, 1996). Yet, whereas social mobility in advanced economies has stalled since the 1990s (often seen in the context of post-industrialisation and labour market dualisation), it has received increasing attention in academic and policy circles. For instance, the OECD's *Broken Social Elevator* report (2018a) introduces the notions of 'sticky floors' and 'sticky ceilings' to capture the inheritance of both social disadvantages and advantages. The research demonstrates how the socio-economic backgrounds of parents strongly influence the education and labour market status of their children. Notably, education, once praised for promoting social mobility, seems to have become an important obstacle to social mobility with the rise of educational inequalities. It is true that more egalitarian societies, such as Nordic countries, continue to achieve greater social mobility than countries with higher inequality (Esping-Andersen, 2009; OECD, 2018a), but the 'broken elevator' has become a pressing concern for policy-makers around the OECD world.

In post-industrial societies, however, a major challenge to the post-war welfare paradigm and to modern societies more generally comes from not only new social risks and associated social inequality but also wider demographic concerns (Harper, 2006; Dorling and Gietel-Basten, 2018). Across the developed world, fertility rates have declined substantially, and no OECD country has seen them at the replacement rate of 2.1 children per woman since 1980. While some countries (such as France and Sweden) have fertility rates that are only moderately below replacement levels, many other countries (especially in Southern Europe and East Asia) present fertility rates outside the 'safety zone' –above 1.5 births per woman. At the same time, life expectancy has risen remarkably, with all OECD countries having experienced an increase in life expectancy of at least 10 years since 1970. On average, a newborn today can expect to reach the age of 80. These falls in fertility and gains in life expectancy have led to rising old-age dependency ratios, specifically the number of individuals aged 65 or older per 100 people aged 20 to 64. In the mid-1970s, the old-age dependency ratio stood at around 20 and, since then, it has increased to nearly 30. Future increases are expected to come much more quickly, and current projections suggest a doubling of the old-age dependency ratio over the next 45 years. Unsurprisingly, countries with very low fertility rates can expect the fastest and steepest increases (OECD, 2019). These demographic changes have major implications for social welfare systems, labour markets and families. Most obviously, population ageing involves considerable fiscal challenges for pensions and long-term care systems. The long-term care sector, characterised by high personnel turnover, also faces a labour supply problem, which is expected to be exacerbated further in coming years. With regard to labour markets, shrinking workforces make it imperative to fully capitalise on working-age populations; and skills shortages and mismatch have already become critical issues, dampening economic progress. These developments have, in many countries, moved pro-natal policies to the forefront of debate in political and policy circles.

## Policy and politics of social investment

In this context, social investment policies can present a critical tool for governments to respond to greater social inequality and the decline in social mobility. While social protection remains important for redistributive justice, the argument that more proactive social policies are needed to address the challenges of post-industrial labour markets has been gaining considerable momentum in both academic and political debates and since the mid-1990s. As discussed earlier, the welfare state of the Golden Age was primarily ascribed the responsibility of providing benefits in the event of income loss. In contrast, social investments present a policy strategy that proactively facilitates labour market participation. The criticism of 'activation discourse', which sought to make social policies more 'employment-friendly', was particularly targeted at both labour market policy and family policy, in which governments (with some notable exceptions, such as Nordic countries) made little effort to support work–family reconciliation (Cox, 1998; Clasen, 2000; Taylor-Gooby, 2004). Capturing the main policy orientation of social investments, Anton Hemerijck, a key author in this area, describes these policy strategies as attempts 'to "prepare" families and societies to respond to the new risks of a competitive knowledge economy, by investing in human capital and capabilities from early childhood through old age, rather than in policies that simply "repair" damages after moments of economic and personal crisis' (2017: 4).

The notion of 'preparing rather than repairing' is at the very heart of the approach, and it seems to gain ever more relevance in knowledge-based economies, which increasingly require highly skilled and adaptable workers who can cope with technological and workplace changes during their career. The social investment approach evidently displays a strong human capital and labour market orientation. Morel et al (2012) describe social investments as policies that not only improve human capital but also help make better use of it, with the objective of promoting greater social inclusion. Here, Hemerijck (2017) coined the rather useful terms 'stocks' and 'flows' to distinguish these two different functions that social investment policies can serve; with the former in Hemerijck's words being concerned with 'raising the quality of the "stock" of human capital and capabilities over the life course' and the latter 'easing the "flow" of the contemporary labour-market and life-course transition' (Hemerijck, 2017: 19). In this context, Hemerijck (2017) draws on Schmid's (1998) analytical and normative ideal of 'transitional labour markets', which are described as institutional arrangements that facilitate the flow between the labour market and different activities. For instance, further education policy can provide a mechanism for temporal withdrawal from the labour market to improve one's human capital stock in order to promote greater adaptability in increasingly fast-changing labour markets and workplaces, thus presenting a tool to prevent low or obsolete skills that are associated with a greater risk of social exclusion.

The human capital and labour market orientation of social investments make these economic policy agendas, in addition to more conventional social policy agendas that are primarily concerned with social inclusion in post-industrial societies. Moreover, the social inclusion rationale is also increasingly perceived as an economic policy and innovation agenda. Well beyond traditional social policy advocacy, international organisations (such as the OECD and the International Monetary Fund, which are associated with a neoliberal rather than a social-democratic value orientation) have started making a case for greater inclusiveness as a means of promoting economic development because growing inequality is increasingly seen as hindering economic growth and prosperity (Ostry et al, 2014; Dabla-Norris et al, 2015; OECD, 2015; OECD, 2018b). For instance, the OECD's (2016) *Productivity-Inclusiveness Nexus* provides a prominent economic argument for tackling social polarisation, showing that rising inequality and declining social mobility undermine economic productivity and, ultimately, the innovative capacity of societies. Hence, the international inclusive growth discourse, with its economic rationale, has, in principle, shown that a paradigm shift in economic and social policy for greater inclusiveness is imperative for sustainable growth strategies (see also Deeming and Smyth, 2019).

With their capacity to facilitate growth, social investment strategies could be considered policies 'for the market' (Iversen, 2005) that present opportunities for cross-class coalition-building, rather than 'politics against markets' (Esping-Andersen, 1985), which views social policy as part of a class struggle with social democracy and organised labour being the main drivers of progress (see also Korpi, 1983, 2006). Indeed, in the welfare politics of post-war Sweden, Swenson (2004) finds employer support for building a social-democratic welfare state, including for social investment policies (most notably, human capital-oriented active labour market policies and employment-oriented family policies) because these were thought to improve the supply of skilled labour. Therefore, businesses benefitted from and supported them (see also Bonoli, 2005). Even in latecomer countries, there is some indication that employers may support employment-oriented family policy expansion for 'business reasons', but cross-class coalition-building in the area of social investments remains a political challenge, with some employers remaining rather sceptical (Fleckenstein and Seeleib-Kaiser, 2011; Seeleib-Kaiser and Toivonen, 2011; Fleckenstein and Lee, 2014).

While the potential for cross-class coalitions might be seen as favourable to the emergence of social investment policies, the 'impatience' of politics undermines the political feasibility of these policies. The costs of these policies are incurred immediately (eg, start-up and running costs of childcare infrastructure), but the benefits (eg, the promotion of women's employment and improved human capital from early education) might only be seen after considerable delay. Politicians, with a firm focus on electoral politics, tend to prioritise policies with immediate returns, which increase their chances to stay in or enter office (Ferrera, 2017). Yet survey data suggests that social investment policies attract remarkable popular support across different electoral groups. Thus, social investment policies might take time to produce desirable social outcomes, but electoral returns can be 'harvested' immediately, including returns from groups that do not personally benefit from the social investments (most notably pensioners) (Garritzmann et al, 2018).

## Issues in social investment: critiques

Social investment is not without controversies. One of the most frequently discussed issues is whether social investment comes at the expense of social protection policies (Cantillon, 2011; Deeming and Smyth, 2015). In less-developed, East Asian welfare states with spending 'headroom', social protection and social investment do not seem mutually exclusive, but the issue is more controversial in 'mature' welfare states. In the context of 'permanent austerity' (Pierson, 2001), which is seen as making it increasingly difficult to expand aggregate social spending, critics suspect trade-offs between social investments and social protection policies. It is true that cash-providing and redistributive social policies tend to have downsized, whereas the rhetoric of social investment contributing to the recommodification of labour has been rising considerably. Yet empirical findings have not found a clear trade-off relationship between the two types of spending (Vandenbroucke and Vleminckx, 2011; Nikolai, 2012; Kuitto, 2016). A recent study by Kim and Choi (2019), however, argues that a positive relationship was found in the period 1981–95 but has disappeared or, in some cases, turned negative between 1996 and 2010.

Another related issue is the so-called Matthew effect, derived from a well-known quote from the Bible: 'to them that has, shall be given' (Cantillon, 2011; Bonoli et al, 2017; Busemeyer et al, 2018). In other words, the vulnerable tend to benefit less from social investment policies compared to the better-off, suggesting a middle-class bias in social investment strategies because of the disproportionate use of social services, such as childcare by the middle class, whereas lower socio-economic classes (eg, migrants) typically present a poor up-take of childcare services and training programmes. This effect is likely even more pronounced in higher education. Without doubt, the degree of the Matthew effect depends on the policy design of each social investment policy, but its existence could significantly undermine the welfare state's capacity to counteract rising inequality and declining social mobility.

The concept of social investment has also been questioned more fundamentally. In recent years, it has become increasingly common to distinguish passive, compensatory social spending (such as old-age security and unemployment protection) and active social investment spending (such as childcare, education and training). While somewhat intuitive, this ideal–typical distinction faces difficulties in practice. Most prominently, Nolan (2013) argues that 'passive-looking' social protections, such as unemployment benefits, also have an investment function. Critically, unemployment protection provides the resources needed for nutrition to maintain one's human capital when unemployed, and furthermore, it supports searching for an adequate job rather than the 'next best' job, which might devalue previously accumulated human capital. Secondly, decent social protection facilitates risk-taking rather than risk-avoiding behaviours, which is a core component of entrepreneurship in knowledge-based economies (Mkandawire, 2007; Koo et al, 2019). Filippetti and Guy (2016) show that social insurance benefits could encourage socially beneficial risk-taking in vocational education and training. Finally, economically secure families contribute to the formation of children's human capital (Bell et al, 2017). Accordingly, the growth of social investment spending at the expense of social protection might not be able to achieve its goal, and might even aggravate income inequality.

Another issue is related to the fall of fertility rates that European and East Asian countries have experienced. Low fertility rates were widely associated with the increase in women's employment participation (see Zaidi and Morgan, 2017). Initial theorising of the second demographic transition emphasised value changes at the heart of falling fertility. It was argued that greater individualisation has not only driven women's labour market participation but also translated into falling marriage and rising divorce rates, among other effects. These developments, including a dramatic drop in fertility rates, were seen as a permanent and irreversible trend towards 'less family' (Lesthaeghe and Surkyn, 1988; Lesthaeghe, 1995). If this assessment were true, policies would have little capacity to affect fertility. However, empirically, we observe considerable variation in fertility, with, counter-intuitively, the most familialistic countries of Continental and Southern Europe as well as East Asia displaying particularly low levels of fertility. What is more, we observe a recent reversal of the fertility decline in a number of low-fertility countries. Nordic countries, for example, with high female employment participation but extensive work–family reconciliation policies have fertility rates near the replacement level, for which Castles (2003) coined the notion of 'turning the world upside down'. Notably some of the countries that have expanded work–family reconciliation support have recently seen a recovery from exceptionally low fertility rates, lending support to Esping-Andersen's (2015) argument for a 'return of the family' (see also Esping-Andersen and Billari, 2015). This presents a remarkable shift in social policy. Traditionally, general family support policies (such as child allowance and tax subsidies) enjoyed the greatest prominence in attempts to support families. Christian-democratic policy, mobilising considerable financial resources to support male-breadwinner families, exemplified this policy strategy (Korpi, 2000); and in more recent times, Japan's return to traditional family policy presents a prominent example (Boling, 2015). In other words, 'investing' in the family was understood as direct financial support for the family. Considering the Scandinavian experience, attention shifted towards work–family reconciliation policies to support families and promote fertility. Increased female employment participation might have, at first, suppressed fertility, but work–family reconciliation policy, rather than general family support, has apparently facilitated the recovery of fertility rates. Thus, employment-oriented family policy has the capacity to promote not only female employment and child development, but also fertility, potentially also making these policies pro-natal policy tools.

Yet some scholars question whether social investment policies put the 'cart before the horse' (Nolan, 2017; Saraceno, 2017). Welfare states should prioritise human welfare and gender equality, but it is suggested that they have reoriented their policy objectives to issues such as boosting female employment and increasing fertility rates. In this process, social investment policies have been instrumental in promoting economic growth and extending the financial basis of the welfare state to support an ageing population, while neglecting the value of care work. For instance, the rhetoric of economic competitiveness and the financial sustainability of the welfare state plays an important role in the expansion of childcare provisions in Japan and Korea. Besides, while pro-natal policies are more emphasised, many governments show less concern about child poverty (which has a huge negative impact on human capital building), and they are less willing to invest in active labour market programmes to increase productivity. Unlike childcare policy, in recent years most OECD countries have hardly expanded vocational training. Instead, retrenchment has dominated recent developments in labour market policy. Also, as more parents experience income and job insecurities because of changing labour markets in the increasingly knowledge-based, digital capitalism, it is becoming more difficult to expect that children grow up in a stable and supportive environment, with detrimental long-term consequences for human capital formation.

## Aims and scope of the book

This book has the two-fold aim of advancing the academic study of social investment policies through the comparative perspective and advancing policy knowledge to inform social policy-making and encourage better social policies that address the challenges of post-industrialisation and the associated increase in social inequality across the OECD. More specifically, we study social investment policies in Europe and East Asia, looking at three key domains – labour market, family and education – to better understand the socio-economic and socio-political conditions for success and failure in the rise of social investment policies, in addition to understanding social outcomes.

The comparison of European and East Asian experiences is particularly intriguing. Not only have social investment policies recently enjoyed considerable prominence in the two regions (offering a great number of empirical observations), the comparison between Europe and East Asia also provides an original and unusual research design, allowing the study of social investment policies in very different political and economic contexts. While a social investment 'turn' has commonly been found, European states have transformed their traditional, cash-heavy welfare states, whereas East Asian states have attempted to introduce and strengthen social investment in addition to existing private investment (for instance the notorious case of shadow education that involves private supplementary tutoring of school-age children). Productive social policy has gained much momentum in these countries, but we observe considerable variation in policy expansion cross-nationally and across policy domains. The study of European and East Asian experiences helps us better understand the *roads* and *barriers* toward social investment policies, with important lessons for social policy-making.

Addressing the issue of a long-term policy strategy for redesigning welfare states, we also critically assess the opportunities and limits of social investment policies for better outcomes. To better understand the implications, we pursue the question of how to best prepare all citizens for the challenges of increasingly knowledge-based societies, which is thought to require greater investment in skills to better cope with changing labour markets. Simultaneously, we look at how to reduce income and gender inequalities, and facilitate social mobility. In this volume, we examine various social policies from a life-course perspective. Social investment in the life-course perspective assumes that capacity and 'learning in any one stage must be seen in connection with what happened earlier and what is to happen' (Kvist, 2015: 136).

Every life stage matters for social investment – from early childhood education to active ageing without isolation in the later stages of life. Various risks faced by individuals at one life stage increase vulnerability in successive stages of their life course, with huge implications for social mobility and well-being; it is therefore vital to approach social investment from the life-course perspective (Hemerijck, 2017).

Accordingly, we focus on policies for children and young people, such as childcare, early childhood education and the social investment-focused aspects of education. Here, we look at not only secondary and tertiary education, but also public and private social investment, including the analysis of so-called shadow education, with regard to impact on income inequality and social mobility. Moreover, much attention is paid to work–family reconciliation and employment-oriented family policies, which are of great importance to women in particular and their ability to engage in the labour market. Furthermore, we consider vocational and training policies for the wider working-age population. Finally, we include long-term care and grandparenting in our analysis of social investments because major social benefits are commonly associated with improving long-term care and involving grandparents in the upbringing of children. Analysing policies and politics of social investment, we critically examine the implications of de-institutionalisation and de-standardisation of the family, learning and work, all of which significantly affect and shape new life courses in contemporary societies. From the empirical analysis of this wide range of social investment policies, we seek to derive policy implications and specific policy recommendations.

The contributions in this book develop a strong case for integrated welfare reform programmes that combine social *investments* at different life stages with meaningful social *protection* mechanisms and labour market *regulation* – addressing the increased social polarisation associated with labour market dualisation across European and East Asian welfare capitalism. In other words, only multi-dimensional reform strategies can be expected to deliver the promise of greater social equality and human capabilities over the life course. Critically, the research in the book underlines that policy-makers need to consider the impact of private social investments (most notably shadow education) in welfare reform strategies. Even though the public–private mix has received considerable attention in comparative welfare state research, this is not true for social investment research; and while arguments about the Matthew effect enjoy considerable prominence in the literature, the discussion is limited to the public sphere. This presents a substantial gap, as shadow education reinforces if not amplifies existing social inequalities with detrimental effects on social mobility. Thus, reform strategies must consider both the public and private dimensions of social investments, and the latter can be viewed as being driven, to a considerable extent, by increased anxieties in the face of labour market dualisation and social polarisation. We argue that this reinforces the imperative for a multi-dimensional approach to welfare reform, combining greater efforts in social investment, protection and labour market regulation. Neglecting any of these three dimensions can be expected to severely compromise the delivery of greater of social equality. Also, contributions to the book show that national reform strategies need to carefully consider existing policy settings and institutional complementarities in policy design, suggesting the presence of multiple pathways toward greater equality. This makes a case for great attention to, but also caution over, policy transfers. Hence, while policies can 'travel' between countries, including between far-away continents, a simplistic search for best practices might not deliver the desired policy outcomes. The research in this book demonstrates that social policy innovations informed by international policies can be pursued by national policy-makers, who appear to have more discretion than often assumed in approaches emphasising path-dependent development.

## Outline of the volume

In Chapter 2, Samuel Mohun Himmelweit and Sung-Hee Lee examine work–family policy expansions in England, Germany, Japan and Korea and argue that the different extents of expansion observed in the four countries can be explained by how much each country realised the potential of social investment as a polysemic international idea. According to the authors, the ambiguous and multi-faceted nature of social investment gives the idea the potential to act as a 'coalition magnet', because it allows different political actors to promote social investment using various interpretations and rationales. In Germany and Korea, we see parties from both the left and right championing work–family reconciliation policies, with their own rationales, as solutions for a wide range of issues – from promoting gender equality and female employment, to boosting fertility and investing in children. Although the German and Korean cases demonstrate how polysemic versions of social investment can facilitate the building of broad political coalitions for ambitious policy reform, the English and Japanese cases show the opposite can also be true. In England, the different dimensions of work–family reconciliation policy never came

13

together to form an overarching polysemic idea. In Japan, work–family reconciliation has been overwhelmingly viewed as a tool for boosting fertility, whereas other aspects (such as maternal employment and gender equality) have been paid little attention. Mohun Himmelweit and Lee suggest that policy-makers who are seeking significant social investment reforms should define their goals as broadly as possible, because the polysemy of the social investment idea allows the building of broad political coalitions in support of reforms.

In Chapter 3, on shadow education in Korea, Sonia Exley studies the consequences of excessive private social investment and the government's struggle to tackle private tutoring. Korea is a critical case in the study of private social investments because it has the most extensive engagement in shadow education across the OECD world. Exley illustrates the three main ways that the Korean government has endeavoured to curtail private tutoring, and how all these reforms have had limited success to date. First, the government increased public spending on education, seeking reduced class sizes and upgraded school facilities. Second, it attempted to regulate shadow education but only a few measures, such as price ceiling and curfew on private tutoring, were available. Third, numerous reforms were introduced to enhance the fairness of university entrance requirements. Nevertheless, no government effort has translated into a meaningful reduction of shadow education, largely due to the desire of Korean families to stay 'one step ahead' in education and the success of the shadow education industry in exploiting families' anxieties whenever new reforms have been introduced. Exley suggests that the drivers of the shadow education frenzy might lie outside the area of education policy. For instance, she points to the 'hakbul' traditions in Korean society (that is, the strong belief that a degree from a few elite universities is imperative for securing high-status, well-paid jobs) as a driver of excessive shadow education. Also, she refers to research showing that labour market deregulation and the rise of youth unemployment since the 1997 Asian financial crisis has heightened families' anxieties about their children's futures in the ever more insecure Korean labour market. Exley recommends that policy-makers in the West should carefully monitor the growth of shadow education in their countries, even if it is not currently perceived as a serious social problem, as the Korean experience demonstrates that, once normalised, it can be very difficult to curb.

Also dealing with private education, Chapter 4, by Yun Young Kim and Young Jun Choi, analyses Korea Education and Employment Panel (KEEP) data to examine two issues. First, Kim and Choi investigate the relationship of parents' income and education levels with the money and time they spend on private tutoring for their children. Second, they analyse the effect of private social investment on academic performance and labour market outcomes. Their results demonstrate that the income and education levels of parents are related to the educational and labour market performance of children in the following ways. First, families with higher incomes spend significantly more time and money on private tutoring for their children, with the expectation that this would translate into higher grades on the College Scholastic Ability Test, thereby increasing their children's chances of entering a prestigious university. Furthermore, there is evidence that children whose parents spend more money on private tutoring are likely to earn higher wages. Lastly, it can be expected that the education and income of parents have a positive effect on the educational performances of children, and that these different educational performances are reflected in labour market outcomes. In sum, Kim and Choi show that shadow education is a powerful mechanism reinforcing, if not exacerbating, existing social inequalities. Drawing on their empirical results, the authors reject the argument that Korea does not need further social investment in education because of 'education fever'. Instead, they argue for public social investment in education and better social protections, with an emphasis on equal opportunity and redistribution, in order to overcome the decline in social mobility caused by families' private social investment.

In Chapter 5, Niccolo Durazzi assesses the 'employability turn' in higher education across advanced capitalist countries, and the increasing role of higher education as the main locus of skill formation. The chapter analyses patterns of alignment between higher education systems and the need for skills in knowledge-based economies. Durazzi argues that vertically differentiated higher education systems (in which universities are differentiated by their prestige, such as rankings) are compatible with knowledge economies based on high-end services (such as the UK), but not with knowledge economies based on advanced manufacturing (such as Korea). Conversely, horizontally differentiated higher education systems (in which, through the creation of a vocational track, universities are classified as traditional, research-oriented institutions and profession-oriented ones) work in conjunction with both types of knowledge economies. Cases in point are Germany, with its reliance on advanced manufacturing, and the Netherlands, where high-end services are of critical importance. Korea and Germany face the additional challenge of increasing the supply of highly skilled workers in science, technology, engineering and mathematics (STEM), which are crucial for knowledge economies reliant on advanced manufacturing but, nevertheless, often avoided by students, even in the presence of strong positive labour market signals. To address this skills shortage, in Korea, the government introduced financial incentives for universities to adjust their offerings to government skill forecasts, whereas in Germany, the same problem was tackled by the government by expanding universities of applied sciences, whose offerings were more in tune with labour market demands. Thus, to meet the high-skills demand of labour markets, Durrazzi recommends that governments should revive or create a vocational subset of higher education institutions.

Improving labour market transitions during one's life course is one of the core functions of social investment, and, in Chapter 6, Ijin Hong and Jieun Lee investigate whether social investments improve labour market flow by focusing on work–family reconciliation policy and women's labour market participation. Investigating social investment latecomers in East Asia (Japan and Korea) and Southern Europe (Spain and Italy), they find that social investment reform itself does not automatically lead to higher female employment rates, because the effectiveness of work–family reconciliation policy hugely depends on the institutional context. Building on the concept of institutional complementarities, Hong and Lee suggest that, in countries without favourable institutional configurations for women's labour market participation (such as a high proportion of female university graduates, the culture of gender equality in the workplace and a less dualised labour market), family policy reform alone is insufficient to generate a considerable increase in maternal employment. The Korean case explicitly illustrates that, although it is the boldest reformer in work–family reconciliation policy among the four countries, its female employment rate is the second lowest. Hong and Lee point to unfavourable labour market institutions for maternal employment as barriers that prevent family policy from improving mothers' labour market flow.

In Chapter 7, Mi Young An investigates the relationship between social investments and gender equality. She performs a multi-level analysis of the 2012 ISSP survey on Changing Families and Gender Roles to explore micro- and macro-level factors affecting the gendered division of housework in two stages: first, only analysing European countries, and then adding two East Asian countries (Japan and Korea). Her analysis shows that housework division, in both stages, is largely determined by micro-level factors such as education, working hours, gender-role ideology, relative income, and number of children and adults in the household. However, she also finds that some macro-level factors affect the cross-national variation in the gendered division of housework. When analysing the European countries, the results show that parental leave policy influences the gendered division, whereas public childcare expenditure, women's representation in parliament and societies' predominant gender-role ideology are insignificant. More specifically, the gendered division of housework tends to be more unequal in countries with longer parental leave. When Japan and Korea – two countries with a very unequal division of housework – are added to the analysis, the results are different. Both have significant public childcare expenditure – a greater investment in formal childcare is associated with greater gender equality. More importantly, the role of women in parliament is significant, indicating that in countries where women are better represented in politics, the division of housework is more equal. An argues that Japan and Korea have modernised family policies, but with no substantive improvement in gendered political power relations, and concludes that social investment strategies alone are insufficient for significant improvements in gender equality.

As discussed earlier, in the section 'Issues in social investment: critiques', social investment policies have been criticised for their potentially regressive distributive effects, particularly the Matthew effect. In Chapter 8, Jaehyoung Park empirically tests this criticism by examining the effect of social investment policies on employment rates and job quality. Analysing data from eleven OECD countries between 1992 to 2013 with a focus on active labour market and work–family policies, he finds some support for the Matthew effect. Although the analysis rejects the claim that higher expenditures on social investment are related to the growth of atypical employment and increased dualisation of the labour market, it suggests that training and childcare indeed disproportionately benefit medium-educated workers, rather than uneducated and highly educated workers. In other words, social investment policies struggle with reducing inequality (and might even aggravate inequality), not because they necessarily tend to increase non-standard employment associated with lower pay, but because less-educated workers tend to benefit the least from them in terms of improving employment prospects. Rather than interpreting this as evidence against social investment, Park calls for a more careful policy design that allows low-income groups to benefit from social investment policy as well.

Instead of human capital accumulation, which is prominently featured in the social investment literature, Ga Woon Ban draws our attention to skills retention in Chapter 9. Analysing data from the Programme for

International Assessment for Adult Competencies (PIAAC), Ban finds strong empirical support for the so-called use-it-or-lose-it hypothesis, which is that utilising people's skills at work is critical to retaining human capital. Obviously, an unemployed person faces great risks of losing their skills, and unsurprisingly, longer unemployment makes reintegration into the labour market more difficult. Considerable cross-national differences in human capital depreciation across the OECD world point to workplaces as the key site, as differences in workplace organisation may shape differences in how skills are used and, accordingly, differences in human capital depreciation. For instance, very hierarchical work cultures may undermine the use of certain skills and thus facilitate their depreciation, whereas higher levels of task discretion and cooperative culture in the workplace promote skills use and support achieved human capital retention. Considering the differences in skills depreciation, Ban's findings call for tailored policy interventions rather than a one-size-fits-all approach. Countries should take different approaches to preserving human capital, depending on their unique patterns of human capital use and depreciation.

Moving on from the labour market and human capital, in Chapter 10, Hyejin Choi examines the relationship between grandparenting and active ageing by analysing data from time use surveys and longitudinal studies of ageing in England and Korea. Active ageing is a social investment strategy, because involving grandparents in childcare can not only contribute to the accumulation of human capital of grandchildren in terms of intellectual, physical and emotional development, but can also provide meaningful social engagements for senior citizens. Active ageing can prevent the elderly from being left marginalised and fully dependent on the state or family. However, grandparenting can leave the elderly with less leisure time, and it might involve considerable physical exhaustion. Choi's research shows that grandparenting can facilitate active ageing if grandparents are supplementary rather than primary caregivers. In Korea, however, her analysis indicates that many grandparents have to fill the gap left by formal childcare provisions, due to Korean labour market practices, which are not favourable to balancing work and family (eg, long work hours and lack of opportunities for flexible working time). Accordingly, Choi argues that Korean grandparents often face much longer and more intensive childcare and related responsibilities than their English counterparts. Comparing the time use of grandmothers who spend more than half an hour a day on childcare, she shows that the peak time of caregiving in Korea is early in the morning (8–9 a.m.) and late in the evening (5–8 p.m.), whereas in England it is in the afternoon (4–6 p.m.).

Moreover, Korean caregiving grandmothers spent much longer on housekeeping than Korean non-caregiving grandmothers. It is suggested that grandmothers, after the peak morning care time, stay in their children's homes doing household chores because their children have long work hours. This leads to Korean childcaring grandparents experiencing less beneficial active ageing, because they engage less in social and physical leisure activities than the elderly with no childcare responsibilities. In England, by contrast, grandparents with childcare responsibilities were not more or less likely than non-caregiving grandparents to engage in social and physical leisure activities. The findings indicate that work–family balance is critical even for the active ageing of grandparents, because policies allowing shorter and/ or more flexible work time for parents with young children are an important institutional condition supporting grandparenting as a means of active ageing.

In Chapter 11, Jooha Lee presents long-term care as a social investment strategy with clear social and economic returns. Long-term care policies can promote high levels of labour market participation by freeing up family members from unpaid care work while facilitating longer independent living of older people and promoting equity, well-being and quality of life. By reducing the likelihood of informal care, long-term care provisions reduce the hidden costs of informal care, including the loss of tax contributions from family caregivers who are no longer able to undertake paid work. Lee argues that the existing research on social investment policies is often preoccupied with *formal* policy domains (ie, policy content that embodies policy goals, principles and intended outputs), whereas *operational* policy domain (ie, the organisational arrangement and procedures for policy implementation) is paid little attention. By examining the governance of long-term care in England and Korea, he demonstrates that the operational policy domain matters greatly in delivering the intended outcomes of social investment strategies. In the governance of long-term care, England has a more coordinated system with greater local autonomy and a single regulatory agency, whereas Korea has a more fragmented system with weak local autonomy. Lee argues that these differences largely stem from institutional legacies. Korea is characterised by exclusive policy-making authority and fragmented delivery mechanisms without autonomous field-level offices specialised in social welfare. To overcome a top-down, fragmented governance structure in long-term care, Korea can learn from England, where long-term care governance has used more inclusive policy-making, involving not only local authorities but also various civil society organisations and communities, and employed partnerships between public and private actors.

In Chapter 12, Timo Fleckenstein and Soohyun Christine Lee assess developments towards greater social investments and the related politics in Europe and East Asia, in addition to reviewing the policy implications suggested by the contributors to this book volume. Regarding the former, they examine the uneven social investment turn in the two regions and provide insight into the roads and barriers towards greater social investments. One can observe an expansion of social investment in family policy, although there is great cross-national variation in the speed and scope of the expansion. By contrast, labour market policy is characterised by declining efforts to improve the employability of the unemployed and of labour market outsiders. The chapter shows that family and labour market policies, and their very different outcomes, are underpinned by diverse political dynamics, rather than by a politics of social investment. In family policy reform, political parties, motivated by electoral imperatives, are in the driving seat. In Germany and Korea, family policy expanded during the incumbency of the political left and right, indicating a responsiveness of political parties to societal changes. However, in Japan, the expansion was somewhat modest because similar party competition did not emerge in family policy due to the absence of wider societal demands. When it comes to labour market reform, employers (in the Swedish and German cases) and trade unions (in the Italian case) appear to be the critical actors, rather than political parties. The authors suggest that the traditional prominence of social partners in labour market policy-making remains largely intact, but the power balance has shifted towards businesses. Fleckenstein and Lee suggest it is important for policy-makers to understand the specific political dynamics of a given policy area and to devise a strategy for social investment accordingly. The review of policy implications in the second half of the chapter provides the conclusion of the book. The rich empirical work covering Europe and East Asia has allowed the authors of each chapter to draw important lessons for policy and politics, and it is hoped that these will make a small contribution towards welfare reforms that facilitate greater social equality and fairness, reversing the trend towards greater social polarisation that has challenged societies the world over.

### References

Atkinson, A.B. (2015) *Inequality: What Can Be Done?*, Cambridge, MA: Harvard University Press.

Bell, A.M., Chetty, R., Jaravel, X., Petkova, N. and Van Reenen, J. (2017) *Who Becomes an Inventor in America? The Importance of Exposure to Innovation*, Cambridge, MA: National Bureau of Economic Research.

Biblarz, T.J., Bengtson, V.L. and Bucur, A. (1996) 'Social mobility across three generations', *Journal of Marriage and the Family*, 58(1): 188–200.

Boling, P. (2015) *The Politics of Work-Family Policies: Comparing Japan, France, Germany and the United States*, Cambridge: Cambridge University Press.

Bonoli, G. (2005) 'The politics of the new social policies: providing coverage against new social risks in mature welfare states', *Policy & Politics*, 33(3): 431–49.

Bonoli, G. (2007) 'Time matters: Postindustrialization, new social risks, and welfare state adaptation in advanced industrial democracies', *Comparative Political Studies*, 40(5): 495–520.

Bonoli, G., Cantillon, B. and Van Lancker, W. (2017) 'Social investment and the Matthew Effect: limits to a strategy', in A. Hemerijck (ed) *The Uses of Social Investment*, Oxford: Oxford University Press, pp 66–76.

Busemeyer, M.R., Garritzmann, J.L., Neimanns, E. and Nezi, R. (2018) 'Investing in education in Europe: evidence from a new survey of public opinion', *Journal of European Social Policy*, 28(1): 34–54.

Cantillon, B. (2011) 'The paradox of the social investment state: growth, employment and poverty in the Lisbon era', *Journal of European Social Policy*, 21(5): 432–49.

Castles, F.G. (2003) 'The world turned upside down: below replacement fertility, changing preferences and family-friendly public policies in 21 OECD countries', *Journal of European Social Policy*, 13(3): 209–27.

Clasen, J. (2000) 'Motives, means and opportunities: reforming unemployment compensation in the 1990s', *West European Politics*, 23(2): 89–112.

Cox, R.H. (1998) 'From safety net to trampoline: labor market activation in the Netherlands and Denmark', *Governance*, 11(4): 397.

Dabla-Norris, E., Kochhar, K., Suphaphiphat, N., Ricka, F. and Tsounta, E. (2015) *Causes and Consequences of Income Inequality: A Global Perspective*, Washington, D.C.: International Monetary Fund.

Daly, M. and Rake, K. (2003) *Gender and the Welfare State*, Cambridge: Polity.

Deeming, C. and Smyth, P. (2015) 'Social investment after neoliberalism: policy paradigms and political platforms', *Journal of Social Policy*, 44(2): 297–318.

Deeming, C. and Smyth, P. (2019) 'Social investment, inclusive growth that is sustainable and the new global social policy', in C. Deeming and P. Smyth (eds) *Reframing Global Social Policy: Social Investments for Sustainable and Inclusive Growth*, Bristol: Policy Press, pp 11–44.

Dorling, D. and Gietel-Basten, S. (2018) *Why Demography Matters*, Cambridge: Polity.

Durazzi, N., Fleckenstein, T. and Lee, S.C. (2018) 'Social solidarity for all? Trade union strategies, labor market dualization, and the welfare state in Italy and South Korea', *Politics & Society*, 46(2): 205–33.

Emmenegger, P., Häusermann, S., Palier, B. and Seeleib-Kaiser, M. (2012) *The Age of Dualization: The Changing Face of Inequality in Deindustrializing Societies*, New York: Oxford University Press.

Esping-Andersen, G. (1985) *Politics against Markets: The Social Democratic Road to Power*, Princeton, NJ: Princeton University Press.

Esping-Andersen, G. (1999) *The Social Foundations of Postindustrial economies*, Oxford: Oxford University Press.

Esping-Andersen, G. (2009) *The Incomplete Revolution: Adapting to Women's New Roles*, Cambridge: Polity Press.

Esping-Andersen, G. (2015) 'The return of the family', in H. Kriesi, H. Kitschelt, P. Beramendi and S. Häusermann (eds) *The Politics of Advanced Capitalism*, Cambridge: Cambridge University Press, pp 157–76.

Esping-Andersen, G. and Billari, F.C. (2015) 'Re-theorizing family demographics', *Population and Development Review*, 41(1): 1–31.

Ferragina, E. and Seeleib-Kaiser, M. (2015) 'Determinants of a silent (r)evolution: understanding the expansion of family policy in rich OECD countries', *Social Politics*, 22(1): 1–37.

Ferrera, M. (2017) 'Impatient politics and social investment: the EU as "policy facilitator"', *Journal of European Public Policy*, 24(8): 1233–51.

Filippetti, A. and Guy, F. (2016) 'Skills and social insurance: evidence from the relative persistence of innovation during the financial crisis in Europe', *Science and Public Policy*, 43(4): 505–17.

Fleckenstein, T. and Lee, S.C. (2014) 'The politics of postindustrial social policy: family policy reforms in Britain, Germany, South Korea, and Sweden', *Comparative Political Studies*, 47(4): 601–30.

Fleckenstein, T. and Lee, S.C. (2017) 'The politics of investing in families: comparing family policy expansion in Japan and South Korea', *Social Politics*, 24(1): 1–28.

Fleckenstein, T. and Seeleib-Kaiser, M. (2011) 'Business, skills and the welfare state: the political economy of employment-oriented family policy in Britain and Germany', *Journal of European Social Policy*, 21(2): 136–49.

Garritzmann, J.L., Busemeyer, M.R. and Neimanns, E. (2018) 'Public demand for social investment: new supporting coalitions for welfare state reform in Western Europe?', *Journal of European Public Policy*, 25(6): 844–61.

Harper, S. (2006) *Ageing Societies: Myths, Challenges and Opportunities*, London: Hodder Arnold.

Hemerijck, A. (2015) 'The quiet paradigm revolution of social investment', *Social Politics*, 22(2): 242–56.

Hemerijck, A. (2017) 'Social investment and its critics', in A. Hemerijck (ed) *The Uses of Social Investment*, Oxford: Oxford University Press, pp 3–39.

Huber, E. and Stephens, J.D. (2001) *Development and Crisis of the Welfare State: Parties and Policies in Global Markets*, Chicago: University of Chicago Press.

Iversen, T. (2005) *Capitalism, Democracy, and Welfare*, Cambridge: Cambridge University Press.

Kim, Y.Y. and Choi, Y.J. (2019) 'Does social protection crowd out social investment?', *Policy and Society*, 39(2): 208–25.

Koo, J., Choi, Y.J. and Park, I. (2019) 'Innovation and welfare: the marriage of an unlikely couple', *Policy and Society*, 39(2): 189–207.

Korpi, W. (1983) *The Democratic Class Struggle*, London: Routledge and Kegan Paul.

Korpi, W. (2000) 'Faces of inequality: gender, class, and patterns of inequalities in different types of welfare states', *Social Politics*, 7(2): 127–91.

Korpi, W. (2006) 'Power resources and employer-centered approaches in explanations of welfare states and varieties of capitalism: protagonists, consenters, and antagonists', *World Politics*, 58(2): 167–206.

Kuitto, K. (2016) 'From social security to social investment? Compensating and social investment welfare policies in a life-course perspective', *Journal of European Social Policy*, 26(5): 442–59.

Kvist, J. (2015) 'A framework for social investment strategies: integrating generational, life course and gender perspectives in the EU social investment strategy', *Comparative European Politics*, 13(1): 131–49.

Lesthaeghe, R. (1995) 'The second demographic transition in western countries: an interpretation', in K.O. Mason and A.-M. Jensen (eds) *Gender and Family Change in Industrialized Countries*, Oxford: Clarendon Press, pp 17–62.

Lesthaeghe, R. and Surkyn, J. (1988) 'Cultural dynamics and economic theories of fertility change', *Population and Development Review*, 14(1): 1–45.

Lewis, J. (1992) 'Gender and the development of welfare regimes', *Journal of European Social Policy*, 2(3): 159–73.

Lewis, J., Knijn, T., Martin, C. and Ostner, I. (2008) 'Patterns of development in work/family reconciliation policies for parents in France, Germany, the Netherlands, and the UK in the 2000s', *Social Politics*, 15(3): 261–86.

Mkandawire, T. (2007) 'Transformative social policy and innovation in developing countries', *The European Journal of Development Research*, 19(1): 13–29.

Morel, N., Palier, B. and Palme, J. (2012) *Towards a Social Investment Welfare State? Ideas, Policies and Challenges*, Bristol: Policy Press.

Nikolai, R. (2012) 'Towards social investment? Patterns of public policy in the OECD world', in N. Morel, B. Palier and J. Palme (eds) *Towards a Social Investment Welfare State? Ideas, Policies and Challenges*, Bristol: Policy Press, pp 91–116.

Nolan, B. (2013) 'What use is "social investment"?', *Journal of European Social Policy*, 23(5): 459–68.

Nolan, B. (2017) 'Social investment: the thin line between evidence-based research and political advocacy', in A. Hemerijck (ed) *The Uses of Social Investment*, Oxford: Oxford University Press, pp 43–50.

OECD (Organisation for Economic Co-operation and Development) (2008) *Growing Unequal? Income Distribution and Poverty in OECD Countries*, Paris: OECD.

OECD (Organisation for Economic Co-operation and Development) (2015) *In It Together: Why Less Inequality Benefits All*, Paris: OECD.

OECD (Organisation for Economic Co-operation and Development) (2016) *The Productivity-Inclusiveness Nexus*, preliminary version, Paris: OECD.

OECD (Organisation for Economic Co-operation and Development) (2018a) *A Broken Social Elevator? How to Promote Social Mobility*, Paris: OECD.

OECD (Organisation for Economic Co-operation and Development) (2018b) *Opportunities for All: The Framework for Policy Action on Inclusive Growth*, Paris: OECD.

OECD (Organisation for Economic Co-operation and Development) (2019) *Pensions at a Glance 2019: OECD and G20 Indicators*, Paris: OECD.

Orloff, A.S. (1993) 'Gender and the social rights of citizenship: the comparative analysis of gender relations and welfare states', *American Sociological Review*, 58(3): 303–28.

Ostry, J.D., Berg, A. and Tsangarides, C.G. (2014) 'Redistribution, inequality, and growth', *Revista de Economía Institucional*, 16(30): 53–81.

Pierson, P. (2001) 'Coping with permanent austerity: welfare state restructuring in affluent democracies', in P. Pierson (ed) *The New Politics of the Welfare State*, New York: Oxford University Press. pp 410–57.

Saraceno, C. (2017) 'Family relationships and gender equality in the social investment discourse: an overly reductive view?', in A. Hemerijck (ed) *The Uses of Social Investment*, Oxford: Oxford University Press, pp 59–65.

Schmid, G. (1998) 'Transitional labour markets: A new European employment strategy', WZB Discussion Paper, No. FS I, 98–206.

Seeleib-Kaiser, M. and Toivonen, T. (2011) 'Between reforms and birth rates: Germany, Japan, and family policy discourse', *Social Politics*, 18(3): 331–60.

Swenson, P.A. (2004) 'Varieties of capitalist interests: power, institutions, and the regulatory welfare state in the United States and Sweden', *Studies in American Political Development*, 18(1): 1–29.

Taylor-Gooby, P. (eds) (2004) *New Risks, New Welfare: The Transformation of the European Welfare State*, Oxford: Oxford University Press.

Tyree, A. and Treas, J. (1974) 'The occupational and marital mobility of women', *American Sociological Review*, 39(3): 293–302.

Vandenbroucke, F. and Vleminckx, K. (2011) 'Disappointing poverty trends: is the social investment state to blame?', *Journal of European Social Policy*, 21(5): 450–71.

Zaidi, B. and Morgan, S.P. (2017) 'The second demographic transition theory: a review and appraisal', *Annual Review of Sociology*, 43(1): 473–92.

# 2

# Work–family policy expansion and the idea of social investment: the cases of Germany, England, South Korea and Japan

*Samuel Mohun Himmelweit and Sung-Hee Lee*

## Introduction

Since the late 1990s, many countries in the Organisation for Economic Co-operation and Development (OECD) have introduced work–family reconciliation policies aimed at enabling families, and women in particular, to more easily balance the demands of employment and childcare. To this end, early childhood education and care (ECEC) services as well as childcare leave policies have been expanded across welfare states of different traditions and institutional origins, including, notably, East Asian welfare states (An, 2013; Ferragina and Seeleib-Kaiser, 2015; Daly and Ferragina, 2018).

Comparative explanations of this shift have highlighted a number of 'new social risks' that are facing modern welfare states (Bonoli, 2005). First, the decline of permanent, full-time employment that characterised industrial economies has eroded the feasibility of the 'family' wage, which underpinned many states' support of the male-breadwinner model family (Lewis, 1992). Second is a growth in women's employment, which has occurred to different extents in different countries, as a response to the need for higher family incomes but also because of women's demands for inclusion in the public realm (Lewis et al, 2008). Third, the shift to service sector-dominated economies has placed a premium on skills and education, which are increasingly vital for labour market success in a globalised, knowledge economy (Bonoli, 2007). Fourth, there has been a decline since the 1970s of birth rates across high-income countries, a trend that has exacerbated the fiscal and social strains presented by demographic ageing (Castles, 2003). These challenges have created new demands for policies that support women's employment, improve education and address falling birth rates (Mätzke and Ostner, 2010a).

In attempting to meet these challenges, many countries have followed the example of social-democratic welfare states, which had introduced work–family policies in earlier decades (Leira, 1992; Ellingsæter and Leira, 2006). In particular, this has involved increasing the availability, affordability and quality of ECEC and introducing or redesigning parental leave policies in order to encourage mothers to maintain labour market attachment after childbirth. Both the pioneering expansion in social-democratic countries and the more recent changes elsewhere have therefore been understood as constituting a shift away from norms and assumptions based on male-breadwinner model families that have underpinned social policy in most countries since the foundation of modern welfare states (Lewis, 1992). Instead, policies are now based on an assumption of an adult worker model, in which all adults are considered participants in the labour market (Lewis, 2001; Orloff, 2006; Daly, 2011).

As such it can be claimed that the changes mark a path departure in many welfare states away from traditional approaches to family policy. Yet, while expansion has been the rule across OECD countries, there is significant variation in approach (Mätzke and Ostner, 2010b; Ferragina and Seeleib-Kaiser, 2015). Countries vary in the design of their work–family policies, including, inter alia, the length and level of remuneration of parental leave, the amount of leave reserved for fathers, the extent of support for childcare costs, the public–private mix of ECEC provisions, the level of universality or conditionality of ECEC provisions, and the age at which children qualify for ECEC provisions. If social democratic countries pioneered a model of family policy, variation in the constitutive aspects of this model means that the latecomers differ in the extent to which their policy packages have followed the pioneers' example. This variation raises the question of what determines how far different welfare states have shifted towards a social democratisation of family policy.

Most of the relevant comparative literature has focused on the 'path-breaking' nature of the reforms, and seeks to explain how change came about (for example Morgan, 2013; Fleckenstein and Lee, 2014; Estevez-Abe and Naldini, 2016; León et al, 2019). This chapter takes a different approach. It examines variation in the trend of work–family policy expansion, by exploring the reforms in four latecomer countries: Germany, England,[1] South Korea and Japan. These countries were all strong male-breadwinner countries, implicitly or explicitly, in which the state has historically had little or no role in how families brought up their children, beyond provision for those in need (Hantrais, 2004; An and Peng, 2016). However, this situation has fundamentally shifted since the expansion of work–family policies; in each of these countries there is now an acceptance that the state is responsible at least in part for the education and care of pre-school children. Thus, the four countries are emblematic of the wider trend of work–family policy expansion, yet they provide a breadth of cases that are appropriate to the investigation of variations within the broader trend. They represent a mix of approaches: conservative-corporatist (Germany), liberal (England), and a combination of elements of both conservative and liberal welfare states (South Korea and Japan) (Kwon, 1997; Esping-Andersen, 1999).

The ideational literature has highlighted that a major advantage of taking ideas seriously as explanatory variables is that they can serve to illuminate the content as well as the direction of institutional change (Béland, 2009). Underpinning many of the rationales for expansion of work–family policy has been the idea of social investment. The argument put forward here is that the different ways in which work–family policies expanded in these four countries can be related to the content and use of the idea of social investment in the respective countries. Drawing on the concepts of 'polysemy' and 'coalition magnets' from the ideational literature, it is argued that in Germany and South Korea, the social investment discourse was broader and more polysemic in terms of what investment could achieve, whereas in England and Japan social investment was discussed in narrower terms (Béland and Cox, 2016). This led to the idea of social investment in work–family policies being a more successful coalition magnet in the former two countries, attracting support from a wider selection of powerful actors. The result was that there has been greater political consensus about work–family policy expansion in Germany and South Korea, which has led to more sustained and consistent expansion in these two countries, and thus a more dramatic path departure than in England or Japan, where elements of path dependence are more evident.

The chapter is structured as follows. The next section reviews the literature on discourse and ideas, with a particular focus on the concept of social investment. It concentrates on the main theoretical concepts of polysemy and ideas as coalition magnets. The third section examines the use of social investment discourse in each of the cases and relates it back to the discussion of polysemy and coalition magnets; it focuses on the ways in which policy-makers defined the relevant policy problems and policy goals of work–family policy expansion. The final section offers some conclusions and suggestions for further research.

## Social investment, polysemy and coalition magnets

The social investment perspective represents a different approach to social policy from the social protection focus of post-1945 welfare states and the residual safety-net approach of neoliberalism (Morel et al, 2012a; Gingrich and Ansell, 2015). Social investment involves using state resources to improve individuals' resilience against social risks, rather than as compensation for them. Such use of resources, the argument goes, is beneficial for the individual but also for society as a whole. As such, the concept of social investment has been central to calls for expansion of work–family policies; indeed, such policies are an archetypical example of the social investment perspective (Morel et al, 2012b; Hemerijck, 2017). The investment in these policies brings a number of potential benefits at both the individual and collective levels. First, they are key to raising maternal employment rates, especially for single mothers. Maternal employment increases the labour supply, the available skills to the economy and potential tax revenue, and is also considered to bring long-term benefits in that it helps prevent children growing up in poverty, which is damaging for future life chances (OECD, 2006, 2007). Second, ECEC services represent an investment in human capital. Quality pre-school education is related to better school-readiness and therefore better outcomes throughout school education (OECD, 2017a). Furthermore, early education is also associated with better social outcomes in the longer term, particularly for children from disadvantaged backgrounds, which implies significant savings for the state in the future (Heckman, 2006). Third, investment in ECEC is part of a skills agenda enabling countries to transition towards the knowledge economies of the future (Lister, 2003). Fourth, leave policies have also been seen to be important in maintaining mothers' connection to the labour market after childbirth, thus avoiding the skill depreciation that can occur with long periods away from employment. This is especially relevant given the high levels of education women are achieving across many high-income countries (OECD, 2017b). Finally, work–family policies have also been related to the issue of falling birth rates and demographic ageing, with analysis showing that countries with extensive work–family reconciliation policies are those where the birth rate has remained near the replacement rate (Thévenon and Gauthier, 2011).

Social investment therefore is a multi-faceted idea, within which different elements can be brought to the fore and behind which there is not necessarily a shared consensus on a single meaning. For example, Jenson (2010) has shown that the 'social investment state' called for by

Giddens (1998) which would invest in human and social capital was more limited and supply-side focused than the 'child-centred social investment strategy' of Esping-Andersen et al (2002). This ambiguity has acted as a 'mechanism of diffusion' for the overall idea of social investment: through its promotion by academics and international organisations, the concept has spread to countries with very different social, political and ideological contexts (Jenson, 2010). As Ambiguity has also been shown to be a powerful trait in terms of improving an idea's political fortunes. For example, Hall's work on Keynesianism notes that the inherent ambiguity of Keynesian ideas 'enhanced their power in the political sphere. By reading slightly different emphases into these ideas, an otherwise disparate set of groups could unite under the same banner'(1989: 367). Similarly, Schmidt and Thatcher argue in relation to neoliberalism that '[t]he very generality and plasticity of neo-liberalism, which make the concept seemingly amorphous and difficult to define precisely, are key reasons for its resilience' (2013: 27). These examples use a number of different terms (ambiguity, generality, plasticity) to capture a fundamental concept that Béland and Cox (2016) have labelled 'polysemy'. Ideational literature has argued that polysemy is a key feature of politically successful ideas, as it enables the idea to function as a coalition magnet. That coalitions may contain internal variance in their interpretations of central ideas has also been noted in policy analysis literature. This literature has highlighted that the wider a set of potential interpretations, the broader the potential coalition around those interpretations can be, and therefore the more likely it is to lead to some form of policy change. Empirically, this feature has been shown to important in social policy change (Baumgartner and Jones, 1993; Sabatier and Jenkins-Smith, 1993). In his account of French welfare state reform, Palier finds that 'ambiguous agreement' is a key feature of policy change, arguing that ideas which can 'aggregate different – and even contradictory – interests, based on different, and sometimes contrasting, interpretations of the consequence' are a crucial feature of change (2005: 138). It is reasonable to conclude therefore, that in general, polysemic ideas will attract the broadest support: they will function more strongly as coalition magnets than more narrowly defined ideas.

The polysemic character of ideas has two implications for comparative analysis. First, that internationally diffuse ideas may appear with different emphases in different countries (Béland, 2009). Ideas are influenced by a wide set of factors including political circumstances, national normative traditions, institutional structures and policy trajectories (Campbell, 2004; Schmidt, 2006). Second, in this cross-national variation, the level of polysemy is also likely to vary. In some countries an internationally polysemic idea may retain a breadth of meaning whereas in others a narrower version of the same idea may be dominant. This is likely to be linked to the political fortunes of that idea: as noted above, the broader a coalition that can coalesce around an idea, the more likely it is to achieve its aims.

The empirical cases explored in the next sections highlight how these concepts can help explain variation in policy change. In each case, the analysis focuses on the initial period of reform and on the ways in which government documents and politicians referred to work–family policies. First, they show that the polysemy of social investment ideas means that the discourse around the expansion of work–family policy has varied in the four countries, and, in particular, that it was more polysemic in Germany and South Korea than in England and Japan. Second, they demonstrate that the countries in which the local version of social investment was more polysemic have seen a broader political coalition coalesce around reform to work–family policies. And third, that the countries which have a broader political coalition for reform of work-family policies have indeed seen a more coherent and sustained expansion of these policies, and thus a more dramatic path departure.

## Germany

With its employment-based social insurance schemes and strong focus on status preservation, the (West) German welfare state was the archetypical 'conservative-corporatist' welfare regime (Esping-Andersen, 1990). Central to this was the notion of subsidiarity, in which welfare provisions were centred on providing a male, industrial worker with a family wage and relying on the family for the provision of care. Germany's welfare state therefore provided relatively few services and relied on families and traditional gender roles for its functioning: the epitome of a strong male-breadwinner model welfare state (Ostner, 2010). Until the mid-1980s, this model was reflected in family policies which encouraged women to leave the labour market at childbirth (Ostner, 1991). In 1986, the introduction of parental leave ushered in a new 'sequential' model of female labour market engagement: withdrawal from the labour market at childbirth and subsequent return to part-time employment once the child reached school age (Blome, 2016).[2] Despite a right to a part-time kindergarten for children aged three and over being enacted in 1996, Germany lagged behind other European countries in its provision of ECEC, which compounded the effect of encouraging mothers to leave the labour market for significant periods (Bleses and Seeleib-Kaiser, 2004). The Red–Green government, elected in 1998, initially only modified this situation with a reform to parental leave in 2000.[3] However, after its re-election in 2002, the Social Democratic Party (SPD) family minister Renate Schmidt sought to initiate change.

The new approach specified a broad policy problem: that families were struggling to reconcile work and family responsibilities. While this had previously been acknowledged as a problem for individuals and families, Schmidt recast the problem as a long-term threat to Germany's prosperity:

> Living and working conditions of working parents need to improve. Otherwise, there is a danger that more and more young women and men will not fulfil their wishes for children, or that those who start a family will not be able to develop their professional skills. Both would be difficult to cope with in the future. (SPD, 2001: 305)

This dual problem of difficult work–family reconciliation – that Germany was missing out on both women's skills in the labour market and on babies – was backed up by hard economic evidence (Leitner et al, 2008). From 2003, the Family Ministry commissioned a series of reports and economic analyses on the fiscal benefits of improving the maternal employment rate (for example, Spieß et al, 2003). Rürup and Gruescu (2003) argued that a shrinking population would harm economic growth, and that investment in a sustainable family policy would lead to long-term benefits through an increase in children's learning and subsequent skill development and a reduction in poverty. Schmidt made the claim about demographics explicit in November 2003: 'Germany needs more children if we want to maintain our prosperity' (Schmidt, 2003), breaking a taboo for German politicians, particularly from the SPD (Seeleib-Kaiser and Toivonen, 2011). By presenting demographics as key to prosperity, Schmidt was able to link her agenda to an ongoing high-profile media discussion over demographic ageing and the sustainability of the German social insurance model. Further, by emphasising that improving work–family balance was an investment in future prosperity, the ministry linked the agenda to a growing debate over Germany's educational performance, triggered by the 'PISA shock' of the early 2000s, the outcry which greeted Germany's relatively poor performance in the OECD's comparison of student learning outcomes (Frindte and Mierendorff, 2017).

Thus alleviating families' struggles with work–family balance was linked to Germany's future success in a range of areas. The solutions proposed by the ministry emphasised this breadth of goals and were not solely aimed at easing mothers' access to the labour market, but also at improving quality of life for parents, so that more families would choose to fulfil their *Kinderwunsch* – their desire to have children – as well as to have careers (Bertram et al, 2005; BMFSFJ, 2005; Ristau, 2005). This idea was broad enough for Chancellor Gerhard Schröder to emphasise that the new approach contained no normative prescription, and thus did not threaten traditional notions of subsidiarity and the family: 'Mothers and fathers who decide against gainful employment and for child-raising and family work deserve all our respect and support. But when people are forced, without wanting to, to choose family or work, I think something is wrong in our society' (Bundestag Plenarprotokoll, 2002).

The 2004 Tagesbetreuungsausbaugesetz (TAG) law undertook to increase by 230,000 the number of places available for children under the age of 3 by 2010. Due to the electoral defeat of the Red–Green coalition in 2005, this was the only major reform undertaken by Schmidt's ministry. Yet the new Grand Coalition led by the Christian Democratic Union (CDU) continued the expansive direction of family policy. If anything, the pace of expansion increased under CDU family minister Ursula von der Leyen. In 2006, parental leave was reformed, replacing the two year flat-rate benefit with a 12-month earnings-related benefit, and an extra two 'partner months' available on a use-it-or-lose-it basis. The 2008 Kinderförderungsgesetz (KiföG) built on and extended the TAG, aiming to increase national provisions to 33 per cent of all children under 3 by 2013, which would require the creation of a further of 750,000 new places in childcare facilities, and instituted a universal legal right to a childcare place for all children from their first birthday, which would come into force in 2013 (Blome, 2016).

Thus the redefinition of work–family balance from a narrow idea about individual well-being to a broad idea centred on national prosperity was followed by a period of dramatic reform between 2004 and 2008, spanning two different governments. While the phrase 'social investment' was rarely used, the themes of a social investment approach were clearly central to the discourse (Seeleib-Kaiser, 2017). The successful building of a broad coalition of support for reform was essential to this process. Politicians were able to take elements from the overarching idea to make arguments tailored towards key potential opponents and win broad support from across society. Schmidt and Schröder persuaded business leaders that German competitiveness depended on making better use of women's skills, especially given that by the early 2000s women were achieving higher levels of educational attainment than men, a point made by Schröder in his memoirs: 'never before has there been a generation of women who are so highly qualified … For companies, which will have difficulty finding qualified personnel within a few years, these women are also the qualified workforce of the future' (2006: 439–40, author's translation). This argument proved effective with the major unions and employers' associations, which became active promoters of reform and whose leaders made numerous public appearances alongside Schmidt and von der Leyen (DIHK, 2003; Schmidt and Mohn, 2004; BDA, 2006; Mohn and von der Leyen, 2007). Elsewhere, Schmidt won support within a sceptical SPD for the potentially controversial parental leave reforms,[4] invoking gender equality and the example of Sweden (see Persson, 2005). Von der Leyen continued Schmidt's approach, stating her aim of making 'family-friendliness a trademark of the Germany economy' (Mohn and von der Leyen, 2007: 15). Furthermore, she also supported the idea of partner months, linking it to the demographic issue: 'More men than women exclude a child in their life planning. Something has to change here' (von der Leyen quoted in Vowinkel and Rübel, 2005). The combination of linking work–family balance to Germany's economic and demographic future was crucial in persuading more conservative elements of the Christian Social Union (CSU)[5] of the need for reform (personal interview with former CSU politician, 2018).

Overall, while the phrase 'social investment' was rarely mentioned during the reform of German family policy, both the public discourse, and the shape of the reforms themselves, bear the hallmarks of the social investment perspective. First Schmidt and then von der Leyen were able to create a broad discourse around the notion of sustainable family policy, recasting a relatively narrow issue – work–family balance – into a broadly defined problem for the future prosperity of Germany, which permitted a flexible interpretation of potential solutions. For the SPD, this included concerns about gender equality – both in the labour market and in the household – poverty and inequality; for modernisers in the CDU it could incorporate the demands of business for skilled labour, the demands of women voters and concerns about the financial sustainability of status-preserving social insurance systems; for the more traditional wing of the CDU it could help solve the national 'crisis' of a low birth rate; while across the political spectrum it could address other concerns about Germany's place in the modern world in terms of its educational and economic performance. This polysemic version of social investment helped build a broad alliance in favour of the reforms, which eventually incorporated all major political parties, employer associations, unions and even some religious organisations. The continued high profile of family policy on the political agenda in recent years is evidence of this.

## England

Traditionally, English family policy was extremely meagre, limited to paying residual benefits and providing some 'welfare' daycare services for those 'in need' (Lewis, 2009). In line with the liberal welfare regime's principle of a limited state and reliance on markets, ECEC was considered a private responsibility outside the remit of the government, best delivered by the market, while leave was seen as best arranged between individuals and employers. England was therefore, like Germany, a strong male-breadwinner model welfare state, although this was more a result of a lack of government involvement rather than through explicit promotion (Hantrais, 2004). In this policy vacuum, a market for ECEC provisions had developed, but was expensive and varied greatly in quality and availability (Randall, 2000). Some tentative steps towards reform had been taken in the 1990s, but the Conservative government had shown little appetite for major change, and work–family balance was seen as a private matter, in which the state should not be involved (Randall, 1995).

Labour won the 1997 election and came into government with an approach to work–family policies that was split between two different goals. On the one hand there was a discourse highlighting the long-term benefits of investment in young children: 'children are 20 percent of the population but they are 100 percent of the future' was a frequently used refrain by Labour leaders (Blair, 1999; Brown, 2001, 2002). Labour had promised to 'make education our number one priority', saying it is 'not just good for the individual. It is an economic necessity for the nation' (Labour Party, 1997). Investment in children's education was an investment in the country: 'By investing in [children], we are investing in our future' said the Chancellor of the Exchequer Gordon Brown (1999: 8). The potential benefits of this investment were savings in the costs of long-term social problems: 'for every pound that we invest in a child's early years we shall save many pounds later on everything from support for a child with special educational needs to the payment of income support.' (Hansard, 1999).

The second policy goal was to increase the proportion of mothers, particularly lone parents, in employment, in order to combat child poverty and increase the labour supply. Brown's endogenous growth theory argued that employment was key to increasing the productive capacity of the economy through mobilising unused skills (Crafts, 1996). Labour had positioned its approach to social policy as 'a modern form of welfare that believes in empowerment not dependency' (DSS, 1998: 19), and it placed 'activation' of those not working at its centre. Lone parents were a particular focus, due to the links between lone parent families and child poverty, which Labour aimed to eradicate by 2020 (Blair, 1999). As such, a lack of available and affordable childcare was identified as a barrier to employment, for lone parents in particular, and as an area in which spending could lead to both productivity gains and poverty reduction (see Harman, 2017). Childcare was therefore discussed in economic terms: 'care should be regarded as part of the national economic infrastructure and as important to women as the roads and railways on which they travel to work' (Hansard, 1997). Leave policies were similar, with the government stressing the benefits to the economy of expanded provisions: 'Competitiveness depends on the UK making the best use of the talents of as many people as possible. The larger the number of people – particularly skilled people – to which business can look, the better.' (DTI, 1998: para 5.1).

With its large parliamentary majority, Labour did not need Conservative support for reform. Nevertheless, the party was keen not to alienate organised business, stressing the business case of policies that encouraged mothers to stay in the labour market (DTI, 2000). Furthermore, policy-makers were sensitive to accusations of government overreach and stressed the importance of a childcare market of diverse providers in which parental choice was vital. By adapting such an approach, Labour was able to win the grudging acceptance of leave regulation from organised business and counter any claim from political opponents that these policies represented the nanny state.

Thus Labour's rhetoric about work–family policy reform was split between a rationale for investment in early education based on the benefits for children in the future, and the goal of increasing maternal employment, especially among single parents, which prioritised increasing the availability of childcare and improving leave provisions. This fragmentation perpetuated the long-standing divide between education and care (Lewis, 2013), and was the result of differing processes by which they became Labour policy. The development of early education was a bottom-up process led by child development experts who were linked to Labour through Margaret Hodge, a former local government leader who had pioneered integrated ECEC centres.

The employment agenda, meanwhile, was more closely linked to Brown's Treasury and to Harriet Harman, a high-profile feminist MP, who had been Brown's deputy in the early 1990s and who helped incorporate feminist campaigners' arguments for childcare provisions into Labour's economic programme. This separation of the policies was maintained after 1997 through administrative fragmentation (Eisenstadt, 2011), and was evident in policy design: early education was a universal offer to parents of 3- and 4-year-olds of 12.5 hours per week free childcare for 33 weeks per year, which had to be taken as 2.5 hours daily, conditions which made it difficult to combine with employment.[6] The National Childcare Strategy (DfEE and DSS, 1998), on the other hand, was targeted: while some government funding was available to help launch childcare provisions in low-income areas, the main strategy was to support low-income working parents with the costs of childcare through means-tested in-work benefits. Leave policies, with their focus on the business case, were developed through a process of consultation with employers and parents, which led to a series of incremental reforms that extended maternity leave and increased maternity leave benefits, while doing little to challenge the 'maternalist' focus of leave policies (Daly and Scheiwe, 2010).

After 2002 there were attempts to broaden the policy goals in each of the three areas. Labour's rhetoric on ECEC became more focused on evidence that it could help narrow attainment gaps between children from different social backgrounds (Sylva et al, 2004). Child development now became a key focus of the whole of ECEC, and this served to bring the two sides of ECEC policy together. Nevertheless, while this involved significantly more spending, the overall approach of universal, part-time, early education for 3- and 4-year-olds, supplemented by means-tested financial support for working parents with the costs of market provision remained Labour's model (HMT et al, 2004; Moss, 2014). There was also a shift in rhetoric around leave when the relevant minister, Patricia Hewitt, attempted to broaden the approach, arguing that families required 'real choice' in how to balance work and family life, which would involve more gender-neutral leave (HMT and DTI, 2003). However, she was unable to win the support of employers, who had only begrudgingly supported previous extensions to maternity leave (Hewitt, 2014). Labour had built support for leave policy expansion on the back of a business case; such a case could not be so easily made for fathers and it proved difficult to make any other case given opposition both from the Conservatives and business who claimed that the government was promoting a nanny state (for example *Daily Mail*, 2004).

Overall, the initial expansion of work–family policies in the UK under the Labour governments of 1997–2010 had a social investment focus, but it was split into separate parts: a promotion of education for young children and a promotion of employment for mothers. As such, a broad and polysemic discourse for a package of policy reforms did not emerge, and early education, childcare and leave policies were each developed by separate government departments with separate aims. While each area saw significant reform, and the introduction of free universal early education was new, there were also strong policy continuities with the pre-1997 status quo: targeted support for childcare costs and expansion of maternity leave. Thus leave policies permitted mothers to take time out of the labour market at childbirth, but did little to shift incentives within households about care roles. Further, childcare policy was designed as economic infrastructure and thus focused on the low-income families that the government wanted to move into the labour market. The fragmented nature of the overall discourse meant that while within each policy area opponents were convinced to at least acquiesce to changes (for example businesses were persuaded to accept increased maternity leave in exchange for administrative simplification). Thus change was necessarily incremental and opposition became difficult to overcome when attempts were made to broaden the overall idea.

## South Korea

South Korea belongs to a group of welfare states in East Asia which share the common cultural heritage of Confucianism, a religion that emphasises the role of the family and hard work (Jones, 1993; Goodman and Peng, 1996; Sung, 2003; Walker and Wong, 2005). Confucian principles involve an unconditional obligation for women to take on the roles of housewives and/or caregivers in the family rather than to become active in the labour market (Peng, 2004). However, Confucian philosophy has been challenged by demographic and socioeconomic changes, especially those occurring since the 1990s, such as a rise in the age of first marriage and a concomitant fall in the fertility rate, which has remained persistently low (in 2003, the country recorded the lowest fertility rate among OECD countries at 1.08 children per woman, called 'the 1.08 shock'). This rapid decline in the fertility rate was seen as a serious socioeconomic threat to the future workforce, as it coincided with an increasingly ageing population: the percentage of the population aged over 65 was projected to be 14.5 per cent by 2020 (KNSO, 2003, cited in Peng, 2004). Another significant social change was the dramatic increase between 1960 and 2000 in the number of working women, particularly married women, while the proportion of women working shorter hours and holding temporary jobs had increased (Peng, 2004). Further, there were increases in the number of single mother families and the child poverty rate, both of which became policy issues in South Korea. Even though there remained a strong cultural identity based in Confucianism, these demographic and socioeconomic changes brought to the fore new policy concerns, including debates over the lack of childcare provisions and working families' need for support. Strong commitment to ensuring greater childcare support, especially for working families, was revealed in the statement made by President Roh Moo-hyun (2003–7), who defeated conservative elites, during his address at Women's Week celebrations on 4 July 2003: 'Once you give birth, the government will look after your children' (Presidential Secretary Office, 2004).

This policy recognition of childcare had already begun during the presidency of Kim Dae-jung (1998–2002), which has been identified as the period in which the state began actively intervening in childcare (Byun, 2000; Baek and Seo, 2004; Kim, 2007, 2010; Peng, 2011a, 2011b; An, 2013; Fleckenstein and Lee, 2014; Lee, 2016). The Kim government pursued the ideology of productivism, in which 'social policy is strictly subordinate to the over-riding policy objective of economic growth' (Holliday, 2000: 708; see also Chan, 2002; Peng and Wong, 2008). The Roh government further developed specific coordinated policies to address the linked issues of childcare and work–family balance and adopted a rhetoric of social investment: the policy goal of investing in children's development and work–family reconciliation was associated with a proliferation of social policies and programmes related to ECEC (The Presidential Committee on Ageing and Future Society, 2004; The Committee on the Low Fertility Rate and Ageing Society, 2006). In pursuit of this goal, support for families with children was demonstrated through extended maternity legal protection, maternity and parental leave. Investments in extending childcare and leave policies were taken up as primary policy goals for resolving the low birth rate and promoting women's working participation in the labour market. In fact, the Presidential Committee on Ageing and Future Society, established during the Roh government, announced four policy goals: to 'boost the fertility rate and foster the future work force', to 'alleviate the cost of childcare for parents', to 'increase women's participation in the workforce' and to 'create new job sectors' (The Presidential Committee on Ageing and Future Society, 2004). Subsequently, these policy goals were highlighted in a governmental report issued during the Roh presidency, 'The stable infrastructure for supporting childcare: policy effort to reinforce the socialisation of childcare', which stated that childcare policy was based on the recognition of child well-being as a form of long-term investment in children and women (The Presidential Counsel of Policy Planning Committee, 2007: 5–8).

These policy goals, couched in the language of social investment, can therefore be considered as reflecting the state's concern regarding 'investing in children's development', which subsequently raised the political profile of extending socialised childcare services. Similarly, the policy goal of 'work–family reconciliation' for caregivers and the provision of suitable childcare services became areas politicians were conscious of and, more importantly, acknowledged as requiring attention. These policy goals can be identified as the source of a paradigm shift: a new acceptance that welfare expansion could be viewed as a form of investment, targeting not only children's development, but also reconciling work–life balance tensions in order to increase female employment.

The polysemic concept of social investment was driven forward within a gender-friendly political environment during the two aforementioned governments. It appears that the two presidents were eager to institutionalise 'femocrats' (that is, female bureaucrats) to push for women's interests in public policies. For example, the Kim government founded the Ministry of Gender Equality in 2001 and in 2003, during the Roh government, ministerial responsibility for childcare was transferred from the Ministry of Health and Welfare to the Ministry of Gender Equality in order to consolidate issues of childcare with gender perspectives (Lee, 2013, 2017). This transfer underlined that the approach to the issue of childcare was taken from a gender-aware perspective, although there were criticisms that in reality the transfer could not change the gender stereotype of women's role as caregiver. Despite some controversy over the transfer, most women's associations, such as the Korean National Council of Women and the Korean Women's Association United, were in favour of the shift. The rationale for their stance was perhaps their eagerness to have leverage, as up until then, they had enjoyed little political representation. Through such an approach, the broad concept of social investment was able to absorb elements of the gender-friendly political environment at that time, and this helped construct a broader political coalition of women's groups.

Social investment rationales were acceptable even to conservative parties and the business sector, which tended to be against the expansion of welfare expenditure. This was because they promised economic growth through investing in human resources as well as utilising the female labour force. By linking economic growth to the crisis of inadequate childcare provisions, the expense of welfare expansion was justified as addressing the various risks brought about since the 1990s. Therefore, through using social investment discourse, agreement to raising social expenditure was obtained from the most conservative camps in government. Social investment, conceived of and shaped in this fashion, permitted the construction of a broad coalition between the advocates of conservative national ideology and those who supported the South Korean welfare regime of productivism.

Overall, the idea of social investment was embedded as a political consensus in the South Korean political landscape. It allowed for a coherent and sustained approach to fostering children's development and encouraging women's participation in paid work. With concerns being voiced regarding securing a future national workforce, the matters of supporting childcare and encouraging women to enter the labour market were taken seriously during the Roh administration. This priority has continued to the present day and free childcare for children aged up to 5 was expanded following the presidential election held in 2012. Free childcare for children aged up to 5 was further extended in 2018 by providing six hours of free childcare for stay-at-home mothers and 12 hours for those seeking employment or requiring long-term childcare, due to their participation in the labour market. Moreover, maternity and parental leave have been increased, currently providing mothers with 90 days paid leave as well as well as allowing both parents to take one year of childcare leave. Men's childcare leave use increased almost fifty times within a decade, reaching 18 per cent in 2018 (Ministry of Health and Welfare, 2019). Thus, the social investment strategy has contributed towards bringing about a shift in perception in South Korean politics that social welfare expenditure can be interpreted as investment for the future.

## Japan

Traditional welfare provisions in Japan have been generally regarded as distinct, taking a 'residual' form (Tabata, 1990: 2) known as 'Japanese-type welfare society', which emphasises the role of informal self-help, mutual aid, and market- and enterprise-based provisions (Hill, 1995; Esping-Andersen, 1996; Goodman and Peng, 1996; Kono, 2005). Following the global oil shock in the 1970s, the Japanese government suppressed any increase in the state's involvement in welfare by enhancing the role played by other sectors, specifically family and corporate enterprises. This residual approach to welfare remains in place and has been classified as a 'familialist welfare approach' (Ochiai, 2009; Song, 2014). In the face of ongoing modernisation, Japanese cultural heritage became a hindrance and was considered to be standing in the way of the rapid development of a progressive capitalist economy. As a consequence, many traditions, including Confucianism, have been watered down. However, some aspects of Confucian culture, such as its hierarchical rules and traditional social norms including stereotyped gender roles within the family remain strong. In particular, with respect to childcare for infants, there is a persisting cultural view on good mothering which maintains that infants under 3 years old should be looked after by their mothers to ensure proper development (Boling, 2015).

As in South Korea, this traditional belief in the woman's role as caregiver has been challenged by Japan's demographic transition towards an aged society. Concerns regarding the declining birth rate, which occurred some years earlier than in South Korea (Japan's '1.57 shock' happened in 1989), feature particularly strongly. The low fertility rate was seen as a threat to Japan's prolonged economic growth due to its impact on the labour force of the future (Cabinet Office, 2011; JILPT, 2013). At the same time, the proportion of older people in the population was rising sharply, along with demand among for social services. This demographic crisis alarmed the central government and an inter-ministry meeting was launched in 1990 to devise policy measures to address the problem (Suzuki, 2006; Peng, 2011a). This initiative was followed by the formulation of the Basic Direction for Future Child Rearing Support Measures in December 1994, known as the Angel Plan. Following this, in December 1999, the government issued the New Angel Plan for the period between 1999 and 2004, asserting the need to improve gender equity and working conditions. The Junichiro Koizumi government of the conservative Liberal Demographic Party (2001–6) was strongly committed to increasing the fertility rate. For example, during this government, the Ministry of Health, Labour and Welfare announced the 'Measures for Decreasing Children Plus One' encouraging local governments as well as companies to support child-rearing. Moreover, the Koizumi government announced the New, New Angel Plan, emphasising the role of local government and companies in providing childcare support and improving gender equity (Suzuki, 2006).

Subsequent administrations the Democratic Party of Japan (2009–12) also attempted to address the issue of low birth rate and the long waiting lists for childcare centres by setting up a Zero Waiting List Team. The problem of long waiting lists for childcare centres became a major political issue and remains one of the many unresolved childcare issues, especially in the major cities of Japan. This is attributed to the lack of government support for working families as well as the lack of funding for licensed childcare centres. Nevertheless, the political commitment during the Koizumi government could be seen as a progressive step as it developed an emphasis on the role of corporate enterprises that challenged conventional beliefs regarding good mothering. Although the policy goals were not elaborated through a social investment discourse as such, they still demonstrate the Koizumi government's commitment to supporting families' needs for childcare with some degree of awareness of gender equality issues at work, although primarily due to the pressing need to increase the birth rate. However, the political commitment to improving childcare provisions and gender equality was not as strong under the Koizumi's successor, the conservative Shinzo Abe, who returned to power in 2012. Even though he pledged to provide childcare for all children, his main concerns were stimulating economic growth and increasing the workforce available to the labour market, which were seen as ways of addressing the crisis of 'too few children'. In 2015, the cabinet called for intensive efforts to overcome this 'critical situation' whereby the number of children had dwindling to the point that it would shake Japan's societal and economic foundations (*The Japan Times*, 2015). The over-riding concern of the long-term economic recession due to the low birth rate was fully revealed in Abe's address during the meeting for 'Overcoming population decline and vitalising the local economy' held in September 2014, at which he stated: 'Creating local communities, in which young people can work with peace of mind, where it is possible to raise children and hold dreams and hopes for the future, is the path to overcoming Japan's population decline'. Thus economic recovery has been prioritised over further work–family policy reforms as a remedy to the birth rate problem.

As for statutory leave policies, the conservative government passed the Child Care Leave Act in 1991, which was extended to become the Child Care and Family Care Leave Act in 1995. However, under this, the income replacement benefit was only 30 per cent of pre-leave earnings and lasted for up to a year. Men could only take leave for the first eight weeks if their partner was not working. The level of the benefit payment was increased to 50 per cent income replacement with effect from 2007. This revision also extended the Act to help part-time workers, who had had no coverage up until that time (Rebick, 2011).

However during the Abe administration, the introduction of leave lasting up to three years, meant that many mothers could stay at home to look after their children themselves (Estevez-Abe and Kim, 2014; An and Peng, 2016). From one point of view this could be interpreted as a pragmatic solution to the politically salient issue of long waiting lists for childcare places, as it served to manage demand from parents of very young infants. Alternatively, this somewhat contradictory step could be taken as simply reflecting conventional beliefs regarding the obligations of mothers to remain at home as caregivers. Further, only 6.2 per cent of men avail of childcare leave, compared to 82.2 per cent of women (Ministry of Health, Labour and Welfare, 2019, cited in JILPT, 2019).

Compared to South Korea, there were similar or perhaps even more challenging demographic changes in Japan, but the idea of social investment does not seem to have been brought forward as a mainstreaming policy discourse. We argue that this is a result of the specific ways of engaging with the policy discourse. While concerns were voiced regarding the low fertility rate, the prolonged economic recession and labour force supply, the idea of social investment discourse was hardly engaged with in the policy goals. It is hard to judge whether the lack of engagement with social investment discourse has led to unsuccessful policy reforms in the long run, but it has led to contradictory policies, such as in the extension of leave provisions. However, it is clear that the Japanese government did not succeed in preventing fertility decline, and the fertility rate dropped further to 1.26 in 2006, becoming the lowest low rate in the country's history (OECD, 2020).

No single factor explains all policy outcomes, but we argue that the Japanese government's efforts to take actions on declining fertility steered away from fully developing the idea of social investment, and was not sufficiently developed to enable a political coalition for work–family policy reform to coalesce around it. For example, gender issues related to childcare were neglected in the policy-making processes in Japan (Boling, 2008; Imai and Sato, 2011). The role of coalition members, such as women's groups in the case of South Korea or conservative parties in Germany, has been made clear in previous sections. It is difficult to find any evidence showing political coalitions formed with civil organisations in the case of Japan, which points to the conclusion that work–family issues were scarcely touched upon from a broader perspective than just a focus on the birth rate (Peng, 2002; Gelb, 2003). Rather, the steps that were taken could be viewed as supporting elements of a primarily pro-natalist agenda.

Further, the long-standing policy problem of childcare waiting lists has remained unresolved and the ongoing debate about integrating services for pre-schoolers (3- to 5-year-old children) and daycare centres (for children up to age 5) raises doubts regarding whether this offers any real solution to the problem. This is because the debate has remained one-dimensional and fails to address issues relating to unsatisfactory service quality in non-licensed childcare centres and the increasingly inadequate wages for the staff employed in them. Despite the amount of social expenditure increasing, the budget allocation for expenditure targeted at families with children is extremely low compared to other developed countries (National Institute of Population and Social Security Research, 2004; Irigoyen, 2016). According to OECD data on social welfare expenditure in 2015, in Japan 43 per cent was spent on programmes for the elderly, such as pensions, while only 6 per cent was spent on child benefits and childcare services. This is in contrast to South Korea, where only 28 per cent of social expenditure was allocated for older people, while families with children were allocated 12 per cent.

Overall, Japan's approach to work–family policy was relatively narrow and superficial. The shortage of childcare facilities presented private-sector providers with an easy opportunity, which they readily took up given the lack of government action. The reasons for this governmental failure might be related to the institutional legacy of the Japanese-type welfare society, which emphasises the role of the family and corporate enterprises in providing welfare. However, two additional reasons may be responsible. First, the issue of childcare was rarely approached from the context of gender relations, which might be the fundamental reason for the continuing low birth rate. Second, the locally developed version of social investment did not go beyond the primary issue of the birth rate and could therefore neither create an effective political coalition for reform, nor evolve to be polysemic in nature.

## Conclusion

As this detailed investigation of work–family policies has demonstrated, policies such as ECEC services and parental leave have been expanded to differing extents in each of the four countries. Arguably, the reforms have been more consistent and sustained in Germany and South Korea than in England or Japan. In the former countries, both leave policies and ECEC services have been overhauled, with a sequence of reforms keeping work–family policies high on policy-makers' agendas. South

Korea has even gone as far as to introduce universal free childcare. England has reformed its ECEC policies, but since 2010 the issue has only sporadically been on the government's agenda, and provisions remain expensive and of varying quality. Leave policies retain a maternalist approach. In Japan, while childcare has been expanded, reforms have been piecemeal and momentum has been halting, with periods of political interest followed by relatively little attention from policy-makers.

This chapter has argued that the extent and logic of reform can be linked to the idea of social investment. Following Jenson (2010), it was argued above that social investment is a polysemic international idea, which would be translated differently in different national contexts. Indeed, the four cases demonstrate that this is the case. The arguments in each of the countries stressed social investment justifications for a greater state role in easing work–family balance conflicts, but the aims emphasised were different. These included reversing low birth rates, increasing the sustainability of public services by improving the ability of women to have both careers and families, improving human capital formation through a focus on child development, increasing economic productivity by increasing maternal employment, and combating child poverty and inequality through improving family incomes and education.

Further, it was argued that not only would different elements of social investment be emphasised in different national contexts, but that some countries would see a more polysemic local version of social investment, while others would develop a more narrowly defined view. The empirical investigation of the four cases backs up this prediction. In Germany, the arguments for intervention focused on the problem of families choosing not to fulfil their 'desire for children' which led to social and economic costs for Germany as a whole. Thus the social investment rhetoric was focused on employment and education but also on work–family balance as a social issue, linking it to wider concerns about educational outcomes, demographic ageing and gender equality. In South Korea, like in Germany, the social investment arguments related to both economic and demographic concerns, and were linked to a legacy of productivist welfare. ECEC in particular was seen as an investment that would lead to multiple benefits, particularly in terms of child development and maternal employment. In England, instead of a broad social investment discourse, leave, childcare and early education policy each had their own rationales, which were rarely combined into a coherent overall strategy. Thus England presents a case in which a series of different ideas did not come together to form an overarching polysemic idea. As such, a cogent case was not made for the state to intervene within the family, for example to attempt to encourage more fathers to take on care responsibilities, something that Germany was able to do. The focus of reforms in Japan was overwhelmingly on its low birth rate, with comparatively less attention on social investment concepts such as maternal employment, gender equality in the workplace or child development. This meant that ECEC was merely one tool of many that governments could use to combat the national crisis of the low birth rate, and, unlike in the other three countries, work–family reconciliation policies remained something of a partisan issue. This can be seen in the lack of enthusiasm among conservative governments for continued childcare expansion and the introduction of longer leave policies.

Finally, the chapter posited a relationship between polysemy of ideas and the ability of that idea to act as a coalition magnet (Béland and Cox, 2016). Without being able to specify the causal direction, it is notable that both South Korea and Germany have seen broad and sustained coalitions for work–family policy reform supported by parties across the political spectrum and also by employers, unions and women's groups. England has seen both political parties commit to reform, but with less progress since Labour left power in 2010 and notable opposition from employers to any further reform of leave policies. In Japan it is notable that coalitions hardly coalesced around work–family reconciliation policies at all.

By drawing on the details of these four cases, this chapter has made a case for considering the impact of social investment as an *ideational* force in politics. It has argued that ideas can have particular political power when they are imbued with an ambiguity that can appeal to a range of political actors. Such polysemic ideas can act as coalition magnets and attract broad support for policies that may seem surprising in some cases, for example in the German CSU acquiescing to partner months that encourage fathers' participation in childcare. On the other hand, a more narrowly defined social investment idea can constrain political reform, as Patricia Hewitt discovered when she was unable to make the case for more gender-neutral parental leave in England. However, this is not to claim, of course, that other factors are unimportant: we have seen in the examples that institutional legacies, such as the English reliance on market provision or Japanese familialism, play powerful constraining roles on the potential for significant reform.

Further, a polysemic idea does not imply a completely coherent agenda. German policy-makers have been accused of taking two steps forward, one step backwards in terms of their failure to enact reform of tax splitting, which provide incentives for married women to withdraw from the labour market (Müller and Wrohlich, 2014). South Korean reforms have been criticised for their lack of attention to the significant discrimination women face in the labour market or the lack of enforcement of the new parental leave policies.

Nevertheless, the findings in this chapter offer some lessons on effective policy-making. In particular, policy-makers looking to undertake significant reforms would do well to define their goals as broadly as possible, which allows flexibility in how the discourse is interpreted by different groups and also allows coalition partners to add elements to it. Evidence from Germany and South Korea suggests that government control of the agenda is useful in setting out a polysemic idea, that a top-down approach to agenda-setting has the best chance of creating a powerful coalition magnet. The story of reform in England, however, suggests that bottom-up agenda-setting can be effective in achieving immediate policy goals, but is less effective in building longer-lasting coalitions for change. Furthermore, the top-down approach does not imply a rigid grip on the agenda. In both Germany and South Korea the governments actively sought to win support by incorporating elements that were important to key stakeholders in their discourse. In Germany, this was particularly the case with employers, while in South Korea it involved reaching out to women's groups. Both examples demonstrate that coalition-building may involve significant compromises with potential opponents.

Overall, this chapter has demonstrated one way in which ideas can matter in politics. They can be made to appeal to broad coalitions that can allow particular agendas to withstand partisan changes in governments, win support from unlikely sources and enjoy long periods of sustained political attention.

## Notes

[1] ECEC policy differs in each of the four nations of the United Kingdom. This chapter concentrates on England, the largest of the four.

[2] After a series of incremental expansions, this parental leave law provided parents with up to three years job-protected leave, and a flat-rate benefit for two years.

[3] This reform facilitated greater flexibility through providing a right to part-time work and offering a 'budget option' of a higher benefit for a shorter period of time.

[4] There was concern within the SPD leadership that the reforms were regressive in that they resulted in higher income families gaining more from the new earnings-replacement benefit, while low income families received a net cut in the overall benefit (Henninger et al, 2008).

[5] The CSU is the more socially conservative, Bavarian 'sister party' of the CDU.

[6] Every 4-year-old was given a place by 1999 and the roll-out of provisions for 3-year-olds was completed by 2003. The amount of free early education was

increased in 2004 to 15 hours per week for 39 weeks and was made more flexible. It was further extended to 20 per cent of the most disadvantaged 2-year-olds by 2010.

## References

An, M.-Y. (2013) 'Childcare expansion in East Asia: changing shape of the institutional configurations in Japan and South Korea', *Asian Social Work and Policy Review*, 7(1): 28–43.

An, M.-Y. and Peng, I. (2016) 'Diverging paths? A comparative look at childcare policies in Japan, South Korea and Taiwan', *Social Policy and Administration*, 50(5): 540–58.

Baek, S.-H. and Seo, M.-H. (2004) 'Youngyua boyukbub gaejunge ttareun boyuksisuljang mit boyukgyosa jakyukchedo yeongoo' [A study of the qualifications required for owners and care workers at childcare centres under the new Childcare Act], *Korea Journal of Child Care and Education*, 39(12): 171–95.

Baumgartner, F.R. and Jones, B.D. (1993) *Agendas and Instability in American Politics*, Chicago: Chicago University Press.

BDA (2006) *Familie schafft Zukunft* [Family Creates the Future], Berlin: Bundesvereinigung der deutschen Arbeitgeberverbände.

Béland, D. (2009) 'Ideas, institutions, and policy change', *Journal of European Public Policy*, 16(5): 701–18.

Béland, D. and Cox, R.H. (2016) 'Ideas as coalition magnets: coalition building, policy entrepreneurs, and power relations', *Journal of European Public Policy*, 23(3): 428–45.

Bertram, H., Rösler, W. and Ehlert, N. (2005) 'Zeit, Infraskruktur und Geld: Familienpolitik als Zukunftspolitik' [Time, infrastructure and money: family policy as policy for the future], *Politik und Zeitgeschichte*, 23–24: 6–15.

Blair, T. (1999) 'Beveridge Lecture', 18 March, Toynbee Hall, London. Available from: http://www.bris.ac.uk/poverty/downloads/background/Tony%20Blair%20Child%20Poverty%20Speech.doc [Accessed 1 July 2020].

Bleses, P. and Seeleib-Kaiser, M. (2004) *The Dual Transformation of the German Welfare State*, London: Palgrave Macmillan.

Blome, A. (2016) *The Politics of Work-Family Policy Reforms in Germany and Italy*, London, New York: Routledge.

BMFSFJ (2005) *Nachhaltige Familienpolitik: Zukunftssicherung durch einen Dreiklang von Zeitpolitik, finanzieller Transferpolitik und Infrastrukturpolitik* [Sustainable Family Policy: Securing the Future through a Triad of Time Policies, Financial Transfers and Infrastructure Policies], Berlin: Bundesministerium für Familie, Senioren, Frauen und Jugend.

Boling, P. (2008) 'Demography, culture, and policy: understanding Japan's low fertility', *Population and Development Review*, 34(2): 307–26.

Boling, P. (2015) *The Politics of Work-Family Policies: Comparing Japan, France, Germany and the United States*, Cambridge: Cambridge University Press.

Bonoli, G. (2005) 'The politics of the new social policies: providing coverage against new social risks in mature welfare states', *Policy and Politics*, 33(3): 431–49.

Bonoli, G. (2007) 'Time matters: postindustrialization, new social risks, and welfare state adaptation in advanced industrial democracies', *Comparative Political Studies*, 40(5): 495–520.

Brown, G. (1999) 'A scar on the nation's soul', *Poverty*, 104: 8–10.

Brown, G. (2001) 'Budget statement', House of Commons, 3 July.

Brown, G. (2002) 'Statement by the Chancellor of the Exchequer on the 2002 Spending Review', House of Commons, 15 July.

Bundestag Plenarprotokoll (2002) *14. Wahlperiode, 230. Sitzung, 18 April, 22772D*, Gerhard Schröder.

Byun, W.S. (2000) *Hangukhajokui Byunhwawa Yeosungui Yeokhal Mit Jiwie Gunhan Yeongu* [A Study of Changes to the Korean Family and to Women's Roles and Status], Seoul: Korean Women's Development Institute.

Cabinet Office (2011) *Survey of Work-Life Balance and Its Impact on the Recent Economic Climate*, Tokyo: Government of Japan.

Campbell, J.L. (2004) *Institutional Change and Globalization*, Princeton, NJ: Princeton University Press.

Castles, F.G. (2003) 'The world turned upside down: below replacement fertility, changing preferences and family-friendly public policy in 21 OECD countries', *Journal of European Social Policy*, 13(3): 209–27.

Chan, R. (2002) 'Balancing social and economic development in Korea: flexible labor market reforms and productive welfare', *The Journal of Comparative Asian Development*, 1(2): 195–226.

Crafts, N. (1996) '"Post-neoclassical endogenous growth theory": what are its policy implications?', *Oxford Review of Economic Policy*, 12(2): 30–47.

*Daily Mail* (2004) 'Breed for the good of the state', *Mail Online*, 22 September, Available from: www.dailymail.co.uk/columnists/article-318750/Breed-good-state.html [Accessed 17 July 2020].

Daly, M. (2011) 'What adult worker model? A critical look at recent social policy reform in Europe from a gender and family perspective', *Social Politics: International Studies in Gender, State and Society*, 18(1): 1–23.

Daly, M. and Ferragina, E. (2018) 'Family policy in high-income countries: five decades of development', *Journal of European Social Policy*, 28(3): 255–70.

Daly, M. and Scheiwe, K. (2010) 'Individualisation and personal obligations – social policy, family policy, and law reform in Germany and the UK', *International Journal of Law, Policy and the Family*, 24(2): 177–97.

DfEE and DSS (Department for Education and Employment, and Department of Social Security) (1998) 'Meeting the childcare challenge: a framework and consultation document', Cm3959, London: Department for Education and Employment, and Department of Social Security.

DIHK (2003) 'Pressemitteilung des DIHK' [Press release of the DIHK], Berlin: Deutscher Industrie- und Handelskammertag.

DSS (Department of Social Security) (1998) 'A new contract for welfare: new ambitions for our country', Cm3805, Norwich: The Stationary Office.

DTI (Department for Trade and Industry) (1998) 'Fairness at work', Cm3968, London: Department for Trade and Industry.

DTI (Department for Trade and Industry) (2000) 'Work and parents: competitiveness and choice – a green paper', Cm5005, London: Department for Trade and Industry.

Eisenstadt, N. (2011) *Providing a Sure Start: How Government Discovered Early Childhood*, Bristol: Policy Press.

Ellingsæter, A.L. and Leira, A. (2006) *Politicising Parenthood in Scandinavia: Gender Relations in Welfare States*, Bristol: The Policy Press.

Esping-Andersen, G. (1990) *The Three Worlds of Welfare Capitalism*, Princeton, NJ: Princeton University Press.

Esping-Andersen, G. (ed) (1996) *Welfare States in Transition: National Adaptations in Global Economies*, London: Sage.

Esping-Andersen, G. (1999) *Social Foundations of Postindustrial Economies*, Oxford: Oxford University Press.

Esping-Andersen, G., Gallie, D., Hemerijck, A. and Myles, J. (eds) (2002) *Why We Need a New Welfare State*, Oxford: Oxford University Press.

Estevez-Abe, M. and Kim, Y.S. (2014) 'Presidents, prime ministers and politics of care – why Korea expanded childcare much more than Japan', *Social Policy and Administration*, 48(6): 666–85.

Estevez-Abe, M. and Naldini, M. (2016) 'Politics of defamilialization: a comparison of Italy, Japan, Korea and Spain', *Journal of European Social Policy*, 26(4): 327–43.

Ferragina, E. and Seeleib-Kaiser, M. (2015) 'Determinants of a silent (r)evolution: understanding the expansion of family policy in rich OECD countries', *Social Politics: International Studies in Gender, State and Society*, 22(1): 1–37.

Fleckenstein, T. and Lee, S.C. (2014) 'The politics of postindustrial social policy: family policy reforms in Britain, Germany, South Korea, and Sweden', *Comparative Political Studies*, 47(4): 601–30.

Frindte, A. and Mierendorff, J. (2017) 'Bildung, Erziehung [education] and care in German early childhood settings – spotlights on current discourses', *Journal of Pedagogy*, 8(1): 99–120.

Gelb, J. (2003) *Gender Policies in Japan and the United States: Comparing Women's Movements, Rights and Politics*, New York: Palgrave Macmillan.

Giddens, A. (1998) *The Third Way: The Renewal of Social Democracy*, Malden, MA: Polity Press.

Gingrich, J. and Ansell, B.W. (2015) 'The dynamics of social investment: human capital, activation, and care', in P. Beramendi, S. Hausermann, H. Kitschelt and H. Kriesi (eds), *The Politics of Advanced Capitalism*, Cambridge: Cambridge University Press, pp 282–304.

Goodman, R. and Peng, I. (1996) 'The East Asian welfare states: peripatetic learning, adaptive change, and nation-building', in G. Esping-Andersen (ed) *Welfare States in Transition: National Adaptations in Global Economies*, London: Sage, pp 192–224.

Hall, P.A. (1989) 'Conclusion: the politics of Keynesian ideas', in P.A. Hall (ed), *The Political Power of Economic Ideas: Keynesianism Across Nations*, Princeton, NJ: Princeton University Press, pp 361–92.

Hansard (1997) HC Debate, 2 June, vol. 295, col. 14, Harriet Harman.

Hansard (1999) HC Debate, 28 April, vol. 330 col. 301, Margaret Hodge.

Hantrais, L. (2004) *Family Policy Matters: Responding to Family Change in Europe*, Bristol: Policy Press.

Harman, H. (2017) *A Woman's Work*, London: Allen Lane.

Heckman, J.J. (2006) 'Skill formation and the economics of investing in disadvantaged children', *Science*, 312(5782): 1900–2.

Hemerijck, A. (ed) (2017) *The Uses of Social Investment*, Oxford: Oxford University Press.

Henninger, A., Wimbauer, C. and Dombrowski, R. (2008) 'Demography as a push toward gender equality? Current reforms of German family policy', *Social Politics: International Studies in Gender, State and Society*, 15(3): 287–314.

Hewitt, P. (2014) 'Gender discrimination', in C. Clarke (ed) *The 'Too Difficult' Box: The Big Issues Politicians Can't Crack*, London: Biteback Publishing.

Hill, M.J. (1995) *Social Policy: A Comparative Analysis*, New York: Prentice Hall.

HMT, DfES, DWP and DTI (Her Majesty's Treasury, Department for Education and Skills, Department for Work and Pensions, and Department for Trade and Industry) (2004) 'Choice for parents, the best start for children: a ten year strategy for childcare', London: HM Treasury, Department for Education and Skills, Department for Work and Pensions, and Department for Trade and Industry.

HMT and DTI (Her Majesty's Treasury and Department for Trade and Industry) (2003) 'Balancing work and family life: enhancing choice and support for parents', London: HM Treasury, Department for Trade and Industry.

Holliday, I. (2000) 'Productivist welfare capitalism: social policy in East Asia', *Political Studies*, 48(4): 706–23.

Imai, J. and Sato, Y. (2011) 'Regular and non-regular employment as an additional duality in the Japanese labour market: institutional perspective on career mobility', in Y. Sato and J. Imai (eds) *Japan's New Inequality: Intersection of Employment Reforms and Welfare Arrangements*, Japan: Trans-Pacific Press, pp 1–31.

Irigoyen, C. (2016) *Tackling the Declining Birth Rate in Japan*, Available from: https://www.centreforpublicimpact.org/case-study/tackling-declining-birth-rate-japan [Accessed 21 July 2020].

*Japan Times, The* (2015) 'Cabinet seeks to raise percentage of men taking paternity leave to 80% by 2020', 20 March, Available from: https://www.japantimes.co.jp/news/2015/03/20/national/cabinet-seeks-to-raise-percentage-of-men-taking-paternity-leave-to-80-by-2020/ [Accessed 17 July 2020].

JILPT (Japan Institute for Labour Policy and Training) (2013) 'Labour situations in Japan and its analysis: detailed exposition 2012/2013', Tokyo: The Japan Institute for Labour Policy and Training.

JILPT (Japan Institute for Labour Policy and Training) (2019) 'Recent statistical survey reports', Available from: https://www.jil.go.jp/english/estatis/esaikin/2019/documents/e201906.pdf [Accessed 21 July 2020].

Jenson, J. (2010) 'Diffusing ideas for after neoliberalism: the social investment perspective in Europe and Latin America', *Global Social Policy*, 10(1): 59–84.

Jones, C. (1993) 'The Pacific challenge', in C. Jones and C.J. Jones (eds) *New Perspectives on the Welfare State in Europe*, London: Routledge, pp 184–203.

Kim, Y.-M. (2007) 'Sahoitoojajungchakegwa Hanguk Sahoijungchaekui Mirae' [Korean Academy of Social Welfare Sahoitoojajungchaek Symposium], 6 February, Seoul: Korean Academy of Social Welfare.

Kim, Y.-M. (2010) *Hanguk Bokjigukga Sungkyuk Nonjang 1* [The Debates on the Korean Welfare Regime 1], Seoul: Ingangwa Bokji.

Kono, M. (2005) 'The welfare regime in Japan', in A. Walker and C. Wong (eds) *East Asian Welfare Regimes in Transition: From Confucianism to Globalisation*. Bristol: Policy Press, pp 117–44.

Kwon, H.-J. (1997) 'Beyond European welfare regimes: comparative perspectives on East Asian welfare systems', *Journal of Social Policy*, 26(4): 467–84.

Labour Party (1997) 'New Labour: because Britain deserves better', Labour Party manifesto, London: Labour Party.

Lee, S.-H. (2013) 'The impact of gender politics on the socialisation of care in South Korea', unpublished PhD thesis, University of Bath.

Lee, S.-H. (2016) 'Has childcare become less of a burden in South Korea? Exploring the nature of pre-and post-reform childcare provision', *Asian Journal of Women's Studies*, 22(4): 414–42.

Lee, S.-H. (2017) 'The socialization of childcare and a missed opportunity through path dependence: the case of South Korea', *Social Politics: International Studies in Gender, State and Society*, 24(2): 132–53.

Leira, A. (1992) *Welfare States and Working Mothers: The Scandinavian Experience*, Cambridge: Cambridge University Press.

Leitner, S., Ostner, I. and Schmitt, C. (2008) 'Family policies in Germany', in I. Ostner and C. Schmitt (eds) *Family Policies in the Context of Family Change*, Wiesbaden: VS, Verlfur Sozialwissenschaften, pp 175–202.

León, M., Pavolini, E., Miró, J. and Sorrenti, A. (2019) 'Policy change and partisan politics: understanding family policy differentiation in two similar countries', *Social Politics: International Studies in Gender, State and Society*, jxz025, Available from: https://doi.org/10.1093/sp/jxz025 [Accessed 8 October 2020].

Lewis, J. (1992) 'Gender and the development of welfare regimes', *Journal of European Social Policy*, 2(3): 159–73.

Lewis, J. (2001) 'The decline of the male breadwinner model: implications for work and care', *Social Politics: International Studies in Gender, State and Society*, 8(2): 152–69.

Lewis, J. (2009) *Work–Family Balance, Gender and Policy*, Cheltenham: Edward Elgar.

Lewis, J. (2013) 'Continuity and change in English childcare policy 1960–2000', *Social Politics: International Studies in Gender, State and Society*, 20(3): 358–86.

Lewis, J., Campbell, M. and Huerta, C. (2008) 'Patterns of paid and unpaid work in Western Europe: gender, commodification, preferences and the implications for policy', *Journal of European Social Policy*, 18(1): 21–37.

Lister, R. (2003) 'Investing in the citizen-workers of the future: transformations in citizenship and the state under New Labour', *Social Policy and Administration*, 37(5): 427–43.

Mätzke, M. and Ostner, I. (2010a) 'Introduction: change and continuity in recent family policies', *Journal of European Social Policy*, 20(5): 387–98.

Mätzke, M. and Ostner, I. (2010b) 'Postscript: ideas and agents of change in time', *Journal of European Social Policy*, 20(5): 468–76.

Ministry of Health and Welfare (2019) *Social Security Factbook*, Seoul: Ministry of Health and Welfare.

Mohn, L. and von der Leyen, U. (eds) (2007) *Familie gewinnt: Die Allianz und ihre Wirkungen für Unternehmen und Gesellschaft* [Family profits: the alliance and its effects on businesses and society], Gütersloh: Bertelsmann-Stiftung.

Morel, N., Palier, B. and Palme, J. (2012a) 'Beyond the welfare state as we knew it?' in N. Morel, B. Palier and J. Palme (eds), *Towards a Social Investment Welfare State: Ideas, Policies and Challenges*, Bristol: Policy Press, pp 1–30.

Morel, N., Palier, B. and Palme, J. (eds) (2012b) *Towards a Social Investment Welfare State: Ideas, Policies and Challenges*, Bristol: Policy Press.

Morgan, K.J. (2013) 'Path shifting of the welfare state: electoral competition and the expansion of work-family policies in Western Europe', *World Politics*, 65(1): 73–115.

Moss, P. (2014) 'Early childhood policy in England 1997–2013: anatomy of a missed opportunity', *International Journal of Early Years Education*, 22(4): 346–58.

Müller, K.-U. and Wrohlich, K. (2014) 'Two steps forward – one step back: evaluating contradicting child care policies in Germany', *DIW Discussion Paper*, No. 1396, Berlin: Deutches Institüt für Wirtschaftsforschung (DIW).

National Institute of Population and Social Security Research (2004) 'Child related policies in Japan', Available from: http://www.ipss. go.jp/s-info/e/childPJ2003/childPJ2003.pdf [Accessed 17 July 2020].

Ochiai, E. (2009) 'Care diamonds and welfare regimes in East and South-East Asian societies: bridging family and welfare sociology', *International Journal of Japanese Sociology*, 18(1): 60–78.

OECD (Organisation for Economic Co-operation and Development) (2006) *Starting Strong II: Early Childhood Education and Care*, Paris: OECD.

OECD (Organisation for Economic Co-operation and Development) (2007) *Babies and Bosses: Reconciling Work and Family Life*, Paris: OECD.

OECD (Organisation for Economic Co-operation and Development) (2017a) *Starting Strong 2017: Key OECD Indicators on Early Childhood Education and Care*, Paris: OECD.

OECD (Organisation for Economic Co-operation and Development) (2017b) *Pursuit of Gender Equality: An Uphill Battle*, Paris: OECD.

OECD (Organisation for Economic Co-operation and Development) (2020) 'Fertility rates'. Available from: https://data.oecd.org/pop/fertility-rates.htm [Accessed 15 July 2020].

Orloff, A.S. (2006) 'From maternalism to 'employment for all." In J.D. Levy (ed) *The State after Statism: New State Activities in the Age of Liberalization*, Cambridge, MA: Harvard University Press, pp 230–68.

Ostner, I. (1991) 'Ideas, institutions, traditions – West German women's experience 1945–1990', *German Politics & Society*, 24/25 (Winter): 87–99.

Ostner, I. (2010) 'Farewell to the family as we know it: family policy change in Germany', *German Policy Studies*, 6(1): 211–44.

Palier, B. (2005) 'Ambiguous agreement, cumulative change: French social policy in the 1990s', in W. Streeck and K.A. Thelen (eds) *Beyond Continuity: Institutional Change in Advanced Political Economies*, Oxford: Oxford University Press, pp 127–44.

Peng, I. (2002) 'Social care in crisis: gender, demography, and welfare state restructuring in Japan', *Social Politics: International Studies in Gender, State and Society*, 9(3): 411–43.

Peng, I. (2004) 'Postindustrial pressures, political regime shifts, and social policy reform in Japan and South Korea', *Journal of East Asian Studies*, 4(3): 389–425.

Peng, I. (2011a) 'Social investment policies in Canada, Australia, Japan, and South Korea', *International Journal of Child Care and Education Policy*, 5(1): 41–53.

Peng, I. (2011b) 'The good, the bad and the confusing: the political economy of social care expansion in South Korea', *Development and Change*, 42(4): 905–23.

Peng, I. and Wong, J. (2008) 'Institutions and institutional purpose: continuity and change in East Asian social policy', *Politics and Society*, 36(1): 61–88.

Persson, G. (2005) 'Das schwedische Projekt des Elterngeldes' [The Swedish project of parental leave], *Neue Gesellschaft – Frankfurter Hefte*, 52(7/8): 39–41.

Presidential Secretary Office (2004) *Roh Moo-hyun Daetongryung Yeonsulmoonjib: Je Il Gwon* [Collection of President Roh Moo-hyun Speeches: Volume 1], Seoul: Presidential Secretary Office.

Randall, V. (1995) 'The irresponsible state? The politics of child daycare provision in Britain', *British Journal of Political Science*, 25(3): 327–48.

Randall, V. (2000) *The Politics of Child Daycare in Britain*, Oxford: Oxford University Press.

Rebick, M.E. (2011) 'Gender inequality in the workplace in Japan', in Y. Sato and J. Imai (eds) *Japan's New Inequality: Intersection of Employment Reforms and Welfare Arrangements*, Tokyo: Trans-Pacific Press, pp 71–95.

Ristau, M. (2005) 'Der ökonomische Charme der Familie' [The economic appeal of the family], *Politik Und Zeitgeschichte*, 23/24: 16–23.

Rürup, B. and Gruescu, S. (2003) *Nachhaltige Familienpolitik im Interesse einer aktiven Bevölkerungsentwicklung* [Sustainable Family Policy in the Interest of Active Population Development], Berlin: Bundesministerium für Familie, Senioren, Frauen und Jugend.

Sabatier, P.A. and Jenkins-Smith, H.C. (1993) 'The advocacy coalition framework: assessment, revisions and implications for scholars and practitioners', in P.A. Sabatier and H.C. Jenkins-Smith (eds) *Policy Change and Learning: An Advocacy Coalition Approach*, Boulder, CO: Westview Press, pp 211–35.

Schmidt, R. (2003) 'Speech to SPD party conference', Bochum: SPD Parteitag.

Schmidt, R. and Mohn, L. (eds) (2004) *Familie bringt Gewinn: Innovation durch Balance von Familie und Arbeitswelt* [Family Brings Profits: Innovation through balance of Family and Working Life], Gütersloh: Bertelsmann Stiftung.

Schmidt, V.A. (2006) *Democracy in Europe: The EU and national polities*, Oxford: Oxford University Press.

Schmidt, V.A. and Thatcher, M. (2013) 'Theorizing ideational continuity: the resilience of neo-liberal ideas in Europe', in V.A. Schmidt and M. Thatcher (eds) *Resilient Liberalism in Europe's Political Economy*, Cambridge: Cambridge University Press, pp 1–51.

Schröder, G. (2006) *Entscheidungen: Mein Leben in der Politik* [Decisions: My Life in Politics], Hamburg: Hoffmann and Campe Verlag.

Seeleib-Kaiser, M. (2017) 'The truncated German social investment turn', in A. Hemerijck (ed) *The Uses of Social Investment*, Oxford: Oxford University Press, pp 227–34.

Seeleib-Kaiser, M. and Toivonen, T. (2011) 'Between reforms and birth rates: Germany, Japan, and family policy discourse', *Social Politics: International Studies in Gender, State and Society*, 18(3): 331–60.

Song, J. (2014) 'Labour markets, care regimes and foreign care worker policies in East Asia', *Social Policy and Administration*, 49(3): 376–93.

SPD (2001) 'Parteitag der SPD in Nürnberg – 19. Bis 22. November 2001 – beschlüsse' [Party conference of the SPD in Nuremburg – 19–22 November 2001 – resolutions], Nürnberg: Sozialdemokratische Partei Deutschlands.

Spieß, C.K., Schupp, J., Grabka, M., Heisken-De New, J.P., Jakobeit, H. and Wagner, G.G. (2003) *Abschätzung der Brutto-Einnahmeneffekte öffentlicher Haushalte und der Sozialversicherungsträger bei einem Ausbau von Kindertageseinrichtungen* [Estimation of the Gross Revenue Effects on Public Budgets and Social Security Institutions when Expanding Child Daycare Facilities], Gutachten des Deutschen Instituts für Wirtschaftsforschung Berlin. Baden-Baden: Bundesministeriums für Familie, Senioren, Frauen und Jugend.

Sung, S. (2003) 'Women reconciling paid and unpaid work in a Confucian welfare state: the case of South Korea', *Social Policy and Administration*, 37(4): 342–60.

Suzuki, T. (2006) 'Fertility decline and policy development in Japan', *The Japanese Journal of Population*, 4(1): 1–32.

Sylva, K., Melhuish, E., Sammons, P., Siraj-Blatchford, I., Taggart, B. and Elliott, K. (2004) 'The effective provision of pre-school education (EPPE) project: findings from the pre-school period', Research Briefing No. RBX15-03.

Tabata, H. (1990) *The Japanese Welfare State: Its Structure and Transformation*, Tokyo: University of Tokyo, Institute of Social Science.

The Committee on the Low Fertility Rate and Ageing Society (2006) *Saromaji Plan: Je Ilcha Jechulsan goryung Sahui Gibongyehoick* [Saeromaji Plan: The First Low Fertility Rate and Ageing Society Basic Plan], Seoul: The Committee on the Low Fertility Rate and Ageing Society.

The Presidential Committee on Ageing and Future Society (2004) *Je Ilcha Yoogajiwon Jeongchaek Bangan: Mirae Inryeok Yangsung Mit Yeosungui Gyungje Hwaldong Chamyeo Hwackdaereul Wihan Yuga Jiwon Jungchack Bangan* [The first childcare policy support: childcare support for fostering future labour force and extending women's economic participation], Seoul: The Presidential Committee on Ageing and Future Society.

The Presidential Counsel of Policy Planning Committee (2007) *Anjungjeok Janyueyangyook Jiwonchekye Guchuk: Gongboyuck Gangwharul Wihan Noryuck* [Stable childcare supports: the efforts to enhance public childcare provisions], Seoul: The Presidential Counsel of Policy Planning Committee.

Thévenon, O. and Gauthier, A.H. (2011) 'Family policies in developed countries: a "fertility-booster" with side-effects', *Community, Work and Family*, 14(2): 197–216.

Vowinkel, H. and Rübel, J. (2005) 'Ursula von der Leyen im Interview mit der Welt am Sonntag' [Ursula von der Leyen in interview with the World on Sunday], *Welt am Sonntag*, 20 December, Available from: https://www.bmfsfj.de/bmfsfj/aktuelles/reden-und-interviews/ursula-von-der-leyen-im-interview-mit-der-welt-am-sonntag/101276?view=DEFAULT [Accessed 17 July 2020].

Walker, A. and Wong, C. (2005) 'Introduction: East Asian welfare regime', in A. Walker and C. Wong (eds) *East Asian Welfare Regimes in Transition: From Confucianism to Globalisation*, Bristol: Policy Press, pp 3–20.

# 3

# Private education in South Korea: lessons for the West from past mistakes

*Sonia Exley*

## Introduction

> I had a chance to talk about private education with a Western researcher a number of years ago. For us it's a real headache, the private education. It's really serious and may be the most serious social problem... But the Western researcher, he kind of envied the Korean parents. They are willing to spend their money for their children, and that increases the level of human resources in the country, so what a desirable phenomenon! But that researcher doesn't understand this really serious social problem in Korea. (interview with a Korean National Assembly politician, February 2017)

Advocates of government social investment strategies across the world almost always highlight the critical importance for societies of spending on education. Developing human capital through education spending is often viewed as being almost a silver bullet for solving countries' problems – boosting economic growth, promoting equality of opportunity and preventing 'wasted talent' among disadvantaged groups. At the same time, one typically neglected area of policy analysis relates to families' simultaneous *private* spending on education, particularly in unequal societies, and the ways this spending may at times actually undermine key aims associated with the government's social investment efforts. Rather than reducing educational inequalities, these are often maintained through families' private spending, as parents seek to ensure their children remain one step ahead of the game. Over time, problems of education *overconsumption* can arise which are suboptimal not only for growth but also for citizens' wellbeing, even if they do drive apparently positive outcomes such as countries' high performances in international education league tables. Where strong, long-term incentives exist in a society for families to buy private alongside public education, private tutoring industries can grow dramatically in size and can become very difficult for governments to regulate – again compromising many aims of public social investment. The quote above from a South Korean politician in 2017 highlights such problems in the context of one particular society – South Korea – where families' private spending on 'shadow education' outside the formal school day is known to have reached a staggering 2.79 per cent of the national GDP in 2006 (Kim and Lee, 2010: 261).

What lessons might societies in the West, where families' private spending on education remains relatively modest to date but is growing, take from parts of the world where such spending has over time arguably become out of control? Here, experiences in East Asia, and in particular South Korea, a country with some of the highest spending on commercial shadow education in the world and where the phenomenon is commonly viewed as being 'the enemy of the public school system' (OECD, 2014: 93), may provide valuable insights into government agendas that both facilitate and constrain private education. This chapter seeks to deliver some such insights, considering policy lessons and recommendations not only for South Korea but also for Western societies where spending on private education is growing. The chapter draws on data from a 2017 research project in which interviews were carried out by the author with 29 experts and key stakeholders in the South Korean education system.

## Public education spending: a panacea for all ills?

Scholars and policy-makers who emphasise the value of social investment agendas in social policy have for many years now highlighted the particular importance for societies of investing in public education. Cultivation of human capital (Becker, 1964) through government spending on education – especially early on in people's lives (see, for example, Heckman, 2011) – is often discussed in policy circles as being a panacea that can cure almost all societal ills in the post-industrial era. Children can be future-proofed – made resilient and productive so they never have to rely on government social protection later in life – in large part through spending on early childhood education and care. Wasted talent can, through public spending, be put to productive use among categories of young people who have previously been failed by inter-generational transmissions of disadvantage, poor home learning environments and public schools, which were in the past under-funded. Under-employed adults can, will and must become re-skilled as part of the government's adult learning agendas. In turn, national and international economies can be boosted, social disadvantage fought and inequalities narrowed, so societies will be much more efficient and equitable in their production and allocation of resources overall.

## Private education spending: undermining public social investment

Alongside public education, however, we must also consider the fundamental reality that individuals and their families also spend privately on education. Such private spending can of course in many ways be considered a good thing in any society, enhancing as it does human wellbeing and individuals' capabilities (Sen, 1999) to live a good life while also complementing government efforts to boost productive human capital. However, private spending on education can also at times undermine the aims of public social investment. In societies where marked social inequalities exist – as is the case in most countries globally today – education credentials almost always come to be viewed in part as positional goods where their value depends on their scarcity. People invest privately in education in order to have more of this not only in absolute terms, but also in order to have more relative to others, signalling their own superiority within hierarchies such as competitive labour markets. Where governments seek to narrow inequalities through public spending on education, focusing particularly on the outcomes of disadvantaged groups, within unequal societies, others with existing competitive advantage will very often seek to preserve that advantage by investing yet more, effectively maintaining inequalities (Lucas, 2001).

In such contexts, when both public and private spending ratchet up – governments spending more in order to improve opportunities for all, but families in turn spending yet more again in order to pull the ladder up behind themselves as best they can – important implications can arise for whole societies. Because links between education spending and economic growth are complex within macroeconomics (see for example Pritchett, 2001; Wolf, 2002), instances can regularly be observed in societies where certain forms of increased education spending do not lead to major growth. Phenomena such as qualification inflation can in such instances often be noted, where people must demonstrate ever-greater education credentials to do the same jobs they would previously have done without those credentials. Chang (2011: 188) describes such inflation as being akin to being in a theatre where some people are standing up to watch a performance and, as a result, in the end everyone must stand in order to be able to see. Once everyone is standing, no one is actually relatively any better off, but everyone is more uncomfortable than when they were sitting down.

Rising engagement with private (on top of public) education in unequal societies can in turn arguably lead to education overconsumption. Financial burdens are created for many, particularly those who are disadvantaged and for whom private education costs constitute a larger proportion of their household income. Problems of student overwork, sleep deprivation and stress emerge among young people – extremes of what scholars such as Lareau (1987) and Vincent (2012) have called the 'concerted cultivation' of children, and Ball (2010) terms 'hyperdevelopmentalism'. Impacts on public education also emerge – this becomes residualised as the 'need' for high private spending becomes normalised. Such residualisation arguably strengthens an undesirable link (from a social justice point of view) between individuals' family backgrounds and their educational attainment, because access to high-quality education becomes increasingly determined by what families can afford to pay (Gurun and Millimet, 2008; Jerrim, 2017).

Overall, then, where governments seek to promote strong and effective public social investment policies in education, it seems reasonable to argue that they should also consider how far private investments in education might simultaneously compromise their progress towards policy goals. Where private education spending by families is found to hamper such progress, it is critical that governments seek to understand, and tackle through policy, key dynamics within societies that drive such spending.

## East Asian 'reference societies' from which the world can learn

Social (and particularly education) policy scholars across the world in recent years have shown ever-growing interest in what are clearly some quite remarkable national cultivations of human capital and educational achievement in East Asian countries since the latter half of the twentieth century. Since the early 2000s in particular, East Asian countries have regularly achieved top scores in international education league tables such as the Organisation for Economic Co-operation and Development (OECD) Programme for International Student

Assessment (PISA), and as a result they have become 'reference societies' in the field of comparative education (Sellar and Lingard, 2013; Waldow et al, 2014). Researchers have been eager to uncover exactly what drives East Asian success in education – from Confucian cultural norms, through 'mastery' of pedagogical methods in the classroom, to intensive parenting styles at home.

At the same time, considering the role of financing in such success, while productivist East Asian governments have certainly prioritised education relative to other areas of public spending during the twentieth and twenty-first centuries, how much spending overall on education has come from private, rather than public, sources? Moreover, given the presence of stark inequalities in East Asia (Chandra et al, 2016), to what extent might success have been accompanied by escalating private education costs for families as they seek to secure a competitive advantage, with implications for societies in general and for poorer groups in particular?

If success has indeed been accompanied by escalating private education spending, then perhaps there are once again messages that Western societies might heed from East Asia regarding possible policy efforts to monitor, manage and curb this spending. Such may be valuable even in a time where governments 'prefer not to know too much' (Bray and Kwo, 2013: 491) about such spending given the extent to which nations are also focusing increasingly on the transformative possibilities of public social investment (Van Kersbergen and Hemerijck, 2012). Private tutoring or shadow education is certainly a phenomenon that many authors have documented as having undergone a 'massive worldwide increase' in recent years (Park et al, 2016: 232).[1] Within Western societies, a proliferation of local, national and international tutoring franchises has emerged during the 2010s in particular. Such franchises have been part of a wider and ever-intensifying global education industry, wherein networked education actors outside the state have increasingly marketed and sold not only tutoring but a multitude of other education services transnationally (Ball, 2012; Verger et al, 2016).

> Today, nearly everywhere in the world, students take part in a myriad of structured academic activities after the formal school day ends. (Park et al, 2016: 232)

Bray (2011, 2020) has shown in detail concerns which may be highlighted in Europe regarding fast-rising private tutoring costs for families. Parents across the continent are spending billions annually on tutoring, and their spending has grown in scale and intensity over time, particularly in Southern, Central and Eastern Europe. Sutton Trust research shows that in England and Wales in 2019, 27 per cent of children aged 11–16 had received private tutoring, compared with just 18 per cent in 2005. In London in 2019, the figure was 41 per cent (Sutton Trust, 2019). Private tutoring as an industry has been estimated at approximately £2 billion in England and Wales (McInerney, 2017).

## The South Korean case

South Korea (hereafter Korea) is a country which might be considered extreme in almost all respects outlined so far in this chapter. In OECD PISA data terms, it has ranked consistently among the top nations with respect to student achievement in maths and reading at age 15. Korea is a society often described as having undergone an 'education miracle' during the second half of the twentieth century, when a national manpower plan guided national education (among other) spending over a 30-year period, driving the Korean economy to grow by almost 10 per cent every year and transforming the country from being in a state of virtual economic ruin following the 1950–53 Korean War into one of the Four 'Asian Tigers' in the 1990s (KEDI, 2011). Korea joined the OECD in 1996.

Korea is, however, also a society today characterised by 'education fever' (Seth, 2002). Despite there being moderate public spending on education in the country, commercial private tutoring or shadow education for children outside their daily lives in school constitutes a major national industry – at one point in recent years, spending on this made up 2.79 per cent of the country's GDP (Kim and Lee, 2010: 261). Far from being seen as a source of national pride, Korean governments have for decades viewed shadow education as being 'the enemy of the public school system' (OECD, 2014: 93). Waldow et al (2014) highlight Korean media reports of an education system in 'crisis'. Families make vast financial sacrifices in order to pay for private tutoring and more than four in ten consider themselves 'edupoor' (Kim, 2016). Children spend large amounts of time in the country's more than 100,000 private *hagwons* (cram schools) (Byun, 2014). Pressure on families to engage in shadow education is believed to contribute to not only low fertility rates in Korea (World Bank, 2020) but also substantial stress, depression and even suicide among young people (Kim, 2016). Why does this happen and how have governments sought to tackle the problem of shadow education spending in Korea?

Given the size and scale of the private education 'problem' in Korea, arguably more than anywhere else in the world, national policy experts in the country have become strongly attuned to observing relationships between private tutoring expenditures on one hand and particular social trends and government policy reforms on the other (Lee et al, 2010). In efforts to prevent the residualisation of public education and consequent impacts, particularly for poorer families, Korea can be thought of as having become over time something of a laboratory for testing the effects of different government policy reforms on families' demand for shadow education. Korean governments have deployed a range of different policy reforms in order to tackle private education nationally – from increasing public spending on education and reforming how public schools are organised; through the regulation of private education providers; to reforms to the fairness of university entrance requirements in Korea. All such reforms have had limited impact to date on families' demand for private tutoring, which has regularly risen over time. Why do Korean experts and key education system stakeholders believe this has been the case? The relative ineffectiveness of so many policies in Korea that have not achieved their objectives may provide important lessons for countries in which public social investment is believed to matter and in which private tutoring is on the rise, but has not (yet) become a truly major phenomenon, thus allowing 'opportunities to avert some of the major problems experienced by countries in which it has become engrained in cultures and daily lives' (Bray, 2011: 15).

## Research methods

The data presented in this chapter draws from a 2017 case study of the Korean education system by the author that sought to explore key factors underpinning the rise of, and efforts to regulate and curb families' demand for private tutoring in Korea. Semi-structured interviews were carried out with 29 policy experts and key stakeholders in the Korean education system. Interviewees included one former *Saenuri* (conservative) government education minister and one former vice minister; advisers within the Korean Ministry of Education, Science and Technology; government researchers; National Assembly politicians from the centre-left Minjoo political party; education scholars and representatives from the Seoul Metropolitan Office of Education (SMOE); Korea's teacher unions; education non-governmental organisations (NGOs); and the tutoring industry itself. Some interviews were carried out in English by the author alone, while others were carried out with the aid of two Korean interpreters familiar with the aims of the research project. In one instance, due to a last-minute cancellation, it was necessary to collect a respondent's insights via email. In five instances, interviewees were interviewed in groups of two or more. A thematic analysis of the interview data was carried out using NVivo 11. In order to boost accuracy, interview data was triangulated with government policy documents, literature published by Korean think tanks and a large body of secondary academic literature on Korean shadow education.

## Improving public education in Korea

One key factor in Korea often cited as driving families' demand for private tutoring has been the perceived problems in Korean public education. Government spending on school-level education in Korea as a proportion of GDP (3.5 per cent in 2015) is not particularly low compared with that of other OECD countries. However, criticisms have nevertheless long been levelled at a system well-known for its dense, standardised national curriculum, and its heavy reliance on rote learning and multiple choice testing. In such a context, critics argue that incentives for public school teachers to innovate are weak. Parents' organisations have described staff within public education as being at times complacent, giving students insufficient personalised attention and focusing predominantly on encouraging simple memorisation. Even in the face of a dense national curriculum, Korean parents also perceive public schools as doing too little to prepare children for what are today extremely competitive and ever-changing Korean university admissions arrangements (particularly the famed *Suneung* or College Scholastic Ability Test – CSAT). All of the above makes tutoring 'outside the state' in Korea, and engagement with a shadow education industry, which is conversely typically described as being *hyper-responsive* to families' ever-changing needs, seem very necessary (see for example Dang and Rogers, 2008).

Since the 1990s, government policy efforts in Korea to improve public education and so to curb demands for shadow education have, at the same time, also been manifold. Policies have been introduced, for example, that have sought to reduce public school class sizes substantially and to upgrade facilities. Since 2015, governments have also aimed to slim down content and give students more subject choice in the public school curriculum – part of a package of reforms referred to as the 'normalisation' of Korean education. Content at each stage of the curriculum has been scrutinised to ensure this is more manageable for students (hence reducing the need for private tutors), and rules now stipulate that public exams must not test students on material beyond that which has been covered in class. Greater experimentation has also been encouraged, with more student-centred methods of teaching, learning and assessment, and with more qualitative forms of feedback to students in order to deepen learning. Notably, a Free Semester Programme was introduced in 2013 in Korean middle schools as part of promoting 'happy education'. During Free Semesters, students are freed from taking exams and encouraged instead to explore areas such as the arts, physical activities and future career options (KICE, 2017).

While such reforms may well improve substantially the amount of creativity, deep learning and personalised attention that students experience in Korean public education, for many parents they have done little to ease anxieties regarding students' preparations for university applications. Indeed, in the wider context of competitive CSAT exams, student-centred learning and reduced curricular content may even drive families to engage even further with private tutoring. As by one official from some highlighted:

> Student-centred learning is very forward thinking; however parents are very worried about college entrance exams. The school system ... has changed but college entrance has not. Parents are worried and they want to see how much accomplishment the students have. Before they could see 'A-plus, B, C' and they could check. But now they cannot even check because it's all descriptive – 'they are doing this, they have proved this' and so on. In that sense they want to send their kids to private education. (SMOE official)

In the light of families' persistent anxieties about college entrance specifically, governments have again tried to help. Simultaneously remaining mindful of the equity implications of private tutoring in a society where not all will be able to afford the same amount or quality of shadow education, in 2004 it was announced that the Korean Educational Broadcasting Service (EBS), originally founded in 1990 in order to transmit educational lectures to the whole Korean public via television and radio, would begin broadcasting lectures specifically geared towards preparing students for college entry. The Korean government's aim here was to offer a high-quality alternative to commercial shadow education for families less able to pay (Bae et al, 2010). The government also announced that 70 per cent of all questions in the annual nationwide CSAT exam would, from that point onward, be based on EBS content. Lectures were delivered by prominent academics and famous Korean private tutors, and they were accompanied by purchasable textbooks. The same year, a national Cyber Home Learning System was additionally established, allowing children to receive government-funded, personalised support online for self-directed learning (Hwang et al, 2010).

A further relevant measure in recent years has been the introduction, since 2006, of national 'after-school' programmes in public schools (see for example Lubienski and Lee, 2013). Such programmes offer in large part additional academic teaching for students in key subjects such as maths, Korean and English. They are not free for most but they are offered at a heavily government-subsidised rate (Choi and Choi, 2016), with voucher schemes to eliminate private costs altogether for the poorest families. Many programmes follow curricula closely matching what is offered in local private *hagwons* and the programmes typically also deploy contracted local private teachers who otherwise work in those *hagwons*.

After-school programmes have, experts argue, been both popular and beneficial, particularly for young people from poorer families and in rural parts of the country where both high-quality public schooling and high-quality private tutoring can be in short supply. Given the geographical patchiness of high-quality education in Korea, EBS lectures broadcast on television and radio, and the decision to base most CSAT questions on these lectures, have also been found to have benefitted students in poorer parts of the country (Bray and Lykins, 2012).

While expanding access for less-advantaged groups to gradually improving public education in all its varying forms does primarily tackle educational inequalities at the bottom of the socio-economic ladder, what impact did such reforms have on more advantaged groups in Korean society? Here government policy-makers have lamented one particularly important problem – affluent groups largely tend to equate 'expensive' with 'high-quality' when it comes to education, whether costly private tutors actually provide such high quality or not. According to one former vice-minister of education, publicly subsidised after-school clubs also have higher student–teacher ratios than do private *hagwons*. Moreover, in the words of one Seoul *hagwon* owner, even where public schools seek to contract tutors from local *hagwon* markets in order to teach in publicly subsidised after-school clubs, remuneration structures are such that *hagwons* tend to send their 'worst people'. Another unfortunate by-product of EBS lectures being central to CSAT preparation is that the efforts to move public school teachers away from more didactic methods of teaching, such as watching television in class and memorising from textbooks, have been undermined.

For all these reasons, and, as many Korean education experts have reported, with the underlying psychology of seeking to stay one step ahead in education, many families in Korea send their children to both publicly subsidised after-school programmes and private *hagwons*. The most elite families in Korea, concentrated in areas such as Gangnam in Seoul, typically use highly expensive private *hagwons* only (outside of school), or (even more expensive and often famous) private tutors on a one-to-one basis at home.

## Reining in private education through regulation

Challenges which clearly do exist in Korean public education aside, however, it is additionally worth considering a simultaneous reality that the powerful shadow education industry in the country also stands to gain from highlighting problems in the public sector. 'Anxiety marketing' is a much-discussed technique among Korean providers of private education, wherein parents' fears regarding their children's futures are consciously exploited, suggesting that unless they purchase supplementary services, they children will fall behind and ultimately lose out in the fierce competition for places in leading universities and jobs with top employers. Anxiety marketing has been reported by Korean interviewees to even specifically target parents whose children have upcoming Free Semesters – semesters designed in large part specifically to relieve the intensive study pressure that students in Korea face:

> They say, 'if you don't send your kids to private institutes you are not good parents, your children will be left behind'. So if you want to send your kids to better schools [universities] you have to send your kids to private institutes. They try to make that kind of propaganda by using anxiety marketing. (former vice-minister of education)

> They have been really successful in marketing, [a] kind of anxiety marketing. When you get advice from the private tutoring company, they say 'your kid will never go to Seoul National University if you just go to [government] schools' … and if you spend more on private tutoring it does

not necessarily lead to more learning, it does not necessarily lead to a higher [CSAT] score ... but more important is parents' perception. (former minister of education)

Obviously when you have only one child then, you know, they will just believe that and they will invest whatever they have. (Ministry of Education Adviser)

As such, perhaps curbing families' consumption of private education needs to be not only a matter of improving public education, but also of controlling how much providers are able to sell or parents are able to buy. Over the decades, therefore, there have been extensive Korean government policies trying to regulate private tutoring. In 1980, under the military government of President Chun Doo-hwan, the country formally banned commercial private tutoring, though this ban was gradually relaxed during the 1990s and was formally declared unconstitutional in 2000. Since the 1990s, governments have made several efforts to impose greater fee transparency and locally determined price ceilings on Korean *hagwons* (Kim and Park, 2010; Kim and Chang, 2010). In 2006, a national requirement was created for provincial governments to impose nightly curfews on *hagwons* (Choi and Choi, 2016). In Seoul, *hagwons* today are required to close at 10 p.m. and public officials patrol the city's neighbourhoods in order to ensure this curfew is obeyed. As part of the 2015 normalisation reforms in Korean public education, private tutors delivering tutoring inside government schools as part of after-school programmes are also now barred from teaching students curricular material in advance of their scheduled syllabus in school (a policy referred to as the ban on 'prior learning'). One National Assembly politician interviewed for this project reported that in some elite private *hagwons*, students learn curricular material up to five years in advance of when it will be covered in school. Such accelerated learning can have disruptive effects on public classrooms, as students are at different stages in their understanding of curricular material. Difficulties are caused in particular for the least affluent students who tend to be furthest behind.

Attempts to regulate private tutoring have, on the whole, had limited impact. When commercial tutoring was banned during the 1980s, many have argued, it only reduced families' aggregate expenditures, in the sense that less-affluent groups found themselves priced out of what quickly became a thriving illegal market. Among richer families, costs are said to have escalated often as tutors began to add risk premiums to what they had previously charged (Choi and Choi, 2016). In the decade after the ban on private tutoring was lifted in 2000, spending increased substantially yet again – this time as a result of pent-up demand.

Moreover, price ceiling and curfew policies regulating private tutoring have on the whole applied only to *hagwons*, they cannot regulate time or money spent by families on tutoring at home. While in some instances *hagwons* have found their profits constrained – including by the reported growth of cultural norms against students studying after 10 p.m. – they also find ways to get around regulations, for example by accepting cash payments beyond their formally advertised prices and by having teachers supervise 'self-directed learning' rather than teaching after 10 p.m.:

> With the 10 p.m. curfew, some *hagwons* just turn off the light, or have the students on the bus and drive on the motorway while teaching. There is also some corruption between the public servants and the *hagwons*, and they let them know when someone is coming [to inspect]. (Korean parent and NGO activist)

Policy instances where only the more affordable end of the tutoring market is regulated (for example after-school programmes where prior learning is banned) cannot help at times risking broadening rather than narrowing educational inequalities, as they restrict the study patterns of less-advantaged students but do far less to curb the accelerated learning of others. However, even if prior learning were to be banned for all students throughout all forms of shadow education, it is very difficult to actually prove that students are learning certain topics in advance, rather than simply deepening existing learning that is appropriate for their age and level. Representatives of right-leaning parents' organisations in Korea have, moreover, argued vociferously that notions such as restricting parents' freedom to invest in their children or children's rights to learn ahead of the national curriculum are morally unacceptable. Article 31 of the Korean Constitution declares an explicit right and indeed responsibility of parents to provide their children with an education suited to their abilities. While many policies, such as *hagwon* curfews and (some) restrictions on prior learning persist, many argue that instead of trying to restrict private tutoring, the government ought to be addressing more fundamental factors driving the demand for such tutoring in the first place.

## Reforming university admissions procedures

One final key area which governments have sought to reform in order to curb shadow education demand is university admissions arrangements. The CSAT exam, which high-school students take every November, has in its current form been the predominant method universities have used to rank and select students since the 1990s. Multiple-choice testing in CSAT, however, though trusted by many for the extent to which it provides a transparent and objective method of assessing students, is also a form of assessment highly conducive pedagogically to students seeking to boost scores by cramming in *hagwons*. CSAT exams, and also additional exams and interviews set by individual universities, have over several decades been subject to numerous reforms. Since the early 2010s they have been targeted by policy-makers as part of the normalisation agenda. Questions today must cover only material that is part of students' mainstream school curriculum. Efforts have also been made more broadly by policy-makers to amend universities' predominant focus on CSAT relative to more qualitative and holistic assessments of student merit. Under President Lee Myung Bak (2008–13), universities began receiving financial incentives to deploy new admissions officers and to give greater weight in their admissions procedures to more qualitative and holistic data about students. The primary focus here has been students' high-school achievements, including information such as overall grade-point average (GPA), involvement in extra-curricular activities,[2] and teachers' written assessments of the students' performance and potential:

> If you just rely on test scores, it's the easiest way the private tutors can sell themselves. [To] change the system of selecting students, [so it is] not just based on test scores, but based on other things, especially other things that were made by teachers, is really the point. (former minister of education)

Have these reforms reduced families' demand for *hagwon* cramming? Experts and stakeholders are doubtful. Representatives of parents' organisations have highlighted that, even under the new rules, quantitative test scores still matter because GPA is a factor, and teachers' apparently more holistic assessments of student performance end up being at least partly based on test performance. Many parents also lack faith in the large amount of discretionary power that has been given to teachers whose subjective judgements now play a significant role in determining students' admission to universities. Increased focus on what happens inside school also means that students must now find new, additional ways to stand out, and this creates new anxieties for parents, particularly in schools where segregated pupil intakes mean that all students in a cohort are similar in their levels of achievement. Private tutoring companies have responded quickly to these new anxieties, promising to help ensure students maintain an 'edge' and 'win' in all sorts of extra-curricular, intra-school competitions – science experiments, art projects, musical performances, sports competitions – particularly in a time when CSAT and university exams have been made 'easier'. Such policy outcomes have led to a broad backlash against 'irregular' university admissions, most recently under the Minjoo President Moon Jae-in, and a Ministry of Education decision that universities should once more place greater emphasis on CSAT scores (Bahk, 2019).

## Beyond the realm of education policy

Shadow education in Korea today, and the size and extent of the Korean private tutoring industry, seem almost entirely culturally normalised. Fleckenstein and Lee (2019: 183) describe a society locked in to a 'pathological equilibrium' in this regard, even in a time of improvements to public education. Private shadow education companies are reportedly employing at least 2.2 per cent of the national workforce (Korea Research Institute for Vocational Education and Training, 2009). This fact, together with such companies' role in driving Korea to a high position in international education league tables, gives them great lobbying power over Korean governments to ensure favourable conditions for themselves, including constraints on regulation.

What are the root causes for the Korean government's failure to curb demand for private tutoring? In order to better understand this, we might need to look beyond the realm of education policy into wider competitive pressures that have long been endemic in Korean society and have worsened in recent decades.

Competitive 'education fever' (see for example Seth, 2002; Lee et al, 2010) is a phenomenon very often discussed in Korean and other Asian societies (Jerrim, 2019). The phrase refers to a strong cultural preoccupation with students' educational achievement and with the importance of family involvement in children's education. Such preoccupations in Korea stem largely from the broad dominance Confucian cultural norms, as well as more local *hakbul* traditions (Oh,

2011) that have historically conferred great societal status in Korea on individuals securing positions in universities with high 'name value' at the top of a fixed higher education hierarchy (above all the SKY – Seoul National, Korea and Yonsei – universities) and the nature of the Korean economy, which has historically been driven strongly by human resources (KEDI, 2011).

Such factors constitute in themselves important explanations as to why demand for private tutoring may be in high in Korea. However, education fever has also become much worse in recent decades as a result of shifting economic realities. Since the 1997 Asian financial crisis, Korean citizens have witnessed dramatic economic change as Korea has gone from being a high growth, comparatively egalitarian society with strong government-regulated national wage structures to one characterised by slow growth, neoliberal deregulation, rising labour market dualism and falling social mobility (Park, 2010; Yujin, 2016). Youth unemployment has grown over time and the country today has high proportions of young people not in employment, education or training (OECD, 2016). High-status, well-paid jobs have long been concentrated in a small number of powerful *chaebols* (conglomerates) – Hyundai, LG, SK, Lotte and Samsung – that dominate the Korean economy. However, these *chaebols* have also shrunk their core workforces in Korea, outsourcing and moving jobs abroad (Snyder, 2018).

All interviewees in this project asserted a sense that a changing social fabric and a growing belief that the 'winner takes all' (Fleckenstein and Lee, 2019: 182) in Korean society has heightened families' anxieties about their children's futures, constituting a clear factor 'beyond education policy' that would drive demand for shadow education. Pressure on students to achieve highly in CSAT has become enormous in a context where not even those from SKY universities are today guaranteed 'top jobs'. Pressure and tutoring start early in students' lives, with many in middle school being further compelled to compete academically in high-stakes tests for access to elite selective high schools such as 'special purpose' and 'autonomous private' high schools (Kang et al, 2007; KEDI, 2011; Exley, 2020). Parents' motivations to ensure their children have access to such schools relate directly to their anxieties about competition for the most prestigious universities and in turn jobs with top employers – selective education at both school and university in Korea ultimately send powerful signals to employers that one's children must be 'the best'.

For Korean governments to tackle shadow education demand at its roots, then, unified policy-making approaches are needed. Labour market policy needs particular attention, alongside education policy, especially after youth unemployment reached record levels of 12.5 per cent in 2016. Labour market dualism, arising in large part from the practices of *chaebols*, must be tackled directly and greater government support is needed for the creation of new, high-quality employment opportunities through small and medium enterprises (on this front, see the recent Korean establishment of a Ministry for small and medium enterprises and start-ups). Taxation policies may also be considered for the purposes of redistributing wealth and income. In 2016, Korea was measured in an International Monetary Fund report as being the most unequal country in the Asia-Pacific region (Chandra et al, 2016). The 2017 election of Moon Jae-in provides some hope, as it led to a raft of government promises to tackle inequality and to raise minimum wages:

> The serious inequality of wealth and income is threatening the nation's democracy. (President Moon, June 2017, quoted in Jung, 2017)

Finally, historically residualist Korean public social protection must be revisited. The enormous stakes attached to university entry, creating despair among young people, at least in part reflect fears about future poverty in a time where many past egalitarian regulations of private sector wages and offer people security throughout their lives no longer exist. Koreans have good reason to fear what will happen to them in times of unemployment, ill health, disability and old age. Almost half of Korea's older people live in poverty (OECD, 2017) and in 2018 Korea devoted just 11.1 per cent of its GDP to public social spending, compared with a 20.1 per cent OECD average (OECD, 2020).

## Learning lessons: the value of unified policy strategies

What lessons might be learnt, then, by both Korea and Western societies, where private education spending has risen recently even in Nordic states (see, for example, Hallsen and Karlsson, 2019; Bray, 2020) and many countries today seem almost to be sleepwalking into a situation where worryingly large tutoring industries are taking root?

One first key lesson for *all* societies must surely be that wherever governments are truly committed to public social investment strategies as a means to enhance national efficiency or narrow inequalities, it would seem highly important for them to remain mindful of families' underlying incentives for engaging in substantial, competitively motivated private education spending. There are strong grounds, too, when we look at the Korean 'pathological equilibrium' today (Fleckenstein and Lee, 2019: 183), for arguing that policy-makers worldwide must pay attention *before* complex tutoring industries are already thoroughly entrenched, rather than after tutoring industries become too dominant and difficult to regulate. In this sense, problems might be considered time critical.

In order to tackle parents' underlying incentives to pay for private supplementary tutoring, governments across the world today must think truly broadly about policy, considering ways in which different factors are connected and accepting a need for unified reforms. Reducing private tutoring consumption is, as Korean governments have learnt, never going to be simply a matter of, for example, improving public education, altering college admissions procedures or restricting shadow education supply through law. It is instead a matter that goes far beyond the realm of education policy alone, and one that should lead us to question how far education can ever be treated as a 'magic bullet' or the primary 'insurance' that people need to protect themselves and their families against a risk of future poverty.

Major private investments in education have been shown in this chapter to relate strongly to families' anxieties regarding children's future destinies in a country where government social protections have long been residual, good jobs have become much harder to come by, and a formerly somewhat egalitarian social and economic order has become much more unequal. Such dynamics suggest implications not only for education systems, but also for labour market policy, for social security design and indeed for wider strategies to tax and spend that fundamentally affect how equal or unequal societies are allowed to become. East Asia is regularly characterised today as being a region substantially different to many others in terms of how far Confucian culture has for centuries sustained a strong focus on education. At the same time, growing private education spending, as families try in ever-more uncertain times to guard against downward mobility, is becoming an increasingly global middle class phenomenon. To borrow from Ball:

> The drive for guaranteed success and advantage over others within changing economic and labour market conditions and increased regional and global competition for work is related to anxieties within middle class families about social reproduction, or what American writer Ehrenreich (1989) calls the 'fear of falling' ... Given the extent to

which middle class families rely on qualifications and other forms of symbolic capital to address and assuage these fears, education in all of its forms becomes an even greater focus of activity and investment and is ever more thoroughly commodified. (2010: 160)

In such contexts it is imperative that governments consider possible negative implications not only for families who *can* afford such investment, but even more crucially for those who cannot.

## Notes
[1] There are too many works on this subject to document here, but see for example Baker and LeTendre, 2005; Aurini et al, 2013; Bray, 2017.
[2] Importantly the mention of extra-curricular activities outside school in students' university applications was recently forbidden under President Park Geun-hye.

## References

Aurini, J., Davies, S. and Dierkes, J. (eds) (2013) *Out of the Shadows: The Global Intensification of Supplementary Education*, Bingley: Emerald.

Bae, S., Oh, H., Kim, H., Lee, C. and Oh, B. (2010) 'The impact of after school programs on educational quality and private tutoring expenses', *Asia Pacific Education Review*, 11(3): 349–61.

Bahk, E.J. (2019) 'Colleges to focus more on CSAT', *The Korea Times*, [online] 28 November, Available from koreatimes.co.kr/www/nation/2019/11/181_279483.html [Accessed 26 July 2020].

Baker, D.P. and LeTendre, G. (2005) *National Differences, Global Similarities: World Culture and the Future of Schooling*, Stanford, CA: Stanford University Press.

Ball, S.J. (2010) 'New class inequalities in education: why education policy may be looking in the wrong place', *International Journal of Sociology and Social Policy*, 30(3/4): 155–66.

Ball, S.J. (2012) *Global Education Inc: New Policy Networks and the Neoliberal Imaginary*, London: Routledge.

Becker, G. (1964) *Human Capital* (3rd edn), Chicago: University of Chicago Press.

Bray, M. (2011) *The Challenge of Shadow Education: Private Tutoring and its Implications for Policy Makers in the European Union*, Brussels: European Commission.

Bray, M. (2017) 'Schooling and its supplements: changing global patterns and implications for comparative education', *Comparative Education Review*, 61(3): 469–91.

Bray, M. (2020) 'Shadow education in Europe: growing prevalence, underlying forces, and policy implications', *East China National University Review of Education*, Online First, Available from: https://doi.org/10.1177%2F2096531119890142 [Accessed 8 October 2020].

Bray, M. and Lykins, C. (2012) *Shadow Education: Private Supplementary Tutoring and its Implications for Policy Makers in Asia*, Mandaluyong City: Asian Development Bank.

Bray, M. and Kwo, O. (2013) 'Behind the façade of fee-free education: shadow education and its implications for social justice', *Oxford Review of Education*, 39(4): 480–97.

Byun, S. (2014) 'Shadow education and academic success in Republic of Korea', in H. Park and K. Kim (eds) *Korean Education in Changing Economic and Demographic Contexts*, Singapore: Springer, pp 39–58.

Chandra, S.J., Kinda, T., Kochhar, K., Piao, S., and Schauer, J. (2016) *Sharing the Growth Dividend: Analysis of Inequality in Asia*, Washington DC: International Monetary Fund.

Chang, H. (2011) *23 Things They Don't Tell You About Capitalism*, London: Penguin.

Choi, H. and Choi, A. (2016) 'Regulating private tutoring consumption in Korea: lessons from another failure', *International Journal of Educational Development*, 49: 144–56.

Dang, H. and Rogers, F.H. (2008) 'The growing phenomenon of private tutoring: does it deepen human capital, widen inequalities or waste resources?', *World Bank Research Observer*, 23(2): 161–200.

Exley, S. (2020) 'Selective schooling and its relationship to private tutoring: the case of South Korea', *Comparative Education*, 56(2): 218–35.

Fleckenstein, T. and Lee, S. (2019) 'The political economy of education and skills in South Korea: democratisation, liberalisation and education reform in comparative perspective', *The Pacific Review*, 32(2): 168–87.

Gurun, A. and Millimet, D.L. (2008) 'Does Private Tutoring Pay Off?', Institute for the Study of Labor (IZA) Discussion Paper 3637, Bonn: IZA.

Hallsen, S. and Karlsson, M. (2019) 'Teacher or friend? Consumer narratives on private supplementary tutoring in Sweden as policy enactment', *Journal of Education Policy*, 34(5): 631–46.

Heckman, J.J. (2011) 'The economics of inequality: the value of early childhood education', *American Educator*, 35(1): 31–5.

Hwang, D., Yang, H. and Kim, H. (2010) *E-learning in the Republic of Korea*, Moscow: UNESCO.

Jerrim, J. (2017) *Extra Time: Private tuition and Out-of-School Study*, London: Sutton Trust.

Jerrim, J. (2019) 'Why do East Asian children perform so well in PISA? An investigation of Western-born children of East Asian descent', *Oxford Review of Education*, 41(3): 310–33.

Jung, M.H. (2017) 'Economic inequality is threatening democracy', *The Korea Times*, [online] 11 June, Available from: http://www. koreatimes.co.kr/www/nation/2018/09/356_230989.html [Accessed 26 July 2020].

Kang, Y., Park, S., Jung, H. and Park, J. (2007) *A Study on the Effect of Special High School Policy in Korea*, Seoul. KEDI.

Kim, J. and Chang, J. (2010) 'Do governmental regulations for cram schools decrease the number of hours students spend on private tutoring?', *KEDI Journal of Education Policy*, 7(1): 3–21.

Kim, J.H. and Park, D. (2010) 'The determinants of demand for private tutoring in South Korea', *Asia Pacific Education Review*, 11(3): 411–21.

Kim, S. and Lee, J. (2010) 'Private tutoring and demand for education in South Korea', *Economic Development and Cultural Change*, 58(2): 259–96.

Kim, Y.C. (2016) *Shadow Education and the Curriculum and Culture of Schooling in South Korea*, New York: Palgrave Macmillan.

KEDI (Korean Educational Development Institute) (2011) *Brief Understanding of Korean Educational Policy*, Seoul: KEDI.

KICE (Korean Institute for Curriculum and Evaluation) (2017) *Issues and Implementation of the 2015 Revised Curriculum*, Seoul: KICE.

Korea Research Institute for Vocational Education and Training (2009) *2008 Survey on Private Education Providers*, Seoul: Ministry of Education, Science and Technology.

Lareau, A. (1987) 'Social class differences in family-school relationships: the importance of cultural capital in education', *Sociology of Education*, 60(2): 73–85.

Lee, C.J., Lee, H. and Jang, H. (2010) 'The history of policy responses to shadow education in South Korea: implications for the next cycle of policy responses', *Asia Pacific Education Review*, 11(1): 97–108.

Lubienski, C. and Lee, J. (2013) 'Making markets: policy construction of supplementary education in the United States and Korea', in J. Aurini, S. Davies and J. Dierkes (eds) *Out of the Shadows: The Global Intensification of Supplementary Education*, Bingley: Emerald, pp 223–43.

Lucas, S.R. (2001) 'Effectively maintained inequality: education transitions, track mobility, and social background effects' *American Journal of Sociology*, 106(6): 1642–90.

McInerney, L. (2017) 'Future schools: core subjects only, parents pay for the rest', *The Guardian* [online], 21 March. Available from: www.theguardian.com/education/2018/mar/21/schools-core-subjects-parents-pay-sport-music [Accessed 26 July 2020].

OECD (Organisation for Economic Cooperation and Development) (2014) *Strong Performers & Successful Reformers in Education: Lessons from PISA for Korea*, Paris: OECD.

OECD (Organisation for Economic Cooperation and Development) (2016) *Government at a Glance: How Korea Compares*, Paris: OECD.

OECD (Organisation for Economic Cooperation and Development) (2017) *Pensions at a Glance 2017: OECD and G20 Indicators*, Paris: OECD.

OECD (Organisation for Economic Cooperation and Development) (2020) 'Social Spending Data'. Available from: https://data.oecd.org/socialexp/social-spending.htm [Accessed 26 July 2020].

Oh, J. (2011) 'High school diversification against educational equality: a critical analysis of neoliberal education reform in South Korea', *Asia Pacific Education Review*, 12(3): 381–91.

Park, H., Buchmann, C., Choi, J. and Merry, J.J. (2016) 'Learning beyond the school walls: trends and implications', *Annual Review of Sociology*, 42: 231–52.

Park, S.Y. (2010) 'Crafting and dismantling the egalitarian social contract: the changing state-society relations in globalizing Korea', *The Pacific Review*, 23(5): 579–601.

Pritchett, L. (2001) 'Where has all the education gone?' *World Bank Economic Review*, 15(3): 367–91.

Sellar, S. and Lingard, B. (2013) 'Looking East: Shanghai, PISA 2009 and the reconstitution of reference societies in the global education policy field', *Comparative Education*, 49(4): 464–85.

Sen, A. (1999) *Development as Freedom*, Oxford: Oxford University Press.

Seth, M. (2002) *Education Fever: Society, Politics and the Pursuit of Schooling in South Korea*, Honolulu, HI: University of Hawai'i Press.

Snyder, S.A. (2018) *South Korea at the Crossroads: Autonomy and Alliance in an Era of Rival Powers*, New York: Columbia University Press.

Sutton Trust (2019) *Private Tuition Polling 2019*, London: Sutton Trust.

Van Kersbergen, K. and Hemerijck, A. (2012) 'Two decades of change in Europe: the emergence of the social investment state', *Journal of Social Policy*, 41(3): 475–92.

Verger, A., Steiner-Khamsi, G. and Lubienski, C. (2016) 'The emergence and structuring of the global education industry: towards an analytical framework', in A. Verger, G. Steiner-Khamsi and C. Lubienski (eds) *World Yearbook of Education: The Global Education Industry*, London: Routledge, pp 3–23.

Vincent, C. (2012) *Parenting: Risk, Responsibilities and Respect*, London: Institute of Education.

Waldow, F., Takayama, K., and Sung, Y.K. (2014) 'Rethinking the pattern of external policy referencing: media discourses over the "Asian tigers'" PISA success in Australia, Germany and South Korea', *Comparative Education*, 50(3). 302–21.

Wolf, A. (2002) *Does Education Matter? Myths About Education and Economic Growth*, Harmondsworth: Penguin.

World Bank (2020) 'Fertility rate, total (births per woman)', Available from: https://data.worldbank.org/indicator/SP.DYN.TFRT.IN?year_high_desc=false [Accessed 26 July 2020].

Yujin, Y. (2016) *A Study of Social Cohesion and Social Mobility in Korea with Policy Recommendations*, Sejong: Korean Institute for Health and Social Affairs.

# 4

# How do family background and shadow education affect academic performance and labour market outcomes in South Korea? Reasons for redistributive social investment

*Yun Young Kim and Young Jun Choi*

## Introduction

Researchers argue that social investment policies contribute not only to equal opportunity and human capital development, but also to the sustainability of welfare states. In that respect, these policies are regarded as the new vanguard of the welfare state (Morel et al, 2012). Yet, in the west, many criticise the role of social investment policies, as they tend to place too much focus on the (re)commodification of labour and are unable to cope with increasing inequality. In fact, scholars suspect social investment policies create a Matthew effect (Bonoli et al, 2017). However, many commentators note that East Asian welfare regimes do not need social investment policies to enhance human capital, as these countries are well-known for highly commodified labour and high rankings in the Programme for International Student Assessment (PISA).

However, these commentators seem to largely neglect the social outcomes of education policies in East Asian countries. Behind the scenes of their remarkable educational achievements, these countries seem to suffer from decreasing social mobility. For example, in South Korea (hereafter Korea), once praised for its active upward social mobility, the media has frequently referred to the country's increasing social inequality and reduced social mobility using the terms 'gold spoon' and 'dirt spoon'. Unlike decreasing social mobility, overall education expenditure in Korea is 8 per cent of GDP, and public expenditure has increased from 3 per cent in 2000 to more than 5 per cent in 2015 (World Bank, 2018). This could mean that the education policy and expenditure has not been able to reverse the labour market dualisation and has failed to secure an equitable outcome. Therefore, it is still important to look at education policy from the perspective of social investment.

This chapter aims to explore the role of education and social investment, with special attention on the effects of shadow education on social mobility in Korea. There has been much social and political discussion about social mobility, but few empirical studies have been conducted. This study analyses how family background and shadow education influence educational attainment and, subsequently, how educational attainment affects incomes, using data from the Korea Education and Employment Panel (KEEP). Then, since this 'broken social elevator' is not a problem faced only by Korea – most Organisation for Economic Co-operation and Development (OECD) countries have 'sticky ceilings' and 'sticky floors' (OECD, 2018) – we discuss the direction social investment policies should take to reboot social mobility. We argue that in order to minimise the effects of family background on educational attainment and labour market outcomes, social investment policies should actively play a redistributive role.

## Social mobility and causal mechanisms

Social mobility can be categorised within a generation and across generations (Causa and Johansson, 2011). Social mobility within a generation is mainly measured by income mobility. For example, a typical method of studying social mobility within the same generation is to measure income levels of a group in their 30s and then again for the same group when they reach their 40s, to detect the class changes over time. Inter-generational social mobility is normally measured by looking at changes in the income levels of parents and their children. Although social mobility within a generation has ample implications for income equality and equal opportunity (Krugman, 1992; Jarvis and Jenkins, 1998), this chapter will focus on social mobility across generations, which has become more problematic in advanced welfare states (OECD, 2018).

The state of social mobility across generations is well illustrated by the 'Great Gatsby curve' proposed by Alan Krueger, former chairman of the White House Council of Economic Advisors, in 2012. His theory explains the relationship between the degree of income inequality and inter-generational mobility (IGM) in various countries. By comparing the degree of income inequality and the IGM indicator, he discovered that there is a general tendency for IGM to be lower in places with higher social inequality. For example, Nordic countries tend to have higher social mobility (Esping-Andersen, 2009). However, it is also clear that inequality has widened across the world (Piketty, 2014), and accordingly, social mobility has reduced (OECD, 2018). As social and economic policies have failed to correct existing inequality, advanced welfare states have also failed to produce success for those from disadvantaged backgrounds. Low social mobility is not only producing inequitable social outcomes, such as weakening social capital (Putnam, 2016), it is also harming the economy, as many workers miss opportunities to become innovators due to their family backgrounds (Bell et al, 2019). In other words, low social mobility could decrease the availability of good human capital and subsequently weaken the sustainability of the welfare state.

What are the factors and mechanisms weakening social mobility? The literature uniformly suggests that parentage and family backgrounds are the most important factors in predicting an individual's social mobility. Chetty et al (2014) investigated social mobility in the US using the data for approximately 40 million people and found that a 10 per cent increase in parental income leads to a 3.4 per cent increase in the income of their offspring on average. Causa and Johansson (2011) analysed the recent IGM patterns of the OECD and obtained empirical results indicating that the socioeconomic backgrounds of parents show significant positive correlation with the educational and labour market outcomes for their children. There are a number of studies also emphasising the importance of class and parents' educational attainment (Davis-Kean, 2005; Beller, 2009). Though there are fewer studies, similar results are also found for Korea. Kim (2015) shows how the economic status of a family affects students' educational performance and school choice, which has important implications for social mobility in Korea. Choi and Min (2015) confirm that the higher the level of education and income of parents, the better the educational outcomes are for their offspring.

Scholars point out two possible factors other than family backgrounds that contribute to social mobility. The first is education and social investment policy. Causa and Johansson (2011) find that government policies on education and childcare play an important role in explaining differences in IGM across countries. Yet, education and social investment policies do not always enhance social mobility. In Korea, Yeo (2008) points out that in the twentieth century, education used to be seen as something that enhanced social mobility, rather than perpetuating inequality. However, more recent results raise the concern that education might be contributing to the inheritance of poverty and inequality across generations (Kim, 2015). The education system, supported and surrounded by shadow education, especially neglects the distribution of opportunities to inter-class competition, acting instead as a mechanism that creates serious gaps in opportunity between classes and reproduces the unequal structure of the existing society. This means that the accessibility to educational opportunities for low-income groups is diminished and inequality is eventually perpetuated. This form of the Matthew effect has been witnessed in Europe, as the middle and upper classes take advantage of the opportunities these policies create (Pintelon et al, 2013; Bonoli et al, 2017).

Another possible factor that has been under-researched is shadow education. Out-of-school education or shadow education has been increasing in many countries, as competition becomes more intense. Korea is a typical example of this. In 2015, private tutoring spending was an estimated 350,000 won (about US$300) per student; the higher the monthly average incomes of households, the higher the private tutoring expenditure and participation rates were (National Statistics Office, 2016). In wealthy districts, the total shadow education spending per student was reported to be more than US$1,000 (Lee et al, 2015). As shadow education increases, it is predicted that it will strongly affect social mobility, but there are few studies that examine this. Many studies on shadow education focus on why people choose it (Lee and Shouse, 2011) or policy responses to rein it in (Lee et al, 2010).

In this context, we would like to establish the first long-term panel data and test the state of social mobility in Korea, paying special attention to shadow education. While we look at family and parental backgrounds, we hope to gauge indirectly the effectiveness of existing education (ie, the extent to which education policy reduces the socio-economic gap) and social investment policies by examining how visible the effects of shadow education are.

## Research methods

### Data

Despite the topicality and academic significance of the subject, few studies regarding social mobility have been conducted, due to the limited data available. With regard to the inheritance of wealth and education level, existing studies have used data from the Korea Labour Income Panel Survey (KLIPS) (Choi and Min, 2015). KLIPS generates pertinent variables through a retrospective method. It asks respondents about their parents' occupations and incomes at a certain time in the past, mostly around the time when the respondents were 14 years old. Therefore, the accuracy of the responses is not guaranteed, since it relies on the memories of the respondents and their knowledge of their parents' financial details.

This study utilises data from KEEP, a panel survey, rather than the retrospective survey data. Even though KEEP is not a long-term survey – it only covers the years 2004–2015 – the wage and income levels are measurable because a majority of the participants of the first survey, who were middle- and high-school students at the time, had already entered the labour market by the time the tenth survey was conducted. Moreover, KEEP also has the advantage of direct information related to the education and income levels of the respondents' parents gathered in the first survey. In this sense, KEEP data is the most suitable for studying class mobility and unequal opportunity between generations in Korea.

To be more specific, KEEP provides the only nationally recognised statistics that can be used to figure out the transition paths of middle- and high-school students to the labour market. In 2004, a total of 6,000 students – 2,000 third-grade, middle-school students; 2,000 third-grade, regular high-school students; and 2,000 third-grade, technical high-school students – were selected as research subjects and, as of March 2016, the survey results up to 2014 (the 11th wave) have been released. An in-depth, multi-lateral analysis can be conducted to examine the effects of various socio-economic factors on social mobility using the data that has been accumulated for these 11 years.

## Analytic variables

The analysis was carried out based on the batch of 2004 third-grade, middle-school students. Since the first survey in 2004 contains the education and income levels of students' parents, the effect of parent's social class on their children's academic performance, measured by the university entrance and College Scholastic Ability Test (CSAT) scores, can be analysed. The second KEEP survey traces whether the first survey respondents went to high school or not, and which types of high schools they entered. Thus, the process of entering high school can be analysed according to the characteristics of parents. The third-grade, middle-school students started entering university from the fourth survey in 2007. Whether students entered university and how they did on the CSAT exams can be identified through the fourth survey in 2007 to the sixth survey in 2009. As major variables of this study, first, we measure the parents' education level. Second, parents' economic class is measured based on the household monthly income reported in the first survey. Table 4.1 shows the advancement of the education level of the third-grade, middle-school students.

Next, in order to estimate the direct and indirect effects of parents' socio-economic status and shadow education on the subjects' income, a path analysis was implemented. Socio-economic status (SES) is a latent variable estimated by measuring three types of variables – academic ability, economic level and parental occupation. As previously mentioned, this study aimed to estimate how parent's socio-economic status directly and indirectly, through children's private education, influences children's primary income. In a bid to analyse the path model, which possesses a latent variable, STATA 14.0 will be used.

The following is the basic information on the sample in the study. The parental education level was divided into three parts: Below high-school graduation, graduated from high school and graduated from junior college or higher. When both parents are present, we use father's education level, and mother's education level when a father is not present. The statistics of the third-grade, middle-school students' parental income levels are indicated in Table 4.2.

Table 4.2 indicates the average monthly income and the proportion of income indexes of the parents of the third-grade, middle-school students. First of all, the average monthly income of 1,933 households in which household income was observable, is 3.01 million won, with

**Table 4.1:** Advancement of the education level of third-grade, middle-school students

|  | 1st wave | 2nd wave | 3rd wave | 4th wave | 5th wave | 6th wave |
|---|---|---|---|---|---|---|
| **Parental variables** | Education Income | | | Income | | |
| **Student variables** | | High-school entrance | | Early graduates<br><br>College entrance | High-school graduates<br><br>College entrance | High-school graduates<br><br>College entrance (including repeaters) |
| | | Score in the tenth grade | | Early graduates<br><br>The CSAT score | High-school graduates<br><br>The CSAT score | High-school graduates<br><br>The CSAT score (including repeaters) |

Source: Based on data from KEEP (2017)

**Table 4.2:** Household income and income quintile share for parents of third-grade, middle-school students

|  | Average | Median | Minimum value | Maximum value | Sample size |
|---|---|---|---|---|---|
| Household income (per month, in 10,000 won) | 301 | 270 | 0 | 3,000 | 1,933 |

|  | 1 Quint | 2 Quint | 3 Quint | 4 Quint | 5 Quint |
|---|---|---|---|---|---|
| Income Quint (household) | 286 | 503 | 497 | 324 | 323 |
| Income Quint ratio (%) | 14.8 | 26.0 | 25.7 | 16.7 | 16.7 |

Source: Based on data from KEEP (2017) and Choi and Min (2015)

a median value of 2.7 million won. In order to classify this into income indexes, the household equalised income, which considers the number of household members, must be calculated. The boundary values of the first to the fifth income quintile of Korea in 2004 are shown on the National Statistical Office website. Therefore, the income quintiles of the cohort households are defined based on these boundary values.

Since the parental education level does not change with time, the parental education level variable of the first survey (2004) can be used. However, household income changes every year after the first survey. Thus, this chapter takes the household income to be the average value of household income from the first survey (2004) to the fourth survey (2007). As in Table 4.2, household equalised income was calculated and households were divided into five groups based on the boundary values of the indexes of Korea's 2007 income quintile presented by the National Statistical Office.

## Analytic results

### Parents' background – shadow education[1]

The income bracket is likely to be passed down to children through investments in education. Figures 4.1 and 4.2 show how children's shadow education time and spending differ based on their parents' education and income levels. Figure 4.1 shows the shadow education time according to guardians' education levels. As parents' education level rises, especially when it is over college, children's private education time increases. If guardians have an education level of graduating from a junior college and higher, the share of children spending more than 9 hours per week participating in shadow education is approximately 41 per cent, whereas only 20.8 per cent of children in the same group spend less than 4.5 hours per week.

**Figure 4.1:** Parents' education levels and children's shadow education time

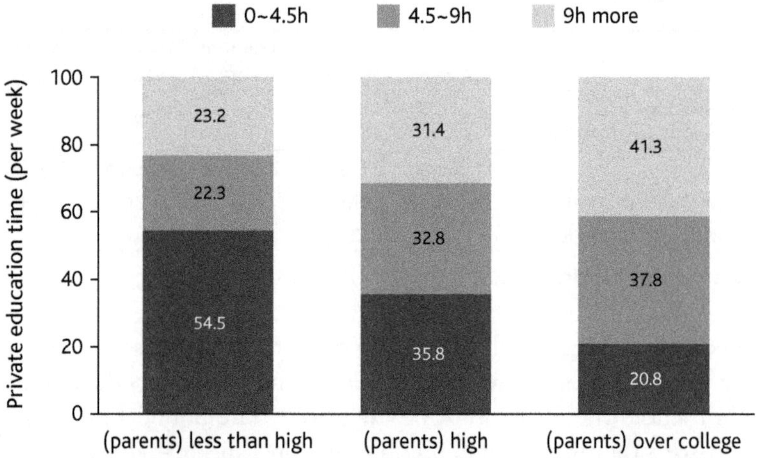

■ 0~4.5h    ■ 4.5~9h    □ 9h more

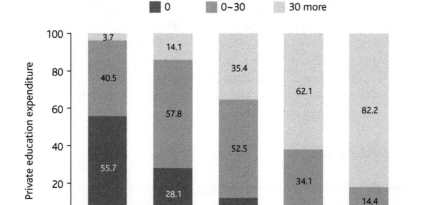

Source: Authors' own calculation

**Figure 4.2:** Parents' income levels and children's shadow education

■ 0    ■ 0~30    □ 30 more

Source: Authors' own calculation

However, more than half of children of parents with less than a high-school education, spend less than 4.5 hours per week participating in shadow education. Figure 4.2 indicates children's shadow education spending based on parents' income levels. As expected, spending on shadow education increases as household income gets higher. Among the first income quintile, 55 per cent of children do not receive any shadow education, but only 3.4 per cent do not among children of the fifth income quintile.

## Shadow education – college scholastic ability test grade

How does shadow education influence entrance examinations? As shown below, the relationship between shadow education and CSAT scores has been suggested based on KEEP data collected over a four-year period. We researched the period from the third grade of middle school to the third grade of high school in 2007. The average shadow education spending was divided into the following quartiles: Section 1 (0), Section 2 (from 10,000 won to 200,000 won a month), Section 3 (from 210,000 won to 450,000 won a month), and Section 4 (450,000 won or more a month). When referring to the bar graph in the figure, 67 students classified as grade 4, the highest performers, spent an average of 450,000 won or more on shadow education, whereas only 29 students did not spend any money on shadow education. In particular, 221 students classified as grade 1 did not spend any money on shadow education. It is generally observed that higher shadow education expenses led to better CSAT scores. However, a marked CSAT score difference was not clearly identified between group 2 (200,000 won or less) and group 3 (from 210,000 won to 450,000 won).

**Figure 4.3:** Shadow education – CSAT scores

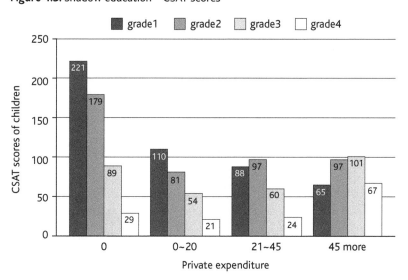

Note: Here grade indicates the CSAT scoring level.
Source: Authors' own calculation

## Parents' background – college scholastic ability test grade

In a situation where the university entrance rate is higher than 75 per cent, entering a prestigious university can be more important than the mere fact of going to a college, because entering a prestigious university can have a greater influence on labour market performance amid worsening job market conditions for college graduates. In this context, Figure 4.4 and Figure 4.5 show how children's CSAT scores differ according to their parent's education and income levels, since higher scores increase the possibility of entering a prestigious university.

Figure 4.4 indicates the rate of children's CSAT grades based on their parents' education levels. As the education level of parents increases, the proportion of the highest performers, those reaching grade 4 on the CSAT, increases greatly. When guardians have an education level of graduating from a college and higher, the rate of children achieving grade 4 is 40 per cent. As the education level of parents becomes higher, the investment and performance toward children's education becomes bigger may become the most important factor. On the other hand, if parents have an education level of less than high school, the rate of children achieving a CSAT grade of 4 is less than 1 per cent. In this case, it is very difficult for children to enter a prestigious university on CSAT scores alone. Figure 4.5 indicates children's rate of CSAT

**Figure 4.4**: Parents' education levels and children's CSAT scores

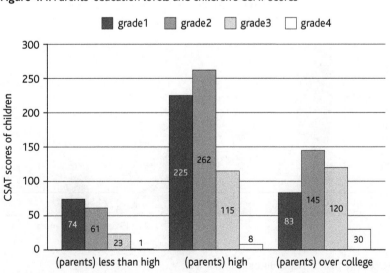

Source: Authors' own calculation

**Figure 4.5:** Parents' income levels and children's CSAT scores

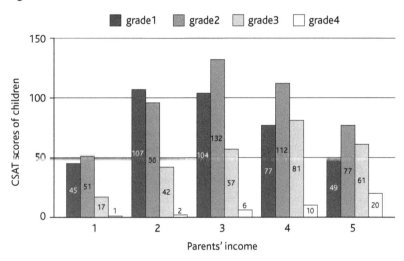

Source: Authors' own calculation

grades according to parent's income level. Similar to the previous figure, as the income level goes higher, the share of grade 3 and 4 scores becomes markedly higher.

## Path analysis

In this section, a path analysis is conducted in order to explore the influence of family background and shadow education on educational attainment and, subsequently, how educational attainment affects labour market income.[2] In this study, as shown in Table 4.3, six statistical variables are presented, consisting of two endogenous variables (CSAT score, children's income in the labour market), two parametric variables (shadow education, self-study), and six endogenous variables (parents' education, parents' income, personal grade, sex, and region), based on a literature review.

All independent, parametric, and dependent variables utilised for this study share close relationships. In addition, the path coefficients related to 'parents' background' variables reveal a direct effect. Direct effect is where a variable has a direct impact on another variable. Indirect effect refers to path effects through an intermediate variable and more. Personal grade, gender and residence are related to indirect effects. Total effect is defined as the sum of total direct effect and total indirect effect generated between variables. The relationship of independent variables (exogenous variables), dependent variables

**Table 4.3:** Analytic variables

| Variables | | | Operationalisation |
|---|---|---|---|
| Endogenous variable | CSAT scores (sat_m)[a] | | Continuous variable: M |
| | Children's income (income) | | Continuous variable: reflecting inflation |
| Parameter variables | Shadow education[b] | | Private education time: mean of Korean, English, mathematics |
| | Self-study[c] | | Self-study time per week |
| Exogenous variables | Parents | Parents' education (father6_1)[d] | Less high=1 High=2 More University=3 |
| | | Parents' income (h_meincome) | Continuous variable |
| | Personal factors | Personal grade (mh_grade) | School grades (1st [highest] to 10th [lowest])[e] |
| | | Personal sex (dum_gender1) | Man=1/Woman=0 |
| | | Personal region (dum_region1) | Seoul=1 Metropolitan city=2 Others=3 |
| | | Personal region | Seoul=1 Capital area=2 Other=3 |

Notes:

[a] From now on, the parenthesis is the abbreviation of analytic variable used in Figure 4.7: 4.8.

[b] Self-study is an exogenous variable when Shadow education is a parameter variable (see path model 1)

[c] Shadow education is an exogenous variable when self-study is a parameter variable (see path model 2)

[d] The reason why the variable abbreviation is father is to take the father value first and then the mother variable.

[e] The lower CSAT score means the higher grade.

Source: Based on data from KEEP (2017)

(endogenous variables) and path structure, including exogenous and endogenous variables, is expressed in Figures 4.6 and 4.7.

Based on the above arguments, we make the following hypotheses that:

- H1: Parents' income is positively associated with shadow education.
- H2: Parents' education is positively associated with shadow education.
- H3: Shadow education is positively associated with children's income.
- H4: CSAT is positively associated with children's income.

- H5: Parents' income is positively associated with children's income.
- H6: Parents' education is positively associated with children's income.
- H7: Shadow education is positively associated with CSAT scores.
- H8: Parents' income is positively associated with CSAT scores.
- H9: Parents' education is positively associated with CSAT scores.

'Children's income' and 'CSAT score' variables may be influenced by parents' backgrounds (income, educational level). Two parameter variables (shadow education, and self-study) may also be directly affected by parents' background (income, educational level).

### Path analysis: shadow education

The results of the path analysis are shown in Figure 4.6 and Table 4.4. In the positive direction, statistically significant results were parents' income → shadow education (+), parents' education → shadow education (+), region (Seoul) → shadow education (+), parents' education → children's income (+). In the negative direction, statistically significant results were shadow education → CSAT (–), parents' education → CSAT (–), CSAT → income (–) (lower CSAT grades indicate better test performance). In other words, shadow education is influenced by parents' socio-economic backgrounds and it is an important factor for CSAT scores. CSAT scores are also seen to influence children's incomes.

To sum up, the higher parents' income/education levels, the better the university entrance outcomes of children, because the parents

**Figure 4.6:** The model of path analysis focusing on shadow education

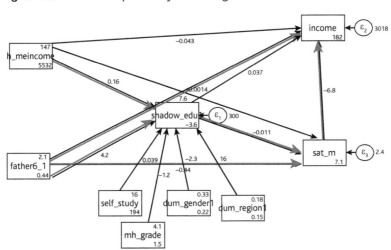

**Table 4.4:** The results of path coefficient focusing on shadow education

| Hypothesis | Hypothesised relationship | Path coefficient | P-value |
|---|---|---|---|
| H1 | Parents' income → Shadow education (+) | 0.1573695 | (0.000)*** |
| H2 | Parents' education → Shadow education (+) | 4.210277 | (0.001)** |
| H3 | Shadow education → Children's income (+) | 0.0365745 | (0.781) |
| H4 | CSAT → Children's income (–) | –6.772608 | (0.000)*** |
| H5 | Parents' income → Children's income (+) | –0.0433556 | (0.302) |
| H6 | Parents' education → Children's income (+) | 7.618677 | (0.064)* |
| H7 | Shadow education → CSAT (–) | –0.0111048 | (0.003)** |
| H8 | Parents' income → CSAT (–) | –0.0014226 | (0.230) |
| H9 | Parents' education → CSAT (–) | –0.4440094 | (0.000)*** |

*p<0.1, **p<0.05, ***p<0.001.

investment more in shadow education, which leads to better CSAT scores and eventual labour market outcomes. However, parents' income/education levels are not directly related to children's income in the labour market. That is, the relationship follows a series of path processes.

**Table 4.5:** Correlation of path coefficient focusing on shadow education

| Variables | Parents' income | Parents' education | Shadow education | SAT |
|---|---|---|---|---|
| Shadow education | 0.1573695 | 4.210277 | | |
| | (0.000)*** | (0.001)** | | |
| Children's income | –0.0433556 | 7.618677 | 0.0365745 | –6.772608 |
| | (0.302) | (0.064)* | (0.781) | (0.000)*** |
| CSAT | –0.0014226 | –0.4440094 | –0.0111048 | |
| | (0.230) | (0.000)*** | (0.003)** | |

*p<0.1, **p<0.05, ***p<0.001.

## Path analysis: self-study

This section is the results of path analysis using self-study as a parameter. As shown in Figure 4.7 and Table 4.6, the following are the statistically significant results: parents' education → self-study (+), self-study → CSAT (–), parents' education → CSAT (–), CSAT → income (–), parents' education → income (+). Parents' income had no influence on self-study time, but education level had a strong effect. Self-study time had a strong influence on university entrance results. In addition,

**Figure 4.7:** The model of path analysis focusing on self-study

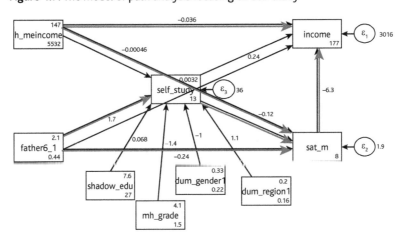

**Table 4.6:** The results of path coefficient focusing on self-study

| Hypothesis | Hypothesised relationship | Path coefficient | P-value |
|---|---|---|---|
| H1 | Parents' income → Self–study (–) | –0.0004564 | (0.909) |
| H2 | **Parents' education → Self–study (+)** | **1.663336** | **(0.000)*** |
| H3 | Self-study → Children's income (+) | 0.2437907 | (0.577) |
| H4 | **CSAT → Children's income (–)** | **–6.34349** | **(0.000)*** |
| H5 | Parents' income → Children's income (+) | –0.0359502 | (0.322) |
| H6 | **Parents' education → Children's income (+)** | **7.504197** | **(0.068)*** |
| H7 | **Self-study → CSAT (–)** | **–0.1222608** | **(0.000)*** |
| H8 | **Parents' income → CSAT (–)** | **–0.0032193** | **(0.000)*** |
| H9 | **Parents' education → CSAT (–)** | **–0.2427888** | **(0.017)**** |

*p<0.1, **p<0.05, ***p<0.001.

those with high self-study times went on to have higher incomes. Shadow education was not directly related to income in the labour market, but was affected by location variables (Seoul). Self-study time was not influenced by the location variable.

Of the common points of influence for shadow education and self-study, parents' education level were the most important variable. Also, shadow education and self-study have a strong influence on university entrance results. As shown in Figures 4.8 and 4.9, since the incline of the correlation degree between private education and university entrance results was –0.1119 and the incline of the correlation degree between self-study and university entrance results was –0.5025, the influence of self-study time is greater.

**Figure 4.8:** Relationship between shadow education and CSAT −0.1119 (p<0.000)

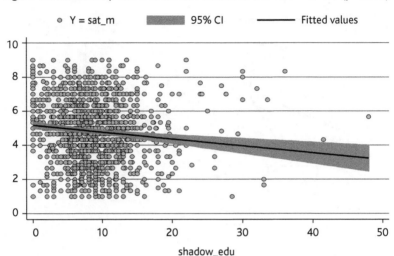

**Figure 4.9:** Relationship between self-study and CSAT −0.5025 (p<0.000)

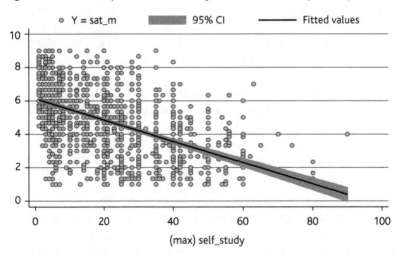

Both shadow education and self-study time influenced the short-term effect (CSAT score). As in previous literature, this study also confirms the effects of shadow education on academic performance (Dang and Rogers, 2008; Ryu and Kang, 2013), and its effects on entering a prestigious university (Ono, 2007; Gurun and Millimet, 2008; Zhang, 2013). However, this study has not discovered a long-term effect on salary at a person's first workplace. It might be because the time period is insufficient to capture the incomes of the students, as some advanced to graduate schools rather than entering the labour market. If that is not the case, as the analyses revealed, parents' education is the most important determining factor. In other words, education has not altered or mediated the effect of parents' background on children's labour market outcomes. In fact, it is also noticeable that self-study time, though not influenced by parents' income, is heavily determined by the parents' education level. In sum, it echoes the concerns on social mobility in Korea, and it seems that education policies have not weakened the role of parental factors in children's educational opportunities and the labour market.

## Conclusion

This study analysed class mobility and inequality of opportunity between different sets of parents and children using KEEP data. It was able to identify the education level and educational performance of children, their entry into the labour market, and performance in the labour market by tracking students from 2004 over a period of 10 years. Based on this finding, this study examined how the characteristics of parents' education and income levels were related to children's educational and labour market performances.

The following are the results regarding children's educational performance and their performance in the labour market. First, money and time spent on private education increase as the education and income levels of parents increase. Second, as the money and time spent on private education grow, the proportion of children achieving first- and second-grade scores on the CSAT increases and they are more likely to enter prestigious universities. Third, there is a strong tendency for the eventual incomes of children to be higher when spending on private education is higher. Fourth, the education and income levels of parents do not directly affect children's CSAT grades and incomes. The third-grade, middle-school students, who had just entered the labour market, exhibited this pattern. However, for the third-grade, high-school students, who have a longer period of work experience, parents' income levels were more clearly reflected in their wages. It can therefore be concluded that the education and income levels of parents have a positive effect on the education levels of their children, and the different educational performances are reflected in the quality of employment.

When looking at the results so far, parents' education and income levels are seen to have a more direct influence on expenses and time spent in private education, and this affects children's CSAT scores. They are also expected to influence their performance in the labour market. In other words, as the media and politicians feared, social mobility in Korea is poor. According to this study's results, since parental background characteristics are significantly reflected in children's education levels and wages, it can be concluded that the probability of rising from humble beginnings will reduce with time. The main path of this kind of mechanism is the difference of parents' class bringing about differences in investment in shadow education, and children's educational performance.

The study results have ample implications for social investment and education policies. First of all, education reforms are still very much required in the Korean context. Although Korea appears to be shining based on its PISA position in the OECD, the country has faced uphill battles against increasing inequity and inequality of opportunities. Unlike the heyday of the country's economic growth, when social mobility was highly visible, the 'Korean dream' is disappearing. Self-study time is still important to academic performance, but it is also highly influenced by family background and private education in Korea. As American scholars, such as Bell et al (2019), observe, Korea is losing 'potential Einsteins'. In this respect, it is wrong to conclude that the country does not need further social investment in education. Instead, Korea should develop education policies from a social investment perspective, with more emphasis on equal opportunity and a redistributive function, in order to overcome weakening social mobility. In other words, public investment should be strengthened.

The social investment paradigm should not only target the improvement of human capital but also play a 'buffering role' for families with children. Korea spends about 10 per cent of its GDP on welfare and has just introduced a child allowance in 2018 for children aged 0–5 years, yet it still does not have sickness benefits and unemployment assistance. That is, very few benefits have been provided for the working-age population. Also, Korea has become known as the least redistributive welfare and tax system, according to the OECD (Joumard et al, 2013). With low social spending with a welfare system that fails to properly redistribute resources, people have had to rely on private educational investment to provide security for their children through good jobs. This has led to extreme educational and positional competition, particularly as de-industrialisation and globalisation have permeated deeper into the labour market. That is why those setting social investment policies in Korea should look into the context of the weak welfare state and go beyond the human capital strategy. As Hemerijck (2017) implies, decent social protection is essential for social investment.

Thus, the government's educational policies need to improve to provide equal opportunity in order to reduce the effects of parent's class on children's educational performance. Moreover, since the differences in educational level may have arisen from individual choices, and have nothing to do with government policy, policies or social efforts to reduce private investment in education are necessary to relieve social stratification.

## Notes

[1] Bray (1999) used 'private education' as shadow education' to emphasise the meaning of private education as a negative system for public education. The term we use is shadow education, but the analytic indicator uses private education time and expenditure, so it can be used together in the title of the analysis table.

[2] In particular, the Partial Least Square method (hereinafter, 'PLS method') is chosen for this study. PLS verifies the significance through a statistical t-test after correcting standard errors, by using bootstrapping (Wolfle, 2003). The statistical package used for PLS analysis in this study is STATA 14.0.

## References

Bell, A.M., Chetty, R., Jaravel, X., Petkova, N. and Van Reenen, J. (2019) 'Who becomes an inventor in America? The importance of exposure to innovation', *The Quarterly Journal of Economics*, 134(2): 647–713.

Beller, E. (2009) 'Bringing intergenerational social mobility research into the twenty-first century: Why mothers matter', *American Sociological Review*, 74(4): 507–28.

Bonoli, G., Cantillon, B. and Van Lancker, W. (2017) 'Social investment and the Matthew Effect', in A. Hemerijck (ed) *The Uses of Social Investment*, Oxford: Oxford University Press, pp 66–76.

Bray, T.M. (1999) *The Shadow Education System: Private Tutoring and Its Implications for Planners*. Paris: UNESCO International Institute for Educational Planning.

Causa, O. and Johansson, Å. (2011) 'Intergenerational social mobility in OECD countries', *OECD Journal: Economic Studies*, 2010(1): 1–44.

Chetty, R., Hendren, N., Kline, P. and Saez, E. (2014) 'Where is the land of opportunity? The geography of intergenerational mobility in the United States', *The Quarterly Journal of Economics*, 129(4): 1553–623.

Choi, P. and Min, I. (2015) '부모의 교육과 소득수준이 세대 간 이동성과 기회불균등에 미치는 영향 [A Study on Social Mobility across Generations and Inequality of Opportunity]', *Social Science Research*, 22(3): 31–56.

Dang, H.A. and Rogers, F.H. (2008) 'The growing phenomenon of private tutoring: does it deepen human capital, widen inequalities, or waste resources?', *The World Bank Research Observer*, 23(2): 161–200.

Davis-Kean, P.E. (2005) 'The influence of parent education and family income on child achievement: the indirect role of parental expectations and the home environment', *Journal of Family Psychology*, 19(2): 294–304.

Esping-Andersen, G. (2009) *Incomplete Revolution: Adapting Welfare States to Women's New Roles*, Cambridge: Policy Press.

Gurun, A. and Millimet, D.L. (2008) *Does private tutoring payoff?* Forschungsinstitut zur Zukunft der Arbeit (IZA) DP No. 3637, Bonn: Institute for the Study of Labor.

Hemerijck, A. (ed) (2017) *The Uses of Social Investment*, Oxford: Oxford University Press.

Jarvis, S. and Jenkins, S. (1998) 'How much income mobility is there in Britain?', *The Economic Journal*, 108(447): 428–43.

Joumard, I., Pisu, M. and Bloch, D. (2013) 'Tackling income inequality', *OECD Journal: Economic Studies*, 2012(1): 37–70.

KEEP (Korean Education and Employment Panel) (2017) *1 Wave in 2004 ~ 11 Wave in 2015*, Sejong: Korea Research Institute for Vocational Education and Training.

Kim, H. (2015) 'Direction of Education Policy for Restoring Social Mobility', *KDI FOCUS*, 54: 1–15.

Krugman, P. (1992) 'The rich, the right, and the facts', *The American Prospect*, 11(Fall): 19–31.

Lee, C.J., Lee, H. and Jang, H.M. (2010) 'The history of policy responses to shadow education in South Korea: implications for the next cycle of policy responses', *Asia Pacific Education Review*, 11(1): 97–108.

Lee, E., Kim, S., Ahn, K., Park, Y., Oh, C., Hwang, S. and Hong, S. (2015) '명문대 간다면 月1000만원 아깝지않아...집도 팔았어요 [Willing to spend 10 million won a month to get my child into a prestigious college...we sold our house for it]', *Maeil Business News Korea*, 20 September, Available from: http://news.mk.co.kr/newsRead.php?year=2015&no=907864 [Accessed in 18 September 2016].

Lee, S. and Shouse, R.C. (2011) 'The impact of prestige orientation on shadow education in South Korea', *Sociology of Education*, 84(3): 212–24.

Morel, N., Palier, B. and Palme, J. (2012) 'Beyond the welfare state as we knew it', in N. Morel, B. Palier and J. Palme (eds) *Towards a Social Investment Welfare State*, Bristol: Policy Press, pp 1–30.

National Statistics Office (2016) 'Shadow education expenditures survey in 2015', Daejeon: National Statistics Office.

OECD (Organisation for Economic Co-operation and Development) (2018) *A Broken Social Elevator? How to Promote Social Mobility*, Paris: OECD, Available from: https://doi.org/10.1787/9789264301085-en [Accessed 26 December 2018].

Ono, H. (2007) 'Does examination hell pay off? A cost–benefit analysis of "ronin" and college education in Japan', *Economics of Education Review*, 26(3): 271–84.

Piketty, T. (2014) *Capital in the XXI century*, Cambridge, MA and London: Belknap Press.

Pintelon, O., Cantillon, B., Van den Bosch, K. and Whelan, C.T. (2013). 'The social stratification of social risks: The relevance of class for social investment strategies', *Journal of European Social Policy*, 23(1): 52–67.

Putnam, R.D. (2016) *Our Kids: The American Dream in Crisis*, New York: Simon & Schuster.

Ryu, D. and Kang, C. (2013) 'Do private tutoring expenditures raise academic performance? Evidence from middle school students in South Korea', *Asian Economic Journal*, 27(1): 59–83.

Wolfle, L.M. (2003) 'The introduction of path analysis to the social sciences, and some emergent themes: An annotated bibliography', *Structural Equation Modeling*, 10(1): 1–34.

World Bank (2018) 'Government expenditure on education,' Washington: World Development Indicator, Available from: https://data.worldbank.org/indicator/SE.XPD.TOTL.GD.ZS?locations=KR/ [Accessed 12 December 2018].

Yeo, E.G. (2008) 'A study of the influence of education on social mobility', *Health and Social Welfare Review*, 28(2): 53–80.

Zhang, Y. (2013) 'Does private tutoring improve students' National College Entrance Exam performance? A case study from Jinan, China', *Economics of Education Review*, 32: 1–28.

# 5

# Employability, higher education and the knowledge economy

*Niccolo Durazzi*

## Introduction

Over the last two decades, policy-makers across advanced capitalist countries have strived to modernise their welfare states. A policy idea attracting significant interest has been that of 'social investment' (Morel et al, 2012; Van Kersbergen and Hemerijck, 2012; Hemerijck, 2015, 2017). Turning welfare states into social investment states means primarily thinking about social and public policies as tools to improve individuals' skills through the life-course. Indeed, 'better skills' make people less vulnerable to economic shocks and technological changes, and more likely to reap the benefits of employment opportunities in knowledge-based economic sectors, such as advanced manufacturing and dynamic services (Nelson and Stephens, 2012; Gingrich and Ansell, 2015; Garritzmann et al, 2017; Kenworthy, 2017). Unsurprisingly, education policy at all levels – from early childhood education and care all the way up to lifelong learning – has been charged with the task of increasing individuals' employability and has therefore taken centre stage within the social investment agenda (Nikolai, 2012; Gingrich and Ansell, 2015; Ansell and Gingrich, 2018). This chapter assesses the employability turn in higher education policy across advanced capitalist countries and the increasing role of higher education as the main *locus* of skill formation by analysing patterns of alignment between higher education systems and skills needs in knowledge-based labour markets.

The chapter focuses in particular on the inter-connections between different types of higher education systems (as commonly defined in education literature by the prevalence of vertical or horizontal differentiation), and different types of knowledge economy (with respect to the relative importance attached to advanced manufacturing or dynamic services). The focus on different higher education–knowledge economy combinations is justified on empirical grounds. Indeed, the aim of better connecting higher education systems and labour markets has been pushed across countries and it has been often aided by international organisations such as the Organisation for Economic Co-operation and Development (OECD) (Robertson, 2005; Prokou, 2008; Marginson, 2009; Capano and Piattoni, 2011). Yet, the process of alignment has not necessarily followed a common pattern across countries: research shows wide variation in the policies put in place by governments and a host of different interactions between employers, governments and the higher education sector (Ballarino, 2011; De Weert, 2011).

Similarly, the cross-national push towards a closer alignment between the labour market's skills needs and higher education provisions does not seem to have reached similar outcomes across countries. Figure 5.1 compares the responses from employers over nearly two decades to the question posed by an international survey asking them to rate on a 0–10 scale whether their university systems meet the needs of a competitive economy. Figure 5.1 returns some puzzling trends. In particular, both graphs (the top one focusing on selected individual countries and the bottom one on groups of countries) show that East Asian countries – often praised for their outstanding educational performance – come at the bottom of the employers' survey. At the same time, the very different higher education systems of the Anglo-Saxon, Continental European and Scandinavian countries seem to all perform equally well. What explains these puzzling patterns?

This chapter investigates such variation by examining the complementarity – or lack thereof – between higher education systems and national knowledge economies in four countries, each having a different higher education–knowledge economy combination (see Table 5.1), thus adopting a diverse cases research design (Seawright and Gerring, 2008).

The chapter argues that vertically differentiated higher education systems are compatible with knowledge economies based on high-end services (the UK case), but not with knowledge economies based on advanced manufacturing (the Korean case); conversely, horizontally differentiated higher education systems work in conjunction with both types of knowledge economies (the German case with respect to advanced manufacturing and the Dutch case with respect to high-end services). From a policy perspective, therefore, this chapter runs counter to conventional wisdom in recent higher education policy, which has been promoting vertical differentiation and competition among universities, and provides evidence that horizontal differentiation remains a viable – if not desirable – policy option, at least as far as the process of skill formation in higher education is concerned. In other

**Figure 5.1:** Employers' satisfaction with higher education

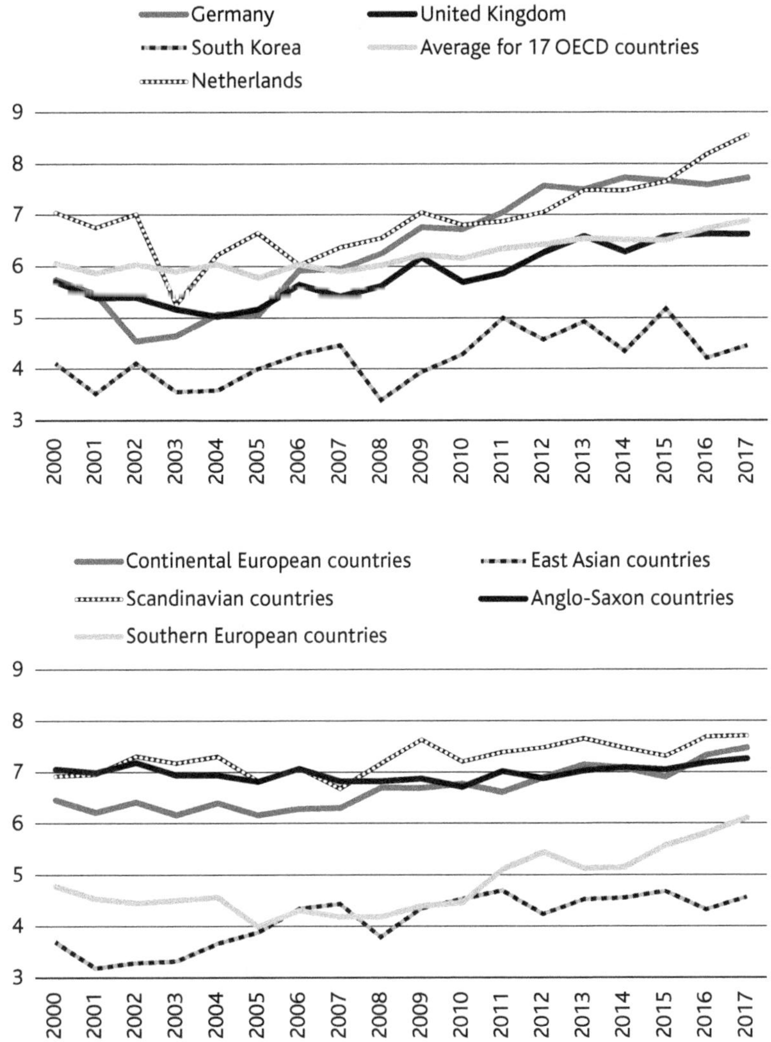

Source: author's calculations based on IMD competitiveness survey

**Table 5.1:** Case selection according to higher education–knowledge economy combinations

|  | HE: vertically differentiated | HE: horizontally differentiated |
|---|---|---|
| KE: dynamic services | UK | Netherlands |
| KE: advanced manufacturing | South Korea | Germany |

Source: created by the author

words, it is suggested that decentralised cooperation (cf. Culpepper, 2001) between a designated sub-sector of the higher education system and individual firms or their associations might be superior in terms of high skill formation compared to market-based interactions among (prospective) students, individual universities and employers. This chapter is structured as follows: the next section proposes a theoretical framework to understand the relationship between higher education systems and knowledge-based labour markets; this is followed by two sections illustrating the framework through concise country case studies of Britain, South Korea, Germany and the Netherlands; the final section provides the conclusions, including policy implications, emerging from the analysis.

## The complementarities between higher education systems and knowledge-based labour markets

Higher education systems have certainly been subject to common cross-national pressures. These trends have been fleshed out at length in particular by the ideational literature that shows how policy-makers across countries have attempted to reframe their higher education systems as tools to sustain national economic competitiveness (see, for example, Brown et al, 2004; Dale, 2005; Olssen and Peters, 2005; Robertson, 2005; George, 2006; Warhurst, 2008; Capano and Piattoni, 2011; Peters et al, 2014). Among other things, this literature points to a development taking place across higher education systems over the last two decades: university systems have seen their traditional autonomy from other societal actors eroding and they have been increasingly asked to serve economic purposes. Policy-makers and employers have been demanding that universities align their educational offerings with labour market needs (OECD, 2008, 2012; Regini, 2011).

But how should these different patterns of alignment be conceptualised? This section suggests that both the structure of the higher education sector and that of the knowledge economy shape the dynamics underpinning the process of skill formation in higher education (Durazzi, 2019; Durazzi and Benassi, 2020). A common approach to classifying higher education systems has been to distinguish between vertically and horizontally differentiated systems (Teichler, 1998; Kyvik, 2004; Goglio and Regini, 2017). The former aims at differentiating 'between the more and the less competitive universities as regards the amount of financial and symbolic resources provided to them' through research and teaching assessments as well as national and international rankings (Goglio and Regini, 2017: 320–1). The latter aimed at differentiating higher education systems through the creation of 'a vocational track, in which tertiary education institutions close to the productive system were especially in tune with labour demand, without having to profoundly modify the missions and features of traditional academic institutions, namely, universities' (Goglio and Regini, 2017: 321). Horizontal differentiation was a particularly fashionable policy option in the 1960s and 1970s, while vertical differentiation became increasingly popular in higher education policy since the 1990s, in conjunction with the widespread use of international rankings and league tables (Hazelkorn, 2015). Higher education systems do not always fit neatly in either category, as they often contain elements of both horizontal and vertical differentiation. Yet, it is certainly possible to discern a dominant logic – either vertical or horizontal – in contemporary higher education systems. The four cases that will be discussed in this chapter offer clear examples of both. In the British and South Korean cases, vertical differentiation dominates. In both countries, some universities are commonly perceived as more prestigious than others, think for instance of Oxbridge or Russell Group universities in the UK and the SKY trio (Seoul National, Korea and Yonsei Universities) in South Korea, and students typically strive for a place in those institutions. Rankings are widespread and they are considered important factors of choice when students decide which universities to attend (Hazelkorn, 2007; Marginson and Van der Wende, 2007). Vertical differentiation co-evolved with high marketisation, for example in the form of above-average shares of private financing. The co-evolution of these two features is captured in Figure 5.2, which shows a positive relationship between the degree of private financing of higher education (as a proxy for marketisation) and the extent to which students choose where to study based on rankings (as a proxy for vertical differentiation).

These systems are found most prominently in Anglo-Saxon and East-Asian countries and they conform closely to the idea of 'academic capitalism', wherein interaction between universities and students and among universities are shaped by market-like mechanisms (Slaughter and Leslie, 1997; Slaughter and Rhoades, 2004). In these settings, fee-paying students are the main stakeholders of universities, who need to attract them to remain financially viable. The interaction between vertically differentiated higher education systems and knowledge-based labour markets are expected to be mediated by student choices: students who are well informed on the labour market returns of various degrees are expected to drive universities' offerings towards those degrees that are most sought-after by the labour market (Barr,

**Figure 5.2:** The co-evolution of marketisation and vertical differentiation in Western European higher education systems

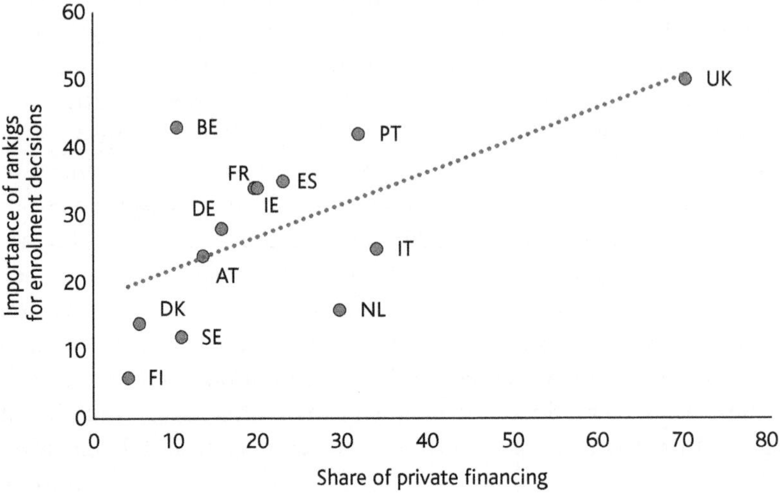

Source: author's calculations based on Gallup (2009) and OECD (2014)

2004). However, this view needs to be qualified in at least three ways. First, research in the sociology of education shows that labour market considerations play a role in students' choices, but that a number of other factors also affect such choices (Briggs, 2006) and therefore perfect matching between students' choices and labour market signals cannot be assumed. Second, a mismatch between labour market prospects and students' choices seem to be most prominent in the science, technology, engineering and mathematics (STEM) subjects, which tend to be avoided by students even though they often offer above-average returns on the labour market (Osborne et al, 2003). Third, in vertically differentiated systems, students tend to base their choices more on the reputation of individual institutions than on the expected labour market returns of a particular degree (Geiger, 2002).

The German and Dutch systems provide examples of higher education systems that maintain significant horizontal differentiation. In both countries, *Fachhochschulen* and *hogescholen* (commonly referred to as universities of applied sciences) were established and developed in the late 1960s and the 1970s respectively. The creation of these institutions meant that traditional research-based universities could to a significant extent retain their distance from labour market concerns, which were instead channelled through universities of applied sciences. Typically, universities of applied sciences offer degrees in those disciplines that are demanded by the labour market (eg, engineering, business administration) and they have close connections with local companies and their associations. Indeed, employers are the main stakeholders in universities of applied sciences. Education in these institutions is therefore highly applied, geared towards practice and often involves fairly sizeable periods of work experience. Provided that the sector of universities of applied science is large enough to accommodate the demands of strategic segments of the labour market, traditional universities in these settings tend to be relatively insulated from the demands of employers. Horizontal differentiation co-evolved with public financing of higher education and low competitive pressures on universities (see Figure 5.2). Research universities and universities of applied sciences in these systems are best characterised as equal but different – ie, the two groups of institutions tend to be internally homogeneous, but perform radically different functions (Teichler, 1996, 1998; Teichler et al, 1996). The prestige of individual universities being relatively equal across groups, students in these systems – particularly those students enrolling in universities of applied sciences – seek a return on their educational investments based on the degree, and not so much on the institution. Degree offerings, in turn, are shaped by close cooperation between universities of applied sciences and various labour market actors.

How are these two systems expected to complement national knowledge economies? To answer this question, it is needed to dig deeper into the internal configurations of knowledge economies. Although characterised by the common need for higher-level skills and the increasing use of high technology in production processes (OECD, 2004, 2005), national knowledge economies also have significant differences. In particular, some knowledge economies are heavily geared towards the so-called dynamic services (eg, finance, consultancy, and information and communication technology), while others rely on advanced manufacturing. Countries pursuing the former type of knowledge economy are the Anglo-Saxon countries and the Netherlands (Hassel and Palier, 2017; Thelen, 2019). East-Asian and Continental European countries, conversely, rely to a greater extent on advanced manufacturing (Hassel and Palier, 2017). Scandinavian countries tend to take an intermediate position (Thelen, 2019).

Both types of knowledge economies are require highly skilled workers and therefore rely significantly on higher education to meet their skills needs. However the sets of high skills are different and have implications for the complementarity between higher education systems and knowledge-based labour markets. A crucial distinction is to be found in the extent to which the high-skills needs of different knowledge economies are relatively broad (ie, the discipline of graduates is not of primary importance) or narrow (ie, graduates from particular disciplines are needed). Broad skills needs are typically to be found in service-based knowledge economies: in sectors such as consultancy or finance, employers seek highly skilled individuals who possess analytical and inter-personal skills but they tend to focus less on whether graduates come from a particular discipline background. For example, both political science and physics graduates can be successfully employed across a vast majority of positions in these sectors. Narrow skills needs tend to characterise knowledge economies based on advanced manufacturing. In this context, a significant number of positions will need graduates in well-defined disciplines that tend to be around the STEM subjects, and in particular engineering (see section 2.1 in Durazzi, 2018 for more details of and empirical evidence on the high skill needs across different knowledge economies).

Having defined the key principles that are expected to govern the higher education–labour market relationship across vertically and horizontally differentiated higher education systems, and having reviewed the high-skills needs of different knowledge economies, it is now possible to advance some hypotheses regarding the complementarity – or lack thereof – between higher education systems and national knowledge economies. Starting from vertically differentiated systems, it has been noted that in these cases the higher education–labour market relationship is strongly mediated by student choices. But it has also been noted that these choices are often driven by the prestige of particular universities and not so much by the labour market prospects of particular degrees. Moreover, STEM degrees tend to be avoided even in the presence of significant labour market signals. Combining these expectations with the insights around the skills needs of different knowledge economies, it is hypothesised that vertically differentiated systems are compatible with service-based knowledge economies, as they have rather broad skills requirements. However, vertically differentiated systems might run into problems in the provision of high skills for knowledge economies reliant on advanced manufacturing. These economies have narrow skills needs, and they require graduates from particular disciplines (STEM and engineering in particular), which is something that vertically differentiated systems might struggle to deliver, resulting in skill mismatches or skill shortages.

Horizontally differentiated systems, meanwhile, include two distinct sub-sets: a vocationally oriented sub-set working in close cooperation with employers and their associations, and a research-oriented sub-set that is largely insulated from external demands. In these contexts,

**Figure 5.3:** A framework of higher education–knowledge economy interactions

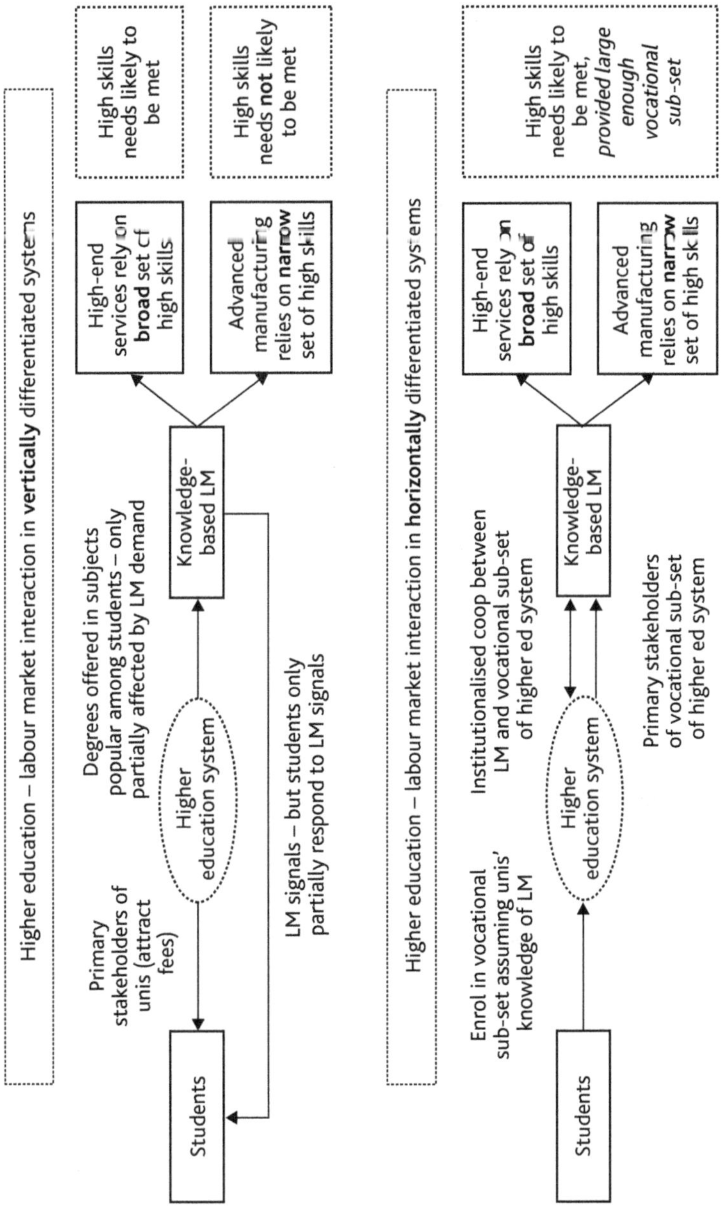

Higher education – labour market interaction in **vertically** differentiated systems

High skills needs likely to be met

High skills needs **not** likely to be met

High-end services rely on **broad** set of high skills

Advanced manufacturing relies on **narrow** set of high skills

Knowledge-based LM

Degrees offered in subjects popular among students – only partially affected by LM demand

LM signals – but students only partially respond to LM signals

Higher education system

Primary stakeholders of unis (attract fees)

Students

Higher education – labour market interaction in **horizontally** differentiated systems

High skills needs likely to be met, *provided large enough vocational sub-set*

High-end services rely on **broad** set of high skills

Advanced manufacturing relies on **narrow** set of high skills

Knowledge-based LM

Institutionalised coop between LM and vocational sub-set of higher ed system

Primary stakeholders of vocational sub-set of higher ed system

Higher education system

Enrol in vocational sub-set assuming unis' knowledge of LM

Students

Source: created by the author

the alignment of high-skills provision and knowledge-based labour market is at the outset automatic, regardless of the type of knowledge economy, to the extent that this is dealt with for a significant part by the vocational sub-set of the higher education system (Witte, 2006; Witte et al, 2008). The key issue, however, is whether the vocational sub-set will be large enough, given that the research-oriented component of the higher education system is unlikely to be responsive to labour market demands. The key challenge in these systems from the perspective of policy-makers seeking to align higher education provisions and labour market needs will be to channel a sufficient number of students into universities of applied sciences to avoid skill mismatches and shortages. The different mechanisms of higher education–knowledge economy interactions are summarised in Figure 5.3. These will be illustrated through case studies in the next two sections.

## Britain and South Korea: vertically differentiated systems in the knowledge economy

Britain and South Korea have higher education systems that are ostensibly highly similar. They are both characterised by strong vertical differentiation and high reliance on private financing, chiefly tuition fees. Recruiting students is therefore a core concerns for universities in these countries, as their organisational survival is directly affected by student numbers (see Figure 5.4).

Yet, the two countries also have starkly different economic structures. Korea has some of the highest employment and gross valued added (GVA) in manufacturing among OECD countries, while the UK is among the lowest scorers in both indicators, as it is a knowledge economy significantly geared towards high-end services (Hassel and Palier, 2017). In both countries, the role of higher education as an important component in the transition to the knowledge economy featured prominently in government agendas since the mid-1990s (Suh and Chen, 2007; Wilson, 2012). However, the patterns of alignment between higher education and the labour market played out differently.

In Britain, the need to align higher education with the knowledge economy was made particularly explicit in the Dearing Report, a bi-partisan review of higher education policy carried out in the mid-1990s, which argued that higher education should be expanded to meet the needs of the knowledge economy and that the provision of transferable skills was particularly crucial for a knowledge economy that had been de-industrialising at fast pace and that was heavily geared

**Figure 5.4:** Share of private financing of higher education in selected OECD countries

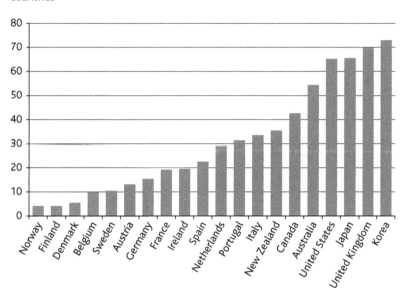

Source: OECD (2014)

towards the service sector (Dearing, 1997). at the same time, successive governments from the mid-1990s onwards increasingly liberalised the higher education sector, creating in essence a real market for higher education (Shattock, 2012), in which universities are exposed to a set of inter-related competitive pressures: they compete for students and their fees, for public funds, and for position in rankings and league tables. Thus, students became the transmission belt between universities and skills needs of the labour market. As explained by several stakeholders in the British higher education sector, students seek a return on their investment in higher education and universities are aware that they themselves benefit from students' employment outcome, because these are factored into rankings (Durazzi, 2018, 2020a, 2020b). As such, universities have been proactively engaging with employers to provide the high skills needed by the labour market (CFE Research, 2014; University Alliance, 2015). Because the British knowledge economy is structurally geared towards high-end services, the provision of general skills was particularly prominent (Durazzi, 2018, 2019). Universities involved a cross-section of employers that offer jobs to their graduates and these invariably included service-sector firms – even for departments that are traditionally thought of as being closer to the manufacturing sector, such as engineering.

The interaction between universities seeking employers' views and the dominance of service-sector employers led to a prioritisation of general skills in universities' curricula, including team-work, analytical skills, business awareness and IT skills (CBI, 2009; CBI and NUS, 2011).

In Korea, universities were subject to similar competitive pressures as in Britain, but the labour market – unlike Britain's – is heavily geared towards the advanced manufacturing (Durazzi, 2019). As a result, the pattern of alignment between higher education and the knowledge-based labour market differed significantly. In particular, as higher education was deeply liberalised in the mid-1990s, heightening the vertical differentiation of the system and increasing competition for students among universities, the allocation of students-to-disciplines proved problematic for a knowledge economy reliant on advanced manufacturing (KEF, 2005, 2006; Yonezawa and Kim, 2008). Indeed, while students strive to access the most prestigious institutions, their degree choices have not been significantly influenced by labour market signals. In particular, as predicted by the sociology of education, students have tended to avoid STEM disciplines, despite their being in demand high in the labour market. Universities too have had no incentive to change their educational offerings because of students' preferences. Employers lamented the resultant high-skill shortages and the government put in place public policies to rectify this problem. In particular, a report by the Ministry of Labour argued that Korea was bound to face an over-supply of humanities and social sciences graduates and an under-supply of engineers (Park, 2016). Accordingly, the government deployed the Programme for Industry-Matched Education (PRIME) that provided financial incentives on a competitive basis to universities that provided credible plans to reduce their intake of students in humanities and social sciences, and increase their intake of students in engineering (MOSF, 2015). The policy stirred up some controversy across South Korean campuses, as it has been accused of bringing higher education too close to the demands of employers, disregarding to an extent the purely educational nature of a university degree (Huh and Lim, 2016; Lee and Byeon, 2016). Yet, it was also perceived as an attractive source of funding for universities: as new entrants in higher education are bound to decrease due to demographic developments, universities looked with increasing interests at alternative sources of funding (Durazzi, 2018). Moreover, being selected to take part in government policies was also perceived by universities as a good public relations strategy, which would signal quality education to prospective applicants (Durazzi, 2018). Preliminary evidence shows that PRIME has the potential to address some of the skill shortages created by a vertically differentiated higher education system, although implementation is only in its initial phase and evidence of its impact is therefore still tentative (Cho et al, 2018).

## Germany and the Netherlands: horizontally differentiated systems in the knowledge economy

Moving on to the second pair of case studies – Germany and the Netherlands – the focus shifts to higher education systems where vertical differentiation is relatively weak, and horizontal differentiation is relatively strong. Horizontal differentiation takes the form of two distinct sub-sets of higher education institutions in both countries: research universities and universities of applied science. Yet, the two sub-sectors differ in the two countries in terms of their relative weight. Traditionally, universities of applied sciences have accommodated the vast majority of students in the Netherlands, while the reverse is true for Germany (see Table 5.2).

The two countries also display radically different knowledge-based growth strategies: the Netherlands embraced a knowledge-based growth centred on high-end services (such as finance), while Germany 'doubled down' on its traditional areas of strength by furthering its advanced manufacturing sector (Thelen, 2019).

How then did the alignment between higher education and the labour market played out in the two countries? In the Netherlands, the alignment of higher education provisions and the needs of the knowledge-based labour market proved unproblematic (Witte, 2006; Witte et al, 2008) as borne out by Figure 5.1, in which Dutch employers had the highest satisfaction levels. Of particular relevance to understanding this smooth alignment is the skewed distribution of higher education students towards universities of applied sciences. The latter have traditionally had employers as their key stakeholders and have striven to provide an educational offer that meets the needs of the labour market. As such, when the salience of higher education–labour

**Table 5.2:** Distribution of higher education students in Germany and the Netherlands

| Country | Share of students in universities (%) | Share of students in professionally oriented higher education institutions (%) |
|---|:---:|:---:|
| Germany | 76 | 24 |
| Netherlands | 37 | 63 |

Source: Huisman and Kaiser (2001: 19)

market alignment increased in the mid-1990s in the Netherlands, as in most advanced capitalist countries, key actors (such as the government, employers and the higher education sector itself) coalesced to maintain the status quo (Witte, 2006). This allowed the large universities of applied sciences to be a crucial link between the higher education sector and the skills needed in knowledge-based labour markets. A notable initiative has been the development of the 'ICT Bachelor', developed in conjunction by the association of universities of applied sciences (the HBO-i) and Dutch employers (HBO-i, 2010). Through this initiative, universities of applied sciences embedded ICT components across very different degrees, ranging from ICT and business administration to ICT and software engineering, with courses developed in conjunction with a vast cross-section of firms across the high-end services, covering sectors as diverse as software development, management consultancy and finance (HBO-i, 2010: 74).

In Germany, as in Korea, the pressures to align higher education provisions and labour market needs gained salience in conjunction with concern over the lack of STEM skills in general and of engineers in particular. This became most prominent in the mid-2000s, when employers put the expansion of STEM skills at the heart of their demands, as the shortage of 70,000 engineers in 2007 alone was perceived as a threat to the manufacturing-based German knowledge economy (BDA, 2008; BDA et al, 2011). As a response, the government launched the Higher Education Pact in 2007, allocating public funds to finance additional enrolment in higher education (Diessner et al, 2020; Durazzi, 2018; Durazzi and Benassi, 2020). The policy initiative had two main goals. First, universities of applied sciences were to be expanded more than traditional research-oriented universities. Second, STEM subjects had to be expanded the most under the new policy (BMBF, 2009, 2014). As such, the German government aimed to bring the distribution of students between sub-sectors of the higher education system closer to that of the Netherlands, ie, privileging the expansion of the vocational subset. Indeed, several studies showed that employers valued the practical orientation of graduates from universities of applied sciences (Durazzi, 2018). Such appreciation is particularly pronounced in the advanced manufacturing sector. For example, a recent survey of engineering companies praised the skills provided by universities of applied sciences and found among other things that the 'integration of practical semesters and modules is stronger in universities of applied sciences than in [research-oriented] universities' (VDI, 2016). The link between employers and universities of applied sciences was also fostered by so-called dual-study programmes (Graf, 2013, 2018; Thelen,

2019; Durazzi and Benassi, 2020). These are work-based programmes in which students spend part of their time at a higher education institution (predominantly universities of applied sciences) studying towards an undergraduate degree (predominantly in engineering) and part of their time at firms (predominantly large employers in the manufacturing sector). Importantly, the degrees on offer depend on the needs of companies collaborating with a university of applied science and students apply to the company, not the university. This model has distinctive advantages for all the parties involved. Employers get graduates in the disciplines they need and they socialise students to the firm's environment during their studies, students are very likely to land a job right upon graduation; and universities of applied sciences strengthen their role in the (local) economy by supplying employers' skills needs. Thus, as expected, the German case suggests that a vocational subset of higher education represents a crucial link with the skills needed in knowledge-based labour markets, provided that the subset is large enough to supply these skills in sufficient quantity. Unlike in the Dutch case, German universities of applied sciences needed 'additional' expansion to make the transition to the knowledge economy. This was achieved through joint efforts by the government (through the Higher Education Pact) and employers (through the establishment of growing numbers of dual-study programmes).

## Conclusion

What lessons can be learnt from these four cases? In all countries, the need to align higher education provisions to labour market needs and increase individuals' employability in fast-changing societies became a salient issue from the mid-1990s onwards. In Britain and the Netherlands, although differing significantly in their higher education systems, this alignment was relatively unproblematic. Given the predominance of high-end services and the relative flexibility in terms of high-skill needs of employers in this sector, universities adjusted their curricular offerings either out of competitive pressures (in the case of Britain) or because aligning curricular offerings to labour market demands is central to their mission (in the case of Dutch universities of applied sciences, where a majority of students are enrolled). Korea and Germany faced the additional challenge of shaping the supply of high skills towards STEM subjects, which are crucial for knowledge economies reliant on advanced manufacturing, but often avoided by students even in presence of positive labour market signals. In Korea, a vertically differentiated system created the conditions for students to compete for a place in prestigious institutions, without paying significant attention to the particular discipline of their degrees. In turn, universities had no incentive to deviate from the demands of students, whose tuition fees made them the primary stakeholders. The result was a shortage of STEM graduates. When this shortage became a pressing problem, the government intervened to shape the supply of STEM skills and provided the financial incentives for universities to adjust their offerings to match government skills forecasts. In Germany, the same problem was solved by expanding universities of applied sciences that have strong links with employers and have traditionally offered degrees in the disciplines most in demand in the labour market.

The lesson emerging from the comparative analysis is clear: although recent higher education policy across countries has privileged a vertical differentiation of higher education systems, the cases show that – as far as high-skill formation is concerned – horizontal differentiation remains a viable – if not preferable – option. It is instructive in this respect to note that the case in which the adjustment to the needs of the knowledge economy was most straightforward was the Dutch case, as a large and vibrant vocational subset of institutions guaranteed the supply of the bulk of high skills required by the knowledge-based sectors of the Dutch labour market. And indeed, the German response to the concern over lack of STEM skills was to move in the 'Dutch direction', by expanding enrolments in universities of applied sciences. While the British case was also relatively unproblematic, the Korean case revealed the problems of supplying STEM skills through a vertically differentiated highly competitive higher education system. The heightening problems of skills mismatch and shortage triggered a top-down government intervention. While this intervention might have ameliorated the problem to an extent, it appears rather rigid, with governments first need to release skills forecasts, and then universities adjusting their educational offerings, resulting in a lengthy process that might not be able to keep up with the fast-changing skill requirements of knowledge-based labour markets. Following the literature on skill formation and building on the evidence presented in this chapter, it is suggested that decentralised cooperation (Culpepper, 2001, 2003; Emmenegger et al, 2019) might be a more agile and effective way of coordinating the supply of skills with the needs of the labour market. In this respect, it seems a particularly effective strategy for governments to strengthen, revive or even create a subset of vocational higher education institutions that are charged with the task of providing local labour markets with the high skills needed through direct cooperation with individual firms and/or their associations.

# References

Ansell, B. and Gingrich, J. (2018) 'Skills in demand? Higher education and social investment in Europe', in P. Manow, B. Palier, and H. Schwander (eds) *Welfare Democracies and Party Politics: Explaining Electoral Dynamics in Times of Changing Welfare Capitalism*, Oxford: Oxford University Press, pp 225–56.

Ballarino, G. (2011) 'Redesigning curricula: the involvement of economic actors', in M. Regini (ed) *European Universities and the Challenge of the Market: A Comparative Analysis*, Cheltenham: Edward Elgar Publishing, pp 11–27.

Barr, N. (2004) *The Economics of the Welfare State*, Oxford: Oxford University Press.

BDA (Bundesvereinigung der Deutschen Arbeitgeberverbänd) (2008) *Bacherlor Welcome – Mint-nachwuchs Sichern!* [Confederation of German Employers' Associations], Berlin: Bundesvereinigung der Deutschen Arbeitgeberverbände.

BDA, HRK, and BDI (2011) *Take Two Cohorts of Students as an Opportunity and Increase Higher Education Pact*, Berlin and Bonn: Bundesvereinigung der Deutschen Arbeitgeberverbände, Hochschulrektorenkonferenz, Bundesverband der Deutschen Industrie e.V.

BMBF (Bundesministeriums für Bildung und Forschung) (2009) *Verwaltungsvereinbarung Zwischen Bund und Ländern Gemäß Artikel 91b abs. 1 nr. 2 des Grundgesetzes über den Hochschulpakt 2020 (Zweite Programmphase)* [Administrative agreement between Federal government and the states according to article 91b/1/2 of the basic law of the Higher Education Pact 2020], Berlin: Bundesministeriums für Bildung und Forschung.

BMBF (Bundesministeriums für Bildung und Forschung) (2014) *Verwaltungsvereinbarung Zwischen Bund und Ländern Gemäß Artikel 91b abs. 1 nr. 2 des Grundgesetzes über den Hochschulpakt 2020* [Administrative agreement between Federal government and the states according to article 91b/1/2 of the basic law of the Higher Education Pact 2020], Berlin: Bundesministeriums für Bildung und Forschung.

Briggs, S. (2006) 'An exploratory study of the factors influencing undergraduate student choice: the case of higher education in Scotland', *Studies in Higher Education*, 31(6): 705–22.

Brown, P., Hesketh, A. and Williams, S. (2004) *The Mismanagement of Talent: Employability and Jobs in the Knowledge Economy*, New York: Oxford University Press.

Capano, G. and Piattoni, S. (2011) 'From Bologna to Lisbon: the political uses of the Lisbon "script" in European higher education policy', *Journal of European Public Policy*, 18(4): 584–606.

CBI (Confederation of British Industry) (2009) *Stronger Together: Businesses and Universities in Turbulent Times*, London: Confederation of British Industry.

CBI and NUS (Confederation of British Industry, and National Union of Students) (2011) *Working Towards Your Future: Making the Most of Your Time in Higher Education*, London: Confederation of British Industry and National Union of Students.

CFE Research (2014) *Forging Futures: Building Higher Level Skills through University and Employer Collaboration*, London: Universities UK and UKCES.

Cho, S., Kam, J. and Lee, S. (2018) 'Efficient supply of human capital: role of college major', *The Singapore Economic Review*, 63(5): 1319–43.

Culpepper, P.D. (2001) 'Employers, public policy, and the politics of decentralized cooperation in Germany and France', in P.A. Hall and D. Soskice (eds) *Varieties of Capitalism*, Oxford: Oxford University Press, pp 275–306.

Culpepper, P.D. (2003) *Creating Cooperation: How States Develop Human Capital in Europe*, Ithaca, NY: Cornell University Press.

Dale, R. (2005) 'Globalisation, knowledge economy and comparative education', *Comparative Education*, 41(2): 117–50.

De Weert, E. (2011) *Perspectives on Higher Education and the Labour Market*, Enschede: CHEPS.

Dearing, R. (1997) 'Higher education in the earning society', National Committee of Inquiry into Higher Education summary report, London: NCIHE.

Diessner, S., Durazzi, N. and Hope, D. (2020) 'Reshaping skills, industrial relations and social protection for the knowledge economy: evidence from Germany', EUI Working Paper MWP 2020/07, Florence: European University Institute.

Durazzi, N. (2018) 'The political economy of high skills: higher education in knowledge societies', PhD thesis, London School of Economics and Political Science.

Durazzi, N. (2019) 'The political economy of high skills: higher education in knowledge-based labour markets', *Journal of European Public Policy*, 26(12): 1799–817.

Durazzi, N. (2020a) 'Opening universities' doors for business? Marketization, the search for differentiation and employability in England', *Journal of Social Policy*, [online first], Available from: https://doi.org/10.1017/S0047279420000276 [Accessed 9 October 2020].

Durazzi, N. (2020b) 'The political economy of employability: institutional change in British and German higher education', *Stato e Mercato*, 119(2): 257–88.

Durazzi, N. and Benassi, C. (2020) 'Going up-skill: exploring the transformation of the German skill formation system', *German Politics*, 29(3): 319–38.

Emmenegger, P., Graf, L. and Trampusch, C. (2019) 'The governance of decentralised cooperation in collective training systems: a review and conceptualisation', *Journal of Vocational Education & Training*, 71(1): 21–45.

Gallup (2009) 'Students and higher education reform: special target survey', report, Brussels: European Commission.

Garritzmann, J.L., Häusermann, S., Palier, B., and Zollinger, C. (2017) 'WoPSI – the World Politics of Social Investment. An international research project to explain variance in social investment agendas and social investment reforms across countries and world regions', LIEPP Working Paper, March, no 64. Available from: https://hal.archives-ouvertes.fr/hal-02177824/file/2017-wp64-wopsi.pdf.

Geiger, R.L. (2002) 'The competition for high-ability students: universities in a key marketplace', in S.G. Brint (ed) *The Future of the City of Intellect: The Changing American University*, Stanford, CA: Stanford University Press, pp 82–106.

George, E. (2006) 'Positioning higher education for the knowledge based economy', *Higher Education*, 52(4): 589–610.

Gingrich, J. and Ansell, B. (2015) 'The dynamics of social investment: human capital, activation, and care', in P. Beramendi, S. Häusermann, H. Kitschelt and H. Kriesi (eds) *The Politics of Advanced Capitalism*, New York: Cambridge University Press, pp 282–304.

Goglio, V. and Regini, M. (2017) 'Processes and stages of differentiation in European higher education', *Higher Education Quarterly*, 71(4): 320–37.

Graf, L. (2013) *The Hybridization of Vocational Training and Higher Education in Austria, Germany, and Switzerland*, Opladen: Budrich UniPress.

Graf, L. (2018) 'Combined modes of gradual change: the case of academic upgrading and declining collectivism in German skill formation', *Socio-Economic Review*, 16(1): 185–205.

Hassel, A. and Palier, B. (2017) 'Growth and welfare in global capitalism', paper presented at the RC19 Annual Conference, Chapel Hill, NC.

Hazelkorn, E. (2007) 'The impact of league tables and ranking systems on higher education decision making', *Higher Education Management and Policy*, 19(2): 1–24.

Hazelkorn, E. (2015) *Rankings and the Reshaping of Higher Education: The Battle for World-Class Excellence*, New York: Palgrave Macmillan.

HBO-i (2010) *Bachelor of ICT – domain description*, Amsterdam: HBO-i Foundation. Available from: https://www.hbo-i.nl/wp-content/uploads/2019/01/HBO-i_Bachelor_of_ICT-Engels.pdf [Accessed 9 October 2020].

Hemerijck, A. (2015) 'The quiet paradigm revolution of social investment', *Social Politics*, 22(2): 242–56.

Hemerijck, A. (ed) (2017) *The Uses of Social Investment*, Oxford: Oxford University Press.

Huh, R.-j. and Lim, Y.-j. (2016) 'Conflict over PRIME project occurs between students and authorities', *Ewha Womans University English Newspaper*. Available from: http://evoice.ewha.ac.kr/news/articleView.html?idxno=4801 [Accessed 9 October 2020].

Huisman, J. and Kaiser, F. (2001) *Fixed and Fuzzy Boundaries in Higher Education: A Comparative Study of (Binary) Structures in Nine Countries*, Den Haag: Adviesraad voor het Wetenschaps.

KEF (Korea Employers Federation) (2005) '2005 survey on surplus and shortage of the workforce', Seoul: Korea Employers Federation.

KEF (Korea Employers Federation) (2006) 'Survey on recruitment of entry-level university graduates', Seoul: Korea Employers Federation.

Kenworthy, L. (2017) 'Enabling social policy', in A. Hemerijck (ed) *The Uses of Social Investment*, Oxford: Oxford University Press, pp 89–96.

Kyvik, S. (2004) 'Structural changes in higher education systems in Western Europe', *Higher Education in Europe*, 29(3): 393–409.

Lee, J.-w. and Byeon, H.-j. (2016) 'The PRIME project is now of prime importance to universities', *The Argus*. Available from: http://www.theargus.org/news/articleView.html?idxno=1014 [Accessed 9 October 2020].

Marginson, S. (2009) *The Knowledge Economy and Higher Education*. Paris: OECD.

Marginson, S. and Van der Wende, M. (2007) 'To rank or to be ranked: the impact of global rankings in higher education', *Journal of Studies in International Education*, 11(3-4): 306–29.

Morel, N., Palier, B. and Palme, J. (eds) (2012) *Towards a Social Investment Welfare State?*, Bristol: Policy Press.

MOSF (Ministry of Strategy and Finance) (2015) *Government Announces Comprehensive Measures for Youth Unemployment*, Seoul: Ministry of Strategy and Finance.

Nelson, M. and Stephens, J.D. (2012) 'Do social investment policies produce more and better jobs?', in N. Morel, B. Palier and J. Palme (eds) *Towards a Social Investment Welfare State*, Bristol: Policy Press, pp 205–34.

Nikolai, R. (2012) 'Towards social investment? Patterns of public policy in the OECD world', in N. Morel, B. Palier and J. Palme (eds) *Towards a Social Investment Welfare State*, Bristol: Policy Press, pp 91–115.

OECD (Organisation for Economic Co-operation and Development) (2004) *Innovation in the Knowledge Economy*, Paris: OECD.

OECD (Organisation for Economic Co-operation and Development) (2005) *The Measurement of Scientific and Technological Activities*, Paris: OECD.

OECD (Organisation for Economic Co-operation and Development) (2008) *Tertiary Education for the Knowledge Society*, Paris: OECD.

OECD (Organisation for Economic Co-operation and Development) (2012) *Better Skills, Better Jobs, Better Lives*, Paris: OECD.

OECD (Organisation for Economic Co-operation and Development) (2014) *Education at a Glance 2014: OECD Indicators*, Paris: OECD.

Olssen, M. and Peters, M.A. (2005) 'Neoliberalism, higher education and the knowledge economy: from the free market to knowledge capitalism, *Journal of Education Policy*, 20(3): 313–45.

Osborne, J., Simon, S. and Collins, S. (2003) 'Attitudes towards science: a review of the literature and its implications', *International Journal of Science Education*, 25(9): 1049–79.

Park, H. (2016) 'PRIME: massive government subsidy seeks to reshape higher education in Korea', World Education Services, Available from: https://wenr.wes.org/2016/09/prime-a-massive-government-subsidy-seeks-to-reshape-higher-education-in-korea [Accessed 9 October 2020].

Peters, M., Besley, T. and Araya, D. (2014) *The New Development Paradigm*, New York: P. Lang.

Prokou, E. (2008) 'The emphasis on employability and the changing role of the university in Europe', *Higher Education in Europe*, 33(4): 387–94.

Regini, M. (ed) (2011) *European Universities and the Challenge of the Market: A Comparative Analysis*, Cheltenham: Edward Elgar.

Robertson, S.L. (2005) 'Re-imagining and rescripting the future of education: global knowledge economy discourses and the challenge to education systems', *Comparative Education*, 41(2): 151–71.

Seawright, J. and Gerring, J. (2008) 'Case selection techniques in case study research: a menu of qualitative and quantitative options', *Political Research Quarterly*, 61(2): 294–308.

Shattock, M. (2012) *Making Policy in British Higher Education 1945–2011*, London: McGraw-Hill.

Slaughter, S. and Leslie, L.L. (1997) *Academic Capitalism*, Baltimore, MD: JHU Press.

Slaughter, S. and Rhoades, G. (2004) *Academic Capitalism and the New Economy*, Baltimore, MD: JHU Press.

Suh, J. and Chen, D.H. (2007) *Korea as a Knowledge Economy*, Washington, DC: World Bank Group.

Teichler, U. (1996) 'Diversity in higher education in Germany: the two-type structure', in L.V. Meek, L.C. Goedegebuure, O. Kivinen and R. Rinne (eds) *The Mockers and the Mocked: Comparative Perspectives on Differentiation, Convergence and Diversity in Higher Education*, Oxford: Pergamon, pp 117–37.

Teichler, U. (1998) 'The changing roles of the university and non-university sectors of higher education in Europe', *European Review*, 6(4): 475–87.

Teichler, U., Aamodt, P.O., Rinne, K., Mora, J., de Weert, E. and Brennan, J. (1996) *Higher Education and Graduate Employment in Europe*, Kassel: Bräuning und Rudert.

Thelen, K. (2019) 'Transitions to the knowledge economy in Germany, Sweden and the Netherlands', *Comparative Politics*, 51(2): 295–315.

University Alliance (2015) *Job Ready: Universities, Employers and Students Creating Success*, London: University Alliance.

Van Kersbergen, K. and Hemerijck, A. (2012) 'Two decades of change in Europe: the emergence of the social investment state', *Journal of Social Policy*, 41(3): 475–92.

VDI (Verein Deutscher Ingenieure) (2016) *Ingenieurausbildung: Die Hochschulen „Können" Bologna* [Engineering Education: The University 'can do' Bologna], Düsseldorf: Verein Deutscher Ingenieure.

Warhurst, C. (2008) 'The knowledge economy, skills and government labour market intervention', *Policy Studies*, 29(1): 71–86.

Wilson, T. (2012) *A Review of Business–University Collaboration*, London: Department for Business, Innovation and Skills.

Witte, J. (2006) 'Change of degrees and degrees of change: comparing adaptations of European higher education systems in the context of the Bologna Process', PhD thesis, University of Twente.

Witte, J., Van der Wende, M. and Huisman, J. (2008) 'Blurring boundaries: how the Bologna process changes the relationship between university and non-university higher education in Germany, the Netherlands and France, *Studies in Higher Education*, 33(3): 217–31.

Yonezawa, A. and Kim, T. (2008) 'The future of higher education in the context of a shrinking student population', in *Higher Education to 2030*, Paris: OECD, pp 199–220.

# 6

# Does social investment make the labour market 'flow'? Family policies and institutional complementarities in Italy, Spain, Japan and South Korea

*Ijin Hong and Jieun Lee*

## Introduction

Social investment policies have gained prominence in policy-making reforms and concerned academic literature since the 1990s (Morel et al, 2012). According to Hemerijck (2015, 2017), such reforms are expected to address the problems associated with increasingly flexible career trajectories and labour markets by making transitions in and out of the labour market during one's life course smoother. Instead of simply 'making work pay' through labour market flexibilisation (as the neoliberal tradition had assumed), parental leave, childcare services, 'flexicure' employment relations, and social investment policies are expected to act as 'social bridges', reconnecting workers to the labour market. Such policies aim to ease life-cycle transitions and secure better employment stability at key points of risk (Hemerijck, 2015). Such risks especially affect women, who are more vulnerable to discrimination when entering the labour market, career interruptions due to motherhood and discontinuous careers. Thus, women's employment and employability are central to the social investment approach (Jenson, 2009; Morgan, 2012). Indeed, improving labour market transitions during individuals' life course is one of the core functions of social investment (the flow function), along with the complementary efforts to boost human capital potential (the stock function) and maintain minimum safety nets for the vulnerable in ageing societies (the buffer function) (Hemerijck, 2013, 2015).

But does social investment actually make the labour market flow? In this chapter, we address this question by examining work–family reconciliation policies and women's labour market participation.

While some studies suggest that there is a connection between social investment reform and the labour market (Nelson and Stephens, 2012), how exactly this happens merits deeper scrutiny at the institutional level. Since the 2000s, social investment policies have been introduced, though to varying degrees, in latecomer countries of East Asia and Southern Europe. This chapter focuses on Italy, Spain, Japan and South Korea, arguing that social investment strategies should be context-sensitive and tailored to different structural and institutional configurations if they are to be suitable and effective. These four countries provide particularly interesting cases for analysis because each has enacted important family policy reforms in the last decade, starting from a conservative, male-breadwinner oriented stance. Despite obvious geographical and cultural differences, these countries share similarities such as dualised labour markets, traditional family values and being latecomers in welfare development. As a result, this comparison is particularly useful in disentangling important institutional complementarities that contribute to a smooth labour market flow. We argue that the degree of policy commitment in terms of social investment does not suffice to guarantee a better labour market flow in industrialised countries. In other words, social investment reform has no linear relation with female employment. Rather, contextual institutional complementarities (Draebing and Nelson, 2017) could be as significant as the reform itself. Our research therefore focuses on the institutional features needed to secure a better labour market flow, such as the previous structure of social spending, gender equality culture, the structure of the labour market and trends in tertiary education – all of which are necessary for securing a better flow. By focusing on contextual features, we claim that, in order for social investment reform to be successful, complementary institutional reform is required.

Our research is presented in the following manner: first, we provide background on how social investment relates to female employment according to academic literature. The following section then provides an overview on which institutional configurations one should consider to understand how the labour market flows during women's life cycles. We then analyse specific countries and their institutional configurations; finally, in the conclusion, we present policy recommendations based on our institutional analysis.

## The puzzle: social investment policies and labour market flow

The social investment approach has enjoyed considerable academic support thus far. It especially gained traction with the 2002 book *Why*

*Do We Need a New Welfare State*, edited by Gosta Esping-Andersen, Duncan Gallie, Anton Hemerijck, and John Myles, among others. Additionally, Nobel Prize winner James Heckman's (2006) research supported early childhood education and care (ECEC) services as an important investment strategy aimed at improving life courses for children from disadvantaged families.

Also, due to their academic legacy, social investment policies tend to be quite normative in their policy recommendations, as the European Commission endorsed them at an institutional level (Eurofound, 2016). However, implementing them in practice might not result in the linear changes expected, not to mention the difficulties in pushing through this kind of reform at all. That different social investment functions need to complement one another in order to work properly is already well understood (Draebing and Nelson, 2017), however, just how institutional configurations should be combined to work properly is not yet adequately discussed in the literature. In other words, we believe that more empirical research is warranted to observe whether social investment policies do improve career chances as expected, and, especially, whether they facilitate labour market participation for previously excluded groups (the labour market 'flow' function).

This chapter focuses on women's employment throughout their life courses and on work–life reconciliation policies by taking into consideration a pool of welfare latecomers: Italy, Spain, Japan and South Korea. There are several reasons why comparing Southern Europe and East Asia provides fertile ground for interesting insights (Estevez-Abe et al, 2016). First, they share many similarities in their traditional familialistic cultures, which stress a strong role for women in caregiving responsibilities (Saraceno and Keck, 2010; An, 2017). Hence, they struggle more with work–family reconciliation issues, showing very large levels of gender labour inequality. This then pushes women to have children later or not at all (OECD, 2018a). Comparatively limited public expenditure in family policy illustrates how these welfare latecomers are slowly moving away from the male-breadwinner model. Yet, they also differ in the degree to which they commit to social investment reform, with Spain and South Korea having sought expansion more actively than Italy and Japan (Estevez-Abe and Naldini, 2016). Thus, differences cut across their original welfare regimes' typology (Ferrera, 1996; Holliday, 2000).

Traditionally, welfare states in Southern Europe and East Asia have relied on male-breadwinner families with strong employment protection legislation, making it more costly for employers to hire women (Estevez-Abe, 2006). However, as has been the case for social-democratic, liberal and conservative welfare regimes (Lewis et al, 2008; Fleckenstein and Seeleib-Kaiser, 2011), post-industrialisation and the growth of the services sector have affected these countries and have resulted in labour market flexibilisation and the proliferation of atypical job contracts. Hence, Southern European and East Asian welfare states are also questioning the validity of their traditional male-breadwinner strategies at the policy level, but the success they attained in pushing for family-friendly policies has varied greatly. While South Korea is the most decisive path-shifter in investing in family policy (An and Peng, 2016; Fleckenstein and Lee, 2017a), Italy has been the most reluctant to push for social investment reform (Ascoli et al, 2015; Kazepov and Ranci, 2017), while Japan (Kwon, 2018; Miura and Hamada, forthcoming) and Spain (León and Migliavacca, 2013; León and Pavolini, 2014) fall somewhere in between. In other words, Italy remains the only case of 'unsupported familism' (Saraceno and Keck, 2010), while Spain's efforts to improve family policies, especially gender equality, have been in place since the 2000s. As for Japan, while being less direct in its family policy changes in comparison to South Korea, it has nonetheless pushed for a more balanced strategy of care support by introducing long-term care insurance as early as 2000 (Estevez-Abe and Naldini, 2016).

All things being equal, according to the implicit assumptions of the social investment approach, South Korea should be at the vanguard of improving prospects for women's, especially mothers', participation in the labour market, with Japan and Spain following, and Italy being the least woman-friendly in terms of work opportunities. However, as it is evident from Table 6.1, this does not seem to have been the case: South Korea, despite its herculean efforts to reform social investment policy, trails the other three countries when it comes to increasing female employment, with Spain and Japan showing the best improvements

**Table 6.1:** Female employment rates (percentage of women population in working age), 2000–18

| | 2000 | 2006 | 2009 | 2012 | 2015 | 2018 | Increase since 2000 (%) |
|---|---|---|---|---|---|---|---|
| Italy | 38.78 | 46.17 | 46.60 | 47.01 | 47.10 | 49.28 | +10.5 |
| Spain | 40.42 | 53.14 | 53.72 | 51.81 | 51.99 | 56.24 | **+15.8** |
| Japan | 56.51 | 58.64 | 59.92 | 60.37 | 64.23 | 68.97 | **+12.5** |
| South Korea | 49.56 | 53.22 | 52.53 | 53.46 | 55.50 | 57.08 | +7.5 |
| OECD | – | 56.35 | 56.86 | 56.84 | 58.24 | 60.60 | – |

Note: all data refers to the first quarter of each year.

Source: OECD (2019b)

between 2000 and 2018. The modest achievements of the Italian case hint at the important role that work–family reconciliation policies might play in easing the labour market flow for women. However, considering how puzzling the South Korean case is, clearly merely increasing social investment does not result linearly in a better labour market flow. Some other mechanisms seem to be at play here, which likely include the lack of work opportunities in highly dualised labour markets, as is the case in South Korea.

What, then, improves women's employment prospects during the course of discontinuous careers, apart from social investment reform itself? In the following section, we first demarcate more specifically the role institutional complementarities perform in improving the labour market flow function of social investment policies. Second, we focus on career interruptions during women's life cycles to understand women's opportunities for work.

## Institutional complementarities

Social investment policies work best when combined with a set of institutional configurations, that is, a favourable institutional context (Pfau-Effinger, 2005; Kazepov and Ranci, 2017). Drawing on previous literature (León and Pavolini, 2014; Blossfeld et al, 2015; León et al, 2016; Kazepov and Ranci, 2017; Jurado-Guerrero and Naldini, 2018), we hypothesise that investing in human capital (the 'stock' part of social investment), creating a gender-equal culture and building a favourable labour market structure all facilitate labour market flow. However, a country's previous structure of social spending and external constraints may limit labour market flow.

Family policy instruments, a core component of social investment strategy (Morel et al, 2012), are meant to alleviate the work–family reconciliation problem: childcare services free up women's time for work (Lewis et al, 2008; Hemerijck, 2017) and help women retain working competencies (Budig et al, 2012); leave policies, provided they are not prolonged, are expected to help reconcile working time with family care (Mandel and Semyonov, 2006); family allowances secure resources for work and care, but they also may push women out of work due to heightened responsibilities in the family (Lewis et al, 2008); finally, long-term care services for elderly family members also free up women's time and thus facilitate work opportunities for middle-aged women (Naldini et al, 2014). A proper combination of different family policy provisions may improve not only women's employment levels, but also gender equality (Jenson, 2009).

In fact, social investment policies need to be complemented by adequate investments in human capital stock and a gender-equal culture (Jenson, 2009; Draebing and Nelson, 2017). Investment in human capital stock is expected to improve employment prospects by addressing the new social risk of low and obsolete skills as a result of de-industrialisation (Bonoli, 2005). Additionally, higher commitments to tertiary education are considered an important component of social investment strategies. Finally, childcare, work and family are arranged differently depending on each society's gender culture, or the ideal way to arrange work–family commitments (Pfau-Effinger, 1998). Greater gender equality at work and in households are key in the face of increasing levels of female labour market participation (Esping-Andersen et al, 2002). Of course, whether women's employment prospects improve also depend on opportunities provided by their respective labour market structures. With de-industrialisation (a general feature of European welfare states and other de-industrialised countries), comes a shift away from industry and toward the service sector (Fleckenstein and Lee, 2014) in tandem with both labour market flexibilisation and proliferation of atypical employment contracts. This problem certainly affects women's labour market participation in Southern Europe and East Asia because highly dualised labour markets (characterised by high levels of employment protection legislation) create more rigidity in hiring women with regular contracts. Furthering the problem, employers are incentivised to discriminate against workers who are at higher risk of career interruptions (Estevez-Abe, 2006; OECD, 2018a).

Social investment reform does not suffice when the institutional context hinders progress. Adverse policy legacy is one such hindrance. Bonoli (2007) argues that financial commitments to old welfare programmes might prevent the development of new social policies that address newly emerging risks in society, thus creating a trade-off between the two (the trade-off argument). External constraints, such as the economic crisis and the European Union, limit budgets for social policies at the national level and significantly hinder Southern European countries (Papadopoulos and Roumpakis, 2015; Távora and Rodríguez-Modroño, 2018). Stand-by agreements were stipulated in Italy and Spain under the influence of the European Union, which aimed to implement austerity measures to address the sovereign debt crisis; however, this depressed their economies. This certainly affected the development of care services and family policies in general (León and Pavolini, 2014; Bouget et al, 2015).

## Labour market flow during the life cycle

Before turning to a more detailed country analysis, we will first reflect on how the labour market could flow better across one's life cycle. Suffering from the double burden of work and caring responsibilities at home (Jenson, 2009; Ciccia and Bleijenbergh, 2014), women are disincentivised from participating in the labour market. This problem is especially visible during a woman's child-birthing and child-rearing years (OECD, 2018a). Though certainly important, motherhood is not the only critical point at which women's labour market flow is compromised. Instead, several critical points might arise in a woman's career, starting from her entrance into the labour market and continuing throughout her working years, especially in strong familialistic cultures such as those in Southern Europe and East Asia. According to Hemerijck, one's human capital may be at risk during the following life stages: (1) when transitioning from education to a first job; (2) when having children; (3) when experiencing episodes of labour market inactivity; and (4) when transitioning into retirement (2017: 10).

In the light of these factors, women's employment patterns are affected by a few critical points in the course of their life cycles:

1. Entering the labour market (LM) (Blossfield et al, 2015): Women's entry into the LM after education might already show some degree of disadvantage in comparison to men.
2. Career interruption due to motherhood and child-rearing (OECD, 2018a): This is the much feared 'motherhood penalty', which often interrupts a woman's career.
3. Re-entering the LM (OECD, 2018a): In this case, institutional and policy configurations – especially the availability of ECEC services – should allow a smooth return into the LM following motherhood.
4. Women's mid-life employment: Care responsibilities for frail elderly family members might infringe on women's employment in mid-life (Bouget et al, 2015). Women's double burden of care responsibilities in East Asia has already been emphasised (Yamashita and Soma, 2015), and Southern and Eastern European countries are also more vulnerable to women's unemployment in mid-life than in Western Europe (Naldini et al, 2014).

Next, we focus on the role of institutional complementarities and on critical points of the labour market flow and consider how Italy, Spain, Japan and South Korea are each coping differently with the problem of disruptions in women's employment within their own distinct institutional settings.

## Country cases

### *Italy*

In Italy, employment rates for women are low and their labour market flow has improved only modestly over the past 20 years. Two critical elements stand out regarding Italy's labour market flow: on the one hand, labour market participation rates remain generally low across all age groups; on the other hand, entrance into the labour market is both slow and delayed (see Figure 6.1). Although employment rates have risen slightly over time, the most significant improvement occurred between 1998 and 2017 for middle-aged and elderly women. Problems with entering the labour market are common for both male and female young adults in Italy (Barbieri and Scherer, 2009); however, labour market rigidities are especially problematic for highly educated young women (León and Migliavacca, 2013).

When looking at employment for women across the life cycle, it appears that labour market rigidities are especially problematic at the entry point (ie, for all young cohorts who are forced to rely heavily on fixed-term, contract-based temporary employment as described in Figure 6.2). While there is no evident M-shape in Figure 6.1, which signals career interruptions, the problem is indeed present, especially for low-skilled women. According to an Istituto Nazionale di Statistica (ISTAT) study, 22.4 per cent of mothers who were employed before pregnancy and interviewed two years later had lost their jobs (Ingenere, 2015). Hence, re-entering the LM might be more problematic for women with lower education levels. This contrasts with high-skilled professional women who tend to seek ways to shorten their working hours without exiting the LM altogether (Castagnetti et al, 2018). This strategy is also common for middle-aged women who seek to shorten working hours rather than give up work altogether when caring for an elderly relative (Naldini et al, 2014).

Italy is a representative case of unfriendly contextual conditions for social investment (Kazepov and Ranci, 2017). In particular, family policies are negatively affected by fragmented legislation and poor coordination between institutions and funds (Bouget et al, 2015). As a result, families are often left unsupported (Saraceno and Keck, 2010).

Generally speaking, Italy's family policies are often incomplete and gendered (Bertolini et al, 2015). Italy, like Spain, fares quite well

**Figure 6.1:** The labour market flow: female employment patterns across the life course

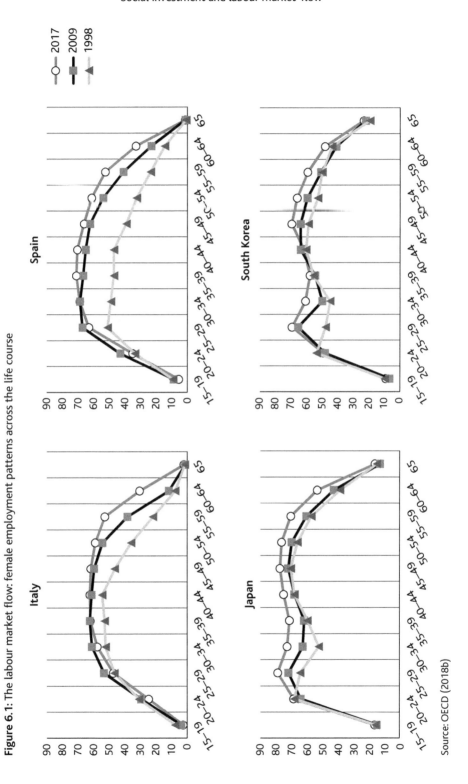

Source: OECD (2018b)

137

in providing childcare services (*asili*) to children between the ages of 3 and 5, whereas childcare facilities for toddlers below 3 years old (*asili nido*) have traditionally been more scarce, often requiring additional support from grandparents (Jurado-Guerrero and Naldini, 2018). Although a comprehensive plan for coordinating public and private services to provide fuller coverage was announced in 2001, as of 2010, Italy had still failed to meet the Lisbon Agenda's goal of covering 33 per cent of children under 3 years of age with childcare services (Canal, 2018). To amend this, Sylvio Berlusconi's government (2001–6) lowered the age threshold for entering childcare service from 36 months to 24 months – the 'spring' childcare services, an initiative that Italy's southern regions particularly favoured (Gambardella et al, 2015). Still, dramatic differences in childcare service provisions exist across different Italian municipalities. Additionally, cities that are better equipped with affordable facilities, such as Milan, Rome or Bologna (Cerea et al, 2015), prioritise the needs of dual-earner, middle-class families, thus discouraging employment for women in lower socio-economic classes (Gambardella et al, 2015).

Italy provides family benefits in the form of tax exemptions for dependent family members or as allowances for families with children (*assegno familare*), with coverage varying depending on household income and on the number of dependent family members (Bergamante, 2018). Cash benefits also fill service coverage gaps in the form of bonuses and vouchers for newborns or adopted children (a provision that increased 53 per cent in expenditure between 2010 and 2014) (Bouget et al, 2015). Italy also offers a one-off lump-sum voucher (which was €800 in 2018) to pregnant women upon completion of their pregnancies (MISSOC, 2018).

Leave policies in Italy are quite lengthy but not well paid, which shows their gendered nature. Maternity leave is five months with an 80 per cent wage-replacement rate, whereas paternal leave is only five days (starting in 2019), which remains far below the European Union's recommendation of 10 days (Ingenere, 2018a). Optional supplementary parental leave can be taken for up to 11 months, with a 30 per cent wage-replacement rate for the first six months only (Bergamante, 2018). Due to the low wage-replacement rate, women are incentivised to use these leave provisions, but take-up remains low among men (Bertolini et al, 2015).

Elderly care in Italy is likewise inadequate and is provided mostly in the form of cash benefits for those in need; this implicitly delegates care responsibilities to the family. Furthermore this pushes working women to seek informal care from female migrants – women who represent 80 per cent of the workforce in Italy's care sector (Ingenere, 2015). Such family policies are patchy and are undermined by weak institutional facilitators.

As for the human capital stock, Italy scores badly in terms of tertiary education for young people between the ages of 30 and 34, of whom only 20 per cent have a university degree – half of Europe's 2020 Strategy target of 40 per cent (Kazepov and Ranci, 2017). Although education does not create an advantage for exiting atypical employment in Italy (Barbieri and Scherer, 2009), it does counteract gender discrimination at work (Castagnetti et al, 2018). However, the gradual increase in the number of female university graduates did not align well with the existing labour market structure, as deregulation had increased the number of precarious workers and, in particular, first entrants to the labour market (Barbieri and Scherer, 2009). The prevalence of small and medium enterprises, along with self-employment, characterises the Italian labour market. This then reflects poorly on the demand for high-skilled human capital: young tertiary-educated individuals' earnings is estimated as only 9 per cent higher than those of high-school graduates, while the OECD difference is, on average, 37 per cent (Barbieri and Scherer, 2009). Public investment in knowledge-intensive economic sectors is a prerequisite for the social investment stock function to work well with the labour market, but Italy has not yet attained these ideal conditions (Kazepov and Ranci, 2017).

A slowly improving gender equality culture has been partially offsetting these limitations in human capital investment and labour market opportunities since 2011. Due to the strong influence of the Catholic Church in Italy, a traditional patriarchal family has been the norm for a long time (Jurado-Guerrero and Naldini, 2018). Nevertheless, some improvements have been made because of a 2011 law on quotas in administrative councils, which requires that at least 20 per cent of board members of public and private companies be women. With women making up 29 per cent of managers in 2015, Italy is above the European average of 21 per cent (Ingenere, 2015). Recent legislative changes also point to a diversification of family models, with Law No.76 of 2016 acknowledging the rights of same-sex civil partnerships, and Law No. 80 of 2015 giving adoptive and foster parents the same rights as those of more traditional families (MISSOC, 2018; Bergamante, 2018).

Despite these improvements in gender culture, strong institutional constraints hinder proper functioning of the social investment strategy in Italy. First, Italy has a strong 'pension state' policy legacy (Hinrichs and Jessoula, 2012), which offers little space to manoeuvre in terms of introducing social investment (SI) policies (the so-called crowding-out effect, see Bonoli and Reber, 2010; León and Pavolini, 2014). Second, the European Union's fiscal consolidation requirements, the magnitude of Italy's public debt and the effects of the 2008 economic crisis all further strained Italy's already weak welfare system – a system characterised by budget limits that triggered downward pressure on wages, privatisation reforms, and welfare cuts (Papadopoulos and Roumpakis, 2015). In particular, the National Fund for Childhood and Adolescence, which was supposed to provide integrated child well-being projects in large metropolitan areas, has been steeply cut since 2008. Furthermore, resources allocated to the National Fund for Social Policies, which supports local welfare systems, decreased by 58 per cent between 2008 and 2014 (Bouget et al, 2015).

In summation, Italy's passive stance towards social investment reform, its low number of university graduates, its structurally non-innovative and segmented labour market, the pressures of austerity policies, and its policy legacy of a pension-oriented welfare state compromise an effective labour market flow, although some improvements in the gender equality culture have been made in the past ten years. While the risk of under-employment affects all age and education groups, low-skilled women are an especially vulnerable demographic (Pistagni, 2011).

## Spain

In Spain, the labour market flow for women has showed considerable improvements since 2000, across all age groups (see Figure 6.1). As in Italy's case, the late entry of younger female workers characterises the Spanish labour market. Nevertheless, although having children negatively affects female labour market participation in Spain, this effect is not immediately visible and remains at similar levels to countries such as Germany and the United Kingdom (León and Migliavacca, 2013). A sizeable proportion of Spanish women are employed and hold relatively good jobs (such as managers, professionals, technicians and clerks): 51 per cent of women between 25 and 29 years old and 44 per cent of women between 50 and 64 years old. The fact that these figures do not differ greatly indicates that there is a certain continuity for professional women, even in middle-age. Presumably, this results from a supply of domestic and care workers in private homes (León et al, 2016). However, general employment growth for women has relied on heavy representation in the secondary labour

**Figure 6.2:** Share (%) of temporary employment by gender and age group in 2017 (dependent work) (gender, age, fixed-term contracts)

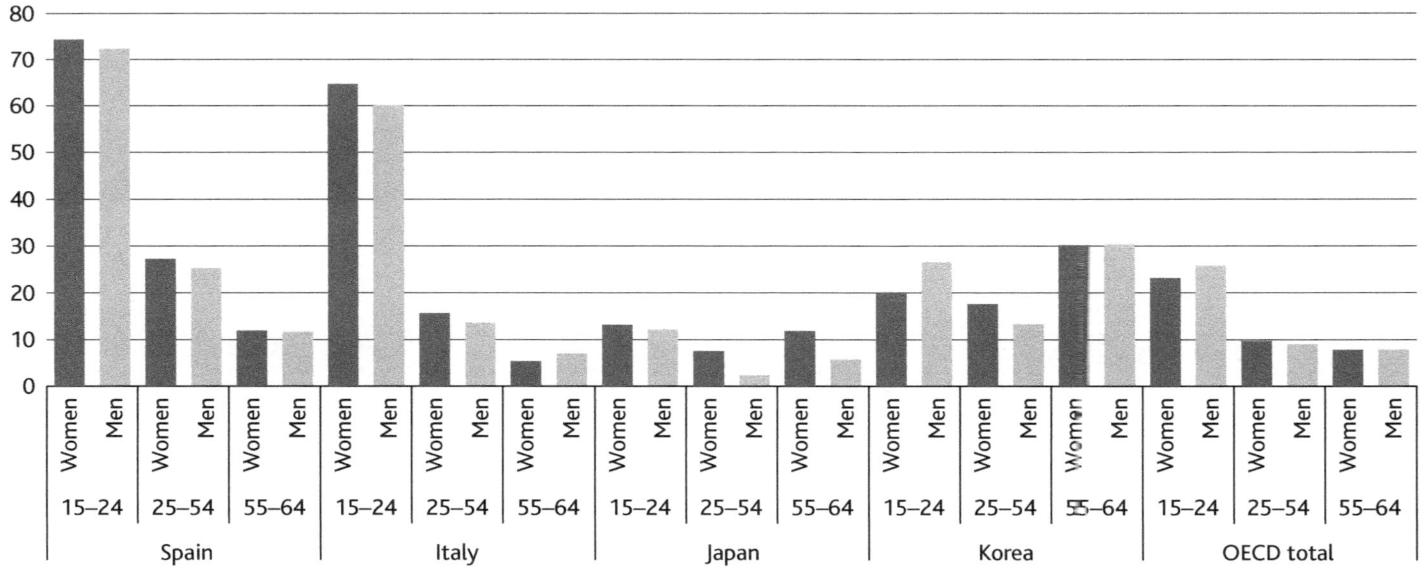

Note: Temporary employment includes both wage and salaried employees whose jobs have predetermined termination dates. National definitions broadly conform to this generic definition, but may vary depending on national circumstances. This indicator is broken down by age group and is measured as a percentage of dependent employees (ie, wage and salaried workers).

Source: OECD (2018b)

market segments, generating a precarious work environment, especially for low-educated female workers (Távora and Rodríguez-Modroño, 2018). Women between the ages of 15 and 54 resort too frequently to fixed-term contracts (see Figure 6.2), markedly more than men do. Additionally, it is increasingly common across all age groups for women working to work in temporary employment in the last 20 years (OECD, 2018c).

In a 'catching up' process that both centre-right (José María Aznar 1996–2004) and centre-left (José Luis Rodríguez Zapatero 2004–11) governments ushered in, Spain has actively promoted social investment reform (León and Pavolini, 2014). However, in many instances, this effort to reform was half-done, as the imperative of budgetary cuts considerably affected work–family reconciliation policies. This was certainly the case for ECEC services: Spain, like Italy, performs well in providing early education to children between the ages of 3 and 5. However, childcare provisions for children under 3 remains patchy and insufficient. In 2008, the implementation of the Educa3 programme addressed this problem and aimed at expanding ECEC provisions for children under 3 years old. This programme initially increased the service coverage ratio to 39 per cent prior to the economic crisis (Távora and Rodríguez-Modroño, 2018), but subsequent social spending cuts considerably reduced its impact. Currently, childcare for children under 3 years old is fragmented, privatised and biased towards working parents (León et al, 2016). Budgetary cuts also affected family cash allowances (cut by half in June 2010), universal childbirth benefits (discontinued in 2011), and regional-level family support for children's development (Bouget et al, 2015). In contrast, leave provisions have been gradually improving, although they remain underfunded for parental leave. Currently women in Spain have the individual right to a 16-week maternity leave that pays 100 per cent of wages, of which six weeks are compulsory for mothers. However, either the mother or the father may use the additional 10 weeks of leave (Ingenere, 2018b). Previously, paternal leave only lasted two days, but in 2007 the individual, non-transferable right for fathers to take fully paid leave was increased to two weeks and further extended to five weeks in 2018 (Távora and Rodríguez-Modroño, 2018). Initially, a lack of funding because of budget restrictions delayed these extensions; however, they were implemented at a later date, showing Spain's commitment to the de-genderisation of care responsibilities. Additionally, parents are also allowed to take unpaid leave for childcare for up to 3 years for each child and is considered a contribution period for pension insurance (MISSOC, 2018).

In 2006, the left-wing government enacted a law addressing long-term care (LTC) for the elderly (*Dependencia Ley*); however, in 2011 budgetary cuts slashed this measure by 5.2 per cent. Furthermore, the lack of adequate financing for LTC was problematic for a full continuation of this programme (León and Pavolini 2014). Because of low public support (Saraceno and Keck, 2010), Spanish families (like Italian families) have increasingly relied on migrants for caring responsibilities in the family; however, this private solution generates a widening inequality of care coverage across social classes (León and Migliavacca, 2013).

These stop-and-go developments in social investment reform notwithstanding, Spain has had encouraging conditions that have facilitated female labour market flow at the institutional level.

First, a rapid increase in women's education level improved the human capital stock in Spain. Between 1989 and 2017, the percentage of women between 25 and 64 years old with tertiary education increased from 8.34 per cent to 38.93 per cent (in Italy the improvement was far more modest at 21.47 per cent in 2017) (OECD, 2019a). In contrast to Italy, employment prospects improved for both high- and low-educated women. As a result, women experienced fewer difficulties when entering the labour market (León and Migliavacca, 2013).

A strategy of labour market structure flexibilisation, along with two subsequent reforms (one between 2010 and 2011, and the other in 2012), increased the availability of highly educated workers. As labour market flexibilisation was pursued, dismissals were easier and less costly, and provided more discretionary power (for competitiveness reasons) to employers – a strong blow to the collective bargaining system, as priority of firm-level (over industry-wide) agreements was accorded in the process. The 2012 reform aimed to boost job creation through subsidies to entrepreneurs and through a new training contract that favoured the youth, workers older than 45, women and the long-term unemployed (Bentolila et al, 2012). These developments undoubtedly created a favourable environment for more employment opportunities for women; however, wage cuts in the public sector and freezing minimum wages disproportionately affected female workers, thus increasing the gender pay gap (Távora and Rodríguez-Modroño, 2018).

A marked departure from familialistic culture has also characterised Spain in the past two decades (León and Migliavacca, 2013). The secularisation of politics has certainly contributed to this, as the centre-right People's Party attempted to modernise and to compete with the socialist party on gender equality issues (León et al, 2016; Estevez-

Abe and Naldini, 2016; Jurado-Guerrero and Naldini, 2018). A series of reforms – such as the 1999 law amending the Workers' Bill of Rights (*Estatuto de los Trabajadores*) to improve maternity and parental protection, the legalisation of same sex marriage and the 2007 equality law increasing the number of female politicians in Spain – promoted a more gender-friendly attitude (León and Pavolini, 2014; León et al, 2016; Jurado-Guerrero and Naldini, 2018). Assuredly, a more marked secularisation of family values had already been in place in Spain in the early 2000s, whereas family de-institutionalisation patterns have only recently been visible in Italy.

Finally, Spain enjoys the comparative advantage of being a welfare latecomer with a relatively light policy legacy when it comes to pension expenditure (León and Migliavacca, 2013; León and Pavolini, 2014). Social expenditure for old age and family 'survivors' in 2015 amounted to 11 per cent of GDP in Spain, in contrast to a more conspicuous 16.1 per cent in Italy (OECD, 2018d), giving this Mediterranean welfare state more leeway for pursuing bolder SI reforms, in support of the crowding out theory (Bonoli and Reber, 2010).

Although Spain has these potentially favourable institutional configurations, external constraints resulting from the economic crisis and fiscal consolidation have strongly affected the Spanish economy. Cuts in budgets for family policies, a move away from universal measures towards more targeted ones, and a postponement or cancellation of SI programmes, such as Educa3, were part of the grim situation confronting Spain (Bouget et al, 2015).

To conclude, Spain is well equipped to become the next successful case of social investment reform, leading to an efficient labour market flow for women. The country has bold policy initiatives addressing new social risks, such as child and elderly care; it has moved gender and family values in a more egalitarian direction; its policy reforms have boosted opportunities for labour market outsiders; and finally, Spain has a prior social expenditure structure that is underdeveloped enough to accommodate significant policy change. Female labour market participation levels have indeed increased rapidly, reaching a level on par with other European countries (León and Migliavacca, 2013). However, the shadow of sovereign debt and the economic crisis of 2008 have loomed large on these institutional preconditions, resulting in the growth of irregular, time-limited employment contracts for working women. In summary, female employment rates have improved considerably in Spain. However, women are over-represented in filling irregular and precarious work positions; this is especially true for the low-educated. Also, this increase in employment might be explained by the 'added worker effects' of women who are forced to be economically active due to increasing male unemployment (Távora and Rodríguez-Modroño, 2018).

## Japan

Female labour market participation in Japan has increased considerably across all age groups since 2000. Regarding the labour market flow during the life cycle of Japanese women, a few points can be noted based on Figure 6.1. First, labour market entry is relatively smooth, starting early and with a fast rate of integration. Women start working as early as their teens (ages 15 to 19) and employment levels have been the highest within our comparison group since 1998. Furthermore, Japanese workers in general attain high levels of labour market participation in their twenties. This might be attributed to the high level of tertiary education and a wider range of employment opportunities (eg, part-time and temporary employment). Traditionally, women were inclined to leave the workforce either after marrying or after having children, and then return to the labour market when their children reached a certain age (Gender Equality Bureau Cabinet Office, 2017). As is evident from Figure 6.1, Japan's pattern of female employment still shows an M-shape: women's employment rate reaches its apex when they are in their twenties, drops in their thirties, rises again in their forties, then gradually falls until they reach 65. This pattern has been maintained for the last 20 years. However, meaningful changes have been observed for middle-age Japanese women. Compared to 1998, female employment in 2017 significantly increased for women between 25 and 39: from 60 per cent to 80 per cent for the 25 to 29 years age group, from 52 per cent to 73 per cent for the 30 to 34 years age group, and from 60 per cent to 72 per cent for the 34 to 39 years age group.

Family policies in Japan have been instrumental mainly in improving declining fertility rates and their main provisions – childcare allowance, childcare services and parental leave schemes – have been continuously reformed since the 1990s. Recent developments were due to the 'Second Stage of Abenomics' under the third Shinzo Abe cabinet, under which labour market activation for women, in addition to public care provisions for children, aided Japan's economic growth strategy (Kwon, 2017).

Childcare allowance has been the primary focus in family policies for the last two decades, with the assumption of mothers assuming the majority of care responsibilities (Ochiai et al, 2007). Because boosting

Japan's fertility rate has been the most urgent issue, the government utilised childcare allowance to reduce families' financial burdens and thus increase the birth rate (Ministry of Health, Labour and Welfare, 1994). As a result, the government has continuously expanded its childcare allowance. Furthermore, the government has continuously raised the age threshold for the allowance from 7 years (2000) to 15 years (2009) (An, 2017; Peng and Chien, 2018). These allowances are provided to parents who take care of their children from infancy to 15 years of age. The previous income threshold was alleviated in 2006 and then eliminated in 2010, but was reintroduced in 2012 as part of the scaling back effort around the time of the 2011 Tohoku earthquake (*Yomiuri Shinbun*, 2011; Fleckenstein and Lee, 2017a).

Public childcare services are not traditionally preferred in Japan because 'a public care service could destroy Japan's beautiful tradition of parents taking care of their children' (Shizuka Kamei, a senior LDP politician in the 1990s, quoted in Osawa, 2000: 16). However, the situation has changed since the late 1990s. In an attempt to meet increasing demand from young parents, the government introduced the Angel Plan (1994) and the New Angel Plan (2000–5), both of which increased the availability and variety of childcare services (An and Peng, 2016). However, long waiting lists are still a problem in major cities. Municipalities ultimately decide who qualifies for such services based on administrative guidelines where full-time working mothers are prioritised over part-time, irregularly employed or unemployed mothers (An and Peng, 2016). Enrolment rates of children younger than 3 years in childcare facilities increased from 11.1 per cent in 1998 to 30.6 per cent in 2014, and for children between the ages of 4 and 5 years, enrolment increased from 83.9 per cent in 1998 to 91 per cent in 2014 (Peng and Chien, 2018).

Japan first introduced parental leave in 1992 and provides a maximum of one year and one month following 14 weeks of maternity leave, if both parents take leave (An, 2017). Although women have increasingly chosen to take parental leave (up from 49.1 per cent in 2002 to 76.3 per cent in 2015), men's take-up rate remains low (from 0.12 per cent in 2002 to 2.03 per cent in 2015) (Ministry of Health, Labour and Welfare, 2016). To boost men's take-up rates, the government introduced the 'daddy month', which lasts for two months (Ministry of Health, Labour and Welfare, 2019). Parental leave showed a positive effect on de-familialisation, with women's rates of returning to work after a first child increasing from 27.4 per cent (2000–4) to 53.1 per cent (2010–13) (National Institute of Population and Social Security Research, 2015).

In contrast to slow developments in childcare services, the introduction of LTC insurance in 2000, with the political motivation of developing a new 'silver' industry was actively pursued (Estevez-Abe and Kim, 2014). With its focus on services, rather than on cash allowances, and on a sufficient range of choices for recipients, the new LTC insurance increased use of formal care at a lower cost to households (Tamiya et al, 2011).

Despite this slow approach to social investment reform, other institutional facilitators have helped improve Japan's female labour market flow.

First, Japan shows a high degree of human capital investment (ie, the human capital stock). Aside from the importance attached to private tutoring, which makes Japan a pioneer among Asian countries (Fleckenstein and Lee, 2017b), Japan has also invested heavily in tertiary education. As for women's educational attainment (OECD, 2018e), 52.2 per cent of women in Japan received tertiary education in 2017, slightly higher than the male equivalent of 50.7 per cent. These numbers are much higher than the OECD average and are estimated at 39.5 per cent for women and 33.4 per cent for men in 2017. Furthermore, the Japanese labour market has a particular, dualised structure that is characterised by a strong corporate culture and a high availability of part-time employment; the full-time/part-time ratio in total employment in Japan reached 29 part-time jobs for every hundred full-time jobs in 2017. The percentage of female part-time employment in Japan is the highest among the countries under observation, especially for women past the labour market entry stage and during their most productive years (25 to 54 years old). High availability of part-time jobs is aligned with labour supply in Japan; indeed, traditional familialism in Japan has shaped the development of part-time jobs. A considerable number of Japanese women prioritise flexible working conditions in order to reconcile working time with family care (Gender Equality Bureau Cabinet Office, 2017). Additionally, the tax and social insurance system has contributed to the traditional male-breadwinner model. Working part-time is the most advantageous way to increase income while benefitting from tax and social insurance contributions in households with a male breadwinner. In fact, Japanese women in part-time jobs said the most significant reason for working part-time was 'not to be a main source of income, but to be supportive to households' (Ministry of Health, Labour and Welfare, 2016). Moreover, rigidities and gender segregation in the labour market became a barrier to women's career development outside part-time jobs (Nemoto, 2016; Kwon, 2017). The gender wage gap in Japan is the second largest in the OECD (OECD, 2018f) and the ratio of women in management positions was only 13 per cent in 2017, while it was 39 per cent in Sweden, 43 per cent in the United States, and 29 per cent in Germany (Yuko, 2019).

Indeed, Japan's gender equality culture has only modestly improved across generations. According to the national survey on 'the joint participation of men and women' in 2000 (Cabinet office, Government of Japan, 2017), only 38 per cent of women and 37.2 per cent of men support the view that 'Women should continue to work after having a child.' This gradually increased, however, to 55.3 per cent for women and 52.9 per cent for men in 2016. Still, Japan – alongside South Korea – scores low on gender equality indicators, such as the wage gap (OECD, 2018f). Furthermore, discriminatory practices towards women persist, as the recent 2018 scandals of rigged entry exams for prestigious medical schools in Japan demonstrate (*The Guardian*, 2018).

Yet, institutional constraints might remain a challenge for the labour market flow in Japan.

In terms of policy legacy, Japan has the relative advantage of being a welfare latecomer. Expenditure for the most typical compensation policy – old age and family survivors – as a proportion of GDP (OECD, 2018d) were moderate throughout the 1990s, making up only 4.8 per cent in 1990. This is far below the average of OECD (6.4 per cent), Spain (7.7 per cent), or of Italy (11.3 per cent). Expenditure rose to 9.4 per cent in 2017, which is higher than the average OECD (7.4 per cent), but lags behind the 2015 figures for Italy (16.1 per cent) and Spain (11 per cent). More problematic is the growth of pension expenditure, which has more than doubled in the last 20 years. Along with the world's highest old-age dependency ratio (47.2 per cent in 2015), this might hinder further commitments to developing social investment policies.

Furthermore, several external constraints might be problematic for the labour market flow. First, Japan is under pressure from its high government debt. According to the International Monetary Fund, Japanese public-sector debt rose to one quadrillion yen (US$10.28 trillion), or 239 per cent of GDP in 2017. Recently, the Japanese government tried to increase tax rates to boost economic growth and alleviate economic risk. The 2011 Tohoku earthquake is also considered an external constraint, as it was the most powerful earthquake ever recorded in Japan. The earthquake caused extensive damage both to the economy and to society, restricting public funds available for social policies. At that time the DPJ-led Japanese government was forced to delay budget increases for child allowance to prioritise reconstruction work. Means testing for the child allowance was reintroduced in 2012 (*Yomiuri Shinbun*, 2011).

Japan's social investment strategy has not been as energetic as South Korea's. Nevertheless, it is generally agreed that Japan has achieved gradual progress on childcare and elderly care policy reforms (Peng, 2014), ultimately resulting in a steady, but 'quiet', social investment strategy (Kwon, 2017; Miura and Hamada, forthcoming). However, higher female employment rates since 2000 owe more to the labour market's abundant provision of part-time work opportunities of a gendered nature (Kwon, 2017).

In sum, sustained high female employment rates in Japan result from a combination of social investment policy reform, high levels of labour force tertiarisation, availability of part-time work, a (still) relatively light policy legacy, and limited budgetary expenses due to high public debt and the 2011 earthquake. Nevertheless, a conservative mindset and institutional pressures persist for women to reduce their working hours (Kwon, 2017), which may stymie career-oriented women from pursuing professional ambitions. Data seems to confirm that part-time employment is mostly an option for low-educated women (see Table 6.2).

**Table 6.2:** Incidence of female part-time work based on educational levels

| | Below upper secondary education (%) | | Upper secondary education (%) | | Tertiary education (%) | |
|---|---|---|---|---|---|---|
| | Full time | Part time | Full time | Part time | Full time | Part time |
| Italy | 48.1 | 51.9 | 61.8 | 38.2 | 68.3 | 31.7 |
| Spain | 42.8 | 57.2 | 56.8 | 43.2 | 68.5 | 31.5 |
| Japan | 40.9 | 59.1 | 50.6 | 49.4 | 74.3 | 25.7 |
| South Korea | 78.2 | 21.8 | 80.6 | 19.4 | 88.0 | 12.0 |
| OECD | 52.1 | 47.9 | 59.2 | 40.8 | 67.1 | 32.9 |

Source: OECD (2018e) and Statistics Bureau of Japan (2014)

## South Korea

In South Korea, career interruptions due to motherhood still seem to affect the **labour market flow** negatively, despite its bold family policy reforms. Korean women's employment is strongly affected both by the lack of opportunities in the labour market and the mismatch between the over-educated workforce supply and the effective labour demand. Looking at comparative data, the motherhood penalty is striking, as the clear M-shape in female labour market participation patterns across the life course attests (see Figure 6.1). Due to postponed marriage and childbirth, this pattern has only been delayed over time, but it is still clearly visible in 2017. Labour market entry is relatively smooth for women in their twenties (León et al, 2016) and women score slightly better than men in fixed-term irregular work, as men delay their entrance into the labour market due to military service duty (see Figure 6.2). However, as seen in Figure 6.2, fixed-term contracts are more common among women between the ages of 25 and 54. Additionally, such contracts prevail among older workers in South Korea, irrespective of gender. The most notable aspect of women's employment in South Korea is their over-qualification, which often excludes them from the labour market. Furthermore, due to the low availability of part-time jobs, women at all levels of education are systematically under-represented in the labour market, with the sole exception of low-educated female workers. Women with a university-level education in South Korea fare much worse than women with comparable levels of education in Spain, Italy or the OECD in general (OECD, 2018e). We hypothesise that, given the choice, highly educated, married women prefer to become housewives rather than to re-enter a labour market with dire working conditions (Jung et al, 2012; OECD, 2018a).

Paradoxically, South Korea's social investment reform has strongly addressed this less-than-ideal labour market. Childcare services represented one of the key programmes of the Vision 2030 for Economic Growth and Welfare strategy set forward by the centre-left government of Roh Moo-hyun (2003–8) (Yang, 2017; Lee and Baek, 2018). Care services were also identified as a way to boost female employment (León et al, 2016; Fleckenstein and Lee, 2017b). Relying on private sector providers rather than public sector providers, and subsidising both childcare institutions and parents through vouchers, childcare services have been continuously expanded. Such services began with families under the poverty threshold (2008) and then expanded to all children from infancy to 5 years old within the lowest 70th percentile of the income bracket (2012). Finally, in 2013, the programme became universal in South Korea under the centre-right government of Park Geun-hye. Co-payments were also eliminated and housewives were guaranteed the same eligibility as working mothers (Yang, 2017). This is truly a merit point in comparison to Italy, Spain, and Japan, all of whom prioritised working women with childcare service provisions over housewives' participation in the labour market. At present, each child younger than 6 is eligible for free childcare and if families opt to care for their child themselves, they are entitled to a child-rearing allowance (*yangyuksudang*) (León et al, 2016), which is a flat-rate cash benefit of approximately 100,000–200,000 won depending on age, place of residence and whether there is a disability. In 2018, another child allowance (*adongsudang*) was introduced in the form of a monthly subsidy of an additional 100,000 won. The government paid up to 90 per cent of families, excluding the top 10 per cent income bracket. In 2019, the benefit was made universal, with a long-term plan to gradually increase its amount (*Korea Bizwire*, 2018a).

Leave policies in South Korea are also undergoing several changes under the progressive Moon Jae-in, who has been president since 2017. Maternity leave (*chulsanjeonhuhyuga*) lasts 90 days with a 100 per cent pay rate up to 1,800,000 won (a number that has been gradually increasing) and this policy has extended to mothers in irregular jobs or self-employment as well, with a maximum of 500,000 won a month. Starting in 2019, paternal leave (*baeujachulsanhyuga*) has been extended from the previous five days (of which two days were unpaid) to 10 days (of which five might be subsidised by the government) (*Sisain*, 2019). Parental leave (*yugahyujik*) can be claimed for children under 8 years old, with each parent entitled to 12 months with a 50 per cent income replacement rate up to a maximum of 1,500,000 won for the first three months and 1,200,000 won for the remainder. In 2017 a bonus was introduced for fathers opting for parental leave ('daddy's month') and in 2019 it was increased from a maximum benefit of 2,000,000 won per month to 2,500,000 won per month, for a maximum of three months (Employment Insurance, 2019).

In 2008, long-term care insurance for the frail elderly was introduced, but – unlike Japan – lacked adequate prior preparation (Chon, 2013). As a result, the insurance was criticised for insufficient coverage levels, high out-of-pocket payments, and low service quality. As of 2015 only 7.1 per cent of the elderly population utilised this service in contrast to 18.5 per cent in Japan (Chung, 2018).

Despite the many improvements in work–family reconciliation policies in South Korea, institutional facilitators favouring a smooth labour market flow are lacking.

The human capital stock is significant in Korean society at all levels of education, tertiary and below. In an educational system geared towards competition and accessing the most prestigious schools, test-taking is overwhelmingly important. As a result, estimates indicate that private tutoring and, notably, household expenditure for private academies (*hagwons*), is now equivalent to 80 per cent of public spending on primary and secondary education (Fleckenstein and Lee, 2017b). South Korea has among the highest levels of enrolment in tertiary education in the world, with 74.9 per cent of women between the ages 25 and 34 holding a university degree in 2017, and 65.1 per cent of men of the same age (OECD, 2018e). The labour market structure is strongly dualised in South Korea, with large industries dominating the primary labour market, SMEs constituting the secondary labour market and limited mobility stymying movement from the latter to the former (Chung and Jung, 2016; Lee and Yang, 2018). Given higher wages and better working conditions, Korean families invest in higher education to acquire the credentials and skills public agencies and large corporations require, but this creates an over-supply of highly educated individuals who are ill-fitted to the labour market's actual demands (Chung and Jung, 2016; Fleckenstein and Lee, 2017b; Choi, 2018). This problem is especially evident for women, as they face discrimination from a corporate culture prone to long working hours that do not favour work–family reconciliation. Estimates indicate that 20.5 per cent of working-age women quit their jobs in 2018 for marriage and family reasons, with women in their thirties constituting the largest percentage at 48 per cent (*Korea Bizwire*, 2018b). The incentive to exit the labour market increases for highly educated women, especially when married to high-income earners (Jung et al, 2012). Re-entering employment following motherhood in South Korea means being segregated in the secondary labour market, in which temporary contracts, self-employment, and unpaid work dominate (OECD, 2018a; Lee and Yang, 2018).

Finally, of all the countries considered here, South Korea fares the worst in terms of gender equality culture, ranking far below the median position in the world. This results from high levels of inequality in women's labour market participation, the gender pay gap and low women's representation in both politics and professional jobs (World Economic Forum, 2018). Assuredly, progress has been made over the years, starting with the Gender-Equal Employment Act (1987) and continuing with the expansion of social care in the 2000s (Presidential Policy Planning Committee, 2018), in which the role of feminist democrats – the so-called femocrats – proved substantial (Estevez-Abe and Kim, 2014). Modest improvements are also visible in the corporate sector with 13.9 per cent female managers in Korean companies in 2014, up from 9.9 per cent in 2010 (Lee, 2016). However, the concept of family in the Basic Law of Healthy Family is still built around a standard nuclear household (Chung, 2018). As a result, all non-standard families, such as single-mother families, are heavily stigmatised. Furthermore, families constituted of children born outside of wedlock are almost non-existent, as they are in Japan.

South Korean governments have enjoyed more room to manoeuvre when addressing new social risks because of the country's weak policy legacy. This has allowed it to introduce social investment policies on top of already existing residual compensation schemes, thus creating a logic of policy layering (Hong et al, 2019). Unlike Spain, Italy and Japan, South Korea also enjoys relatively low levels of public debt, with the fiscal balance visibly deteriorating only after 2008. Additionally, a package of labour market policies aimed at limiting work dismissals efficiently counterbalanced the effects of the economic crisis (Yang, 2017). Nevertheless, Korean families are burdened with high levels of private household debt, which is itself an internal constraint on the budget for social policies (Kim, 2017).

In summation, a conspicuous motherhood penalty still negatively affects working prospects for women and hinders South Korea's labour market flow. A bold universal family policy reform with a clear social investment orientation addressed this issue, but only with limited success. Several institutional features might have worked well with social investment reform: high educational levels of working-age Korean women, a relatively light policy legacy that allows social investment initiatives to create a logic of policy layering and relatively stable socio-economic conditions (limited impact of the 2008 economic crisis and low public debt). However, these elements were apparently insufficient in countering the negative effects of a dualised, discriminatory labour market and limited openness in terms of gender equality culture in the country.

## Conclusion

Italy, Spain, Japan and South Korea have a lot in common: late welfare state development, traditional familialistic culture, low fertility problems and dualised labour markets. However, they differ in the degree of success they have had in improving women's employment opportunities by easing working transitions during their life cycles – the so-called labour market flow function described in social investment literature (Hemerijck, 2013, 2015). When it comes to improving female employment levels, Spain and Japan have fared considerably better than Italy and South Korea (see Table 6.1), notably by improving the labour market flow for the critical life-cycle transition points of motherhood, re-entering the labour market and mid-life employment. Spain has managed to increase female employment across all life cycle stages, labour market entrance still remains slow and arduous for female workers in their teens and twenties. In Japan, women's already high levels of employment has been boosted even further and, most notably, the dip in working continuity during motherhood (ie, the motherhood penalty) has evened out, although the M-shape remains clearly noticeable. In contrast, Italy has only modestly improved its low female employment levels and labour market entry remains difficult for young women; however, re-entering the labour market and mid-life employment have somewhat improved. South Korea's overall labour market flow has improved for female workers, but motherhood remains a stumbling block and weighs heavily in women's family and career choices (see Figure 6.1).

What role did social investment policies play? Again, differences in policy reform span welfare regime categories, with Korea being the boldest reformer, Spain and Japan engaging either in partial or gradual reform strategies (or both), and Italy trailing behind (Estevez-Abe and Naldini, 2016). Considering the important improvements that Spain and Japan have made in their labour market flow for women, we cannot minimise the importance of social investment reform. Nevertheless, closer scrutiny at the institutional level is needed to ascertain why South Korea and Italy both fared worse in their labour market flows, notwithstanding their commitment to social investment going in opposite directions. In particular, South Korea is the most striking case of social investment policy reform in the presence of adverse institutional configurations. Although a light policy legacy and low public debt helped promote a more ambitious social investment agenda and high levels of investment in human capital made this a well-positioned case for success, a conservative working culture and the dualised labour market structure rendered the cost of motherhood too high and often forced women to choose between work and family. This results in erratic female labour market participation patterns and, worse, results in even lower economic activity for the highly educated populace.

Arguably, among different institutional complementarities that might contribute to a better flow function of the labour market, opportunities opening up in the dualised labour markets and improving gender equality culture are the most promising reforms with which to start a discussion on improving the efficacy of social investment policy (for a closer look at institutional complementarities, see Table 6.3).

How can the labour market flow be improved, then? Here, the main policy implication is that social investment reform must find ideal institutional terrain in order to function well. In other words, context

**Table 6.3:** Institutional configurations influencing the flow function of social investment policies

| | Italy | Spain | Japan | South Korea |
|---|---|---|---|---|
| Social investment reform | Minimal | Partial | Gradual | Substantial |
| Female labour market flow | 1. Slow | 1. Slow | 1. Smooth | 1. Smooth |
| | 2. Acceptable | 2. Acceptable | 2. Noticeable M-shape | 2. M-shape |
| | 3. Acceptable | 3. Smooth | 3. Fewer working hours | 3. Bad |
| | 4. Improved | 4. Improved | 4. Acceptable | 4. Acceptable (but secondary labour market) |
| Facilitating institutions — Human capital stock | Low | Medium high | High | High |
| Dual labour market structure | Dominance of low-innovations SMEs | Flexibilisation | Part-time job availability | Secondary, low-skill labour market |
| Gender equality culture | Slowly improving | Improving | Conservative | Conservative |
| Hindering institutions — Policy legacy | High expenditure | Medium high expenditure | Medium high expenditure | Low expenditure |
| Socio-economic conditions | Austerity | Austerity | Public debt | Limited impact |

Source: Author's elaboration

matters and a complementary reform of institutions is also necessary. This chapter presents important lessons in two respects. First, it identifies different critical points of the life cycle that might impede an optimal labour market flow for women. Second, this chapter finds that commitments to social investment reform were met in varying degrees with resistance in different institutional configurations.

Italy and Spain share in common a difficult and patchy flow at labour market entrance and mid-life employment, but the latter had been able not only to push more for social investment reform, but also to improve human capital stock, gender equality culture and working opportunities in a flexible labour market. In the Italian case, bolder steps towards social investment reform might have helped. However, if this reform had been joined with increasing innovation and investment in its labour market structure, and with more investments in human capital stock, then Italy's labour market flow could have improved further. In particular, investing more in tertiary education and incentivising small and medium enterprises to innovate more might be worthy institutional reform strategies to follow, along with social investment reform.

As for South Korea and Japan, they are hard-pressed to make further improvements in their human capital stock, which is already very high. Improvements in the labour market flow in Japan were possible because social investment provisions (albeit partial ones) were coupled with increasing opportunities for part-time work for women. South Korea, despite its bold social investment reforms, had limited improvement in labour market flow because the motherhood penalty continued to loom large. Most problematic is South Korea's rigid labour market structure, which does not allow women to re-enter the labour market at the same levels as their initial entry point. Improving the labour market's dualised structure and pushing for a more gender-equal culture by identifying and sanctioning discriminatory hiring practices might be important institutional reforms to implement.

In conclusion, while the presence of an adequate human capital stock is useful in combination with social investment policies (Draebing and Nelson, 2017), the real difference lies in the labour market and to what degree it accommodates women's non-linear, discontinuous professional careers (OECD, 2018a: 212). Much of this rests with corporate culture and the way in which women are perceived as competent and reliable workers – an attitude that clearly depends on a gender equality culture. Appropriate reform measures, then, should address this corporate culture.

# References

An, M.Y. (2017) 'Welfare states and care arrangements: care time mix approach and its application to Japan and Korea', *Social Policy and Society*, 16(2): 183–98.

An, M.Y. and Peng, I. (2016) 'Diverging paths? A comparative look at childcare policies in Japan, South Korea and Taiwan', *Social Policy & Administration*, 50(5): 540–58.

Ascoli, U., Ranci, C. and Sgritta, G.B. (eds) (2015) *Investire nel Sociale. La Difficile Innovazione del Welfare Italiano* [*Social Investment: The Difficult Innovation of Italian Welfare*], Bologna: Il Mulino.

Barbieri, P. and Scherer, S. (2009) 'Labour market flexibilization and its consequences in Italy', *European Sociological Review*, 25(6): 677–92.

Bentolila, S., Dolado, J.J. and Jimeno, J.F. (2012) 'Reforming an insider-outsider labor market: the Spanish experience', *IZA Journal of European Labor Studies*, 1(1): 4.

Bergamante, F. (2018) 'Kajoksudang [Family allowances]', in I. Hong et al (eds) *Italy Social Security System*, KIHASA & Nanam, pp 207–26, Available from: https://www.kihasa.re.kr/web/publication/research/view.do?menuId=45&tid=71&bid=12&division=001&ano=2411 [Accessed 28 July 2020].

Bertolini, S., Musumeci, R., Naldini, M. and Torrioni, P.M. (2015) 'Working women in transition to motherhood in Italy', *Journal of Romance Studies*, 15(3): 49–70.

Blossfield, H.P., Bochholz, S., Daemmrich, J., Kilpi-Jakonen, E., Kosyakova, Y., Skopek, J., Triventi, M. and Vono de Vilhena, D. (2015) 'Gender differences at labor market entry: the effect of changing educational pathways and institutional structures', in H.P. Blossfeld, J. Skopek, M. Triventi and S. Buchholz (eds) *Gender, Education and Employment: An International Comparison of School-to-Work Transitions*, Cheltenham: Edward Elgar, pp 3–34.

Bonoli, G. (2005) 'The politics of new social policies: providing coverage against new social risks in mature welfare states', *Policy and Politics*, 33(3): 431–49.

Bonoli, G. (2007) 'Time matters', *Comparative Political Studies*, 40(5): 495–520.

Bonoli, G. and Reber, F. (2010) 'The political economy of childcare in OECD countries: explaining cross-national variation in spending and coverage rates', *European Journal of Political Research*, 49(1): 97–118.

Bouget, D., Frazer, H., Marlier, E., Sabato, S. and Vanhercke, B. (2015) *Social Investment in Europe: A Study of National Policies*, Brussels: European Commission.

Budig, M.J., Misra, J. and Boeckmann, I. (2012) 'The motherhood penalty in cross-national perspective: the importance of work–family policies and cultural attitudes', *Social Politics*, 19(2): 163–93.

Cabinet office, Government of Japan (2017) 'Danjokyoudoushakainikansuruyoronchousa [Public survey on the joint society for men and women]', Available from: www.cao.go.jp [Accessed 31 July 2019].

Canal, T. (2018) 'Adong mit boyukseobisu [Childcare services]', in I. Hong et al (eds) *Italy Social Security System*, KIHASA & Nanam, pp 317–42, Available from: https://www.kihasa.re.kr/web/publication/research/view.do?menuId=45&tid=71&bid=12&division=001&ano=2411 [Accessed 28 July 2020].

Castagnetti, C., Rosti, L. and Toepfer, M. (2018) 'Overeducation and the gender pay gap in Italy', *International Journal of Manpower*, 9(5): 710–30.

Cerea, S., Giannone, M., Salvati, A. and Saruis, T. (2015) 'I dilemmi dell'investimento sociale nelle politiche locali per l'infanzia [The dilemmas of social investment for childcare local policies]', in U. Ascoli, C. Ranci and G.B. Sgritta (eds) *Investire nel Sociale: La Difficile Innovazione del Welfare Italiano* [Social Investment: The Difficult Innovation of Italian Welfare], Bologna: Il Mulino.

Choi, S.E. (2018) 'What makes it difficult for highly educated Korean women to participate in the labor market? Heritage of the developmental production regime in Korea', *Journal of the Korean Welfare State and Social Policy*, 2(1): 58–86.

Chon, Y.H. (2013) 'The development of Korea's new long-term care service infrastructure and its results: focusing on the market-friendly policy used for expansion of the numbers of service providers and personal care workers', *Journal of Gerontological Social Work*, 56(3): 255–75.

Chung, M.K. (2018) 'Sahoeseobisuwa gajokjungchek [Social services and family policies]', in B.Y. Ahn, M.K. Chung, D.M. Shin and J.J. Yang (eds) *Welfare State and Social Welfare Policies*, Seoul: Dasan.

Chung, S. and Jung, S. (2016) *Testing the Labor Market Dualism in Korea*, Economic Research Institute, Seoul: The Bank of Korea.

Ciccia, R. and Bleijenbergh, I. (2014) 'After the male breadwinner model? Childcare services and the division of labor in European countries', *Social Politics: International Studies in Gender, State and Society*, 21(1): 50–79.

Draebing, V. and Nelson, M. (2017) 'Addressing human capital risks and the role of institutional complementarities', in A. Hemerijck (ed) *The Uses of Social Investment*, Oxford: Oxford University Press.

Employment Insurance (2019) 'Moseongbohoanne [About motherhood protection]', Available from: www.ei.go.kr [Accessed 31 July 2019].

Esping-Andersen, G., Gallie, D., Hemerijck, A. and Myles, J. (2002) *Why We Need a New Welfare State*, Oxford: Oxford University Press.

Estevez-Abe, M. (2006) 'Gendering the varieties of capitalism: a study of occupational segregation by sex in advanced industrial societies', *World Politics*, 59(1): 142–75.

Estevez-Abe, M. and Kim, Y.S. (2014) 'Presidents, prime ministers and politics of care: why Korea expanded childcare much more than Japan', *Social Policy & Administration*, 48(6): 666–85.

Estevez-Abe, M. and Naldini, M. (2016) 'Politics of defamilialization: a comparison of Italy, Japan Korea and Spain', *Journal of Social Policy*, 26(4): 327–43.

Estevez-Abe, M., Yang, J.J. and Choi, Y.J. (2016) 'Beyond familialism: recalibrating family, state and market in Southern Europe and East Asia', *Journal of European Social Policy*, 26(4): 301–13.

Eurofound (2016) 'The gender employment gap: challenges and solutions', Luxembourg: Publications Office of the European Union.

Ferrera, M. (1996) 'The "southern model" of welfare in social Europe', *Journal of European Social Policy*, 6(1): 17–37.

Fleckenstein, T. and Lee, S.C. (2014) 'The politics of postindustrial social policy family policy reforms in Britain, Germany, South Korea, and Sweden', *Comparative Political Studies*, 47(4): 601–30.

Fleckenstein, T. and Lee, S.C. (2017a) 'The politics of investing in families: comparing family policy expansion in Japan and South Korea', *Social Politics*, 24(1): 1–28.

Fleckenstein, T. and Lee, S.C. (2017b) 'A social investment turn in East Asia? South Korea in comparative perspective', in A. Hemerijck (ed) *The Uses of Social Investment*, Oxford: Oxford University Press.

Fleckenstein, T. and Seeleib-Kaiser, M. (2011) 'Business, skills and the welfare state: the political economy of employment-oriented family policy in Britain and Germany', *Journal of European social policy*, 21(2): 136–49.

Gambardella, D., Pavolini, E. and Arlotti, M. (2015) 'L'investimento sociale alle prese con disuguaglianze sociali e territoriali [Social investment faced with social and territorial inequalities]', in U. Ascoli, C. Ranci and G.B. Sgritta (eds) *Investire nel Sociale. La Difficile Innovazione del Welfare Italiano*, Bologna: Il Mulino.

Gender Equality Bureau Cabinet Office (2017) 'Danjokyodousankahakusho [White paper on the joint participation of men and women]', Available from: www.gender.go.jp [Accessed 1 July 2018].

Heckman, J.J. (2006) 'Skill Formation and the Economics of Investing in Disadvantaged Children', *Science*, 312: 1900–2.

Hemerijck, A. (2013) *Changing Welfare States*, Oxford: Oxford University Press.

Hemerijck, A. (2015) 'The quiet paradigm revolution of social investment', *Social Politics: International Studies in Gender, State & Society*, 22(2): 242–56.

Hemerijck, A. (ed) (2017) *The Uses of Social Investment*, Oxford: Oxford University Press.

Hinrichs, K. and Jessoula, M. (eds) (2012) *Labour Market Flexibility and Pension Reforms: Flexible Today, Secure Tomorrow?*, Basingstoke: Palgrave.

Holliday, I. (2000) 'Productivist welfare capitalism: social policy in east Asia', *Political Studies*, 48(4): 706–23.

Hong, I., Kim, B. and Kwon, E. (2019) 'Measuring social policy change in comparative research: survey data evidence from South Korea', *Journal of Comparative Policy Analysis: Research and Practice*, 21(2): 131–50.

Ingenere (2015) 'Occupazione femminile, fotografia dell'Italia di oggi [Female employment, a snapshot of today's Italy]', 3 November, Available from: www.ingenere.it/articoli/occupazione-femminile-fotografia-italia-di-oggi?fbclid=IwAR098DPpQOrgdyEglFONG MmV0AWb1qG359mgkzwaEPWHFd60qId6qLdiPPc [Accessed 20 December 2018].

Ingenere (2018a) 'Solo cinque giorni per fare i padri?' [Only five days to be a father?], 6 December, Available from: www.ingenere.it/news/solo-cinque-giorni-fare-i-padri?fbclid=IwAR0mIBiGOgPNdoZB eZm94NFonHNRB0y1TFpmCaWhSvOLdFPX_Ay-Hocn_UY [Accessed 20 December 2018].

Ingenere (2018b) 'Paternità, cosa possiamo imparare dalla Spagna [Fatherhood, what we can learn from Spain]', 29 November, Available from: www.ingenere.it/articoli/paternita-cosa-possiamo-imparare-dalla-spagna?fbclid=IwAR3Pvy1Y-lJ2TkvtKk2rcs5uAWhA6giWj TMWQU7T849KOUehqWdDZkbuL_0 [Accessed 20 December 2018].

Jenson, J. (2009) 'Lost in translation: the social investment perspective and gender equality', *Social Politics: International Studies in Gender, State & Society*, 16(4): 446–83.

Jung, E.H., Kim, Y.M. and Kwon, H.J. (2012) 'Donasia sinhungseonjinkuk yeoseonggoyong hangukgua deman bigyo [Female employment in newly developed countries in East Asia: a comparison of Korea and Taiwan]', *Korean Women's Studies*, 28(1): 147–81.

Jurado-Guerrero, T. and Naldini, M. (2018) 'Child and family policy in Southern Europe', in G.B. Eydal and T. Roostgard (eds) *Handbook of Family Policy*, Cheltenham: Edward Elgar, pp 209–22.

Kazepov, Y. and Ranci, C. (2017) 'Is every country fit for social investment? Italy as an adverse case', *Journal of European Social Policy*, 27(1): 90–104.

Kim, D.K. (2017) 'The duality of self-employed business debt and its increase after the Asian financial crisis', *Journal of the Korean Welfare State and Social Policy*, 1(2): 24–50.

*Korea Bizwire* (2018a) 'Gov't to lower child-rearing expenses to tackle low birthrate', 7 December, Available from: koreabizwire.com/govt-to-lower-child-rearing-expenses-to-tackle-low-birthrate/128480?fbclid=IwAR3FGgT6LyXbpLL3PjlpRIJq5Sqge2azod900HjKqgvWr-SnDHD4TPppggk [Accessed 17 January 2019].

*Korea Bizwire* (2018b) '20.5 pct of women quit jobs after marriage', 28 November, Available from: koreabizwire.com/20-5-pct-of-women-quit-jobs-after-marriage/128076?fbclid=IwAR233NnyviMK2vTZVqGAwCGtX8lbtXeGF9mrazM8Nf6kXZ3zye3-Qs7QPno [Accessed 17 January 2019].

Kwon, S.M. (2018) 'Baljeonjuei gukgaeseo sahoitujagukgaro: Ilbonsaraerul jungsimuro [From a developmentalist welfare state to a social investment state: z case study of Japan]', *Korea Social Policy Review*, 25(1): 231–57.

Kwon, S.M. (2017) 'Ilbon yosungduleun patutaimnodongeul jabaljeokuro seontekhanunga [Are "voluntary" part-time workers for women indeed voluntary? A case study of Japan]', *Journal of Japanese Studies*, 46: 5–31.

Lee, H.Y. and Yang, J.J. (2018) 'Who are the outsiders in the dualized labour market in South Korea? A fuzzy set analysis', *Journal of the Korean Welfare State and Social Policy*, 2(2): 31–72.

Lee, S.S.Y. (2016) 'Institutional legacy of state corporatism in de-industrial labour markets: a comparative study of Japan, South Korea and Taiwan', *Socio-Economic Review*, 14(1): 73–95.

Lee, S.S.Y. and Baek, S.H. (2018) 'The social investment approach in the productivist welfare regime: the unfolding of social investment in South Korea and Japan', in G.B. Eydal and T. Roostgard (eds) *Handbook of Family Policy*, Cheltenham: Edward Elgar, pp 111–23.

León, M., Choi, Y.J. and Ahn, J.S. (2016) 'When flexibility meets familialism: two tales of gendered labour markets in Spain and South Korea', *Journal of European Social Policy*, 26(4): 344–57.

León, M. and Migliavacca, M. (2013) 'Italy and Spain: still the case of familistic welfare models?', *Population Review*, 52 (1): 25–42.

León, M. and Pavolini, E. (2014) 'Social investment or back to familism: the impact of the economic crisis on care policies in Italy and Spain', *South European Society & Politics*, 19(3): 353–69.

Lewis, J., Knijn, T., Martin, C. and Ostner, I. (2008) 'Patterns of development in work/family reconciliation policies for parents in France, Germany, the Netherlands, and the UK in the 2000s', *Social Politics*, 15(3): 261–86.

Mandel, H. and Semyonov, M. (2006) 'A welfare state paradox: state interventions and women's employment opportunities in 22 countries', *American Journal of Sociology*, 111(6): 1910–49.

MISSOC (2018) 'Mutual information system on social protection', Available from: www.missoc.org_[Accessed 20 December 2018].

Ministry of Health, Labour and Welfare (1994) 'Kongonokosodatesiennotamenoshisakunokihontekihoukounituite [Basic direction of childcare support policy in the future]', Available from: www.mhlw.go.jp [Accessed 31 July 2019].

Ministry of Health, Labour and Welfare (2019) 'Ikuji, kaigokyuugyouhounitsuite [About the law of parental leave and care leave]', Available from: www.mhlw.go.jp [Accessed 21 November 2020].

Miura, M. and Hamada, E. (forthcoming) 'Quiet diffusion of social investment in Japan', in B. Palier, S. Haeusermann and J. Garritsmann (eds) *The World Politics of Social Investment (Vol. II)*, Oxford: Oxford University Press.

Morel, N., Palier, B. and Palme, J. (2012) *Towards a Social Investment Welfare State? Ideas, Policies and Challenges*, Bristol: Policy Press.

Morgan, K.J. (2012) 'Promoting social investment through work-family policies: which nations do it and why?' in N. Morel, B. Palier and J. Palme (eds) *Towards a Social Investment Welfare State? Ideas, Policies and Challenges*, Bristol: Policy Press, pp 153–80.

Naldini, M., Pavolini, E. and Solera, C. (2014) 'Does caring for the elderly affect mid-life women's employment? Differences across regimes', *Carlo Alberto Notebooks*, 368: 1–15.

National Institute of Population and Social Security Research (2015) 'Daijyuugokaisyusseidoukoukihonchousa (huuhuchousa) [The 15th basic survey on birth trends (married couples)]', Available from: www.ipss.go.jp [Accessed 31 July 2019].

Nelson, M. and Stephens, J.D. (2012) 'Do social investment policies produce more and better jobs?', in N. Morel, B. Palier and J. Palme (eds) *Towards a Social Investment State? Ideas, Policies and Challenges*, Bristol: Policy Press, pp 205–34.

Nemoto, K. (2016) *Too Few Women at the Top: The Persistence of Inequality in Japan*, New York: Cornell University Press.

Ochiai, E., Yamane, M. and Miyazawa, S. (2007) *Ajianokajokutojenda* [Family and Gender in Asia], Tokyo: Keisoshobo.

OECD (Organisation for Economic Co-operation and Development) (2018a) *OECD Employment Outlook 2018*, Paris: OECD.

OECD (Organisation for Economic Co-operation and Development) (2018b) 'Labour force statistics', Available from: stats.oecd.org [Accessed 3 July 2018].

OECD (Organisation for Economic Co-operation and Development) (2018c) 'Permanent temporary employment', Available from: stats. oecd.org [Accessed 3 July 2018].

OECD (Organisation for Economic Co-operation and Development) (2018d) 'Social protection and wellbeing', Available from: stats.oecd. org [Accessed 3 July 2018].

OECD (Organisation for Economic Co-operation and Development) (2018e) 'Educational attainment and outcomes', Available from: stats. oecd.org [Accessed 3 July 2018].

OECD (Organisation for Economic Co-operation and Development) (2018f) 'Gender wage gap', Available from: stats.oecd.org [Accessed 3 July 2018].

OECD (Organisation for Economic Co-operation and Development) (2019a) 'Adult education level (indicator)', Available from: https:// doi.org/10.1787/025421e5-en [Accessed 10 August 2019].

OECD (Organisation for Economic Co-operation and Development) (2019b) 'Employment rate (indicator)', Available from: https://doi. org/10.1787/a452d2eb-en [Accessed 11 January 2019).

Osawa, M. (2000) 'Government approaches to gender equality in the mid-1990s', *Social Science Japan Journal*, 3(1): 3–19.

Papadopoulos, T. and Roumpakis, A. (2015) 'Democracy, austerity and crisis: Southern Europe and the decline of the European social model', S. Romano and G. Punziano (eds) *The European Social Model Adrift*, Farnham and Burlington: Ashgate, pp 189–212.

Peng, I. (2014) 'The social protection floor and the "new" social investment policies in Japan and South Korea', *Global Social Policy*, 14(3): 389–405.

Peng, I. and Chien, Y.C. (2018) 'Not all in the same family: diverging approaches to family policies in East Asia', in G.B. Eydal and T. Roostgard (eds) *Handbook of Family Policy*, Cheltenham: Edward Elgar, pp 236–48.

Pfau-Effinger, B. (1998) 'Gender cultures and the gender arrangement: a theoretical framework for crossnational comparisons on gender', *Innovation: The European Journal of Social Sciences*, 11 (2): 147–66.

Pfau-Effinger, B. (2005) 'Culture and welfare state policies: reflections on a complex interrelation', *Journal of Social Policy*, 34 (1): 3–20.

Pistagni, R. (ed) (2011) *Perchè non Lavori? I Risultati di una Indagine ISFOL sulla Partecipazione Femminile al Mercato del Lavoro* [Why don't you work? The results of a ISFOL survey on female labour market participation], Roma: ISFOL.

Presidential Policy Planning Committee (2018) *Moon Jae-in Jungbu 'Poyonggukga' Bijeongwa Jeonryak* [Moon Jae-in Government's Vision and Strategy of an 'Inclusive State'], Seoul: Presidential Policy Planning Committee.

Saraceno, C. and Keck, W. (2010) 'Can we identify intergenerational policy regimes in Europe?', *European Societies*, 12(5): 675–96.

*Sisain* (2019) '2019 Chulsanhyuga iroeke bakuieotta [The changes in the maternity leave system in 2019]', 1 November, Available from: www.sisain.co.kr/?mod=news&act=articleView&idxno=33592 [Accessed 18 January 2019].

Statistics Bureau of Japan (2014) 'Female employment and educational level', Available from: www.stat.go.jp [Accessed 3 July 2018].

Tamiya, N., Noguchi, H., Nishi, A., Reich, M.R., Ikegami, N., Hashimoto, H. and Campbell, J.C. (2011) 'Population ageing and wellbeing: lessons from Japan's long-term care insurance policy', *The Lancet*, 378(9797): 1183–92.

Távora, I. and Rodríguez-Modroño, P. (2018) 'The impact of the crisis and austerity on low educated working women: the cases of Spain and Portugal', *Gender, Work & Organization*, 25(6): 621–36.

*The Guardian* (2018) 'Tokyo medical school admits changing results to exclude women', 8 August, Available from: www.theguardian.com/world/2018/aug/08/tokyo-medical-school-admits-changing-results-to-exclude-women [Accessed 17 January 2019].

Yamashita, J. and Soma, N. (2015) 'The double responsibilities of care in Japan: emerging new social risks for women providing both childcare and care for the elderly', in R.K.H. Chan, J.O. Zinn and L.R. Wang (eds) *New Life Courses, Social Risks and Social Policy in East Asia*, Oxford and New York: Taylor and Francis.

Yang, J.J. (2017) *The Political Economy of the Small Welfare State in South Korea*, Cambridge: Cambridge University Press.

*Yomiuri Shinbun* (2011) 'Kodomoteate juugatuikouhaishihe hukkouzaigenwoyuusen [Child benefits are abolished after October in order to prioritise recovery funds]', 13 April, Available from: yomiuri.co.jp [Accessed 1 July 2018].

Yuko, A. (2019) 'Gender equality in Japan remains bottom', *NHK*, 25 December, Available from: www3.nhk.or.jp/nhkworld/en/news/backstories/335/?cid=nwd-adwords-all_site_dsa-201905-000 [Accessed 31 July 2019].

World Economic Forum (2018) *The Global Gender Gap Report 2018*, Geneva: World Economic Forum.

# 7

# The social investment approach and gender division of housework across East Asia and Europe

*Mi Young An*

## Introduction

Since the 1990s, the idea of social investment, which advocates the modernisation of welfare systems for sustainable social and economic development by highlighting human capital development, has influenced European welfare states (Jenson and Saint-Martin, 2003). Demographic structural changes have created a need to harvest human resources to enhance employability, and the modernisation of social policy has focused on human capital development of the young (Esping-Andersen et al, 2002). Peng (2014), among others, has argued that the idea of social investment has expanded beyond Western countries. Both Japan and the Republic of Korea (hereafter Korea) have developed social policies to support and incentivise the productive sectors. Those previously left out of the welfare system – women, children, and the elderly – have become targets of social spending.

Although what the social investment approach actually means may vary across East Asia and Europe, just as social investment policy configurations vary, in all countries, social policy changes are significant macro-level factors with implications for changes in the gender division of labour in the private sphere, not least because the idea has been influential in policy interventions targeting the family.

The gender gap in the division of housework has narrowed in most advanced economies (Gershuny, 2000; Gornick and Meyers, 2003; Ellingsaeter and Leira, 2006; Hook, 2006), but women still do the lion's share of housework. The strongly gendered division of labour at home is even more problematic in East Asia. On average, women in East Asian societies spend three to four times more than men doing unpaid work, including household chores and care for the family. The daily proportion of time allocated by men to unpaid work was 4.7 per cent and 3.0 per cent in Japan and Korea respectively, compared to 15.3 per cent and 13.7 per cent for women (OECD, 2020a). Unfortunately, the gap continues to exist despite significant policy interventions in East Asia.

Criticisms of social investment include concerns about gender equality. For example, Jenson (2009: 446) argued that women's demands for equality and attention to their needs are sidelined in favour of the interests of young girls' futures. Others have suggested this is a neoliberal strategy that does not fully address the right to care and maintains an ambiguous stance to the family (Bothfeld and Rouault, 2015; Saraceno, 2015). It is questionable if the social investment approach can ameliorate the structural conditions that hinder women as paid workers, such as the wage gap (Jenson, 2009; Hemerijck, 2017). Lee and Baek (2014) made a similar point, saying the approach is not good enough, as it does not address the structural constraints, such as the dualised labour market that Korean women face in employment decisions. Interestingly, the debates on the social investment approach, specifically its promulgation of family policy, have paid little attention to gender equality within the family in the division of housework.

This chapter addresses the issue of the gender division of housework, focusing on how formal childcare services and parental leave provisions are related to it. It comparatively examines the extent to which family policies are related to housework division in countries in East Asia and Europe. It finds parental leave, which supports women as paid workers, is significant in Europe, but formal childcare services, which support women's deviant gender roles, are significant when the examination is extended to East Asian countries. Gendered political power relations become significant only when we add in Japan and Korea. Neither gender-role ideology nor structural constraints, measured as gender wage gap, was an important macro-level factor. The chapter discusses how these results are related to the social investment approach to family and explains why the division of housework in East Asian countries remains highly gendered.

## The family policy and gender division of housework

Researchers have posited several micro-level mechanisms as driving the division of housework. Drawing on human capital theory, the time availability thesis argues that husbands and wives perform housework based on the amount of time that they have to devote to it (Becker, 1991). The relative resources thesis conceptualises the division of housework as an outcome of negotiation between husbands and wives, who use whatever valued resources they can to strike the best deal for themselves (Blood and Wolfe, 1965). This implies that people who have more resources (eg, education, income) have more bargaining power in negotiating the division of unpaid work (Bianchi et al, 2000; Evertsson and Nermo, 2004). The gender-role ideology hypothesis states that household tasks are allocated on the basis of gender attitudes and values learnt through socialisation (Kamo, 2000). Meanwhile, gender display (Brines, 1994) suggests individuals' behaviour in housework does not always follow what the economic bargaining thesis predicts. Men whose economic dependence is stronger do not spend more time on housework than men who are economically dependent upon their wives; women whose economic independence is stronger do not spend less time on housework than women whose independence is weaker (Bittman et al, 2003; Evertsson and Nermo, 2004).

The gender division of housework also differs by macro-level context and by welfare state or social policy. In her analysis of gender and housework in 22 countries, Fuwa (2004) used International Social Survey Programme (ISSP) 1994 Changing Families and Gender Roles data and found empirical evidence that welfare regimes play a role in the gender division of housework. Conservative regimes tend to have more unequal divisions of housework than liberal ones, and social democratic and former socialist regimes are more egalitarian than liberal ones. Geist (2005) compared the division of housework using the same data as Fuwa and confirmed cross-welfare regime differences in the gender division of domestic labour, with conservative regimes featuring more unequal gender divisions of housework than either social democratic or liberal ones. These two influential studies suggest the type of welfare regime impacts the micro-level gender division of housework. Social democratic regimes enhance gender equality, but liberal regimes do not; they focus on the individual, as an egalitarian ideology underlies the liberal tradition (O'Connor et al, 1999). Meanwhile, conservative welfare regimes often support traditional gender divisions of labour. In an analysis of ISSP 2002 data, Kleider (2015) developed a de-familialisation index to show that the promotion of female employment in family policy influences cross-national differences in housework division: the more that family policy supports female employment, the greater the egalitarian division of housework.

The social investment idea is important for gender inequality at home simply because family policy or work–family policies are a lynchpin of the idea. Morel et al (2012) claimed it can justify government spending in times of austerity. By the same token, Jenson (2012) asserted that social investment embraces voices from both the top and bottom and, hence, can be an efficient tool because it enables individual policies (ie, childcare services) to address multiple issues. In fact, I suggest that it is a powerful idea that can modernise family policy in highly gendered cultural, economic and political contexts. Societies that are highly gendered culturally, economically and politically may actually have quite modern family policies.

In Europe, it is important to recognise that women's political agency advanced despite cross-national differences when the idea prevailed and drove family policy changes. Studlar et al (1998) elaborate how structural changes and modernised perceptions turn into political change, leading to the modernisation of family policies. More specifically, the growth of female employment and corresponding changes in gender role perceptions caused European women to lean more to the left when voting. Where women's employment is high, there is a significant gender gap in political party preference (Iversen and Rosenbluth, 2006; Abendschön and Steinmetz, 2014). Morgan (2013) highlighted that changes in the old electoral constellations made political parties adjust to new realities to win female votes, which then led to a substantive increase in women's participation in top-level policy-making. The percentage of women in the lower chamber of parliament in Germany increased from around 15 per cent in 1990 to more than 30 per cent in 2010 when the country expanded public expenditure on formal childcare and education services from 0.3 per cent of GDP to 0.5 per cent. Corresponding rates of women in parliament increased from about 20 per cent to close to 50 per cent in the Netherlands when the country's spending on formal childcare services increased from 0.3 per cent of GDP to 0.8 per cent. In the UK, the rate of participation was as low as about 5 per cent in 1990, but jumped to around 20 per cent in 2010 when public expenditures on formal childcare services increased from 0.6 per cent of GDP to 0.8 per cent (Morgan, 2013; OECD, 2020b).

The macro-level context has largely corresponded to policy change in Europe. That is, family policy was modernised as perceptions of work and family were modernised (Ferragina and Seeleib-Kaiser, 2015). As Morgan (2012, 2013) noted, women's employment behaviour evolved in Europe in terms of participation and women's political agency became significant at the same time. Yet debates on parental leave supporting women as caregivers (Knijn and Kremer, 1997) or workers (Jaumotte, 2003; Hofferth and Curtin, 2006) are ongoing, and cross-national differences in the length of parental leave in Europe are significant. Empirical evidence shows that too much and too little parental leave both obstruct continuation of women's paid work (Ruhm, 1998; Jaumotte, 2003; Pettit and Hook, 2005).

This is critically different from East Asian experiences. The Confucian patriarchy has long shaped Korean perceptions, relationships and behaviours (Sechiyama, 2013). Contemporary Japan significantly differs from Korea in this regard. As we will show, Korean married women held highly traditional gender-role ideologies. While women's employment has grown in Korea and Japan, both have had M-shaped age-specific employment patterns, albeit to a lesser degree in Japan. In Peng's view (2004, 2008), women's organisations played an important role in the modernisation of social policies in Japan and Korea, but Fleckenstein and Lee (2017) say that modernisation of family policy occurred without much progress in women's participation in parliament. Similarly, in their work on Japan, Boling (2015) and Schoppa (2010) contended that organised women's groups have been poorly positioned in the development of social policy. The proportions of women parliamentarians in Japan and Korea increased from 7.3 per cent and 5.9 per cent respectively in 2002, to 10.3 per cent and 15.7 per cent in 2012, but remained extremely low compared to their European counterparts (OECD, 2020c).

Both East Asia and Europe are similar in their support of family policy. For example, in 2010, public expenditure on formal childcare services was 0.3 per cent of GDP in Japan and 0.6 per cent in Korea, whereas Austria, Ireland, and Germany spent 0.5 per cent and Switzerland 0.3 per cent (OECD, 2020b). Korea now has 52 weeks and Japan has 44 weeks of paid parental leave – likely neither too long nor too short (OECD, 2020d). However, gendered political power relations seem to evolve differently for East Asia. Severely gendered political power relations in policy-making have remained in place in East Asia more generally, despite the promulgation of advanced family-oriented policy.

Blumberg (1984) argued that male political and ideological dominance affects gender relations at the micro level. Fuwa (2004) found male control or dominance in political, economic and ideological areas at the macro level may act as a 'discount factor' in the power of individual women's resources. Women who lack time or possess progressive gender role ideologies tend to enjoy more equal divisions of housework if they live in societies where women are visible, and are politically and economically empowered.

The above discussion makes the following points. By and large, the welfare state has taken significant steps to support the family and, in many advanced political economies, social investment is key at the ideational level. While a micro-level phenomenon, the gender division of housework can be theorised as gendered power relations at a macro-level in culture, economics and politics. Family policy should have equalising effects on housework division, as it affects women's employment and this, in turn, determines time availability and relative bargaining power. It also affects gender-role perceptions (Bolzendahl and Myers, 2004). Thus, family policy should be a key macro-level factor in terms of gendered power relations. The social investment approach, which essentially was to meet social and economic ends, has modernised family policy even in societies like East Asia, where socio-cultural and/or political context is highly gendered.

An (2020) found gender-role ideology and economic dependence did not matter for married Korean women's housework time but they did for Korean men's housework time. Further a husband whose wife's income is more than half of his spent much less time on housework when he had traditional gender-role ideology compared to a husband with the same level of economic dependence holding a progressive ideology. She suggested housework is a type of power practice and whether individuals allocate time on housework based on economic bargaining power and/or gender-role belief is crucial for gender equality in a society where socio-cultural, structural, political and economic context is highly gendered. Thus, in a comparative context, the important question is whether the effects of the macro-level context vary for East Asia and Europe in the division of housework. The next part of the chapter constitutes the empirical analysis. The goal is to determine how formal childcare services and parental leave provisions are related to the gender division of housework, and how this varies across East Asia and Europe.

## Method

### Data and measurement

The study sample was drawn from the ISSP 2012 survey on Changing Family and Gender Roles. It consisted of married women between 20 and 64 years of age from Austria, Belgium, Denmark, Finland, France, West Germany, Ireland, Japan, Korea, the Netherlands, Norway, Portugal, Sweden, Switzerland and the United Kingdom. Those who were in education, apprentices or trainees, permanently sick or disabled, and retired were excluded.

The dependent variable was the division of housework. The ISSP collects information on who does laundry, grocery shopping, cleaning and cooking. The response categories are: (1) always me; (2) usually me; (3) about equal or both of us; (4) usually my spouse/partner; (5) always my spouse/partner. I created an average response value based on which higher values indicated more equal divisions of housework.

The independent variables were time availability, relative income and gender-role ideology. Married women's time availability was measured using information on weekly working hours. The information on who earned more, husbands or wives, was used to measure married women's income relative to their husbands. The ISSP includes seven response categories: (1) my spouse/partner has no income; (2) I have a much higher income; (3) I have a higher income, (4) we have about the same income; (5) my spouse/partner has a higher income; (6) my spouse has a much higher income; (7) I have no income. Responses were scored as follows: 3 for response 1; 2 for response 2; 1 for response 3; 0 for response 4; −1 for response 5; −2 for response 6; −3 for response 7. Higher values indicate stronger relative income power.

Individuals' gender role ideologies were measured by considering survey responses to five statements: (1) a working mother can be as close to her children as a non-working mother; (2) a pre-school child is likely to suffer if his or her mother is working; (3) family life suffers if a woman has a full-time job; (4) what women really want is home and children; (5) a man's job is to earn money and a woman's job is to look after the home. The response categories were: (1) strongly agree; (2) agree; (3) neither agree nor disagree; (4) disagree; (5) strongly disagree. I reversed the response for the first statement and created an additional measurement, where the variable indicates the average value and a higher value indicates progressive gender-role ideology.

The first level co-variates included respondents' age and its squared term to see age effects. It also included information on education collected using the following responses: (0) no formal education; (1) primary school; (2) lower secondary; (3) upper secondary; (4) post-secondary, non-tertiary; (5) lower-level tertiary; (6) upper-level tertiary. Information on health status was collected using the following responses: (1) excellent; (2) very good; (3) good; (4) fair; (5) poor. Those who reported excellent, very good and good health were grouped together (coded 1), and those who reported fair and poor health were grouped together (coded 2). The number of school-level children aged up to 17 years and pre-school children were included, and the number of adults was included following Kleider (2015). Married women's religion was also considered: those who reported being Catholic or Protestant (coded 2), and others (coded 1). The latter included those with no religion. How religious married women were was measured by attendance at religious services: a higher value indicates being more religious.

Analysis at the macro level focused on spending on childcare and education services as a proportion of GDP, drawn from Organisation for Economic Co-operation and Development (OECD) data for 2010, and on the length of parental leave available to mothers, again drawn from OECD data for 2010 (OECD, 2020b; 2020d). To test for a reverse U-shaped effect, it is squared after standardisation. To explore the effect of gendered political power relations, the proportions of women parliamentarians in 2012 was used, obtained from OECD (2020c). The effects of the gender wage gap in 2010 was also tested using OECD data (OECD, 2020e). Finally, gender-role ideology at the macro level was measured using the average value of micro-level gender-role ideology.

Figure 7.1 shows the macro-level factors. In 2010, Japan's spending was lower than Korea's. Korea's spending was between that of Austria and of Belgium. Parental leave was neither too long nor too short in East Asia; the UK, Belgium and Ireland had relatively short parental leave; while Germany, France, Finland and Portugal had longer leave. The proportion of women in parliament was lowest in Japan, followed by Ireland and Korea. The gender wage gap was highest in Korea, followed by Japan. Korean married women held relatively more traditional gender-role attitudes, followed by married women in Austria and Switzerland. In contrast, Japanese women's gender-role ideology was as progressive as that of their counterparts in the UK, Germany, Ireland and France.

The main effects of the macro-level variables on married women's housework division across East Asia and Europe were estimated using HLM. Models were built for European countries and then Japan and Korea were included to identify differences and similarities between Europe and East Asia. Model 1 is a null model indicating whether the gender division of housework needs to be explained by macro-level factors. Model 2 tested the effects of micro-level factors. Models 3, 4, 5, 6, and 7 tested the main effects of public expenditure on ECEC, parental leave length, gender-role ideology, women in parliament and the gender wage gap, respectively.

## Results

Figure 7.2 shows married women's share of housework in 15 countries across East Asia and Europe. Although in all countries, women do most of the housework, the division of housework is most gendered in East Asia, especially in Japan (1.56) and Korea (1.72). Housework

**Figure 7.1:** Public expenditure on ECEC, parental leave length, gender-role ideology, women in parliament and gender wage gap across East Asia and Europe

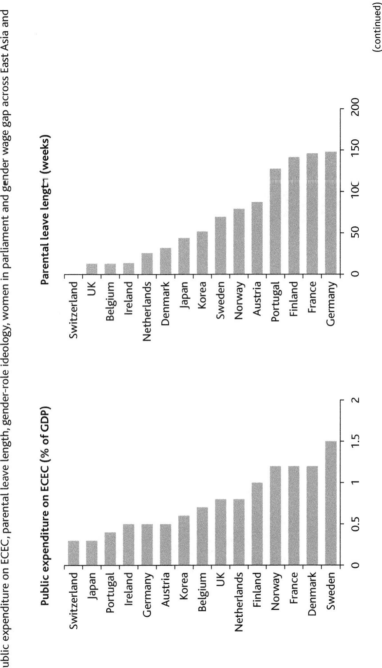

(continued)

**Figure 7.1:** Public expenditure on ECEC, parental leave length, gender-role ideology, women in parliament and gender wage gap across East Asia and Europe (continued)

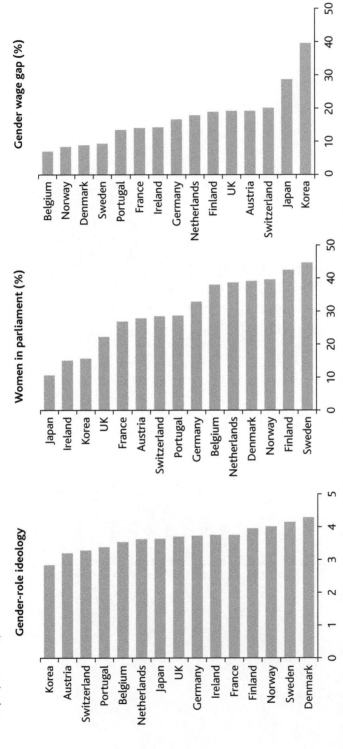

Note: Gender-role ideology is measured by: (1) strongly agree with traditional ideology; (2) agree; (3) neither agree nor disagree; (4) disagree; (5) strongly disagree to a set of five statements about gender roles.

Source: Public expenditure on ECEC (OECD, 2020b); Parental leave length (OECD, 2020d); Gender-role ideology (author's calculation using ISSP 2012 survey, Changing Families and Gender Roles); Women in parliament (OECD, 2020c); Gender wage gap (OECD, 2020e)

**Figure 7.2:** Division of housework for married women

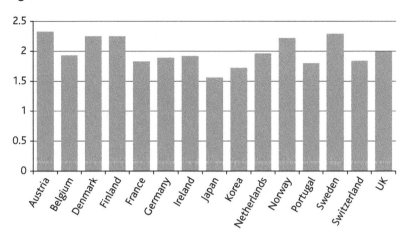

Note: Responses to the question of who does the housework were (1) always me; (2) usually me; (3) about equal or both together; (4) usually my spouse/partner; (5) always my spouse/partner.
Source: Author's calculation using ISSP 2012 Changing Families and Gender Roles

is most equitably divided in Sweden (2.29), Denmark (2.25), Finland (2.25), and Norway (2.22).

Model 1 in Table 7.1 shows that the intraclass correlation coefficient (ICC) of the unconditional model for European countries is 8.5 per cent. Variance in housework division among married women is largely assumed by the micro-level factors, but cross-national variances in housework division need to be explained by contextual factors. Model 2 shows that shorter time availability, stronger relative income power and progressive gender-role ideology are all significant in the division of housework labour, indicating more equal division. Furthermore, the more educated women are, the less housework they do. Although the number of pre-school children is not important, larger numbers of school-level children or of adults correlate with more unequal division. Health status is not a significant factor. Among the macro-level factors, only parental leave provisions is significant (Model 4). It indicates that both too much and too little leave leads to more unequal division of housework.

The two East Asian countries are added to the model in Table 7.2. The ICC indicates that contextual factors explain 11.5 per cent of the variances in married women's share of housework. Model 2 in Table 7.2 indicates that education, gender-role ideology, relative income, number of school-level children and number of adults play the

**Table 7.1:** HLM estimates on the division of housework among married women in 13 countries in Europe

| | Model 1 | Model 2 | Model 3 | Model 4 | Model 5 | Model 6 | Model 7 |
|---|---|---|---|---|---|---|---|
| Intercept | 2.046** | 2.061** | 2.059** | 2.060** | 2.059** | 2.059** | 2.061** |
| | (0.056) | (0.042) | (0.041) | (0.031) | (0.042) | (0.038) | (0.044) |
| Care service expenditure | | | 0.123 | | | | |
| | | | (0.105) | | | | |
| Parental leave length | | | | −0.00004** | | | |
| | | | | (0.00001) | | | |
| Gender-role ideology | | | | | 0.090 | | |
| | | | | | (0.126) | | |
| Women in politics | | | | | | 0.008 | |
| | | | | | | (0.003) | |
| Gender wage gap | | | | | | | 0.004 |
| | | | | | | | (0.008) |
| Age | | −0.012 | −0.012 | −0.012 | −0.012 | −0.011 | −0.012 |
| | | (0.011) | (0.011) | (0.011) | (0.011) | (0.011) | (0.011) |
| Age squared | | 0.00006 | 0.00006 | 0.00006 | 0.00006 | 0.00005 | 0.00006 |
| | | (0.00001) | (0.00001) | (0.00001) | (0.00001) | (0.00001) | (0.00001) |

(continued)

**Table 7.1:** HLM estimates on the division of housework among married women in 13 countries in Europe (continued)

| | Model 1 | Model 2 | Model 3 | Model 4 | Model 5 | Model 6 | Model 7 |
|---|---|---|---|---|---|---|---|
| Education | | 0.048** | 0.048** | 0.048** | 0.048** | 0.047** | 0.048** |
| | | (0.009) | (0.009) | (0.009) | (0.009) | (0.009) | (0.009) |
| Working hours | | 0.004* | 0.004* | 0.004* | 0.004* | 0.004* | 0.004* |
| | | (0.001) | (0.001) | (0.001) | (0.001) | (0.001) | (0.001) |
| Relative income | | 0.073** | 0.072** | 0.071** | 0.072** | 0.072** | 0.073** |
| | | (0.014) | (0.014) | (0.015) | (0.014) | (0.015) | (0.014) |
| Gender-role ideology | | 0.086* | 0.085* | 0.088** | 0.085** | 0.086** | 0.086** |
| | | (0.020) | (0.020) | (0.020) | (0.020) | (0.021) | (0.020) |
| Number of pre-school children | | -0.045 | -0.045 | -0.047* | -0.046* | -0.044 | -0.045 |
| | | (0.023) | (0.023) | (0.023) | (0.023) | (0.023) | (0.023) |
| Number of school-level children | | -0.057** | -0.058** | -0.058** | -0.058** | -0.058** | -0.057** |
| | | (0.014) | (0.014) | (0.014) | (0.014) | (0.014) | (0.014) |
| Number of adults | | -0.047* | -0.047* | -0.048* | -0.047* | -0.047* | -0.047* |
| | | (0.016) | (0.016) | (0.016) | (0.016) | (0.016) | (0.016) |
| Health status | | -0.049 | -0.050 | -0.048 | -0.049 | -0.047 | -0.049 |
| | | (0.036) | (0.036) | (0.036) | (0.036) | (0.036) | (0.036) |

(continued)

179

Table 7.1: HLM estimates on the division of housework among married women in 13 countries in Europe (continued)

| | Model 1 | Model 2 | Model 3 | Model 4 | Model 5 | Model 6 | Model 7 |
|---|---|---|---|---|---|---|---|
| Religion | -0.030 | -0.030 | -0.031 | -0.031 | -0.032 | -0.033 | -0.030 |
| | (0.030) | (0.030) | (0.030) | (0.030) | (0.030) | (0.030) | (0.030) |
| Religious service attendance | | 0.006 | 0.006 | 0.007 | 0.006 | 0.005 | 0.007 |
| | | (0.006) | (0.006) | (0.006) | (0.006) | (0.006) | (0.006) |
| **Random effect** | | | | | | | |
| Time availability slope | | 0.003* | 0.003* | 0.003* | 0.003* | 0.003* | 0.003* |
| | | (0.00001) | (0.00001) | (0.00001) | (0.00001) | (0.00001) | (0.00001) |
| Relative income slope | | 0.038* | 0.040* | 0.041* | 0.040* | 0.041* | 0.040* |
| | | (0.001) | (0.001) | (0.001) | (0.001) | (0.001) | (0.001) |
| Gender–role ideology slope | | 0.045 | 0.046 | 0.041 | 0.046 | 0.049 | 0.044 |
| | | (0.002) | (0.002) | (0.001) | (0.002) | (0.002) | (0.001) |
| ICC | 0.085 | 0.053 | 0.051 | 0.028 | 0.054 | 0.043 | 0.060 |
| Number of cases | 2,452 | 2,452 | 2,452 | 2,452 | 2,452 | 2,452 | 2,452 |

*p<0.5, **p<0.01.

Note: These models were built using full maximum likelihood.

**Table 7.2:** HLM estimates on parameters on the division of housework among married women in 15 countries across East Asia and Europe

| | Model 1 | Model 2 | Model 3 | Model 4 | Model 5 | Model 6 | Model 7 |
|---|---|---|---|---|---|---|---|
| Intercept | | 1.997** | 1.995** | 1.998** | 1.957** | 1.996** | 1.997** |
| | | (0.043) | (0.042) | (0.044) | (0.044) | (0.035) | (0.042) |
| Care service expenditure | | | 0.274* | | | | |
| | | | (0.107) | | | | |
| Parental leave length | | | | -0.00002 | | | |
| | | | | (0.00002) | | | |
| Gender-role ideology | | | | | 0.143 | | |
| | | | | | (0.123) | | |
| Women in politics | | | | | | 0.012* | |
| | | | | | | (0.003) | |
| Gender wage gap | | | | | | | -0.009 |
| | | | | | | | (0.005) |
| Age | | -0.020* | -0.019 | -0.020 | -0.019 | -0.192 | -0.019 |
| | | (0.008) | (0.010) | (0.010) | (0.010) | (0.010) | (0.010) |
| Age squared | | 0.0001 | 0.0001 | 0.0001 | 0.0001 | 0.0001 | 0.0001 |
| | | (0.00009) | (0.0001) | (0.0001) | (0.0001) | (0.0001) | (0.0001) |

(continued)

Table 7.2: HLM estimates on parameters on the division of housework among married women in 15 countries across East Asia and Europe (continued)

| | Model 1 | Model 2 | Model 3 | Model 4 | Model 5 | Model 6 | Model 7 |
|---|---|---|---|---|---|---|---|
| Education | | 0.049** | 0.048** | 0.049** | 0.049** | 0.048** | 0.049** |
| | | (0.007) | (0.008) | (0.008) | (0.008) | (0.008) | (0.008) |
| Gender-role ideology | | 0.079** | 0.076** | 0.080** | 0.078** | 0.077** | 0.079** |
| | | (0.018) | (0.020) | (0.020) | (0.020) | (0.020) | (0.020) |
| Working hours | | 0.003* | 0.003* | 0.003* | 0.003* | 0.003* | 0.003* |
| | | (0.001) | (0.001) | (0.001) | (0.001) | (0.001) | (0.001) |
| Relative income | | 0.072** | 0.072** | 0.072** | 0.071** | 0.071** | 0.071** |
| | | (0.012) | (0.012) | (0.013) | (0.013) | (0.013) | (0.013) |
| Number of pre-school children | | -0.044 | -0.044** | -0.044** | -0.045* | -0.044** | -0.045* |
| | | (0.023) | (0.021) | (0.021) | (0.021) | (0.021) | (0.021) |
| Number of school-level children | | -0.059** | -0.060** | -0.060** | -0.060** | -0.060** | -0.060** |
| | | (0.007) | (0.013) | (0.013) | (0.013) | (0.013) | (0.013) |
| Number of adults | | -0.043* | -0.043* | -0.044* | -0.043* | -0.043* | -0.044* |
| | | (0.010) | (0.014) | (0.014) | (0.014) | (0.014) | (0.014) |
| Health status | | -0.050 | -0.052 | -0.051 | -0.051 | -0.050 | -0.052 |
| | | (0.038) | (0.030) | (0.030) | (0.030) | (0.030) | (0.030) |

(continued)

**Table 7.2:** HLM estimates on parameters on the division of housework among married women in 15 countries across East Asia and Europe (continued)

| | Model 1 | Model 2 | Model 3 | Model 4 | Model 5 | Model 6 | Model 7 |
|---|---|---|---|---|---|---|---|
| Religion | | −0.010 | −0.013 | −0.010 | −0.012 | −0.016 | −0.014 |
| | | (0.033) | (0.028) | (0.002) | (0.023) | (0.028) | (0.028) |
| Religious service attendance | | 0.009 | 0.008 | 0.009 | 0.009 | 0.007 | 0.008 |
| | | (0.005) | (0.006) | (0.006) | (0.005) | (0.006) | (0.006) |
| **Random effect** | | | | | | | |
| Time availability slope | | 0.003* | 0.003* | 0.003* | 0.003* | 0.003* | 0.003* |
| | | (0.00001) | (0.0001) | (0.0001) | (0.0001) | (0.0001) | (0.0001) |
| Relative income slope | | 0.035* | 0.035* | 0.036* | 0.036* | 0.036* | 0.036* |
| | | (0.001) | (0.001) | (0.001) | (0.001) | (0.001) | (0.001) |
| Gender-role ideology slope | | 0.051 | 0.054 | 0.052 | 0.051 | 0.053 | 0.050 |
| | | (0.002) | (0.003) | (0.002) | (0.002) | (0.002) | (0.002) |
| ICC | 0.115 | 0.071 | 0.060 | 0.069 | 0.062 | 0.043 | 0.063 |
| Number of cases | 2,992 | 2,992 | 2,992 | 2,992 | 2,992 | 2,992 | 2,992 |

*p<0.5, **p<0.01.

Note: These models were built using full maximum likelihood.

same role as in the models for European countries shown in Table 7.1. However, in this case, a larger number of pre-school children means unequal housework division.

Models 3–7, analysing the effect of macro-level factors, show spending on care services matters, in that housework division is more equal in a country spending more on childcare and education services. The main effects need to be interpreted with caution, however. Notably, as a proportion of GDP, Korea (0.6) spends more on ECEC than Austria (0.5), Germany (0.5), Ireland (0.5), Portugal (0.4) and Switzerland (0.3) (Figure 7.1), yet the division of housework is more unequal there; the division is 2.33, 1.89, 1.92, 1.8 and 1.84 in Austria, Germany, Ireland, Portugal and Switzerland, respectively. Japan spends the same amount on ECEC as Switzerland but has a more unequal division of housework.

Parental leave does not have a main effect when East Asian countries are added to the model. This suggests the parental leave is an issue for both academic and political debate regarding gender equality in European countries. Parental leave in East Asia is theoretically well designed to have strong equalising effects, but as both countries studied have strongly gendered division of housework, statistically there are no main effects. UK, Ireland and Belgium have relatively short parental leave, which ought to have a negative effect on housework division (Figure 7.1); yet their gender division of housework is more equal than in Japan and Korea.

As the analysis is extended to Japan and Korea, the proportion of women in parliament is the most significant main effect. The result indicates that in a country where women are weakly represented in parliament, the division of housework is likely to be more gendered. As in the European case, however, the macro-level gender-role ideology and the gender wage gap show no effects.

## Conclusion

This chapter comparatively analysed the gender division of housework across East Asia and Europe, and asked how the state's investment in the family might be related to it. The multi-level modelling analyses generate several important findings. First, the results show that housework division is largely influenced by individual-level factors, including education, gender-role ideology, relative income, number of children and number of adults. Second, the cross-national variances in gender division of housework differ by macro-level contextual factors. Specifically, in Europe, married women's share of housework is related to length of parental leave. Cultural, political, and economic contexts do not matter for cross-national differences in the gender division of housework, nor does the degree of state's investment in formal childcare and education services. However, state investment in childcare services shows cross-national differences in the gender division of housework when the two East Asian countries are added to the analysis. The results indicate that public spending on ECEC is lower in a comparative context and the macro level factor is statistically related to gendered division of housework, as married women do almost all of housework in the two East Asian countries. Most importantly, women's proportion in parliament played a role. I suggest the state's investment in family to meet social and economic ends may foster the modernisation of family policy. But the East Asian cases show the limits of modernisation in a country where power relations in politics are highly gendered.

There is little doubt that the social investment idea is powerful enough to modernise family policy, with implications for gender equality at home in the division of housework. As women's political agency evolves, we may expect more investment in ECEC in East Asian countries, as European experience tells us. Yet the East Asian countries, especial Korea, have already made extensive spending increases in ECEC, without much women's political agency. A further increase in public expenditure on ECEC in East Asia may be a feasible social investment, but it is questionable how far more investment in family will lead to equalising effects in the division of housework.

## References

Abendschön, S. and Steinmetz, S. (2014) 'The gender gap in voting revisited: women's party preferences in a European context', *Social Politics*, 21(2): 315–44.

An, M.Y. (2020) 'Economic dependence, gender-role beliefs, and housework hours of husbands and wives in Contemporary Korea', *Journal of Asian Sociology*, 49(2): 193–218.

Becker, G.S. (1991) *A Treatise on the Family* (Enlarged edition), Cambridge, MA: Harvard University Press.

Bianchi, S.M., Milkie, M.A., Sayer, L.C. and Robinson, J.P. (2000) 'Is anyone doing housework? Trends in the gender division of household labor', *Social Forces*, 79(1): 191–222.

Bittman, M., England, P., Sayer, L.C., Folbre, N. and Matheson, G. (2003) 'When does gender trump money? Bargaining and time in household work', *American Journal of Sociology*, 109(1): 186–214.

Blumberg, R.L. (1984) 'A general theory of gender stratification', *Sociological Theory*, 2: 23–101.

Blood, R.O. and Wolfe, D.M. (1965) *Husbands and Wives: The Dynamics of Married Living*, New York: Macmillan.

Bolzendahl, C.I. and Myers, D.J. (2004) 'Feminist attitudes and support for gender equality: opinion change in women and men, 1974–1998', *Social Forces*, 83(2): 759–89.

Bothfeld, S. and Rouault, S. (2015) 'Families facing the crisis: is social investment a sustainable social policy strategy?', *Social Politics*, 22(1): 60–84.

Boling, P. (2015) *The Politics of Work-family Policies: Comparing Japan, France, Germany and the United States*, Cambridge: Cambridge University Press.

Brines, J. (1994) 'Economic dependency, gender and the division of labor at home', *American Journal of Sociology*, 100(3): 652–88.

Esping-Andersen, G., Gallie, D., Hemerijk, A. and Myers, J. (eds) (2002) *Why do We Need a New Welfare State?*, Oxford: Oxford University Press.

Evertsson, M. and Nermo, M. (2004) 'Dependence within family and the division of labor: comparing Sweden and the United States', *Journal of Marriage and Family*, 66(5): 1272–86.

Ellingsaeter, A.L. and Leira, A. (2006) *Politicising Parenthood in Scandinavia: Gender Relations in Welfare States*, Bristol: The Policy Press.

Hofferth, S.L. and Curtin, S.C. (2006) 'Parental leave statutes and maternal return to work after childbirth in the United States', *Work and Occupations*, 33(1): 73–105.

Ferragina, E. and Seeleib-Kaiser, M. (2015) 'Determinants of a silent (r)evolution: understanding the expansion of family policy in rich OECD countries', *Social Politics*, 22(1): 1–37.

Fleckenstein, T. and Lee, S.C. (2017) 'The politics of investing in families: comparing family policy expansion in Japan and South Korea', *Social Politics*, 24(1): 1–28.

Fuwa, M. (2004) 'Macro-level gender inequality and division of household labor in 22 countries', *American Sociological Review*, 69(6): 752–67.

Geist, C. (2005) 'The welfare states and the home: regime differences in the domestic division of labour', *European Sociological Review*, 21(1): 23-41.

Gershuny, J. (2000) *Changing Times: Work and Leisure in Post-industrial Society*, Oxford: Oxford University Press.

Gornick, J.C. and Meyers, M.K. (2003) *Families that Work: Policies for Reconciling Parenthood and Employment*, New York: Russell Sage Foundation.

Hemerijck, A. (ed) (2017) *Uses of Social Investment*, Oxford: Oxford University Press.

Hook, J.L. (2006) 'Care in context: men's unpaid work in 20 countries, 1965–2003', *American Sociological Review*, 71: 639–60.

Iversen, T. and Rosenbluth, F. (2006) 'The political economy of gender: explaining cross-national variation in the gender division of labor and the gender voting gap', *American Journal of Political Science*, 50(1): 1–19.

Jenson, J. (2009) 'Lost in transition: the social investment perspective and gender equality', *Social Politics*, 16(4): 446–83.

Jenson, J. (2012) 'Redesigning citizenship regimes after neoliberalism: moving towards social investment', in N. Morel., B. Palier and J. Palme. (eds) *Towards a Social Investment Welfare State? Ideas, Policies and Challenge*, Bristol: Policy Press, pp 61–90.

Jenson, J. and Saint-Martin, D. (2003) 'New routes to social cohesion? Citizenship and the social investment state', *Canadian Journal of Sociology*, 28(1): 429–51.

Jaumotte, F. (2003) 'Labour force participation of women: empirical evidence on the role of policy and other determinants in OECD countries', *OECD Economic Studies*, 37, Paris: Organisation for Economic Co-operation and Development.

Kamo, Y. (2000) '"He said, she said": Assessing discrepancies in husbands' and wives' reports on the division of household labor', *Social Science Research*, 29(4): 459–76.

Knijn, T. and Kremer, M. (1997) 'Gender and the caring dimension of welfare states: toward inclusive citizenship', *Social Politics*, 4(3): 328–61.

Kleider, H. (2015) 'Paid and unpaid work: the impact of social policies on the gender division of labour', *Journal of European Social Policy*, 25(5): 505–20.

Lee, S.S. and Baek, S. (2014) 'Why the social investment approach is not enough: the female labour market and family policy in the Republic of Korea', *Social Policy and Administration*, 48(6): 686–703.

Morel, N., Palier, B. and Palme, J. (eds) (2012) *Towards a Social Investment Welfare State? Ideas, Policies and Challenges*, Bristol: Policy Press.

Morgan, K. (2012) 'Promoting social investment through work-family policies: which nations do it and why?', in N. Morel., B. Palier and J. Palme. (eds) *Towards a Social Investment Welfare State? Ideas, Policies and Challenge*, Bristol: Policy Press, pp 153–80.

Morgan, K. (2013) 'Path shifting of the welfare state: electoral competition and the expansion of work-family policies in Western Europe', *World Politics*, 65(1): 73–115.

O'Connor, J., Shaver, S. and Orloff, A.S. (1999) *States, Markets, Families: Gender, Liberalism and Social Policy in Australia, Canada and Great Britain*, Cambridge: Cambridge University Press.

OECD (Organisation for Economic Co-operation and Development) (2020a) 'Family database', Paris: OECD.

OECD (Organisation for Economic Co-operation and Development) (2020b) 'Social expenditure', Paris: OECD.

OECD (Organisation for Economic Co-operation and Development) (2020c) 'Women in Parliament', Paris: OECD.

OECD (Organisation for Economic Co-operation and Development) (2020d) 'Gender Equality Data', Paris: OECD.

OECD (Organisation for Economic Co-operation and Development) (2020e) 'Gender wage gap', Paris: OECD.

Peng, I. (2004) 'Postindustrial pressures, political regime shifts, and social policy reform in Japan and South Korea', *Journal of East Asian Studies*, 4(3): 389–425.

Peng, I. (2008) 'Welfare policy reforms in Japan and South Korea: cultural and institutional factors', in W. van Oorschot., M. Opielka and B. Pfau-Effinger (eds) *Culture and Welfare State: Values and Social Policy in Comparative Perspective*, Cheltenham: Edward Elgar, pp 162–82.

Peng, I. (2014) 'The social protection floor and the "New" social investment policies in Japan and South Korea', *Global Social Policy*, 14(3): 389–405.

Pettit, B. and Hook, J. (2005) 'The structure of women's employment in comparative perspective', *Social Forces*, 84(2): 779–801.

Ruhm, C.J. (1998) 'The economic consequences of parental leave mandates', *Quarterly Journal of Economics*, 108(1): 285–317.

Sechiyama, K. (2013) *Patriarchy in East Asia: A Comparative Sociology of Gender*, Boston, MA: Brill.

Studlar, D.T., McAllister, I. and Hayes, B.C. (1998) 'Explaining the gender gap in voting: a cross-national analysis', *Social Science Quarterly*, 79(4): 779–98.

Saraceno, S. (2015) 'A critical look to the social investment approach from a gender perspective', *Social Politics*, 22(2): 257–69.

Schoppa, L. (2010) 'Exit, voice, and family policy in Japan: limited changes despite broad recognition of the declining fertility problem', *Journal of European Social Policy*, 20(5): 422–32.

# 8

# Employment outcomes of social investment in latecomer countries

*Jaehyoung Park*

## Introduction

In the mid-1990s, a new economy marked by the explosive growth of information and communications technology (ICT) is more strongly dependent on the use of knowledge than ever before across advanced capitalist democracies (OECD, 1996). As knowledge is embodied in human beings, the economy places emphasis on human capital investment which generates a highly skilled workforce, especially in the service sector. Post-industrial societies, coupled with the transition to the knowledge-based economy, have faced new social needs and demands in family life and the labour market, which are labelled 'new' social risks. According to Bonoli (2005) and Taylor-Gooby (2004), new social risks are generally related to three factors: (1) the problem of reconciling work and family life (mostly, care for children or frail elderly family members) as a result of the massive labour market participation of women, (2) the risk of being unemployed or paid low wages due to low/obsolete skills, (3) the risk of insufficient protection in social security schemes for workers engaged in atypical jobs like part-time and temporary work. These new social risks most seriously affect vulnerable groups such as low-skilled workers, women and young people. They are different from the 'old' social risks of industrialised economies – the risk of sickness, unemployment and retirement of the male breadwinner – against which protection is available in the form of unemployment insurance and pensions contingent upon full-time employment.

In the process of economic and social transformation, advanced capitalist democracies have modernised their welfare state settlements, especially by developing social investment policies. As such, a social investment perspective is intended, on the one hand, to sustain the knowledge-based economy, where knowledge accumulation of a skilled workforce entails higher productivity and economic growth, and, on the other, to better address new social risks that people face in successive stages of their life courses (Morel et al, 2012). Above all, the idea is based on an understanding that skill development and facilitation of employment are the best responses to workers' needs and the best prevention against the new risks. As a consequence, central to the work-oriented policy tool are active labour market policies (ALMPs) and work–family policies (WFPs). Childcare, for example, is expected to not only allow children to improve cognitive and non-cognitive abilities through high-quality early childhood interventions, but help mothers of young children to engage in paid employment. The role of ALMPs comprises investment in human capital (eg, training) and other services promoting labour market re-entry (eg, counselling jobseekers and direct job creation). In this regard, we can encapsulate the salient traits of social investment policies: (1) investment orientation shift from ex-post remedies towards ex-ante prevention; (2) social-risk orientation shift from old to new social policies; (3) services orientation shift from cash benefits to social services (Vandenbroucke and Vleminckx, 2011; De Deken, 2013).

However, there is a debate as to whether these policies are biased towards or against the vulnerable groups that are more exposed to new social risks. The potentially regressive distributive effects, often referred to as the Matthew effect, mean that work-related social investment policies could be actually profit those already participating in the labour market, but not the unemployed and low-skilled, who are most likely to be in atypical employment (Cantillon, 2011; Ghysels and Van Lancker, 2011; Cantillon and Van Lancker, 2012; Bonoli et al, 2017). The Matthew effect argument, consequently, means that social investment policies favour the employment of middle- and higher-income households rather than low-income households. This suggests that social investment policies in the long run are responsible for the rise of poverty rates and income inequality, especially when they are funded by retrenching social protections (Cantillon, 2011; Cantillon and Van Lancker, 2012). Therefore, we need to investigate the association between social investment policies and employment outcomes, particularly whether social investment policies influence the employment disadvantages of vulnerable groups. Alongside employment, job quality also matters, because employment growth can be directly linked to the rise of poverty rates despite there being no Matthew effect in terms of employment. In other words, if most jobs produced by social investment policies are low-skilled and temporary, employment grows, but it does not reduce poverty; instead it produces in-work poverty. Although Cantillon (2011) negates this association, some scholars deem social investment policies to be associated with the quality of jobs in a negative way (eg, Bosch, 2009; Eichhorst and Marx, 2011; Bonoli, 2012). However, few studies examine how social investment policies are involved in both employment and quality of employment.

This chapter tests the Matthew effect argument with regard to social inequality in employment. Moreover, it analyses whether social investment policies favour low-quality jobs. For the testing of the two dimensions, employment and job quality, this chapter focuses on two particular policy areas: ALMPs and WFPs. The first section briefly introduces the conflicting evidence for the relationship between social investment and employment outcomes in the literature, and suggests reasons why we need to pay more attention to class differentials in employment and job quality, as well as why we need to differentiate between ALMPs and WFPs at the programme level. The second section describes the data and estimation strategy. The follow section then discusses the results and how they meet the argument. The final section summarises the chapter and suggests some political implications.

## Employment outcomes of social investment

### Revisiting 'the paradox of the social investment state'

There is a question as to why growth in employment does not lead to reduction in relative poverty and income inequality across European countries where social investment strategies are promoted through the Lisbon Strategy in 2000. This problem has been labelled 'a paradox of the social investment state' by Cantillon (2011: 432). More specifically, in the countries with a shift in policy from passive social protection to proactive social investment, which is meant to help people who have traditionally been excluded invest in human capital and facilitate (re)entry to the labour market, there is a correlation between social investment and employment growth but, paradoxically, no correlation between social investment and poverty reduction. This is, Cantillon argues, due to the social stratification of employment between households, rather than the higher incidence of low-quality jobs associated with lower pay. Her argument is confirmed by the findings of Corluy and Vandenbroucke (2013) that between 2005 and 2008, employment growth benefitted work-rich households, where some members are already in work, but did not benefit jobless and work-poor households, thereby showing asynchronism between increasing individual employment rates and poverty reduction.

Cantillon (2011) suggests two explanations for the declining redistributive capacity of social investment states. The first explanation is a resource competition hypothesis, according to which social investment states have moved their resources from social protection policies that relied on traditional income support through cash transfers, to work-related and service-oriented social investment policies which are less redistributive. The second explanation is the re-commodification hypothesis: irrespective of the shift of resources, the emphasis on activation and 'making work pay' of social investment policies weakens traditional social protection, especially resulting in retrenchment in unemployment benefits. The former occurs mainly in the non-Nordic welfare states, but the latter refers to all welfare states including Nordic countries (Vandenbroucke and Vleminckx, 2011).

The resource competition explanation is itself based on two hypotheses. The first hypothesis is the crowding-out effect of social investment policies, which means that the expansion of social investment services takes the fiscal space of traditional cash transfers, which are necessary for the most disadvantaged in a society. Although this crowding out argument reveals the underlying politics of the competition and conflict between the two policies (Noël, 2017), most research does not support the first hypothesis of resource competition (eg, Vandenbroucke and Vleminckx, 2011; Van Lancker and Ghysels, 2013; Noël, 2017), except for Ronchi (2018) who finds that spending for social protection was been crowded out after the financial crisis. Hence, scholars explore whether social investment policies have a detrimental effect on their own goals of equality, irrespective of the changes of traditional protection policies, which is the second hypothesis, the so-called Matthew effect hypothesis.

## Social investment and the Matthew effect

The Matthew effect hypothesis is that social investment policies disproportionately benefit the middle class at the expense of more vulnerable groups (Cantillon, 2011; Cantillon and Van Lancker, 2012; Bonoli et al, 2017). It cites a verse of the Gospel according to St. Matthew (Matthew 25:29): 'For to everyone who has will more be given, and he will have abundance; but from him who has not, even what he has will be taken away'. Although the proponents of the Matthew effect theory focus on a social bias in access to ALMPs and childcare (eg, Van Lancker and Ghysels, 2013; Bonoli et al, 2017), a more explicit example is parental leave. This programme is designed only for participants in the labour market, and low-educated workers working in atypical and low-skilled jobs are less likely to use it.

A number of studies have tested the Matthew effect argument. Some of the research analyses the impact of social investment policies on the equality of outcomes. The underlying assumption here is that if the hypothesis is valid, the expansion of social investment policies will be associated with increases in relative poverty and income inequality. Quantitative micro-analysis on data from European Union Statistics on Income and Living Conditions (EU-SILC) reveals little evidence of this (Verbist et al, 2012; Vaalavuo, 2013; Rovny, 2014; Verbist and Matsaganis, 2013; Burgoon, 2017). For instance, Verbist et al (2012), based on EU-SILC for 2007 and other OECD data, find that publicly provided service benefits (ie, education, healthcare, social housing, childcare and elderly care) contribute to reducing poverty and income inequality in 27 OECD countries and the redistributive effects are larger for poorer groups. This is also confirmed in Vaalavuo (2013). Using the same dataset, Vaaluvo argues that 'new' social spending (childcare, education and elderly care) is more equally distributed among income quintiles than 'old' social spending (unemployment benefits, old age pension and healthcare). Verbist and Matsaganis (2013), using EU-SILC 2007 data for 21 EU countries, show that social investment policies (ie, the total spending of childcare, education and healthcare) have redistributive effects, but these are smaller than for cash transfers. Narrowing down the analysis to ALMPs and childcare, and employing static logit regression analysis on 18 OECD countries around 2004, Rovny (2014) finds more spending on ALMPs and childcare generated lower poverty risk among those with lower education levels. This is also supported by Burgoon (2017), who showed, based on the EU-SILC dataset between 2004 and 2011 for 27 EU member states, that ALMPs correlate negatively with poverty risk of less-skilled males aged 55−64.

Contrary to static evaluations based on micro-data, recent time-series and cross-sectional (TSCS) studies using aggregate data provide conflicting results for the hypothesis (Taylor-Gooby et al, 2015; Van Vliet and Wang, 2015; Hemerijck et al, 2016). For instance, Taylor-Gooby et al (2015) show that ALMPs are linked to lower employment and higher poverty rate in 17 European countries over the years 2001−7, while social investment policies including ALMPs were found by Van Vliet and Wang (2015) to reduce poverty and income inequality for 15 European countries between 1997 and 2007.

Other scholars investigate inequality of access to the services, especially whether the vulnerable suffer from much difficulty in the use of social investment services. There is good evidence of the unequal access to childcare from several studies using micro-data from EU-SILC (Van Lancker and Ghysels, 2012, 2013; Van Lancker, 2013; Bonoli et al, 2017; Campbell et al, 2018; Van Lancker, 2018). For instance, in in-depth case studies of the Flanders region in Belgium, Van Lancker and Ghysels (2012, 2013) show a bias in childcare and parental leave use towards higher-income households. Van Lancker (2013, 2018) also draws a similar conclusion, finding that children with high-income parents (fifth income quintile) benefit more from childcare services more than those with low-income parents (first income quintile) across more than 20 European countries. This holds true for ALMPs where low-skilled workers are underrepresented in terms of participation in programmes (Bonoli and Liechti, 2018).

Taken as a whole, despite a growing number of studies on the effects of social investment policies, the results are inconsistent and unclear in terms of the effects on employment, the main focus of attention in this chapter. Not only do the results depend on the research methods used and social investment policies investigated, they also depend on the scope of countries and time periods studied. The research on equality outcomes of social investment negate the presence of the Matthew effect in employment, but the shape of access biases reveals a likelihood that the unequal use of social investment services may result in the social stratification of work intensity between households, as suggested by Cantillon (2011). This is why we need to take stock of the relationship between social investment policies and employment effect.

## Social investment and job quality

In addition to the impact on employment, we need to analyse the impact of social investment policies on job quality. Even if the policies successfully boost labour force participation and employment for the vulnerable, we cannot take for granted the expectation that employment growth gives rise to desirable distributive performance. Instead, the policies might be responsible for generating low-quality jobs and thereby in-work poverty. This is because working in low-skilled and insecure jobs contributes less to acquisition of higher skills and long-term accumulation of human capital, so precarious workers easily face the risk of unemployment and lose opportunities to improve upward social mobility (Gallie, 2002). Moreover, because those jobs are more likely to be poorly paid than are full-time or permanent jobs, they do not provide substantial, sufficient and steady sources of income (Grzegorzewska and Thévenot, 2014). This may bring about in-work poverty, lower unemployment benefits when out of work and lower pension entitlements after retirement. In this regard, it is important to assess the quality of employment generated by social investment policies as much as the quantity, although Cantillon (2011) argues that job quality is not an issue given the finding that in-work poverty as well as pre-transfer poverty remain largely unchanged.

So what is the impact of social investment policies on job quality? From the perspective of social investment, it is obvious that the desired employment outcomes should be good-quality jobs, not merely more jobs. 'More and better jobs', the agenda of the European Employment Strategy (EES) – part of the Lisbon Strategy in the 2000 European Council – also clarifies this statement. ALMPs, especially training, have a potential to lower the risk of skill obsolescence and increase the likelihood of meeting the demand for skilled labour. Childcare can be also expected to have positive effects on mothers' attachment to the labour market as they become freer from family responsibilities, thereby increasing the probability of not being employed in part-time and/or fixed-term jobs.

On the contrary, some forms of ALMPs with an emphasis on helping the unemployed to return to work quickly may push participants into low-skilled, low-paid and insecure employment. Because such programmes do not help human capital development in the life course, workers can become trapped in a cycle of low-quality jobs and unemployment. Bosch (2009) highlights the adverse effects of ALMPs (especially job-search assistance and monitoring programmes) that put pressure on participants to accept low-wage work in the United States, the United Kingdom and Germany with a 'work-first' model that is characterised by a short duration of unemployment benefits, low net replacement rate and weak ALMPs. Eichhorst and Marx (2011) show that the strong activation supported by Germany's Hartz reforms between 2002 and 2005 allowed growth in the scope of atypical jobs. Thus we cannot assume that both 'more' and 'better' jobs will be automatically achieved at the same time by ALMPs.

Despite the criticality of job quality, there is no literature on analysing the relationship between social investment policies and the incidence of precarious employment. Although Nelsen and Stephens (2012) show that high-quality jobs, measured as jobs in knowledge-intensive services according to the Eurostat classification, are positively associated with social investment, they do not look into the impact on non-standard employment. Social investment policies might be responsible for generating low-quality jobs and thereby the (in-work) poverty trends, or they might be able to get individuals into good-quality work, thereby reducing segmentation or dualisation of labour markets. This is why we need to incorporate job quality into assessments of social investment effects.

## The potential multi-dimensionality of social investment

As we have shown, many studies on the effectiveness of social investment policies go from one extreme to another with respect to choosing a range of social investment policies – either clubbing all policies together, or focusing on one specific policy. This might attenuate the true value of social investment outcomes because it ignores the possibility of the effects being in the opposite direction between policies as well as the possibility of policies excluded in the model affecting outcomes.

The impact of ALMPs and WFPs on labour market outcomes is likely to vary depending on the programmes. According to Bonoli (2010, 2012), ALMPs encompass different policy tools: (1) training programmes that raise the human capital of jobless people whose skills are obsolete (these are most developed in the Nordic countries); (2) direct job creation. which prevents the depletion of human capital by creating public sector jobs (used mainly by Continental European countries); (3) incentive reinforcement, or in-work benefits and sanctions, which force recipients not to settle for unemployment; and (4) employment assistance, such as counselling and matching services, which increase the likelihood of the unemployed quickly finding a job (began in English-speaking countries, but have become common everywhere). The same holds true for WFPs. The main locus of the extension of WFPs is childcare, but maternity and parental leave also seem to have a Matthew effect. It may negatively affect employment of low-skilled workers who have little chance to use the programme, even if they are employed, due to poor working conditions (Del Boca et al, 2009). Therefore, we need to disaggregate ALMPs and WFPs at the programme level in order to better interpret how the impacts of ALMPs and WFPs vary across different types of programmes. Figures 8.1 and 8.2 show the recalibration of ALMPs and WFPs as a percentage of GDP at the programme level across the 11 European countries being studied in this chapter. We can see different trends in the configuration between programmes even within individual countries.

Among ALMPs and WFPs, this chapter focus on training and childcare as major elements of social investment policies. From the perspective of social investment, training is most likely to contribute to human capital accumulation, while childcare can contribute to

**Figure 8.1:** ALMP programmes in 11 European countries, 1990–2013

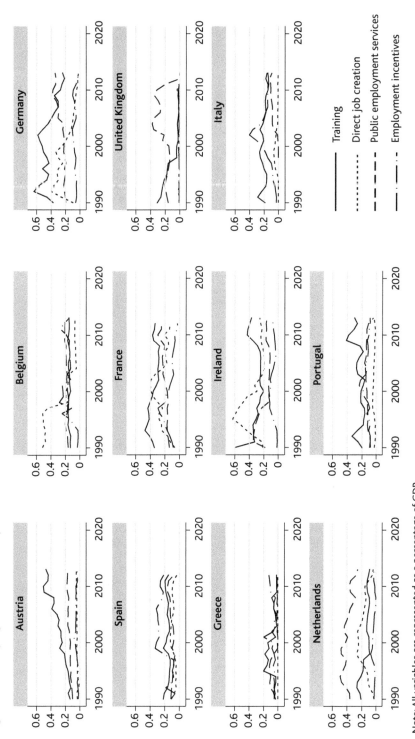

Note: All variables are represented as a percentage of GDP.

Source: OECD Social Expenditure (SOCX) database

**Figure 8.2:** WFP programmes in 11 European countries, 1990–2013

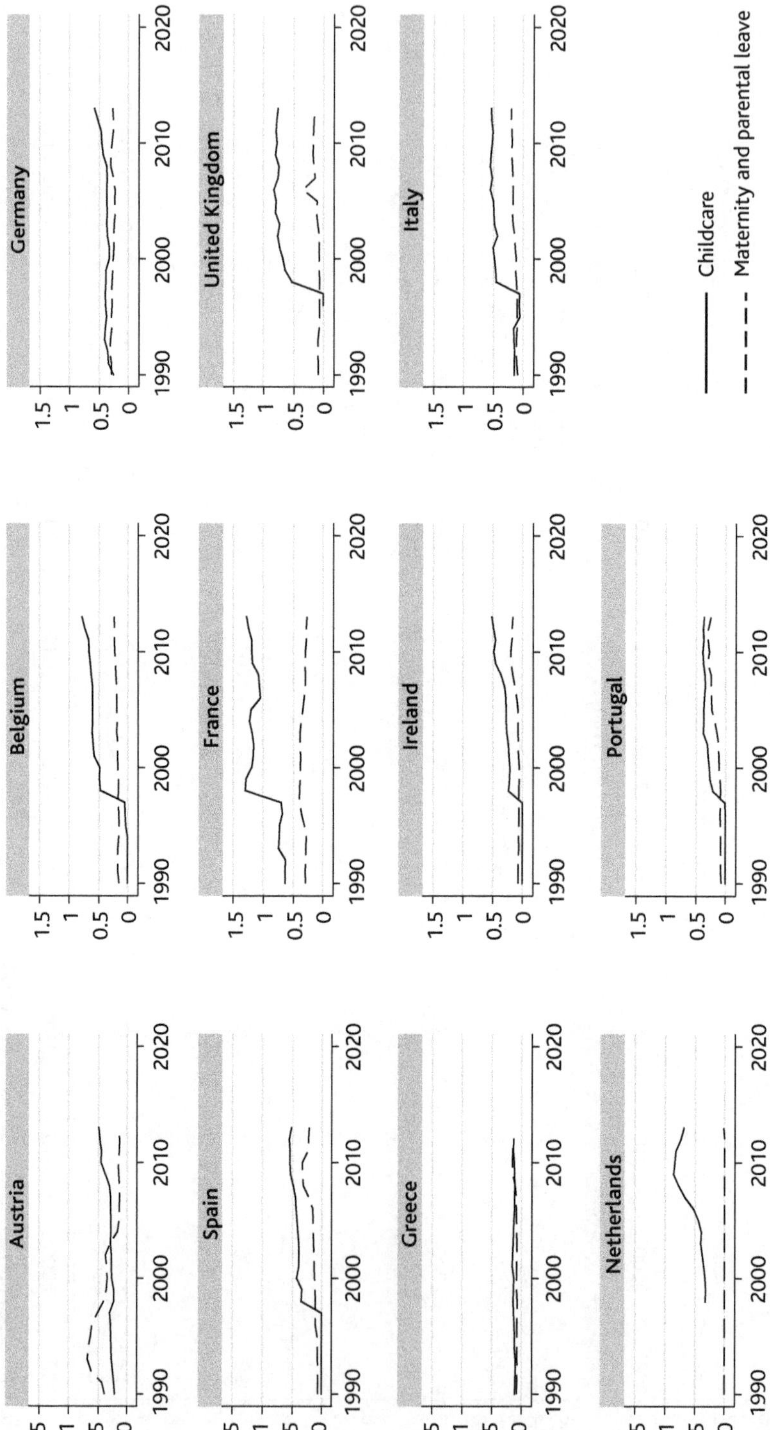

Note: All variables are represented as a percentage of GDP.

Source: OECD Social Expenditure (SOCX) database

making its efficient use by helping mothers participate in the labour market and reconciling paid work and family life. Other ALMPs and maternity/parental leave policies are expected to have different effects on employment, especially for low-skilled workers.

## Data and estimation strategy

To analyse the effectiveness of ALMPs and WFPs on employment and job quality, this chapter focuses on 11 advanced industrialised European countries from 1992 to 2013: Austria, Belgium, France, Germany, Greece, Ireland, Italy, the Netherlands, Portugal, Spain and the United Kingdom, while Nordic countries such as Denmark, Finland, Norway and Sweden are excluded. This is because literature on the Matthew effect describes the adverse effect as particularly pronounced in non-Nordic countries, which are latecomers to the social investment strategy – Continental and Southern European, and Anglo-Saxon countries (eg, Bonoli et al, 2017). By contrast, the Matthew effect does not seem to be strong in the Nordic welfare states, which are pioneers where the high level of social investment yields higher employment rates of low-educated workers, and thus lower poverty rate and income inequality. Therefore, directly analysing the extent to which the impact of social investment policies on employment outcomes is socially stratified in the latecomer countries helps us get a better understanding of the relationship between social investment policies and equality outcomes.

For dependent variables, we employ two different groups of measures of labour market outcomes. The first analysis of the Matthew effect in employment uses total employment rates and female employment rates by education level from the OECD World Indicators of Skills for Employment (WISE). Based on the International Standard Classification of Education (ISCED 2011), the OECD WISE provides employment rates for low-educated (ISCED levels 0–2: early childhood education to lower secondary education), medium-educated (ISCED levels 3–4: upper secondary education to post-secondary non-tertiary education), and highly educated workers (ISCED levels 5–8: tertiary education) for both sexes. In the analysis of job quality, we use the OECD Labour Force Statistics (LFS) data on the share of full-time jobs, involuntary part-time jobs, temporary jobs and low-skilled jobs out of the total number of jobs in a country. The line between part-time and full-time employment is 30 hours a week, based on the OECD LFS. Involuntary part-time jobs are jobs where people who want full-time employment are trapped in part-time jobs. Temporary jobs are the ones conditioned on fixed-term contracts. The OECD LFS does not provide data by education level. As the OECD WISE provides the employment rate of low-educated workers for temporary jobs, instead, we are limited to checking job quality for the most vulnerable group.

The main explanatory variables are six expenditures on ALMPs and WFPs as a percentage of GDP at the programme level: training, public employment services (PES), direct job creation, employment incentives, childcare and maternity/parental leave, which are extracted from the OECD Social Expenditure (SOCX) database. In order to deal with the problem that the expenditures might be affected by unemployment rates and the change of child population from birth to age 5 years old, they are divided by unemployment rate and 0–5 population ratio, respectively (eg, Nelsen and Stephens, 2012; Abrassart, 2015; Hemerijck et al, 2016; Burgoon, 2017).

As control variables for institutional, economic and demographic factors on the labour market, we include unemployment benefits, union density, coordination of wage bargaining, employment protection indicators for regular and temporary workers, output gap, openness, payroll taxes, population ratio of those aged 0–15 years and those over 64 years old. In the first analysis, we add the share of occupations fitting each skill level to exclude demand-side variation that could affect employment rates regardless of social investment policies. The data on the control variables are extracted from OECD's many databases (ie, SOCX, Economic Outlook, Revenue Statistics and Employment Protection), ICTWSS (Database on Institutional Characteristics of Trade Unions, Wage Setting, state Intervention and Social Pacts), and UN World Population.

The analytic technique used in the panel data analysis is the one-step System Generalised Method of Moments (GMM) estimator suggested by Arellano and Bover (1995) and Blundell and Bond (1998). The logic of choosing the estimator in our analysis is as follows. First, most of the regressors in macroeconomic models are not likely to be strictly exogenous so that they are correlated with the error term, leading to the endogeneity problem. To address the problem, one needs to search for adequate instruments for the regressors. However, this is a huge challenge in macroeconomic variables. Instead, we employ the dynamic panel model in which the lagged dependent variable is included in the right-hand side of the equation. GMM estimators in the dynamic panel model use the lagged dependent variables as instruments for past values of the regressors, thereby managing the endogeneity. Second, the System GMM estimator allowing for more instruments through a system combining the first-differenced equations and the levels equations is consistent and more efficient than the Difference GMM estimator proposed by Arellano and Bond (1991) when time series data in short sample periods are persistent over time (Blundell and Bond, 1998). As variables used in our model, especially employment rate and social expenditure, are highly persistent, we employ the System GMM estimator. It has also shown that although two-step estimators are more efficient than one-step estimators, two-step System GMM estimators can have an extremely downward bias in small sample sizes (Blundell and Bond, 1998). Therefore we decided to use the one-step System GMM estimator in our model. In order to evaluate the robustness of the estimators, we employ two model specification tests: the Hansen test of over-identifying restrictions to check the validity of the instruments and the Arellano-Bond tests for AR(1) and AR(2) to check the presence of first-order and second-order serial correlations in the error term of the first-differenced equation.

## Results

In Table 8.1, one-step System GMM estimates covering total employment rate and female employment rate by education level are reported in columns 1−6. Training has a positive and statistically significant impact only on the total employment rate for medium-educated workers and on the employment rate for medium-educated female workers. According to the estimates, more specifically, for every one unit rise in training, there is an increase of 0.340 per cent points of the medium-educated total employment rate at a 5 per cent significance level and 0.288 per cent points of the medium-educated female employment rate at a 0.1 per cent significance level. The significant and positive impact of childcare exists only on the employment rate of medium-educated female workers. This implies that the employment effect of childcare is significantly larger for women than men. Training and childcare does not significantly affect employment rate for low-educated and highly educated (female) workers. Thus, higher levels of training and childcare probably benefit the middle class, suggesting the social investment policies have a Matthew effect.

Examining the other ALMPs and WFPs, PES has a positive and significant effect on employment and the effect is larger for low-educated workers. In contrast, maternity and parental leave seem to have a quasi-Matthew effect in that the detrimental effect on employment is larger for low-educated workers. Direct job creation

**Table 8.1:** Estimated effects on employment rates by educational attainments

| | Dependent variables | | | | | |
|---|---|---|---|---|---|---|
| | Low-educated workers | | Medium-educated workers | | High-educated workers | |
| Independent variables | (1) Total | (2) Women | (3) Total | (4) Women | (5) Total | (6) Women |
| Training | -0.208 | -0.052 | 0.340* | 0.288*** | 0.075 | 0.089 |
| Childcare | 0.056 | 0.028 | 0.104 | 0.172* | 0.072 | 0.055 |
| Public employment services | 0.518** | 0.379* | 0.320** | 0.231 | 0.389** | 0.333*** |
| Direct job creation | -0.064 | -0.079 | -0.047 | -0.067 | -0.194* | -0.207* |
| Employment incentives | 0.271 | 0.061 | 0.030 | -0.105 | 0.211 | 0.192 |
| Maternity and parental leave | -0.343† | -0.178 | 0.127 | 0.109 | -0.135 | -0.135 |
| Unemployment benefits | -0.090† | -0.055 | -0.021 | -0.008 | -0.066 | -0.065 |
| Union density | -0.077† | -0.058 | -0.055† | -0.079*** | 0.072 | 0.098* |
| Coordination of wage bargaining | 0.649*** | 0.275† | 0.795*** | 0.678** | 0.343† | 0.246 |
| Regular EPL | 1.097 | 0.773 | -0.597 | 0.368 | 0.029 | -0.333 |
| Temporary EPL | 0.041 | -0.129 | -0.376 | -0.425 | -0.040 | 0.159 |
| Output gap | 0.264*** | 0.169** | 0.222*** | 0.178*** | 0.180*** | 0.192*** |
| Openness | 0.004 | 0.006 | 0.024* | 0.023* | 0.013 | 0.010 |
| Payroll taxes | -0.109 | -0.011 | -0.035 | -0.033 | 0.178* | 0.080 |

(continued)

**Table 8.1:** Estimated effects on employment rates by educational attainments (continued)

| | Dependent variables | | | | | |
|---|---|---|---|---|---|---|
| | Low-educated workers | | Medium-educated workers | | High-educated workers | |
| Independent variables | (1) Total | (2) Women | (3) Total | (4) Women | (5) Total | (6) Women |
| Under-15 population | 0.266 | 0.018 | 0.143 | 0.154 | -0.145 | 0.111 |
| Over-64 population | 0.185 | 0.063 | 0.416 | 0.179 | -0.102 | 0.232 |
| Low-skilled jobs | 0.004 | 0.055 | | | | |
| Medium-skilled jobs | | | 0.156** | 0.088** | | |
| Highly-skilled jobs | | | | | -0.042 | -0.023 |
| Total employment rate | 0.699*** | | 0.695*** | | 0.659*** | |
| Female employment rate | | 0.819*** | | 0.764*** | | 0.777*** |
| Constant | 0.004 | 3.139 | 2.390 | 2.170 | 27.212** | 8.037 |
| Observations | 193 | 193 | 193 | 193 | 193 | 193 |
| Number of countries | 11 | 11 | 11 | 11 | 11 | 11 |
| Hansen test (p-value) | (1.000) | (1.000) | (1.000) | (1.000) | (1.000) | (1.000) |
| AR(1) test (p-value) | (0.105) | (0.039) | (0.081) | (0.031) | (0.079) | (0.027) |
| AR(2) test (p-value) | (0.221) | (0.199) | (0.381) | (0.771) | (0.183) | (0.709) |

† $p<0.1$, * $p<0.05$, ** $p<0.01$, *** $p<0.001$.

Notes: Command used to obtain estimates of one-step robust System GMM is *xtabond2* in Stata 15, written by David Roodman (2009). Heteroscedasticity-consistent standard errors for sample are in parentheses. The values reported for the Hansen test are the p-values for the null hypothesis that the instrumental variables are uncorrelated with the residuals. The values reported for the AR(1) and AR(2) tests are the p-values for the null hypothesis of no first-order and second-order serial correlation in the first-differenced residuals, respectively.

and employment incentives have no significant impact on low–educated workers, against expectations, nor do they suggest any Matthew effect. Taken together with the estimates of training and childcare, instead of helping low–educated workers reintegrate into the labour market, ALMPs and WFPs may reinforce employment inequality.

Next we assess the effectiveness of ALMPs and WFPs in the dimension of job quality in Table 8.2. In general, the findings show a neutral or positive impact of the social investment policies on job quality (columns 1–4). Higher training efforts significantly decrease employment in involuntary part-time jobs and temporary jobs, but the impacts on employment in both full-time jobs and low-skilled jobs are not significant. Childcare and direct job creation are not associated with job quality, while PES decreases temporary jobs, while employment incentives increase full-time jobs but decrease involuntary part-time jobs. Unlike the impact on employment rate, maternity and parental leave leads to increased likelihood of working in full-time jobs and additionally helps workers avoid temporary jobs. This evidence suggests that mandated paid leave schemes (especially with employment protection) enable parents to reduce the risk of having to unwillingly change from regular jobs to part-time or temporary jobs in order to spend more time with their infants.

When we focus on job quality issues for the vulnerable (columns 5 and 6), PES and direct job creation appear to be more conducive to reducing temporary jobs for low-educated workers. The decline in the share of low-educated workers in temporary jobs does not necessarily mean that low-educated workers move into permanent jobs. This may result from the relative rise of medium- and high-educated workers in fixed-term contract jobs because the variable provided from OECD WISE is defined as persons in temporary employment as a proportion of all employees. However, given the fact that PES significantly reduces employment in temporary jobs, direct job creation has no association with the incidence of temporary jobs (column 3) and these policies do not significantly reduce the employment rate of low-educated workers (columns 1 and 2 in Table 8.1), one could infer a positive impact on the job quality for low-educated workers to some extent. When it comes to ALMPs, the concern that activation tools might push participants into any available low-quality jobs is unfounded in terms of non-standard employment.

In sum, it is clear that higher expenditures on social investment policies are not related to the recent upward trend in atypical employment and to the rising dualisation between labour market insiders and outsiders, at least in terms of job quality. They rather

**Table 8.2:** Estimated effects on job quality

| | | | Dependent variables | | | |
|---|---|---|---|---|---|---|
| Independent variables | (1) Full-time jobs | (2) Involuntary part-time jobs | (3) Temporary jobs | (4) Low-skilled jobs | (5) Temporary jobs for low-educated workers | (6) Temporary jobs for low-educated female workers |
| Training | 0.032 | −0.071** | −0.369† | −0.041 | −0.082 | −0.179 |
| Childcare | −0.004 | −0.031 | 0.013 | −0.006 | −0.027 | 0.006 |
| Public employment services | 0.035 | −0.057 | −0.186† | −0.104 | −0.130* | −0.187* |
| Direct job creation | −0.052 | −0.062 | 0.099 | −0.067 | −0.268** | −0.133 |
| Employment incentives | 0.134** | −0.072† | −0.080 | −0.050 | −0.211 | −0.143 |
| Maternity and parental leave | 0.151* | 0.021 | −0.339* | 0.016 | −0.217 | −0.372 |
| Unemployment benefits | −0.013 | 0.014 | −0.002 | 0.068* | −0.000 | 0.027 |
| Union density | 0.005 | −0.009 | −0.004 | −0.063† | −0.057 | −0.061 |
| Coordination of wage bargaining | 0.060 | −0.086 | −0.104 | −0.021 | −0.133 | −0.185 |
| Regular EPL | −0.095 | −0.468 | 0.787** | 0.052 | 0.609 | 0.964* |
| Temporary EPL | 0.606*** | −0.200* | −0.497* | 0.349† | −0.708** | −0.568* |
| Output gap | 0.048** | −0.043** | 0.077 | 0.008 | 0.121† | 0.172* |
| Openness | −0.000 | −0.000 | 0.003 | 0.009* | 0.009 | 0.003 |

(continued)

**Table 8.2:** Estimated effects on job quality (continued)

| Independent variables | (1) Full-time jobs | (2) Involuntary part-time jobs | (3) Temporary jobs | (4) Low-skilled Jobs | (5) Temporary jobs for low-educated workers | (6) Temporary jobs for low-educated female workers |
|---|---|---|---|---|---|---|
| | | | Dependent variables | | | |
| Payroll taxes | −0.111* | 0.014 | 0.171* | −0.194* | 0.374** | 0.349* |
| Under-15 population | 0.181 | −0.087 | −0.286 | 0.127 | −0.184 | −0.252 |
| Over-64 population | 0.159 | −0.084 | −0.293** | 0.394* | −0.437† | −0.306 |
| Full-time jobs | 0.910*** | | | | | |
| Involuntary jobs | | 0.984*** | | | | |
| Temporary jobs | | | 0.934*** | | 0.855*** | 0.798*** |
| Low-skilled jobs | | | | 0.793*** | | |
| Constant | 1.034 | 5.551** | 10.325 | −1.481 | 12.069* | 11.868 |
| Observations | 212 | 205 | 210 | 199 | 193 | 193 |
| Number of countries | 11 | 11 | 11 | 11 | 11 | 11 |
| Hansen test ($p$-value) | (1.000) | (1.000) | (1.000) | (1.000) | (1.000) | (1.000) |
| AR(1) test ($p$-value) | (0.009) | (0.008) | (0.010) | (0.005) | (0.017) | (0.023) |
| AR(2) test ($p$-value) | (0.488) | (0.854) | (0.271) | (0.248) | (0.317) | (0.272) |

Notes: see Table 8.1.

seem to contribute to restraining the growth of such jobs. Our results thus support the presumption that social investment policies fail to reduce relative poverty because the job growth generated by those policies is socially stratified, biased against low-income households, rather than because they necessarily tend to increase the non-standard employment associated with lower pay (Cantillon, 2011).

The validity of GMM estimates is verified by various tests. The Hansen tests for over-identifying restrictions indicate that the instruments employed are valid. The Arellano-Bond tests for autocorrelation generally identify high first-order serial correlation (although the $p$-value reported for $AR(1)$ in total employment rate for low-educated workers is very close to significance, $p = 0.105$) but not second order correlation in the error terms. In sum, these test statistics confirm a proper specification for the System GMM reported in each column of Tables 8.1 and 8.2.

## Conclusion

In sum, social investment policies, especially training and childcare, have a Matthew effect in that they help medium-educated workers more than poorly and highly educated workers. The latter two groups do not significantly benefit from training and childcare, probably for different reasons. For highly educated workers already participating in the labour market and being at less risk of job loss due to their high skills, training and childcare do not seem to provide additional employment. In contrast, low-educated workers, due to a lack of cognitive and non-cognitive skills, are likely to have less ability to participate in training programmes and make the most of opportunities for employment through them (Abrassart, 2013; Bonoli and Liechti, 2018). In terms of childcare, low-educated workers, especially women, tend to choose unpaid work because they have trouble getting jobs due to their low skills. The additional costs of using childcare services are also often unaffordable for the low-income family (Van Lancker and Ghysels, 2012; Abrassart and Bonoli, 2015). These problems are most severe in the latecomer countries that have inefficient training programmes and no universal childcare services. In terms of job quality, this chapter shows that there are no tangible grounds for suspicion that jobs created by social investment are mainly involuntary part-time, temporary, low-skilled jobs in which low-educated workers are much more likely to be hired. This result supports the idea of Cantillon (2011) that the recent rise of poverty and income inequality is because employment benefits from social investment do not tend to flow more to low-educated workers, not because social investment increases in-work poverty associated with jobs of low quality.

These results yield the following policy implications. First, welfare states must fine-tune social investment programmes to benefit more low-income workers. For low-income women and low-skilled workers, governments should make proper investments in improving both the accessibility of childcare services and the effectiveness of employment programmes, including training. The accessibility of childcare includes both availability and affordability. Lack of centre-based childcare and presence of additional fees for services put low-income workers at a disadvantage. When it comes to ALMPs, street-level civil servants who are in charge of ALMP programmes tend to prefer higher-educated workers who are more efficient in getting jobs in the short term. This hinders low-skilled (or low-educated) workers from participating in ALMPs, especially training, which takes more time to be effective than other programmes. To overcome this problem, governments should prioritise the needs of low-educated households for high-quality and affordable childcare services, and target more ALMP resources on low-skilled workers who are more likely to suffer from an access bias. Properly designed and configured, social investment can have a very clear redistributive effect.

Second, our analysis suggests that welfare states should not rely on social investment policies alone to fight poverty and income inequality for the lowest income groups. If welfare states facing budget constraints enact social investment policies at the expense of income protection for the poor, it will only aggravate the redistributive outcomes. Accordingly, social investment should be complemented by traditional social protections, such as passive income support, what Hemerijck (2017) terms the 'buffer' function. Put differently, the effectiveness of social investment will be greater for low-income groups when governments provide them with a package deal, allowing them to build the necessary capabilities using income protection (Morel et al, 2012).

One problem is a lack of the necessary political support for 'new' investments. The educated middle-classes benefitting more from training and childcare are the most politically important constituency and are not very likely to support a change from the status quo, which would reduce their benefits. Politicians and governments do not seem to undertake reforms that create additional budget pressures to avoid a zero-sum game among social classes. Social investment does not come cheap. If and only if it is properly designed and packaged, will social investment yield both economic and social returns.

# References

Abrassart, A. (2013) 'Cognitive skills matter: the employment disadvantage of low-educated workers in comparative perspective', *European Sociological Review*, 29(4): 707−19.

Abrassart, A. (2015) 'Low-skill jobs or jobs for low-skilled workers? An analysis of the institutional determinants of the employment rates of low-educated workers in 19 OECD countries, 1997−2010', *Journal of European Social Policy*, 25(2): 225−41.

Abrassart, A. and Bonoli, G. (2015) 'Availability, cost or culture? Obstacles to childcare services for low-income families', *Journal of Social Policy*, 44(4): 787−806.

Arellano, M. and Bond, S. (1991) 'Some tests of specification for panel data: Monte Carlo evidence and an application to employment equations', *Review of Economic Studies*, 58(2): 277−97.

Arellano, M. and Bover, O. (1995) 'Another look at the instrumental variable estimation of error-components models', *Journal of Econometrics*, 68(1): 29–51.

Blundell, R. and Bond, S. (1998) 'Initial conditions and moment restrictions in dynamic panel data models' *Journal of Econometrics*, 87(1): 115–43.

Bonoli, G. (2005) 'The politics of the new social policies: providing coverage against new social risks in mature welfare states', *Policy & Politics*, 33(3): 431−49.

Bonoli, G. (2010) 'The political economy of active labor-market policy', *Politics & Society*, 38(4): 435−57.

Bonoli, G. (2012) 'Active labour market policy and social investment: a changing relationship', in M. Nathalie, B. Palier and J. Palme (eds) *Towards a Social Investment Welfare State? Ideas, Policies and Challenges*, Chicago: Policy Press, pp 181−204.

Bonoli, G., Cantillon, B. and Van Lancker, W. (2017) 'Social investment and the Matthew effect: limits to a strategy', in A. Hemerijck (eds) *The Uses of Social Investment*, Oxford: Oxford University Press, pp 66−86.

Bonoli, G. and Liechti, F. (2018) 'Good intentions and Matthew effects: access biases in participation in active labour market policies', *Journal of European Public Policy*, 25(6): 894−911.

Bosch, G. (2009) 'Low-wage work in five European countries and the United States', *International Labour Review*, 148(4): 337−56.

Burgoon, B. (2017) 'Practical pluralism in the empirical study of social investment: examples from active labour-market policy', in A. Hemerijck (eds) *The Uses of Social Investment*, Oxford: Oxford University Press, pp 161−73.

Campbell, T., Gambaro, L. and Stewart, K. (2018) '"Universal" early education: who benefits? Patterns in take-up of the entitlement to free early education among three-year-olds in England', *British Educational Research Journal*, 44(3): 515–38.

Cantillon, B. (2011) 'The Paradox of the social investment state: growth, employment and poverty in the Lisbon era', *Journal of European Social Policy*, 21(5): 432–49.

Cantillon, B. and Van Lancker, W. (2012) 'Solidarity and reciprocity in the social investment state: what can be learned from the case of Flemish school allowances and truancy?', *Journal of Social Policy*, 41(4): 657–75.

Corluy, V. and Vandenbroucke, F. (2013) 'Individual employment, household employment, and risk of poverty in the European Union: a decomposition analysis', in B. Cantillon and F. Vandenbroucke (eds) *Reconciling Work and Poverty Reduction: How Successful are European Welfare States?*, Oxford: Oxford University Press, pp 94–130.

Del Boca, D., Pasqua, S. and Pronzato, C. (2009) 'Motherhood and market work decisions in institutional context: a European perspective', *Oxford Economic Papers*, 61: i147–71.

De Deken, J. (2013) 'Identifying the skeleton of the social investment state', in B. Cantillon and F. Vandenbroucke (eds) *Reconciling Work and Poverty Reduction: How Successful are European Welfare States?*, Oxford: Oxford University Press, pp 260–83.

Eichhorst, W. and Marx, P. (2011) 'Reforming German labour market institutions: a dual path to flexibility', *Journal of European Social Policy*, 21(1): 73–87.

Gallie, D. (2002) 'The quality of working life in welfare strategy', in G. Esping-Andersen (eds) *Why We Need a New Welfare State*, Oxford: Oxford University Press, pp 96–129.

Ghysels, J. and Van Lancker, W. (2011) 'The unequal benefits of activation: an analysis of the social distribution of family policy among families with young children', *Journal of European Social Policy*, 21(5): 472–85.

Grzegorzewska, M. and Thévenot, C. (2014) 'Working-age poverty: what policies help people finding a job and getting out of poverty?', in *Employment and Social Developments in Europe 2013*, Luxembourg: Office for Official Publications of the European Communities, pp 129–71.

Hemerijck, A. (ed) (2017) *The Uses of Social Investment*, Oxford: Oxford University Press.

Hemerijck, A., Burgoon, B., di Pietro, A. and Vydra, S. (2016) *Assessing Social Investment Synergies (ASIS)*, Brussels: European Commission.

Morel, N., Palier, B. and Palme, J. (eds) (2012) *Toward Social Investment Welfare State? Ideas, Policies and Challenges*, Bristol: Policy Press.

Nelsen, M. and Stephens, J.D. (2012) 'Do social investment policies produce more and better jobs?', in N. Morel, B. Palier and J. Palme (eds) *Toward Social Investment Welfare State? Ideas, Policies and Challenges*, Bristol: Policy Press, pp 205–34.

Noël, A. (2017) 'Is social investment inimical to the poor? Or do active labour market and childcare expenditures crowd out income support?', paper presented at the Annual Conference of the Canadian Political Science Association Ryerson University, Toronto, 31 May, pp 1–30.

OECD (Organisation for Economic Co-Operation and Development) (1996) *The Knowledge-Based Economy*, Paris: OECD.

Ronchi, S. (2018) 'Which roads (if any) to social investment? The recalibration of EU welfare states at the crisis crossroads (2000–2014)', *Journal of Social Policy*, 47(3): 459–78.

Roodman, D. (2009) 'How to do xtabond2: an introduction to difference and system GMM in Stata', *Stata Journal*, 9(2): 86–136.

Rovny, A.E. (2014) 'The capacity of social policies to combat poverty among new social risk groups', *Journal of European Social Policy*, 24(5): 405–23.

Taylor-Gooby, P. (2004) 'New risks and social change', in P. Taylor-Gooby (ed) *New Risks, New Welfare: The Transformation of the European Welfare State*, Oxford: Oxford University Press, pp 1–28.

Taylor-Gooby, P., Gumy, J.M. and Otto, A. (2015) 'Can "new welfare" address poverty through more and better jobs?', *Journal of Social Policy*, 44(1): 83–104.

Vandenbroucke, F. and Vleminckx, K. (2011) 'Disappointing poverty trends: is the social investment state to blame?', *Journal of European Social Policy*, 21(5): 450–71.

Vaalavuo, M. (2013) 'The redistributive impact of "old" and "new" social spending', *Journal of Social Policy*, 42(3): 513–39.

Van Lancker, M. (2013) 'Putting the child-centred investment strategy to the test: evidence for the EU27', *European Journal of Social Security*, 15(1): 1–27.

Van Lancker, W. and Ghysels, J. (2012) 'Who benefits? The social distribution of subsidized childcare in Sweden and Flanders', *Acta Sociologica*, 55(2): 125–42.

Van Lancker, W. and Ghysels, J. (2013) 'Who benefits from investment policies? The case of family activation in European countries', in B. Cantillon and F. Vandenbroucke (eds) *Reconciling Work and Poverty Reduction: How Successful are European Welfare States?*, Oxford: Oxford University Press, pp 212–36.

Van Lancker, W. (2018) 'Reducing inequality in childcare service use across European countries: what (if any) is the role of social spending?', *Social Policy and Administration*, 52(1): 271–92.

Verbist, G., Förster, M. and Vaalavuo, M. (2012) 'The impact of publicly provided services on the distribution of resources: review of new results and methods', *OECD Social, Employment and Migration Working Papers*, no. 130, Paris: OECD.

Verbist, G. and Matsaganis, M. (2013) 'The redistributive capacity of services in the European Union', in B. Cantillon and F. Vandenbroucke (eds) *Reconciling Work and Poverty Reduction: How Successful are European Welfare States?*, Oxford: Oxford University Press, pp 185–209.

Van Vliet, O. and Wang, C. (2015) 'Social investment and poverty reduction: a comparative analysis across fifteen European countries', *Journal of Social Policy*, 44(3): 611–38.

# 9

# Estimation of the human capital depreciation rate: an international comparison and policy implications in South Korea

### Ga Woon Ban

## Introduction

Not only does an individual's human capital determine their wages, living standards and quality of life, it is also closely related to productivity, growth and employment at the national level. It plays a significant role in integrating society as well. Despite the considerable effort and political interest in amassing and improving human capital, however, research on how accumulated human capital is maintained or depreciated remains scant. In particular, the importance of estimating the human capital depreciation rate as a starting point for research on human capital depreciation has generally been overlooked, except for the works of Mincer and Polachek (1974), Mincer and Ofek (1982), Carliner (1982), Neuman and Weiss (1995), and Albrecht et al (1999).

Although it is theoretically plausible to consider a human capital depreciation rate, the fact that a variety of factors such as physical ageing, unemployment and technological change affect the depreciation of human capital has led to this scarcity of empirical studies. Neuman and Weiss (1995) differentiated the depreciation of human capital into internal and external depreciation. The former indicates depreciation caused by individual-related reasons, including any loss of physical or mental ability. The latter occurs when the stock of knowledge obtained by learning gradually becomes obsolete owing to environmental changes, corresponding to the so-called vintage effects that Becker (1964) suggested.

However, Rosen (1975), and Weiss and Lillard (1978) argued that distinguishing between these two depreciation factors is impossible since they occur at the same time. As previous studies used wages as dependent variables in estimating the depreciation rate of human capital, both internal and external depreciation were reflected simultaneously in the changes in wages. Groot (1998), and Arrazola and Hevia (2004), who took different approaches, proposed non-linear models that estimated the human capital depreciation rate directly. Specifically, both estimated the depreciation rate of human capital accumulated through formal education by using data collected from the UK and from the Netherlands and Spain, respectively. However, they also estimated the depreciation rate of human capital by using wage data; their estimation of the depreciation rate accordingly reflected internal and external depreciation simultaneously. Due to the limitations of estimation, they could not provide clearer explanations on which of two factors – reduced physical or mental ability and the vintage effects – led to individual wage changes. Based on the limitations and contribution of existing studies, this study attempts to propose a more developed estimation by using data on cognitive skills instead of wage data to estimate the human capital depreciation rate directly, thus reflecting only internal depreciation.

Work environment and lifelong learning as external factors have been regarded as important variables influencing internal depreciation. However, as explained in detail below, existing studies argue that the depreciation of cognitive skills (internal depreciation) in adulthood is not significantly affected by ageing itself until people reach their sixties. Based on these findings, this study, analysing the Program for International Assessment for Adult Competencies (PIAAC) data that was obtained from a sample of people aged under 65, aims to make theoretical and empirical advancements by estimating internal depreciation rates reflecting skills use in the workplace, which could be an important external factor. In other words, this study estimates the human depreciation rate on the assumption that skills use could affect the inner depreciation rate. Thus, physical ageing is not taken into account when the depreciation rate is estimated in the analysis. To sum up, the focus of this study will be the level of skills use in the workplace (as an external factor) which could be a more important variable than biological aging, which affects the internal depreciation of human capital.

Thus, this approach adopts the intellectual challenge and the use-it-or-lose-it hypotheses to explain the depreciation of human capital, which argue that cognitive skills dwindle when individuals are in an environment that provides low levels of intellectual stimulus or they have insufficient opportunities to use their cognitive skills in the workplace and in daily life. These hypotheses have been questioned by many researchers since they were suggested in the 1920s (Salthouse, 2006, 2007; Schooler, 2007). Pazy (2004) supported the use-it-or-lose-it hypothesis by suggesting that not using cognitive skills causes their depreciation. Mincer and Ofek (1982), Krahn and Lowe (1998), and De Grip and Van Loo (2002) similarly reported the depreciation of skills when they are not used.

Fratiglioni et al (2004) and Staff et al (2004) provided results that support for these two hypotheses. In particular, Staff et al (2004) demonstrated that intellectual stimulation received during education and occupational activities increases cerebral reserves and maintains cognitive functioning in old age, thereby explaining the degree to which cognitive skills decrease as people age (Schaie, 1994). Bosma et al (2003a, 2003b) also found that mental load at work negatively affects cognitive impairment as people age. Avolio and Waldman (1990), Finkel et al (2009), Ribeiro et al (2013), Kröger et al (2008), and Ravaglia et al (2002) examined the modifying effects of job complexity and/or occupational type on age-related cognitive decline. Marquié et al (2010) showed that mental stimulation at work influences both the level of cognitive performance and the rate of cognitive change, providing empirical evidence for the use-it-or-lose-it hypothesis.

This study is the first attempt to estimate the depreciation rate of the human capital accumulated by formal education, reflecting only internal depreciation. Moreover, since the degree of internal human capital depreciation that employed individuals face might differ from that the unemployed face, this study proposes a method of estimating depreciation rates by distinguishing both states in one estimation model, since the intellectual stimulation and skills-use opportunities individuals face might vary depending on whether they are in a job. Those employed after formal education may accumulate additional human capital when facing more intellectual challenges, whereas individuals who are unemployed are more likely to experience a significant depreciation of human capital. This study can also be distinguished from previous studies as it expands the scope of the analysis to an international comparison. For the analysis, literacy scores from the PIAAC are used to estimate the depreciation rates of human capital.[1] According to OECD (2013a), literacy is defined as the ability to understand, evaluate, use and engage with written texts to participate in society, achieve one's goals, and develop one's knowledge and potential. However, the literacy proficiencies in the PIAAC are not simply measured by the level of abilities and knowledge related to reading. Rather, it reflects key information-processing skills.

The remainder of this chapter is organised as follows. The following section presents the estimation model developed in this study. After that, an international comparison is conducted using estimates of human capital depreciation rates and results derived from distinguishing the states of employment are suggested. Next, the deterioration rate of skills is calculated and its relationship with skill demand in labour market is examined. Finally, the study is summarised and policy implications are suggested.

## Estimation model for the depreciation rates of human capital

According to Groot (1998), based on the assumption that $t$ years elapsed after an individual $i$ had completed formal education, the current value of human capital $(K_i)$ that the individual $i$ had accumulated through formal education is shown in Eqn. (1). The value for $t$ is obtained by subtracting the number of schooling years $(S_i)$ and 6 from the individual's age:

$$K_i = (1 - \delta_{ni})^t S_i \tag{1}$$

Contrary to previous studies (Groot, 1998; Arrazola and Hevia, 2004), in this work, depreciation rates are assumed to be affected by the various characteristics of individual $i$ $(Z_i)$:

$$\delta_{ni} = \delta_n(Z_i) \tag{2}$$

The relation between individual $i$'s proficiency score $(C_i)$ measured in the PIAAC and the current value of their human capital is:

$$C_i = e^{\beta_K\{1 - \delta_n(Z_i)\}^t S_i + \beta_X X_i + u_i} \tag{3}$$

Eqn. (3) indicates that the current score of an individual's proficiency is determined by the current value of human capital accumulated through formal education and other factors $(X)$. Cognitive skills are influenced by an individual's family background and innate ability (Hanushek et al, 2013). Therefore, we must control for these related variables. Here, $X$ includes gender, language used, status of birth abroad, parents' immigration status, academic backgrounds of the parents and number of books at home. $X$ also includes the learning strategies and the social capital variable. Learning strategies significantly affect an individual's learning performance. Desjardins and Warnke (2012) summarised research on the effect of social capital on cognitive skills. Sharp et al (2010) argued that social participation positively affects an individual's cognitive skills. Responses to the question item on health status were also included as a control variable. Salthouse (2009) reported that a substantial part of the cohort effect could be controlled for using an individual's schooling year and health status. Table 9A.1 shows the control variables and measured indicators in this study.

Taking the natural logarithm of Eqn. (3) leads to Eqn. (4), which is an estimation equation for the cross-sectional data. The key factor to the estimation is how effectively $X$ can control for the endogeneity caused by the unobservable characteristics contained in $u_i$.

$$\ln C_i = \beta_K\{1 - \delta_n(Z_i)\}'S_i + \beta_X X_i + u_i \tag{4}$$

If factors cause systematic differences in the cohort to which an individual belongs (for example, disparate quality of schooling depending on birth year) or if the social and biological changes that individuals experience at a specific age affect their cognitive competencies, these factors may not be sufficiently controlled for by $X$. Hence, depreciation rates for different ages are suggested:

$$\delta_{ni} = \delta_n(Z_i) = \delta_0 + \delta_1 \times age_i \tag{5}$$

Plugging Eqn. (5) into Eqn. (4) leads to:

$$\ln C_i = \beta_K\{1 - (\delta_0 + \delta_1 age_i)\}'S_i + \beta_X X_i + u_i \tag{6}$$

The observed age difference consists of cohort and age effects. For instance, people of different ages exhibit different depreciation rates because of the difference in the quality of education across birth cohorts, in experience after formal education or in degree of biological ageing at a specific age. In cross-sectional data, the cohort and age effects, therefore, cannot be completely distinguished.

Basic cognitive skills comprise two components: cognitive mechanics and cognitive pragmatics. Cognitive mechanics includes concentration, processing speed, reasoning, working memory and spatial perception. It is also called fluid intelligence (or Gf) as it is related to the ability to understand and learn independently of previous knowledge. All other cognitive functions, such as knowledge, skills and wisdom, are categorised as cognitive pragmatics; these types of cognitive skills are often called crystallised intelligence (or Gc) as they are acquired or learnt in advance. Crystallised intelligence is determined by the social and cultural learning environments.

In general, traditional intelligence test scores (G), which are associated with cognitive skills, are stable throughout adulthood. A moderate decline may be expected if the nature of a test reflects the attributes of fluid intelligence more strongly, whereas a modest rise is plausible if a test is more closely related to crystallised intelligence. Desjardins and Warnke (2012) found that crystallised intelligence has a stable age profile in adulthood compared with fluid intelligence. While fluid intelligence dwindles in early adulthood, crystallised intelligence continues to rise slowly. Therefore, an individual's cognitive ability does not shrink greatly, since a decrease in fluid intelligence is accompanied by a sufficient increase of crystallised intelligence. In other words, overall cognitive ability can be preserved by continued learning and experiences. Figure 9.1 illustrates the patterns of fluid and crystallised intelligence and their combination, G. If the measures of the PIAAC are closer to crystallised intelligence than fluid intelligence, the age effect on the depreciation rate is expected to be small.

The decline in cognitive skills by ageing, however, differs significantly among individuals (Figure 9.2). Although G does not show a sharp decline before age 60, some individuals show sharp declines, or even rises. The intellectual stimulation and use-it-or-lose-it hypotheses of interest in this study may be suitably explain these cases. That is,

**Figure 9.1:** Profiles of fluid intelligence and crystallised intelligence

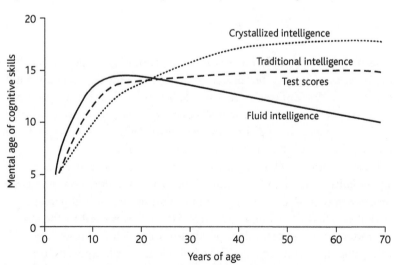

Source: Quoted and reconstructed from Cattell (1987), McArdle et al (2002), and Desjardins and Warnke (2012)

**Figure 9.2:** Individual differences in decrease in cognitive skills

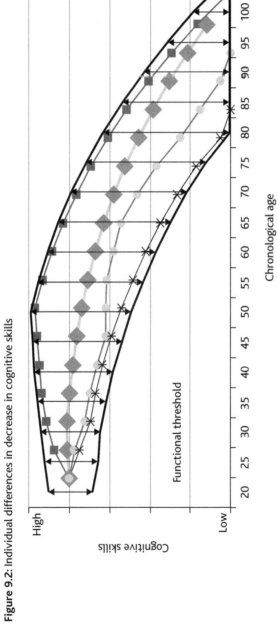

Source: Quoted and reconstructed from Hertzog et al (2008) and Desjardins and Warnke (2012)

individual differences in declining trends may be significant depending on the environments (for example, the intellectual stimulation that individuals receive), even when no general decrease in cognitive skills due to ageing is observed.

Eqn. (4) shows that human capital accumulates during formal education ($S$) and, consequently, cognitive skills increase, whereas human capital depreciates and cognitive skills deteriorate after its completion. This is equivalent to modelling the accumulation and depreciation of human capital by intellectual stimulation, regardless of the biological ageing process. The model used in this study includes the assumption that intellectual stimulation and the frequency of skills use determine the depreciation rates of human capital rather than biological ageing, at least between the ages of 16 and 65 years. Thus, birth cohorts are controlled for by using the age variable in Eqn. (6).

The depreciation that occurs during $t$ years may also vary considerably depending on whether an individual is employed. The intellectual challenge and use-it-or-lose-it hypotheses indicate that the degree of depreciation might differ from individual experiences. Taking into account this point, two distinct depreciation rates are assumed: a depreciation rate with being employed for $t_0$ years and a depreciation rate with being unemployed for $t_1$ years. That is, for $t$ years after the end of formal education, an individual is assumed to face a depreciation rate of $\delta_{n0}$ for $t_0$ years and $\delta_{n1}$ for $t_1$ years, rather than the depreciation rate $\delta_n$. The present value of human capital is now this:

$$(1 - \delta_n)^t S = (1 - \delta_{n0})^{t_0} (1 - \delta_{n1})^{t_1} S \tag{7}$$

Taking the logarithm of Eqn. (7), Eqn. (8) is derived as follows:

$$t \ln(1 - \delta_n) = t_0 \ln(1 - \delta_{n0}) + t_1 \ln(1 - \delta_{n1}) \tag{8}$$

Since $t = t_0 + t_1$, defining $wer = t_0/t$ yields Eqn. (9):

$$\delta_n \cong \delta_{n0} wer + \delta_{n1} (1 - wer) \tag{9}$$

The depreciation rate $\delta_n$ can now be seen as a weighted sum of $\delta_{n0}$ and $\delta_{n1}$. The weight $wer$ is the ratio of years of employment among $t$ years. If one is employed for the entire $t$ years, $wer$ will become 1 and $\delta_n = \delta_{n0}$. Conversely, if one is unemployed for the entire $t$ years, $wer$ will be 0 and $\delta_n = \delta_{n1}$. The calculation of $wer$ with actual data was based on the number of years of working full-time or part-time for more than six months divided by $t$; therefore, some values exceed 1.

In that case, they are turned into 1. Thus, the set of values taken as *wer* is expressed as follows: *wer* = {0,1}.

Since the depreciation rates for the employed ($\delta_{n0}$) and unemployed ($\delta_{n1}$) are expressed by Eqn. (10) and Eqn. (11), respectively, the total depreciation rate ($\delta_n$) is represented as Eqn. (12). Consequently, the estimation equation becomes Eqn. (13) from which $\delta_{01}$, $\delta_{11}$, $\delta_{00} - \delta_{01}$ and $\delta_{10} - \delta_{11}$ can be estimated. By using these estimates, $\delta_{00}$, $\delta_{01}$, $\delta_{10}$ and $\delta_{11}$ are calculated:

$$\delta_{n0} = \delta_{00} + \delta_{10}\ age \tag{10}$$

$$\delta_{n1} = \delta_{01} + \delta_{11}\ age \tag{11}$$

$$\begin{aligned}\delta_n &= \delta_{n0}\ wer + \delta_{n1}\ (1 - wer) \\ &= (\delta_{00} + \delta_{10}\ age)wer + (\delta_{01} + \delta_{11}\ age)(1 - wer) \\ &= \delta_{01} + \delta_{11}\ age + (\delta_{00} - \delta_{01})wer + (\delta_{10} - \delta_{11})wer \times age \end{aligned} \tag{12}$$

$$\begin{aligned}\ln C_i &= \beta_K\{1 - (\delta_0 + \delta_{11}\ age_i + (\delta_{00} - \delta_{01})wer_i \\ &\quad + (\delta_{10} - \delta_{11})age_i \times wer_i)\}^t S_i + \beta_X X_i + u_i \end{aligned} \tag{13}$$

Eqn. (6) and Eqn. (13) are estimated by using the non-linear least squares method.

## Estimation results of human capital depreciation rates

Figure 9.3 illustrates the age–skill profiles measured by literacy proficiency. In most countries, this profile shows a convex shape with its peak in the twenties and thirties age range. Korea shows a significant gap in the level of skills depending on age showing a much faster reduction in literacy proficiency than the OECD average trend.[2] In Japan, skills are maintained after a considerable increase until middle age and decline in older people. No substantial gap in the level of skills across ages is observed in English-speaking countries or former Eastern Bloc communist countries. Italy, a group E country, has a lower skill level than the OECD average at all ages, but its gap across ages is small.

Figure 9.4 and Table 9A.2 show the estimation results of the human capital depreciation rates from Eqn. (6), which do not distinguish between states of employment. The results of estimating the depreciation rates by distinguishing between the employed and unemployed from Eqn. (13) are also shown in Figure 9.4 and Table 9A.3.[3] All the estimates are obtained by using the literacy

**Figure 9.3:** Age–literacy proficiency profiles in OECD countries

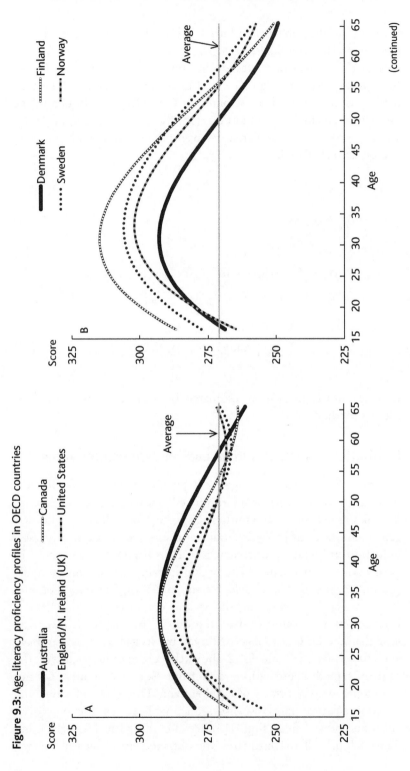

(continued)

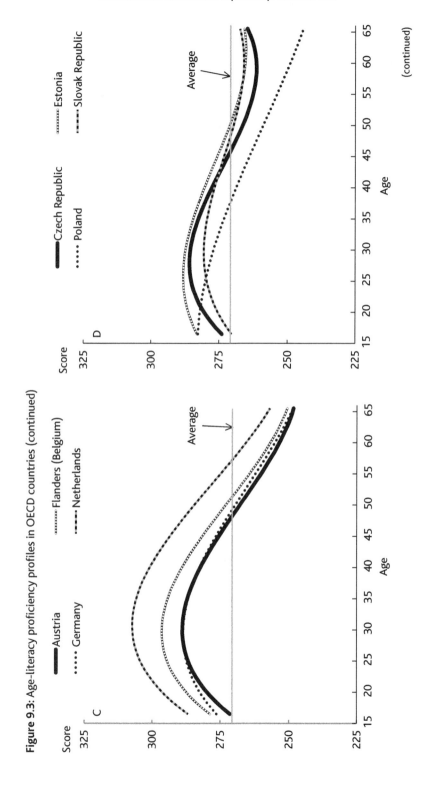

**Figure 9.3:** Age-literacy proficiency profiles in OECD countries (continued)

(continued)

**Figure 9.3:** Age-literacy proficiency profiles in OECD countries (continued)

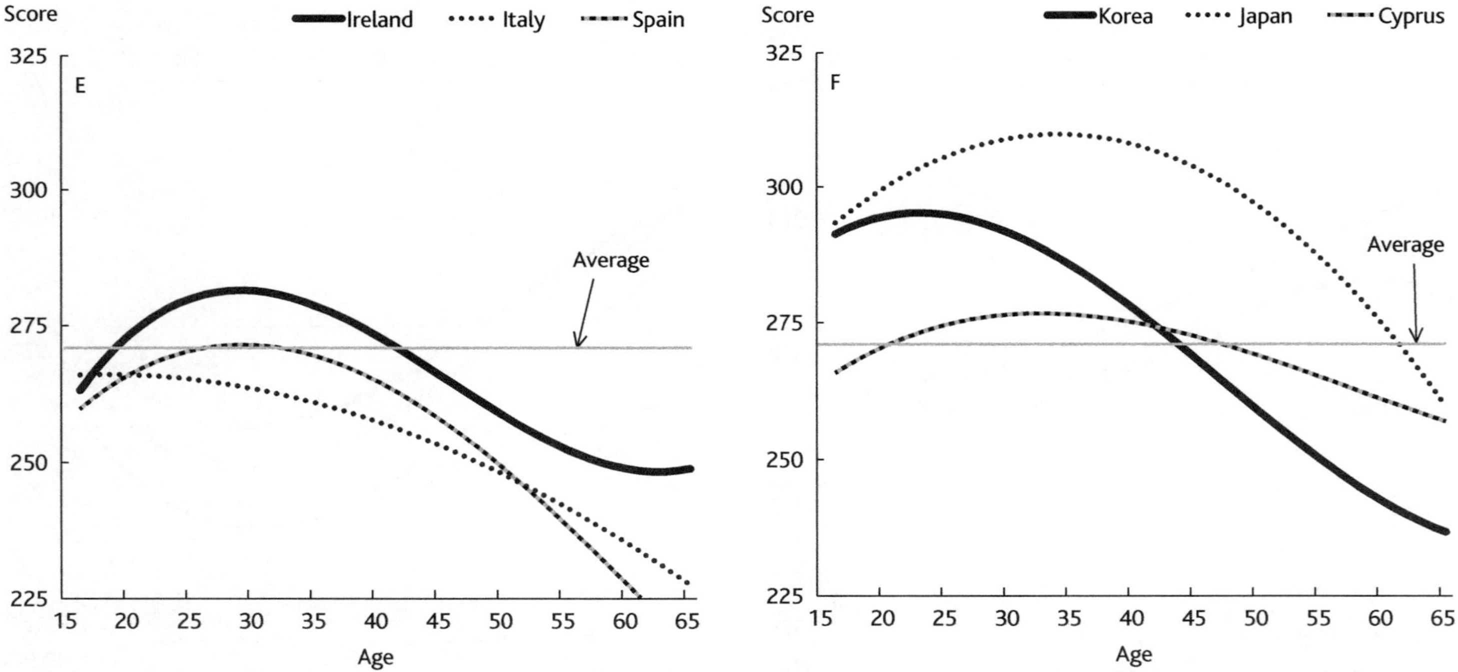

Note: The A–D countries are grouped according to regional or language considerations, with the remainder grouped in E and F. A cubic specification of the trend curves is found to be most accurate in reflecting the distribution of scores by age in most countries. Foreign-born adults are excluded from the analysis.

Source: OECD (2013a)

**Figure 9.4:** Depreciation rates by age in OECD countries

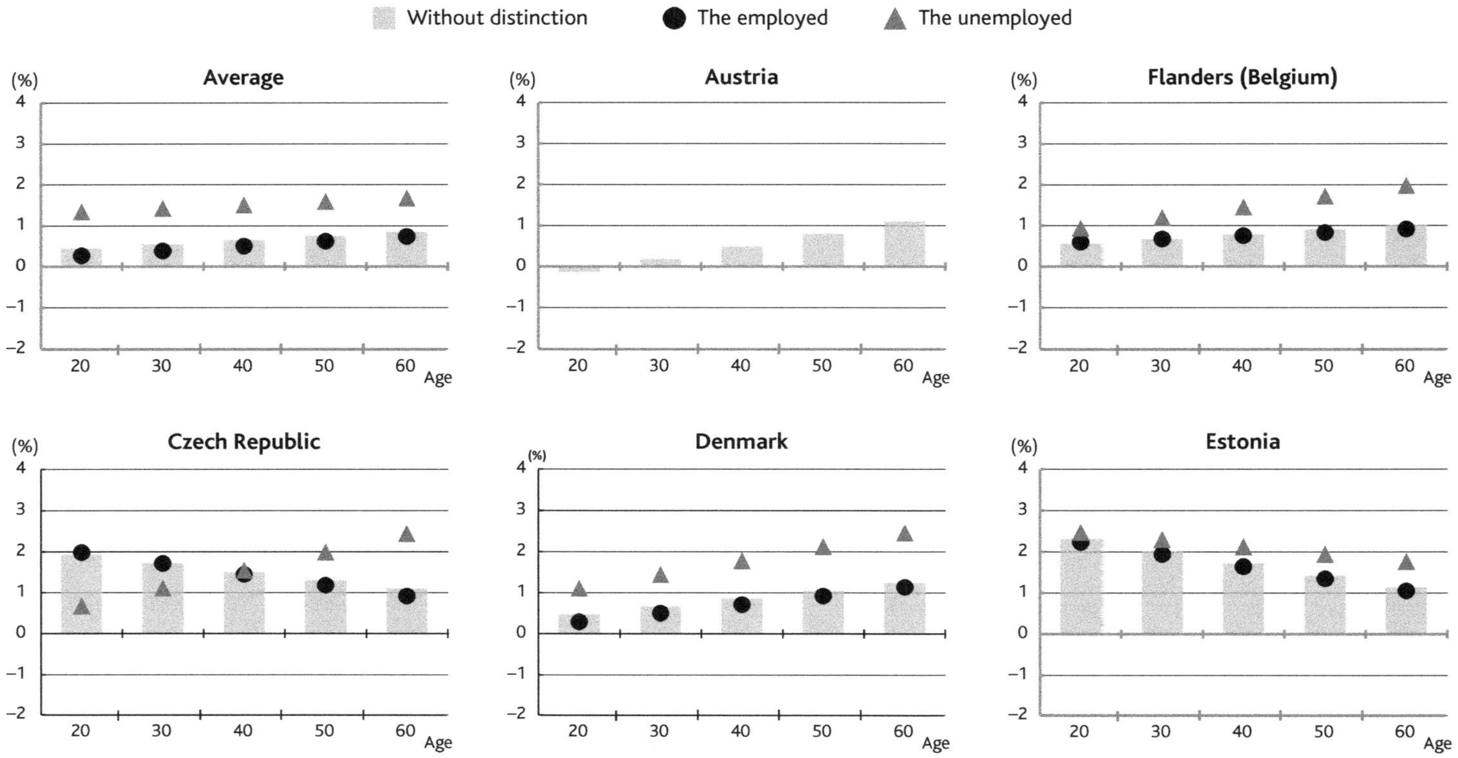

(continued)

**Figure 9.4:** Depreciation rates by age in OECD countries (continued)

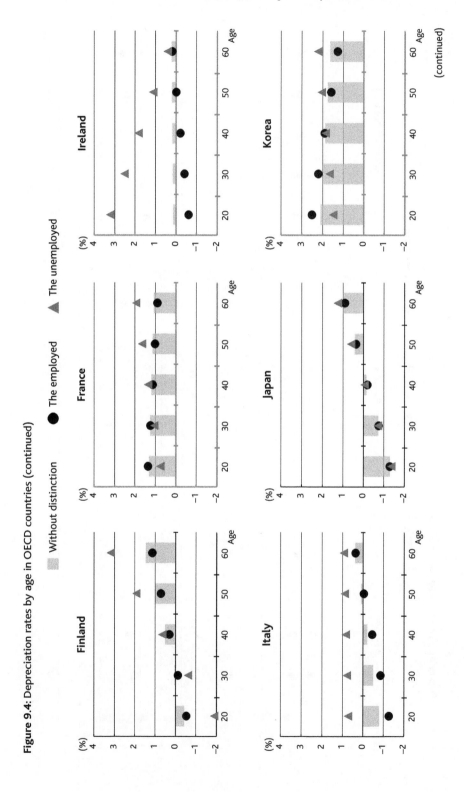

(continued)

**Figure 9.4**: Depreciation rates by age in OECD countries (continued)

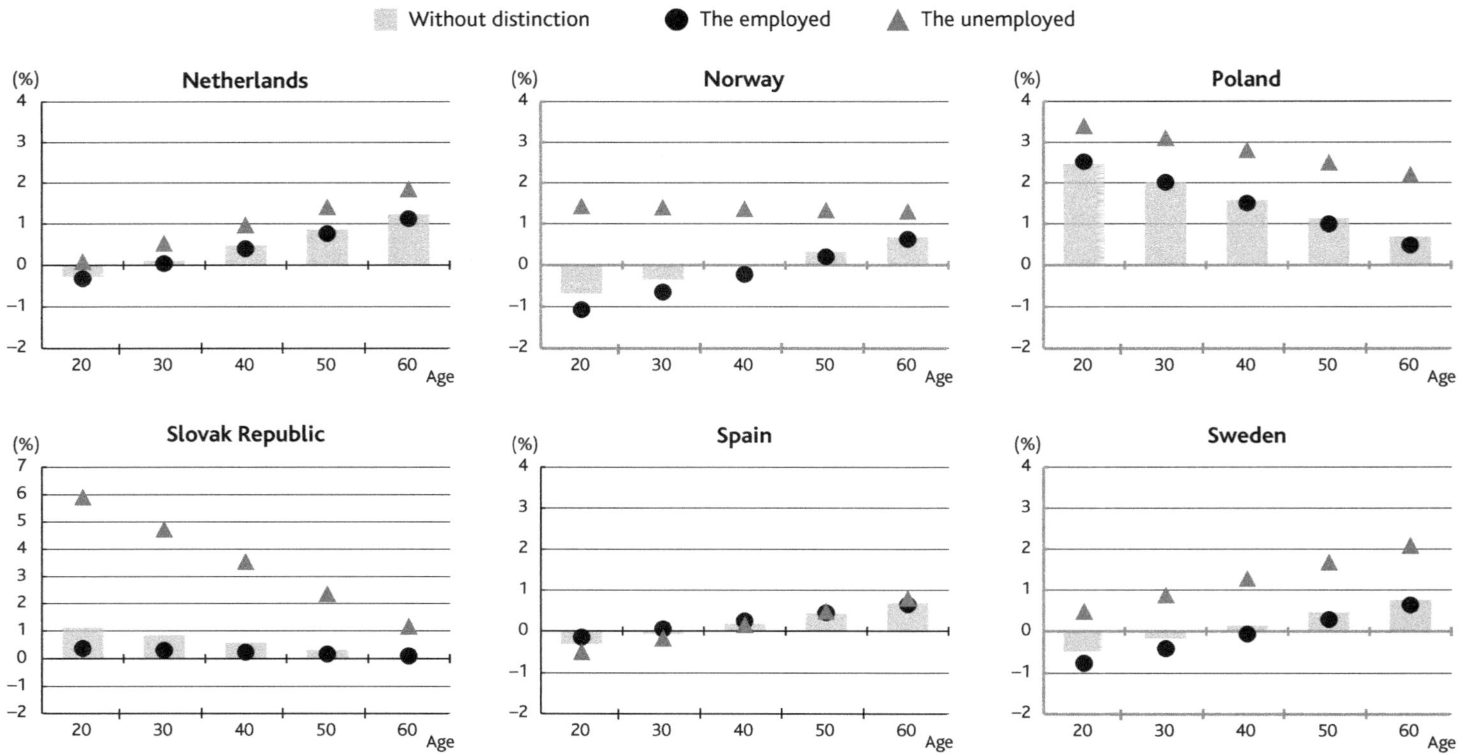


(continued)

Figure 9.4: Depreciation rates by age in OECD countries (continued)

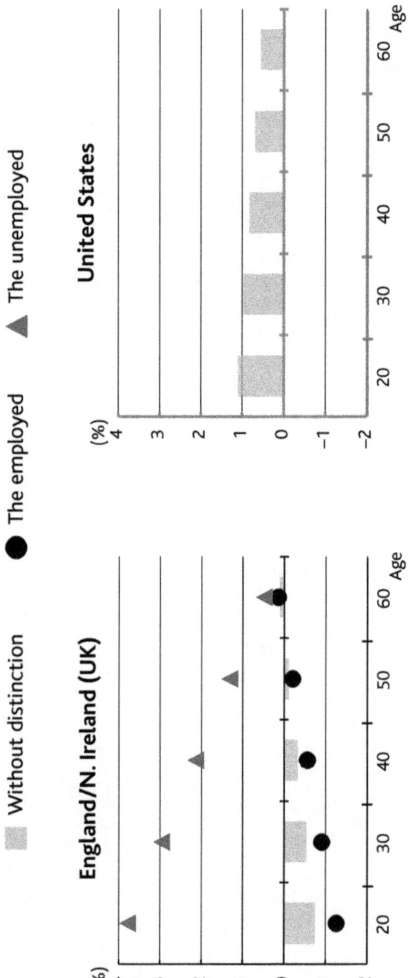

Source: OECD (2012)

proficiency of the PIAAC as a proxy for cognitive skills. As mentioned above, age does not mean one's biological age, but rather birth year.

The OECD average depreciation rate obtained by not distinguishing between states of employment increases as age rises, suggesting that the younger generation experiences a better quality of education and enjoys an environment that is more favorable for the accumulation of human capital, even after formal education, compared with the older generation. However, depreciation is greater among the younger generations in the former Eastern Bloc communist countries, the United States, France and Korea. However, the trends in Korea and France are not statistically significant (see Table 9A.2).

The depreciation rate for the unemployed for the OECD average, as well as for most countries, is higher than that for the employed. According to the intellectual challenge and use-it-or-lose-it hypotheses, individuals receive different amounts of intellectual stimulation depending on their employment status, which lead to distinct depreciation rates. The results of this study thus support these two hypotheses. However, the positive depreciation rates for the young employed in Korea, the Czech Republic and France have larger estimates than those for their young unemployed counterparts.

Figure 9.5 shows the depreciation rates obtained by using median ages but without distinguishing between employment statuses. The OECD average depreciation rate is 0.65 per cent. Arrazola and Hevia (2004) used data from the European Household Panel to estimate the human capital depreciation rates of Spanish wage earners aged 16–64 years in 1994 at 1–1.5 per cent. Conversely, the depreciation rate for Spain estimated in this study is only 0.20 per cent. This could be because the estimate from Arrazola and Hevia (2004) reflects both internal and external depreciation.

Figure 9.6 shows the literacy proficiency scores and depreciation rates together. Korea's level of skills is around the OECD average, whereas its depreciation rate is the highest of all members. The UK has a level of skills similar to that of Korea, but its depreciation rate is the lowest.

Figures 9.7 and 9.8 show comparisons for the depreciation rates depending on the employment statuses based on the median ages of each country. Korea has the highest depreciation rates for the employed, with 1.90 per cent, while the UK has the lowest rate, with −0.56 per cent. Some countries have negative depreciation rates; this can be interpreted as accumulation, which occurs by developing the human capital accumulated from formal education. The depreciation rates for the unemployed have positive estimates in all countries.

**Figure 9.5:** International comparison of human capital depreciation rates without a distinction between states of employment

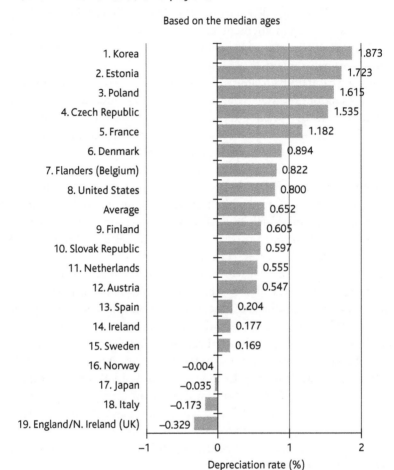

Based on the median ages

Source: OECD (2012)

Slovakia has the highest rate with 3.66 per cent and Japan has the lowest rate with 0.08 per cent.

As shown in Figure 9.9, the depreciation rates in Korea, Poland and Estonia are high for both the employed and the unemployed. The UK and Ireland exhibit low depreciation rates for the employed and high rates for unemployed. Japan, Italy and Spain have low depreciation rates for both the employed and unemployed. However, as shown in Figure 9.6, Italy and Spain have the lowest levels of human capital, whereas Japan has the highest.

The degree of intellectual stimulation or skills use in the workplace and the amount of depreciation are affected by the gap between

**Figure 9.6:** International comparisons of literacy proficiency scores and depreciation rates

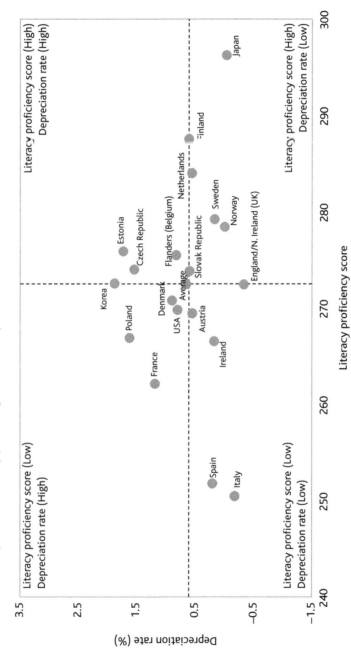

Source: OECD (2012)

**Figure 9.7:** International comparison of depreciation rates for the employed

Based on the employed with median ages

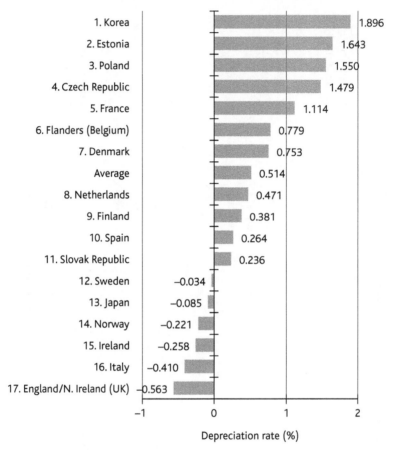

Depreciation rate (%)

Source: OECD (2012)

demand for skills and individuals' skills. No matter how high demand for skills at work is, if the level of skills an individual possesses is above that, the individual will not be intellectually stimulated, and this will lead to depreciation. Conversely, even if demand for skills in the workplace is low, if it is higher than the level of an individual's skills, he or she can accumulate human capital. Figure 9.10 depicts the relationship between the proportion of under-skilled workers and depreciation rates for the employed.[4] The higher the proportion of under-skilled workers is, the lower the depreciation rates for employees are.

**Figure 9.8:** International comparison of depreciation rates for the unemployed

Based on the unemployed with median ages

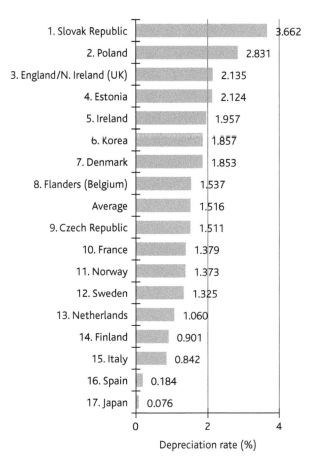

Source: OECD (2012)

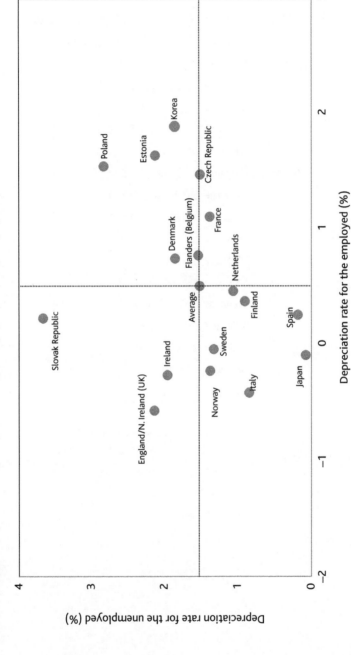

**Figure 9.9:** International comparison of depreciation rates depending on the states of employment

Source: OECD (2012)

**Figure 9.10:** Relationship between under-skilling and depreciation rates for the employed

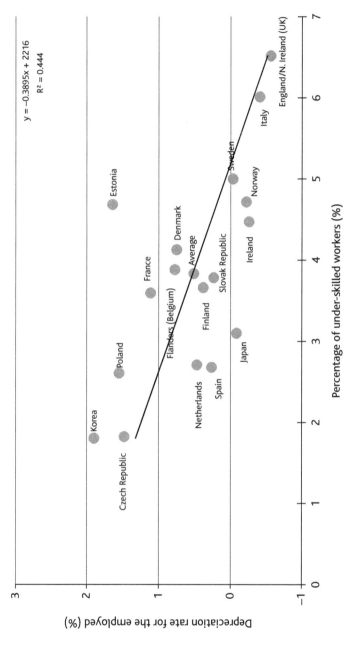

Source: OECD (2012)

## The deterioration rate of skills and its relationship with skill demand

The deterioration rate of skills can be calculated by using the estimation results of Eqn. (13) to derive policy implications for Korea. The deterioration rate of skills is defined as the negative value of the annual average rate of change in cognitive skills after the completion of formal education ($- (\partial \ln C/\partial t)$). Since Eqn. (13) is non-linear, the deterioration rate of skills is calculated by using the average marginal effect. Figure 9.11 shows that the deterioration rate of skills is 0.1 per cent on average for OECD countries compared with 0.3 per cent for Korea, which is the highest among OECD countries. To understand intuitively the meaning of the deterioration

**Figure 9.11:** International comparison of skills deterioration rates after formal education

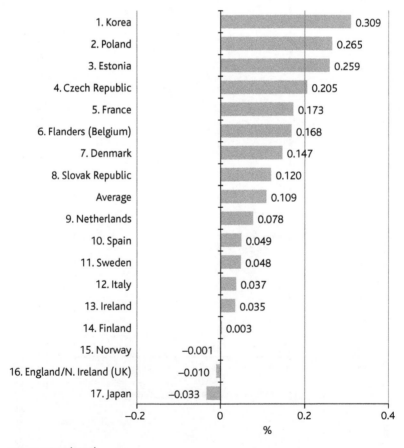

Source: OECD (2012)

rate of skills, an improvement rate of skills due to formal education is calculated (Figure 9.12). Receiving one year of formal education increases cognitive skills by 1.4 per cent on average for OECD countries, compared with a rise of only 1.2 per cent in Korea. In the case of Korea, this 1.2 per cent deterioration in skills occurs four years after formal education is completed. Hence, it is equal to the stock of cognitive skills accumulated from one year of formal education. By contrast, for the OECD average, it takes 13 years for the stock of cognitive skills accumulated by one year of formal education to deteriorate. Among OECD member countries, Korea thus has a considerably larger deterioration rate relative to its accumulation of human capital.

**Figure 9.12:** International comparison of skills improvement rates due to formal education

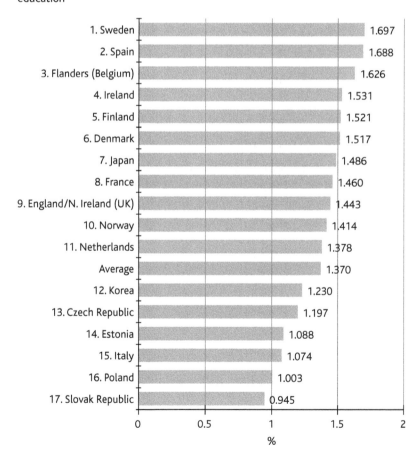

Source: OECD (2012)

The deterioration rate of skills is closely related to several indicators of skill demand in the labour market. First of all, it is negatively related to labour productivity per hour and positively related to working hours (see Figure 9.13). The USD purchasing power parity (PPP) measure is applied to calculate labour productivity. Korea has a low level of labour productivity per hour as well as the longest working hours among the surveyed countries. Regarding labour productivity and working hours as outcomes of skill-friendly technologies the corporate culture adopted by firms, and the institutional environment related to skill demand in the labour market, Figure 9.13 shows a negative relationship between the deterioration rate of skills and skill demand.

In addition, the deterioration rate of skills is negatively related to the hourly wage as well as to years of service. PPP is applied to calculate wages, using the median values. Years of service are the number of years that an employee has worked in his or her current company. These two indicators are also related to skill demand in the labour market.[5] The lower the demand for skills in the labour market is, the greater the deterioration rate of skills is, and Korea has low demand for skills.

Furthermore, the relationship between the deterioration rate of skills and either the wage gap or the minimum wage also supports this argument. The wage gap is calculated by dividing the 90th percentile wage by the 10th percentile wage, and the minimum wage is the hourly wage in 2012 with PPP applied. As Acemoglu and Pischke (1998), and Thelen (2004) emphasised, policies and institutions that enable wage compression create a favourable environment for employers to invest in general skills and increase demand for skills in the labour market. This should also be associated with a lower deterioration rate of skills. Korea has the largest wage gap among the surveyed countries and its minimum wage is also low.[6]

## Conclusion

This study estimated the internal depreciation rates of human capital in OECD countries. Existing studies have examined the quality of formal education, the environment for lifelong learning and the degree to which skills are used at work as factors affecting internal depreciation of human capital. However, the focus of this study was more closely on the skills used in the workplace. In other words, this study emphasises that a low level of skills use in the workplace could be an important factor affecting internal depreciation of human capital.

**Figure 9.13:** Relationship between deterioration rate of skills and skill demand

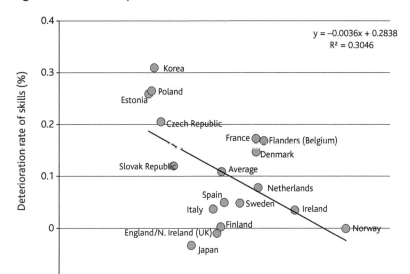

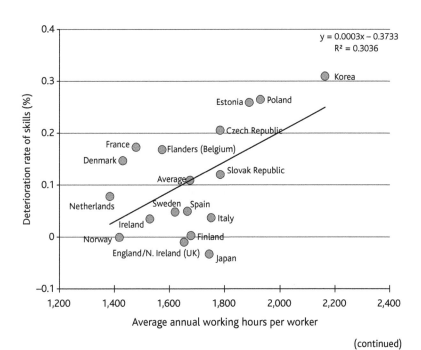

(continued)

**Figure 9.13:** Relationship between deterioration rate of skills and skill demand (continued)

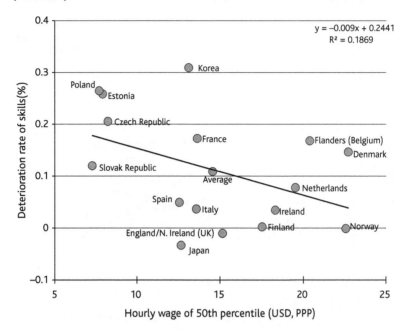

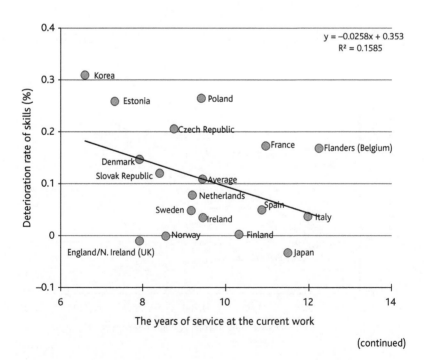

(continued)

**Figure 9.13:** Relationship between deterioration rate of skills and skill demand (continued)

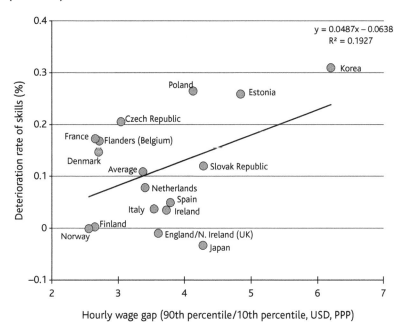

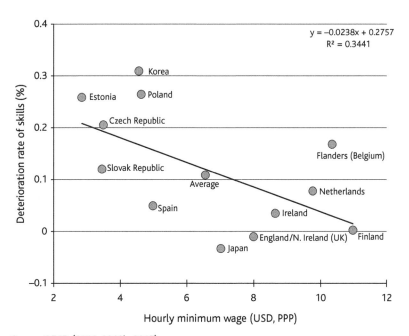

Source: OECD (2012, 2013b, 2015)

Most countries had positive depreciation rates, implying that policy for maintaining human capital is as essential as policy for accumulating it. Different degrees of depreciation across countries are likely to result from differences in the quality of formal education, the degree to which skills are used at work and the environment for lifelong learning. Furthermore, this study found that the depreciation rates for the unemployed are higher than those for the employed in most OECD countries. These findings support the intellectual challenge and use-it-or-lose-it hypotheses with respect to the depreciation of human capital. Thus, the degree of skills use at work was identified as an important factor in human capital depreciation.

The results of the international comparisons in the previous section suggest that even in countries with similar levels of accumulated human capital, different policy strategies should be taken according to their unique conditions. For instance, whereas the levels of human capital in Korea and the UK are similar, Korea's depreciation rates are the highest and the UK's are the lowest among OECD countries. Moreover, Korea has the highest depreciation rate for the employed, whereas the UK has a substantially high depreciation rate for the unemployed. These findings reveal that in countries, including Korea, where higher human capital depreciation among the employed is an issue, the government should promote raising the level of skills used in the workplace to prevent massive loss of human capital that low-skilled jobs cause. On the other hand, the importance of employment policy encouraging the unemployed to find a job should be stressed in the countries such as the UK where the main issue is human capital depreciation for unemployed people.

The results of the Skill Utilization at Work Index, created using various skills use indicators provided by the PIACC,[7] demonstrate that Korea has the lowest level of skill use at work (see Figure 9.14).[8] Level 1 and below were classified as low proficiency level, and levels 4 and 5 were categorised as high proficiency level.[9] Notably, Korea stands at the bottom of the OECD countries list in the degree of skill use at work among those who have very low proficiency in literacy, and the figure for those with the highest level of proficiency is the second lowest after Japan. Korea also displays the lowest ratio of skilled occupations.[10] Compared to other OECD countries, Korea has very low demand for skills. Workers do not tend to get many opportunities to utilise their skills in the workplace, and jobs suitable for professionals are not abundant. This may also be evidence suggesting that the low demand for skills in the Korean labour market is significantly linked to the proficiency curve illustrated in Figure 9.3. It also explains the higher depreciation rate in the Korean workplace that was estimated in the previous section.

Japan, however, exhibits different patterns in the depreciation rate of human capital (see Figure 9.4). Significantly, the country has the highest level of human capital, a low depreciation rate for the employed and the lowest depreciation rate for the unemployed. These are in sharp contrast to Korea, where the depreciation rate for the employed is the highest, and the UK, which has a substantially high depreciation rate for the unemployed. In addition, similar patterns in depreciation rates for both the employed and unemployed by age group in Japan also differ with those in Korea and the UK, where they exhibit completely different patterns. The accumulation of human capital is identified in both employed and unemployed people in their twenties and thirties, and it peaks in the forties, whereas the group in their fifties and sixties show some depreciation of human capital (see Figure 9.4).

Figure 9.14 displays low degrees of skills use and a low proportion of professionals in Japan and Korea. While Korea places last in both lists, Japan is also at the lower end. However, it is a distinctive feature of Japan that despite its low level of skills use in the workplace and having highest literacy proficiency score, the depreciation rate is very low. In Italy and Spain, both of the level of skills use and the depreciation rate are as low as Japan. One of Spain and Italy's contrasting aspects is that they have the lowest levels of human capital (see Figure 9.6). As stated in the previous section, skills use in the workplace is relative. This means that, although the level of skills use in the workplace is low, human capital might not depreciate because the level of human capital is also low. The correlation between the depreciation of human capital in the workplace and under-skilling is identified from Figure 9.10.

Japan also has higher levels of task discretion (Figure 9A.1) and cooperative activities at work (Figure 9A.4). This means that, although both Japan and Korea have hierarchical company cultures and a low proportion of professionals, what makes Japan different seems to be substantially higher levels of autonomy and cooperative culture in the workplace, which Korea lacks. These two factors are regarded as preventing the depreciation of human capital in Japan.

The question of why Korean adults could not fully use their accumulated skills seems to be related to low levels of autonomy during working hours, as well as of task discretion, unlike what workers in other OECD countries have (see Figures 9A.1 and 9A2). Korean workers also hardly engage in problem-solving by themselves and or participate in cooperative tasks due to the pervasive hierarchical

**Figure 9.14:** International comparison of workplace skill utilisation index and the proportion of professionals

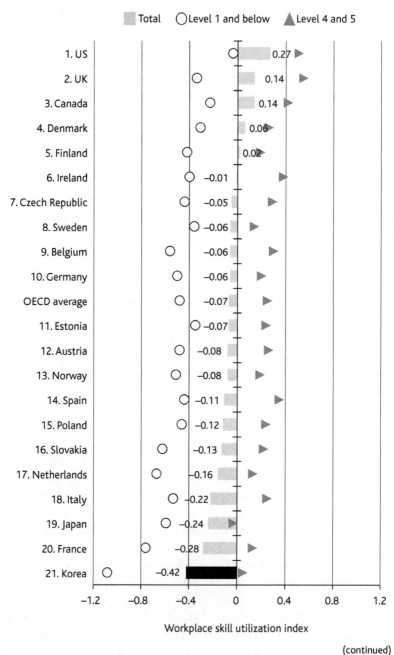

Workplace skill utilization index

(continued)

**Figure 9.14:** International comparison of workplace skill utilisation index and the proportion of professionals (continued)

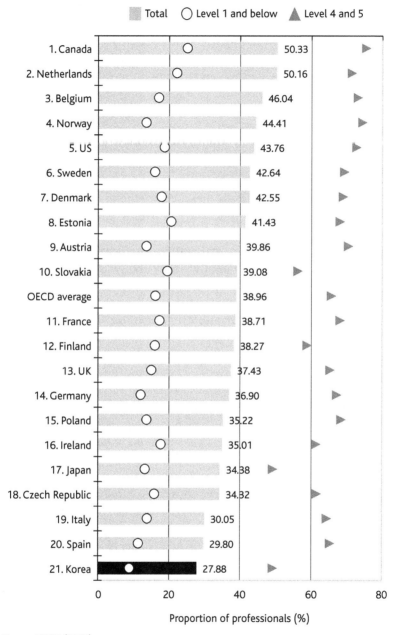

Proportion of professionals (%)

Source: OECD (2012)

organisational culture (see Figures 9A.3 and 9A.4). Furthermore, both the level of learning at work and job satisfaction are substantially lower than those in other countries (see Figures 9A.5 and 9A.6). The organisational culture of autonomy and discretion increases the need for educational training and use of skills from corporations' perspectives. Problem-solving, cooperation and job satisfaction affect the rate of return for education and training in terms of the necessity for skills, the spill-over effect of knowledge, long years of service and motivation for workers. The same is true for learning in workplaces.

In summary, compared to other surveyed countries, a sharply higher depreciation rate of human capital was observed in Korea, which might originate from lower levels of demand for skills in the labour market. In this sense, the country needs to improve utilisation of human capital across individuals' lifetimes. To do this, emphasis should be placed on creating more decent jobs requiring higher levels of skills and improving the quality of jobs. Improving the quality of jobs, including changing organisational cultures to ensure autonomy and discretion for workers, is as important as economic rewards.

Lastly, although it was not verified in this study, lifelong learning should also not be overlooked as an essential factor for reducing the human capital depreciation rate. Strengthening lifelong learning is regarded as a skill supply-side measure, while developing work environments where workers can fully utilise their skills can be considered a demand-side measure to maintain human capital. It is vital to understand the inter-relations between the two. However, existing policies for capacity building have been weighted towards the supply side. In other words, policies taking this approach could not be implemented optimally in situations where the demand side for skills is ignored. This study, rather, puts more emphasis on improving the quality of current jobs, which requires higher levels of skills. In particular, policy interventions to promote autonomous and discretionary organisational culture are essential (see Figures 9A.1 and 9A.2). Lifelong learning, the important supply-side policy, should also be considered in this sense. If governments operate lifelong learning programs to meet individuals' needs for general skills rather than the specific skills that companies need, it will help to establish an organisational culture ensuring autonomy and discretion by raising the bargaining power of labour in labour–management relations in workplace units. That is, skill supply policy will lead to an increase in skill demand.

## Notes

1 The PIAAC was conducted in 2011 and 2012 as an initiative of the OECD among 157,000 adults aged from 16 to 65 years in 24 countries (OECD, 2013a).

2 If these age–literacy proficiency profiles resulted from the cohort effect (differences in quantity and quality of education), the issue of a rapid drop in cognitive ability for older age groups might be overcome as time passes. However, similar trends are also observed when controlling for individuals' years of education, and Korea even shows a steeper decline compared to the OECD average. This phenomenon indicates that the issue of human capital depreciation in the country could be highly associated with policies and systems under which adults have fewer opportunities to learn after school age and many of them cannot fully utilise their skills and abilities at work.

3 Since the length of employment after formal education is longer than the length of unemployment, the depreciation rate of human capital after formal education is more influenced by the depreciation rate for the employed. Thus, the depreciation rate by age without distinction between states of employment is similar to the depreciation rate by age for the employed.

4 Under-skilling was calculated by combining actual literacy scores and the self-reported skill mismatch information according to the method suggested by Pellizzari and Fichen (2013).

5 Years of service are related to the turnover rate. If the turnover rate is high, demand for skills and investment in skills must be low.

6 The minimum wage in Korea almost doubled from ₩4,580 in 2012 to ₩8,350 in 2019. Although the current minimum wage is significantly higher than it was of 2012, the problem of the large wage gap has not been resolved in Korea.

7 This is calculated by standardising the sum of standardised skill utilisation indicators, which includes 12 questions about the frequency with which respondents perform specific tasks in their workplaces. Detailed indicators can be found in Table 9A.4.

8 The analysis includes people who were employed at the time of survey and had been employed at some point within the past five years.

9 Although PIAAC provides six different proficiency levels in literacy scores, the author reclassifies these categories into four levels: Level 1 and below, Level 2, Level 3, and Levels 4 and 5. Therefore, proficiency Level 1 and below means scores below 226 points, and across countries, 15.5 per cent of adults fell into this level. However, proficiency at Levels 4 and 5 indicates scores of 326 points or higher, and 11.8 per cent of adults were at this level.

10 The PIACC classifies respondents' jobs as skilled, semi-skilled white-collar, semi-skilled blue-collar and elementary occupations based on the International Standard Classification of Occupation.

## References

Acemoglu, D. and Pischke, J. (1998) 'Why do firms train? Theory and evidence', *Quarterly Journal of Economics*, 113(1): 79–119.

Albrecht, J.W., Edin, P.A., Sundström, M. and Vroman, S.B. (1999) 'Career interruptions and subsequent earnings: a reexamination using Swedish data', *Journal of Human Resources*, 34(2): 294–311.

Arrazola, M. and Hevia, J.D. (2004) 'More on the estimation of the human capital depreciation rate', *Applied Economics Letters*, 11(3): 145–8.

Avolio, B.J. and Waldman, D.A. (1990) 'An examination of age and cognitive test performance across job complexity and occupational types', *Journal of Applied Psychology*, 75(1): 43–50.

Becker, W.C. (1964) 'Consequences of different kinds of parental discipline', *Review of Child Development Research*, 1: 169–208.

Bosma, H., van Boxtel, M.P.J., Ponds, R.W.H.M., Houx, P.J., Burdorf, A. and Jolles, J. (2003a) 'Mental work demands protect against cognitive impairment: MAAS prospective cohort study', *Experimental Aging Research*, 29(1): 33–45.

Bosma, H., Van Boxtel, M.P.J., Ponds, R.W.H.M., Houx, P.J.H. and Jolles, J. (2003b) 'Education and age-related cognitive decline: the contribution of mental workload', *Educational Gerontology*, 29(2): 165–73.

Carliner, G. (1982) 'The wages of older men', *Journal of Human Resources*, 17(1): 25–38.

Cattell, R.B. (eds) (1987) *Intelligence: Its Structure, Growth and Action*, Amsterdam: Elsevier.

De Grip, A. and Van Loo, J. (2002) 'The economics of skills obsolescence: a review', in A. De Grip, J. Van Loo and K. Mayhew (eds) *The Economics of Skills Obsolescence*, Bingley: Emerald Group Publishing Limited, pp 1–26.

Desjardins, R. and Warnke, A.J. (2012) 'Ageing and skills: a review and analysis of skill gain and skill loss over the lifespan and over time', OECD education working paper no. 72.

Finkel, D., Andel, R., Gatz, M. and Pedersen, N.L. (2009) 'The role of occupational complexity in trajectories of cognitive aging before and after retirement', *Psychology and Aging*, 24(3): 563–73.

Fratiglioni, L., Paillard-Borg, S. and Winblad, B. (2004) 'An active and socially integrated lifestyle in late life might protect against dementia', *The Lancet Neurology*, 3(6): 343–53.

Groot, W. (1998) 'Empirical estimates of the rate of depreciation of education', *Applied Economics Letters*, 5(8): 535–8.

Hanushek, E.A., Schwerdt, G., Wiederhold, S. and Woessmann, L. (2013) 'Returns to skills around the world: evidence from PIAAC', working paper no. 19762, National Bureau of Economic Research.

Hertzog, C., Kramer, A.F., Wilson, R.S. and Lindenberger, U. (2008) 'Enrichment effects on adult cognitive development: can the functional capacity of older adults be preserved and enhanced?', *Psychological Science in the Public Interest*, 9(1): 1–65.

Krahn, H. and Lowe, G.S. (eds) (1998) *Literacy Utilization in Canadian Workplaces*, Ottowa: Statistics Canada.

Kröger, E., Andel, R., Lindsay, J., Benounissa, Z., Verreault, R. and Laurin, D. (2008) 'Is complexity of work associated with risk of dementia? The Canadian Study of Health and Aging', *American Journal of Epidemiology*, 167(7): 820–30.

Marquié, J.C., Duarte, L.R., Bessières, P., Dalm, C., Gentil, C. and Ruidavets, J.B. (2010) 'Higher mental stimulation at work is associated with improved cognitive functioning in both young and older workers', *Ergonomics*, 53(11): 1287–301.

McArdle, J.J., Ferrer-Caja, E., Hamagami, F. and Woodcock, R.W. (2002) 'Comparative longitudinal structural analyses of the growth and decline of multiple intellectual abilities over the life span', *Developmental Psychology*, 38(1): 115–42.

Mincer, J. and Ofek, H. (1982) 'Interrupted work careers: depreciation and restoration of human capital', *Journal of Human Resources*, 17(1): 3–24.

Mincer, J. and Polachek, S. (1974) 'Family investments in human capital: earnings of women', *Journal of Political Economy*, 82(2, Part 2): S76–S108.

Neuman, S. and Weiss, A. (1995) 'On the effects of schooling vintage on experience-earnings profiles: theory and evidence', *European Economic Review*, 39(5): 943–55.

OECD (Organisation for Economic Co-operation and Development) (2012) 'Survey of adult skills', Available from: http://www.oecd.org/skills/piaac/publicdataandanalysis/#d.en.4089 [Accessed 11 October 2020].

OECD (Organisation for Economic Co-operation and Development) (2013a) *OECD Skills Outlook 2013: First Results from the Survey of Adult Skills*, Paris: OECD.

OECD (Organisation for Economic Co-operation and Development) (2013b) 'OECD annual national accounts database', Available from: http://stats.oecd.org [Accessed 23 July 2017].

OECD (Organisation for Economic Co-operation and Development) (2015) OECD 'Labour database', Available from: http://stats.oecd.org [Accessed 13 June 2017].

Pazy, A. (2004) 'Updating in response to the experience of lacking knowledge', *Applied Psychology* ,53(3): 436–52.

Pellizzari, M. and Fichen, A. (2013) 'A new measure of skills mismatch: theory and evidence from the survey of adult skills (PIAAC)', OECD social, employment and migration working Papers, no. 153, London: OECD Publishing.

Ravaglia, G., Forti, P., Maioli, F., Sacchetti, L., Mariani, E., Nativio, V., Talerico T., Vettori, C. and Macini, P.L. (2002) 'Education, occupation, and prevalence of dementia: findings from the Conselice study', *Dementia and Geriatric Cognitive Disorders*, 14(2): 90–100.

Ribeiro, P.C., Lopes, C.S. and Lourenço, R.A. (2013) 'Complexity of lifetime occupation and cognitive performance in old age', *Occupational Medicine*, 63(8): 556–62.

Rosen, S. (1975) 'Measuring the Obsolescence of Knowledge', in F.T. Juster (ed) *Education, Income, and Human Behavior*, New York: National Bureau of Economic Research, pp 199–232.

Salthouse, T.A. (2006) 'Mental exercise and mental aging: evaluating the validity of the "use it or lose it" hypothesis', *Perspectives on Psychological Science*, 1(1): 68–87.

Salthouse, T.A. (2007) 'Reply to Schooler: consistent is not conclusive', *Perspectives on Psychological Science: A Journal of the Association for Psychological Science*, 2(1): 30–2.

Salthouse, T.A. (2009) 'Responses to commentaries by Finch, Nilsson et al, Abrams, and Schaie', *Neurobiology of Aging*, 30(4): 530–3.

Schaie, K.W. (1994) 'The course of adult intellectual development', *American Psychologist*, 49(4): 304–13.

Schooler, C. (2007) 'Use it—and keep it, longer, probably: a reply to Salthouse (2006)', *Perspectives on Psychological Science*, 2(1): 24–9.

Sharp, E.S., Reynolds, C.A., Pedersen, N.L. and Gatz, M. (2010) 'Cognitive engagement and cognitive aging: is openness protective?', *Psychology and Aging*, 25 (1): 60–73.

Staff, R.T., Murray, A.D., Deary, I.J. and Whalley, L.J. (2004) 'What provides cerebral reserve?', *Brain: A Journal of Neurology*, 127(5): 1191–9.

Thelen, K. (ed) (2004) *How Institutions Evolve: The Political Economy of Skills in Germany, Britain, the United States, and Japan*, Cambridge: Cambridge University Press.

Weiss, Y. and Lillard, L.A. (1978) 'Experience, vintage, and time effects in the growth of earnings: American scientists, 1960–1970', *Journal of Political Economy*, 86(3): 427–47.

# Appendix

**Table 9A.1:** Control variables used to measure the depreciation rates of human capital

| Variable | Description | Note |
|---|---|---|
| Gender, family background, health status | Gender | 0. Female<br>1. Male<br>* Dummy coding with female as the reference group |
| | Highest level of education of parents | 1. None of them achieved secondary education or higher<br>2. At least one of them achieved secondary education or higher (excluding tertiary education)<br>3. At least one of them achieved tertiary education<br><br>* Dummy coding with 'none of them achieved secondary education or higher' as the reference group |
| | Number of books in home at age 16 | 1. 10 books or less<br>2. 11 to 25 books<br>3. 26 to 100 books<br>4. 101 to 200 books<br>5. 201 to 500 books<br>6. More than 500 books<br><br>* Dummy coding with '10 books or less' as the reference group |
| | Country of birth and language background | 0. Local birth or use of local language<br>1. Birth abroad and use of foreign language<br><br>* Dummy coding with 'Birth abroad and use of foreign language' as the reference group |
| | Country of the birth of parents | 1. Both of them were born abroad<br>2. One of them was born abroad<br>3. Both of them were born in the homeland<br><br>* Dummy coding with 'Both of them were born abroad' as the reference group |
| | Health status | 1. Excellent<br>2. Very good<br>3. Good<br>4. Fair<br>5. Poor<br><br>* Dummy coding with 'Poor' as the reference group |

(continued)

**Table 9A.1:** Control variables used to measure the depreciation rates of human capital (continued)

| Variable | Description | Note |
|---|---|---|
| Learning strategies | When I hear or read about new ideas, I try to relate them to real life situations to which they might apply. | 1. Not at all |
| | | 2. Very little |
| | | 3. To some extent |
| | | 4. To a high extent |
| | I like learning new things. | 5. To a very high extent |
| | When I come across something new, I try to relate it to what I already know. | * Details are averaged |
| | I like to get to the bottom of difficult things. | |
| | I like to figure out how different ideas fit together. | |
| | If I don't understand something, I look for additional information to make it clearer. | |
| Social capital | In the last 12 months, how often, if at all, did you do voluntary work, including unpaid work for a charity, political party, trade union or other non-profit organisation? | 1. Never |
| | | 2. Less than once a month |
| | | 3. Less than once a week but at least once a month |
| | | 4. At least once a week but not every day |
| | | 5. Every day |
| | | * Dummy coding with 'Never' as the reference group |
| | People like me don't have any say about what the government does. | 1. Strongly agree |
| | | 2. Agree |
| | There are only a few people you can trust completely. | 3. Neither agree nor disagree |
| | | 4. Disagree |
| | | 5. Strongly disagree |
| | If you are not careful, other people will take advantage of you. | * Dummy coding with 'Strongly agree' as the reference group |

*Source:* OECD (2013a)

**Table 9A.2:** Estimation results of depreciation rates without distinction between states of employment

| | | Average | Austria | Flanders (Belgium) | Czech Republic | Denmark | Estonia | Finland |
|---|---|---|---|---|---|---|---|---|
| $\beta_k$ | | 0.018*** | 0.016*** | 0.022*** | 0.017*** | 0.021*** | 0.016*** | 0.020*** |
| Depreciation rate (%) | $\delta_0$ | 0.236* | -0.739 | 0.325 | 2.346*** | 0.0?5 | 2.903*** | -1.372*** |
| | age | 0.010*** | 0.031*** | 0.012* | -0.021 | 0.020*** | -0.029*** | 0.047*** |
| Observations | | 102,767 | 4,732 | 4,528 | 5,625 | 7,0?4 | 6,945 | 5,102 |
| Proficiency scores | | 272.51 | 269.50 | 275.48 | 274.01 | 27C.79 | 275.88 | 287.55 |

| | | France | Ireland | Italy | Japan | Korea | Netherlands | Norway |
|---|---|---|---|---|---|---|---|---|
| $\beta_k$ | | 0.021*** | 0.020*** | 0.013*** | 0.017*** | 0.0?9*** | 0.018*** | 0.018*** |
| Depreciation rate (%) | $\delta_0$ | 1.419*** | 0.105 | -1.381 | -2.442*** | 2.3?3*** | -1.018* | -1.343** |
| | age | -0.006 | 0.002 | 0.029* | 0.057*** | -0.0?2 | 0.037*** | 0.033*** |
| Observations | | 5,088 | 5,124 | 4,454 | 4,762 | 6,4?4 | 4,704 | 4,520 |
| Proficiency scores | | 262.14 | 266.54 | 250.48 | 296.24 | 272.56 | 284.01 | 278.43 |

| | | Poland | Slovak Republic | Spain | Sweden | UK | United States |
|---|---|---|---|---|---|---|---|
| $\beta_k$ | | 0.016*** | 0.011*** | 0.021*** | 0.021*** | 0.0?6*** | 0.024*** |
| Depreciation rate (%) | $\delta_0$ | 3.344*** | 1.646** | -0.802 | -1.095** | -1.18?* | 1.369*** |
| | age | -0.044*** | -0.027** | 0.025*** | 0.031*** | 0.02?1** | -0.014* |
| Observations | | 8,857 | 5,444 | 5,431 | 4,087 | 5,9?4 | 3,862 |
| Proficiency scores | | 266.90 | 273.85 | 251.79 | 279.23 | 272.46 | 269.81 |

Notes:

1): Dependent variables are the natural log of the literacy scores. The result of the control variables in Table 9A.1 is omitted because of a lack of space.

2): * p<0.1, ** p<0.05, and *** p<0.01 significance levels.

Source: OECD (2012)

Table 9A.3: Estimation results of depreciation rates for the employed and unemployed

| | | Average | Flanders (Belgium) | Czech Republic | Denmark | Estonia | Finland |
|---|---|---|---|---|---|---|---|
| $\beta_k$ | | 0.017*** | 0.022*** | 0.017*** | 0.020*** | 0.016*** | 0.019*** |
| Depreciation rate (%) | Estimation $\delta_{01}$ | 1.169*** | 0.421 | -0.209 | 0.433 | 2.833* | -4.429*** |
| | age | 0.008 | 0.026 | 0.044 | 0.034 | -0.018 | 0.127*** |
| | wer | -1.136*** | 0.017 | 2.729 | -0.574 | -0.009 | 3.058** |
| | age × wer | 0.003 | -0.018 | -0.071 | -0.013 | -0.012 | -0.085*** |
| | Calculation $\delta_{00}$ | 0.033 | 0.437 | 2.520 | -0.141 | 2.824 | -1.371 |
| | $\delta_{10}$ | 0.012 | 0.008 | -0.027 | 0.021 | -0.030 | 0.042 |
| | $\delta_{01}$ | 1.169 | 0.421 | -0.209 | 0.433 | 2.833 | -4.429 |
| | $\delta_{11}$ | 0.008 | 0.026 | 0.044 | 0.034 | -0.018 | 0.127 |
| Observations | | 93,872 | 4,523 | 5,599 | 7,037 | 6,925 | 5,093 |

| | | France | Ireland | Italy | Japan | Korea | Netherlands |
|---|---|---|---|---|---|---|---|
| $\beta_k$ | | 0.020*** | 0.018*** | 0.013*** | 0.016*** | 0.019*** | 0.018*** |
| Depreciation rate (%) | Estimation $\delta_{01}$ | 0.164 | 4.631*** | 0.618 | -2.681*** | 1.113 | -0.779 |
| | age | 0.030* | -0.070*** | 0.005 | 0.066*** | 0.019 | 0.044* |
| | wer | 1.409 | -5.656*** | -2.708* | 0.287 | 2.023** | -0.270 |
| | age × wer | -0.041** | 0.091*** | 0.036 | -0.011 | -0.050** | -0.008 |
| | Calculation $\delta_{00}$ | 1.573 | -1.025 | -2.090 | -2.395 | 3.136 | -1.049 |
| | $\delta_{10}$ | -0.011 | 0.020 | 0.041 | 0.055 | -0.031 | 0.036 |
| | $\delta_{01}$ | 0.164 | 4.631 | 0.618 | -2.681 | 1.113 | -0.779 |
| | $\delta_{11}$ | 0.030 | -0.070 | 0.005 | 0.066 | 0.019 | 0.044 |
| Observations | | 5,061 | 5,118 | 4,439 | 4,743 | 6,454 | 4,699 |

(continued)

**Table 9A.3:** Estimation results of depreciation rates for the employed and unemployed (continued)

| | | | Norway | Poland | Slovak Republic | Spain | Sweden | UK |
|---|---|---|---|---|---|---|---|---|
| $\beta_k$ | | | 0.017*** | 0.015*** | 0.010*** | 0.021*** | 0.020*** | 0.015*** |
| Depreciation rate (%) | Estimation | $\delta_{01}$ | 1.503 | 4.011** | 8.291*** | -1.14E | -0.331 | 5.440** |
| | | age | -0.003 | -0.030 | -0.119**** | 0.032* | 0.040 | -0.083** |
| | | wer | -3.418** | -0.479 | -7.796*** | 0.60E | -1.135 | -7.401*** |
| | | age × wer | 0.046* | -0.021 | 0.112** | -0.013 | -0.005 | 0.118 |
| | Calculation | $\delta_{00}$ | -1.915 | 3.532 | 0.495 | -0.542 | -1.466 | -1.961 |
| | | $\delta_{10}$ | 0.042 | -0.051 | -0.007 | 0.022 | 0.035 | 0.035 |
| | | $\delta_{01}$ | 1.503 | 4.011 | 8.291 | -1.143 | -0.331 | 5.440 |
| | | $\delta_{11}$ | -0.003 | -0.030 | -0.119 | 0.032 | 0.040 | -0.083 |
| Observations | | | 4,514 | 8,759 | 5,438 | 5,402 | 4,082 | 5,986 |

Notes:

1): Dependent variables are the natural log of the literacy scores. The result of the control variables in Table 9A.1 is omitted because of a lack of space.

2): * p<0.1, ** p<0.05, and *** p<0.01 significance levels.

Source: OECD (2012)

255

Table 9A.4: Indicators of skills use in PIAAC

| Indicators | | Descriptions | Notes |
|---|---|---|---|
| **Information-processing skills** | | | |
| Reading | At work | Reading documents (directions, instructions, letters, memos, e-mails, articles, books, manuals, bills, invoices, diagrams, maps) | Variables are derived by using two or more related items asking frequency and level of use and applying Item Response Theory. The calculated score is adjusted for the international average to be scaled on 2 with a standard deviation of 1. |
| | In daily life | | |
| Writing | At work | Writing documents (letters, memos, e-mails, articles, reports, forms) | |
| | In daily life | | |
| Numeracy | At work | Calculating prices, costs or budgets; use of fractions, decimal or percentages; use of calculators; preparing graphs or tables; algebra or formulas; use of advanced math or statistics (calculus, trigonometry, regression) | |
| | In daily life | | |
| ICT skills | At work | Using e-mails, Internet, spreadsheets, word processors, programming languages; conducting transactions on line; participating in online discussions (conferences, chats) | |
| | In daily life | | |
| Problem-solving | At work | Facing complex problems (at least 30 minutes of thinking to find a solution) | 1. Never 2. Every few months 3. Once or twice a month 4. A few times a week, not every day 5. Every day |

(continued)

**Table 9A.4:** Indicators of skills use in PIAAC (continued)

| Indicators | Descriptions | Notes |
|---|---|---|
| **Other generics skills** | | |
| Task discretion | Choosing or changing the sequence of job tasks, the speed of work, working hours; choosing how to do the job | Variables are derived by using two or more related items asking frequency and level of use and applying Item Response Theory. The calculated score is adjusted for the international average to be scaled on 2 with a standard deviation of 1. |
| Learning at work | Learning new things from supervisors or co-workers; learning-by-doing; keeping up-to-date with new products or services | |
| Influencing skills | Instructing, teaching or training people; making speeches or presentations; selling products or services; advising people; planning others' activities; persuading or influencing others; negotiating. | |
| Cooperative skills | Cooperating or collaborating with co-workers | 1. None of the time<br>2. Up to a quarter of the time<br>3. Up to a half of the time<br>4. More than half of the time<br>5. All the time |
| Self-organising skills | Organising one's time | 1. Never<br>2. Every few months<br>3. Once or twice a month<br>4. A few times a week, not every day<br>5. Every day |
| Dexterity | Using skill or accuracy with one's hands or fingers | |
| Physical skills (gross) | Working physically for a long period | |

Source: OECD (2013a)

**Figure 9A.1:** International comparison of task discretion

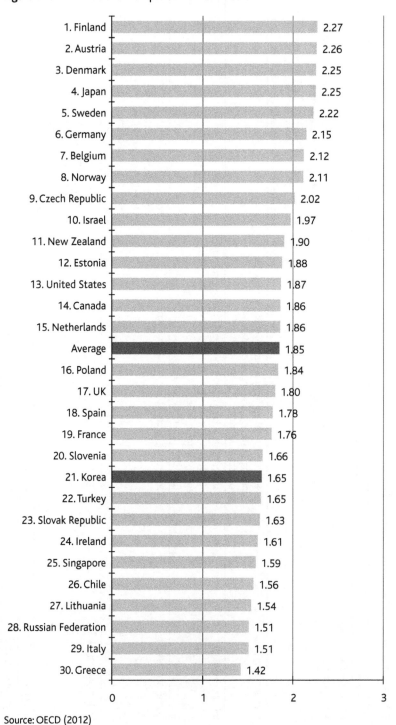

Source: OECD (2012)

**Figure 9A.2:** International comparison of self-organising skills

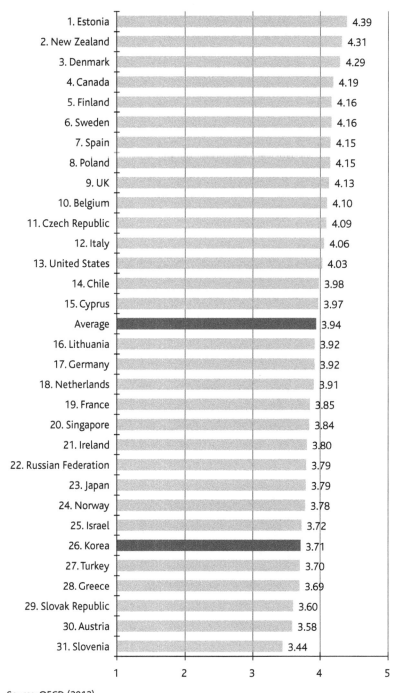

Source: OECD (2012)

**Figure 9A.3:** International comparison of problem-solving skills

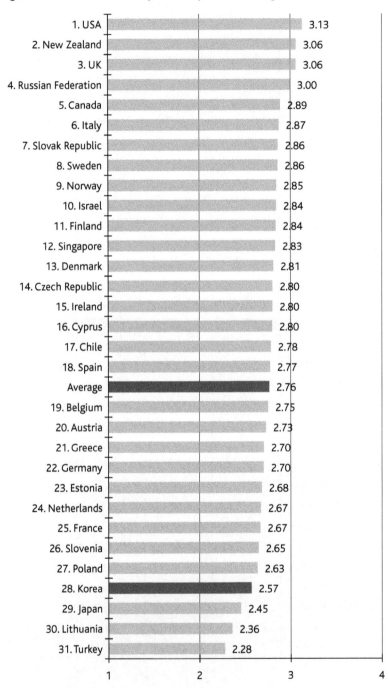

| | |
|---|---|
| 1. USA | 3.13 |
| 2. New Zealand | 3.06 |
| 3. UK | 3.06 |
| 4. Russian Federation | 3.00 |
| 5. Canada | 2.89 |
| 6. Italy | 2.87 |
| 7. Slovak Republic | 2.86 |
| 8. Sweden | 2.86 |
| 9. Norway | 2.85 |
| 10. Israel | 2.84 |
| 11. Finland | 2.84 |
| 12. Singapore | 2.83 |
| 13. Denmark | 2.81 |
| 14. Czech Republic | 2.80 |
| 15. Ireland | 2.80 |
| 16. Cyprus | 2.80 |
| 17. Chile | 2.78 |
| 18. Spain | 2.77 |
| Average | 2.76 |
| 19. Belgium | 2.75 |
| 20. Austria | 2.73 |
| 21. Greece | 2.70 |
| 22. Germany | 2.70 |
| 23. Estonia | 2.68 |
| 24. Netherlands | 2.67 |
| 25. France | 2.67 |
| 26. Slovenia | 2.65 |
| 27. Poland | 2.63 |
| 28. Korea | 2.57 |
| 29. Japan | 2.45 |
| 30. Lithuania | 2.36 |
| 31. Turkey | 2.28 |

Source: OECD (2012)

**Figure 9A.4:** International comparison of cooperative activities at work

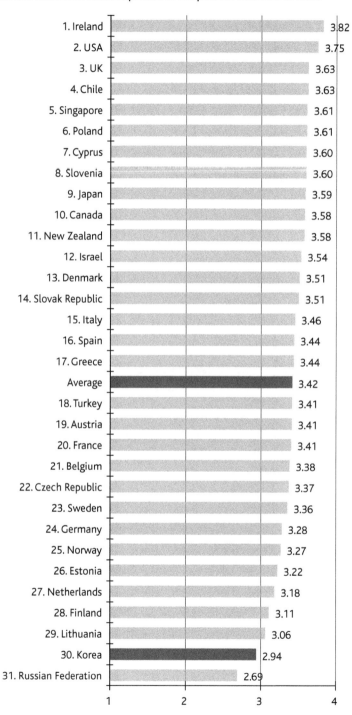

Source: OECD (2012)

**Figure 9A.5:** International comparison of learning at work

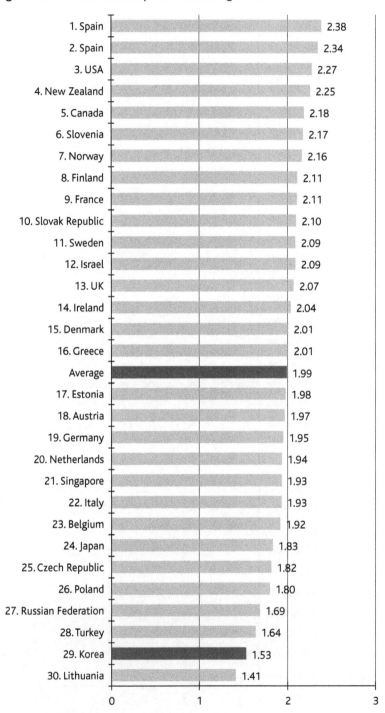

| | |
|---|---|
| 1. Spain | 2.38 |
| 2. Spain | 2.34 |
| 3. USA | 2.27 |
| 4. New Zealand | 2.25 |
| 5. Canada | 2.18 |
| 6. Slovenia | 2.17 |
| 7. Norway | 2.16 |
| 8. Finland | 2.11 |
| 9. France | 2.11 |
| 10. Slovak Republic | 2.10 |
| 11. Sweden | 2.09 |
| 12. Israel | 2.09 |
| 13. UK | 2.07 |
| 14. Ireland | 2.04 |
| 15. Denmark | 2.01 |
| 16. Greece | 2.01 |
| Average | 1.99 |
| 17. Estonia | 1.98 |
| 18. Austria | 1.97 |
| 19. Germany | 1.95 |
| 20. Netherlands | 1.94 |
| 21. Singapore | 1.93 |
| 22. Italy | 1.93 |
| 23. Belgium | 1.92 |
| 24. Japan | 1.83 |
| 25. Czech Republic | 1.82 |
| 26. Poland | 1.80 |
| 27. Russian Federation | 1.69 |
| 28. Turkey | 1.64 |
| 29. Korea | 1.53 |
| 30. Lithuania | 1.41 |

Source: OECD (2012)

**Figure 9A.6**: International comparison of job satisfaction

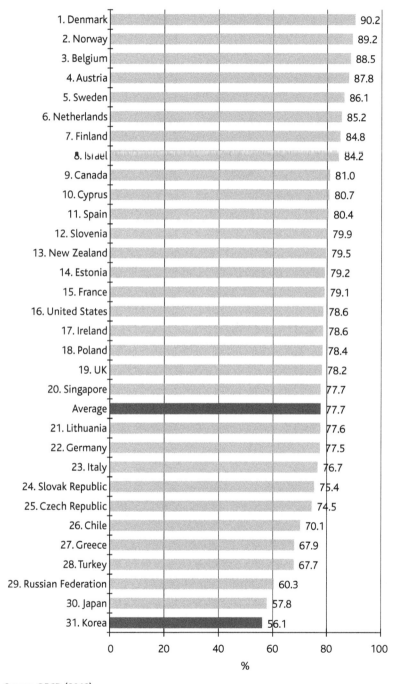

Source: OECD (2012)

# 10

# Changing patterns of grandparenting and their implications for active ageing in England and South Korea

*Hyejin Choi*

## Introduction

Since 2000, social investment has risen up the policy agenda across the globe. The idea is to replace the traditional welfare state strategy – that is, providing direct cash benefits, with a social investment state which focuses on human capital development in order to afford sustainable economic growth and the welfare of the population (Hemerijck, 2007: 12–13). Social investment strategy emphasises preparing rather than repairing, focusing on the roots of social problems. In that regard, social investment strategies call for investing in children to maximise their life-cycle opportunities, from which principle has emerged the key strategy of expanding childcare services. Childcare provisions enable parents, particularly young mothers, to remain in the paid labour market, and improves children's life chances by preparing them for future human capital development (Esping-Andersen et al, 2002).

At the same time, there has been growing interest in the provision of informal childcare that complements formal childcare arrangements. People, especially women, in their fifties and sixties, have relatively low labour market participation rates, but they play a central role in enabling mothers with children under 5 years old to take up or remain in paid work (Hank and Kreyenfeld, 2003; Gray, 2005). Research has also increasingly underlined the importance of grandparenting that facilitates child development, and raising a grandchild simultaneously influences grandparents' motivation to keep healthy and in touch with their grandchildren (Coall and Hertwig, 2011). Thus, it looks like a win–win situation, as grandparenting benefits not only grandchildren but also grandparents. Besides the positive evidence, however, it has also been suggested that grandparenting may have a harmful impact on the grandparents' health and social engagement (Minkler and Fuller-Thomson, 1999; Chen and Liu, 2011; Grundy et al, 2012).

This chapter seeks to understand the equivocal findings of previous studies by analysing multiple aspects of grandparenting, and examines the cost–benefit trade-offs of grandparenting while being mindful of policy contexts such as public childcare services. To examine whether and how childcare programme correlates differ across a wide range of contexts, this study focuses on grandparenting in South Korea (hereafter, Korea) and the United Kingdom. This chapter uses data from the Korea Time Use Survey (K-TUS) and UK Time Use Survey (UK-TUS) to analyse the amount of time spent by older adults in providing childcare, and their general use of time in other activities. Data from the Korea Longitudinal Study of Ageing (KLoSA) and the English Longitudinal Study of Aging (ELSA) are also utilised, which allows us to account for unobservable characteristics at the individual level.

This chapter begins with a brief description of active ageing strategy as a social investment strategy in the context of ageing populations and gives an overview of recent studies that address the connection between grandparenting and grandparents' wellbeing. After a short description of our data sources and methods, we present descriptive findings using UK-TUS/K-TUS. The TUS analysis illuminates the lifestyle differences between caregivers and non-caregivers. I also estimate fixed-effect models using ELSA/KLoSA, which allow us to analyse the inter-relationship between grandparenting and different productive activities. The final section provides a conclusion.

## Literature Review

### Active ageing as a social investment strategy

In Europe, a debate has emerged since the mid-1990s with regard to social investment. According to the European Commission's definition, social investment is about investing in people to strengthen their current and future capacities, and to improve opportunities to participate in society and the labour market (Vandenbroucke and Vleminck, 2011; European Commission, 2013). Social investment stresses prevention rather than cure, by intervening earlier in the life cycle to reduce the need for social benefits later on. In this regard, Esping-Andersen et al (2002) mentioned that the 'child-centred approach' is the core of the European social investment strategy, which is expected to contribute to enhancing human capital and the 'new gender contract' to ensure mothers' labour market participation.

Meanwhile, as life expectancy increases, the European Commission has extended the policy response to social investment in an ageing population (European Commission, 2013). The Social Investment Package (SIP) highlights the importance of older adults in order to prevent a loss of valuable expertise, retain the potential of older people, and strengthen society's human and structural resilience, and argues that we should support healthy and active ageing. Two points clearly emerge with regard to the importance of active ageing as a social investment strategy. First, it is socially favourable to encourage the engagement of older adults in economic and social life. They can be volunteers, caregivers and workers in society, and their participation is an important resource in social capital formulation. Second, the cost of promoting active ageing is much lower than the passive management of older people who are left marginalised and fully dependent on the state and family. Hence active ageing has been emphasised in the Commission's communication 'Towards Social Investment for Growth and Cohesion' and included as one of the investment priorities of the European Social Fund (ESF) in the 2014–20 period.

In this context, grandparenting can be considered a key area of social investment that also helps the family to maintain its dual earning status, and helps accumulation of human capital by grandchildren in terms of intellectual, physical and emotional development. Also, the Active Ageing Index includes grandparenting as an important mode of social engagement along with employment, voluntary activities, physical exercise and educational attainment of older adults (Zaidi et al, 2013).

## Grandparenting and active ageing

Although grandparenting has increasingly emerged as an important area of social investment, much previous literature on grandparental childcare has presented mixed evidence. Some research suggests that grandparenting impedes the ability to engage in productive and social activity. Baker and Silverstein (2008) argue that grandparents who provide primary care are associated with a lack of privacy and leisure time, and a heightened risk of isolation and depression. Arpino and Bordone (2014) also report that having to provide regular childcare has a significant negative effect on the number of activities in which grandmothers participate, such as educational or training courses, volunteering, and participating in political or community organisations. Bulanda and Jendrek (2014) suggest that grandparents raising co-residential grandchildren have a lower probability of participating in volunteer work than grandparents that provide non-regular grandchild care. However, most such studies focused on a particular situation, such as cases in which the grandparents provide full care.

On the other hand, providing childcare on a supplementary basis may have a far different effect on grandparents' outcomes than being a primary caregiver. Providing part-time care may enhance grandparents' sense of purpose in life and help maintain family identity (Giarrusso et al, 2000; Burr et al, 2005; Baker and Silverstein, 2008; Butrica et al, 2009; Arpino and Bordone, 2014; Bulanda and Jendrek, 2014). Some grandparents have reported having a more active lifestyle after assuming a caregiver role (Waldrop and Weber, 2001), and four out of five caregiving grandparents have said they find the experience of raising a grandchild 'extremely rewarding' (Giarrusso et al, 2000). Burr et al (2005) found that caregivers without a heavy care burden were more likely to volunteer and spend more time in volunteering than non-caregivers. Butrica et al (2009) argued that the onset of childcare responsibilities increases the likelihood of volunteering, with greater opportunities to engage in grandchildren's school-related activities. Such research suggests that it is important to consider the type of grandparenting and the amount of time committed to it when considering the effects. It also leads to a debate on the institutional conditions that reduce the care burden of grandparents.

### Institutional conditions for easing the care burden of grandparents

Many studies have sought to specify the conditions and mechanisms that underpin grandparenting characteristics across countries. Igel and Szydlik (2011), using the Survey of Health, Ageing and Retirement in Europe (SHARE), found that informal childcare help is given intensively in Southern European countries because of their high degree of familialism, but it is less common in, for example, the Nordic countries where formal welfare arrangements relieve families of care responsibilities. Hank and Buber (2009) also examined grandparenting patterns in the European setting in the light of the welfare state-related contextual factors that vary across countries. As the availability of institutional childcare has often been suggested to have a significant impact on mothers' employment, they argue that the intensity of grandparent-provided care varies in accordance with the geographic lines of different childcare and employment regimes in Europe.

Lewis et al (2008) found a similar pattern. They explored the ways in which parents in families reconcile employment with childcare in 13 EU member countries: Greece, Belgium and Austria had the biggest proportions of working mothers who use grandparents as the main childcare providers (all three over 40 per cent) rather than formal childcare provisions. The Netherlands, Portugal, Germany, Ireland, Great Britain, Spain and Finland take an average position, with between 34 and 24 per cent of working mothers usually having the grandparents looking after the children. In Sweden, France and Denmark, grandparents are less used as the main childcare source from 6 to 16 per cent (Lewis et al, 2008).

In sum, prior research suggests that the pattern of grandparenting is determined largely by formal childcare arrangements: where there are more formal alternatives, parents rely less on help from grandparents (Hank and Buber, 2009; Igel and Szydlik, 2011). However, most of these studies are confined to Western Europe, so the countries share similar institutional contexts. Although European countries provide a unique opportunity for comparative work, such commonalities often overshadow other contextual variables that might influence the dependent variable.

## Case selection and hypothesis

To examine whether and how childcare programmes are correlated across a wide range of contexts, this study focuses on grandparenting in Korea and the UK. The contexts of the child support system in the two nations have both similarities and differences, and thus offer a unique opportunity for a comparative study. Both countries have several common features. They maintained a residual approach to childcare in the early 1990s, with about 5 per cent of GDP in England and 1 per cent in Korea. Compared to other European countries with a long history of pre-school provisions, state intervention came relatively late and responsibility for childcare was essentially regarded as a private matter in both countries. But in the 2010s, early childhood education had a high political and policy profile in both countries, as the social investment agenda emerged as the centre of political discourse. There has been a considerable development of ECEC provisions in England since 1997 and in Korea since 2003.

However, there are two major differences between the countries that may affect the grandparents' patterns. The first point is the extent of childcare benefits. Although both countries are highly committed to a social investment strategy, Korea has been much faster and bolder in terms of childcare expansion (Fleckenstein and Lee, 2017), while England targeted reform more (Gambaro et al, 2014). Since the presidential election in 2012, the Korean government implemented a universal free childcare programme which guarantees full-time childcare from 10 a.m. to 6 p.m. Meanwhile, in England, despite the progressive government's vision turning increasingly towards universal childcare (Vevers, 2004), the level of benefit was notably limited so that 0–2 year old children have been largely excluded from publicly supported childcare, and 3–4 year old children are entitled to only 15 hours (30 hours for disadvantaged children) per week. This usually means that mothers can use either morning or afternoon childcare session of around 2.5 hours.

The second point is the broader institutional difference between the UK and Korea. Although both countries adopted social investment at the same time, less is known how the services effectively work in their different institutional settings. As mentioned earlier, most previous studies are confined to Western Europe, where the countries share similar labour market cultures. According to OECD data, Koreans worked an average of 2,113 hours in 2015, the second highest among the 35 OECD member countries. In England the average was only about 1,545 hours. Employee-centred flexibility, in which workers have some input and control over the scheduling and length of their work hours, is an important resource for employees, especially working for mothers and their families who are responsible for or support the care of young children (Pocock et al, 2012). In many European countries, including England, female part-time employment (especially for mothers) has increased rapidly since the 1980s, while in Korea labour flexibility for working mothers is still very low.

Reflecting the findings of previous literature, this chapter makes an analytical distinction between the two mechanisms that potentially characterise the patterns of grandparenting. Firstly, we can expect that grandparents in Korea lead more active lifestyles than in England, as Korea's higher levels of childcare infrastructure allow a more or less voluntary decision by grandparents. Previous studies have shown that the availability of childcare service crowds out intensive informal care needs, but brings in non-intensive informal care that benefits mothers who are already employed (eg, Igel and Szydlik, 2011).

Secondly, if the influence of other institutional contexts (such as labour market conditions) is stronger, Korean grandparents may experience more fragmented and contaminated leisure and social engagement, which can be understood as a spill-over effect of domestic and care commitments that could have otherwise been handled by working mothers. Due to the influence of the intensive labour market, the burden of working mothers becomes very taxing, and the domestic/parent role spill-over may compromise the capacity for voluntary decision-making during grandparents' free time, and grandparents can thus be exposed to demands for intensive care from working mothers. By testing this hypothesis, we attempt to clarify the complementary relationship between grandparenting and active ageing in later life.

## Methods

Two paired datasets designed for comparative studies were used for the analyses. The first analysis uses the UK-TUS and K-TUS. These two datasets are obtained from nationally representative samples of households and individuals using clustered, stratified sampling designs. The data is gathered from face-to-face interviews, where all members of a household over the age of 10 are asked to keep track of their activities. Similar sampling and coding procedures, time-diary instruments and instructions to respondents are also used in order to produce valid estimates of changes in time use. The participants are asked to begin journaling at 00:00 (midnight) and record their activities in 10-min slots until 23:50 each day.

We used K-TUS data from 2004 and 2014, and UK-TUS data from 2000 and 2014. Because of the dissimilarities of the survey items, we used the 2004 K-TUS data instead of the 1999 K-TUS data. The data includes the number of people who provide childcare, how much time they spend on these activities (eg, playing, feeding and giving attention) and when they use such time. The respondents' main activity records were requested and compared. We used 55–70 year-old respondents as the sample for childcare. As childcare activities include feeding and dressing, those over 70 were excluded, since there were too few people in this group who actually engage in caring for young children.

To determine whether there were significant differences in time spent on the said non-childcare activities between the childcare-providing older adults and non-caregiving older adults, we utilised ANOVA analysis. We compared the time-use difference of each activity, and developed a single measure, 'active lifestyle variable' – which included voluntary work and participation, meeting friends, theatre and cultural activities, leisure and outdoor activities, sports and physical activities, hobby activities, and reading – to evaluate the overall difference between caregivers and non-caregivers.

However, as the K-TUS does not provide data on the relationship between caregivers and care recipients, we created variables of 'child caregivers' from respondents' reports of time spent during the diary day. Within the sample of respondents aged 55 to 70 years, child caregivers were defined as those who spend more than a half-hour a day on childcare, while those who did not were defined as non-caregivers. Because of this limitation, a precise comparison of grandparents' provision of caregiving is challenging as the TUSs lack information with regard to the relationship between caregivers and care recipients.

Therefore, this chapter utilised the second analysis, based on ELSA and KLoSA data, that included nationally representative samples of English and Korean populations aged over 55. Both datasets were designed to be comparable, and contained detailed information on respondents as well as their children, siblings and parents. Both ELSA and KLoSA have many questions in common. We used data from the first, second and third waves (2004, 2009 and 2014) for those countries that participated in all three waves. The definition of the variables are as follows.

### Dependent variable

In the panel estimation, we measured the three distinctive features of active lifestyle, social engagement (including membership in organisations and frequency of meeting friends), and regular exercise as the dependent variable. To measure the engagement in social activities variable, we used responses to the ELSA and KLoSA questionnaire item, 'Have you done any of these activities in the last four weeks?' with response choices such as: social groups, educational or training course; sport, social or other clubs; religious organisation (church, synagogue, mosque etc); political or community-related organisation.

We also considered the frequency of meeting friends. The ELSA and KLoSA questionnaires ask: 'On average, how often do you do the following with any of these friends, not counting those who live with you?' ELSA has six categories of frequency (three or more times a week, once or twice a week, once or twice a month, every few months, once or twice a year, less than once a year or never). KLoSA employs nine categories for the frequency of meeting friends, so we collapsed some of the KLoSA categories for comparison. Finally, we created a binary variable for physical exercise more than once a week. For ELSA, frequency of participation in vigorous, moderate and light physical activities (more than once per week, once per week, one to three times per month, hardly ever) was used, and for KLoSA frequency of exercise more than once a week was used.

Independent variable We use the self-report question 'During the last twelve months, have you looked after your grandchildren?' to separate grandchild caregivers from non-caregivers. Using this item, we created a binary independent variable that indicated whether the respondent took care of grandchildren or not. However, we did not utilise the childcare time as the independent variable. While KLoSA provides a time measure of grandparenting, the information on the hours of grandparenting in ELSA is limited, since it provides data only on those who live with grandchildren.

A number of control variables were chosen according to a general empirical consensus on the important determinants of participation in social activities. Sociodemographic variables such as age, gender (female = 1), and marital status (if living with a partner = 1; if not living with a partner = 0) are usually found to be negatively associated with level of social participation. Age was measured as a continuous variable from low to high. Gender and education may also affect the level of social engagement, but were omitted from the fixed-effects analysis, since gender and education variables are time-invariant.

To assess household income, we used a scale that divides household income by the square root of household size. This implies that a household of four persons has needs twice as large as one composed of a single person. The population of households was divided into fifths, and these quintiles were arranged from lowest to highest income. We measured employment status with dummy variables where 'employed' was denoted as 1. Self-rated health was measured using a 1–5 ordinal scale based on the following question: 'Regarding your state of health, do you feel it is: excellent, good, average, not so good, or poor?' We also considered functional impairment and depressive symptoms that may adversely affect active lifestyles. Functional impairment was measured as the aggregated number of mobility limitations in activities of daily living ("ADL limitations"). Depressive symptoms were measured using these five items extracted from the 20-item Center for Epidemiological Studies Depression (CES-D) Scale: 'everything I did was an effort', 'felt lonely", 'felt sad', 'felt depressed' and 'sleep was restless', since the KLoSA validates only these five items.

## Results of the study

This study utilised a bivariate and multivariate regression analysis in order to further analyse the differential characteristics of informal caregivers in the two surveys. Some previous studies have utilised instrumental variable regression using the availability of grandchildren as the instrumental variable. Although instrumental variable regression is a powerful method to resolve endogeneity issues, it does not allow for consistent estimation if the instrument variable is correlated with the error term in the explanatory equation (Bound et al, 1995). This issue is especially critical when we estimate the effect on social activities, since the presence of grandchildren is likely to influence grandparents' social engagement (ie, joining clubs), particularly in the Asian context.

Thus, instead of utilising an instrumental variable, we used a fixed-effects panel estimation. We use a Hausman test to decide between fixed and random effects model. Chamberlain (1980) has suggested that the fixed-effects logit model is particularly well suited to control for unobserved heterogeneity in panels with a large number of individuals and a small number of time periods, as in the present case. However, as Chamberlain (1980) also noted, the fixed-effects logit regression can result in a biased outcome as the sum of observations eliminates unobserved heterogeneity from the discrete model. In other words, the logit regression uses only information from individuals who experience a change in the dependent variable over time. To compensate for this weakness, this present study ran a fixed-effects ordinary least squares (OLS) regression as a supplementary analysis to check robustness.

## Evidence from the TUSs

Childcaring older adults between the ages of 55 and 70 years represented 9.3 per cent of UK population in 2000 and 8.6 per cent in 2014, while in Korea these figures were respectively 8.3 per cent and 3.5 per cent. The amount of childcaring time between 2000 and 2014 presents a similar trend. In Korea, the mean weekday minutes spent in childcare decreased from 142.3 minutes per day in 2004 to 125.1 minutes per day in 2014, and for female caregivers from 153 minutes in 2004 to 134.7 minutes in 2014. In England, the mean weekday minutes spent taking care of children was 112.5 minutes per day in 2000 and 122.5 minutes per day in 2014. For female caregivers in England, these figures were 115.6 minutes in 2004 and 121.8 minutes in 2014. The reduction in occurrence and time spent on childcare in Korea is most possibly due to the implementation of a universal childcare programme in 2009. These trends validate the conventional wisdom that universal childcare schemes reduce the caring burden of grandparents. However, although older Korean women became less involved in childcare, they seemed to be engaged in childcare more intensively. In England, the occurrence of grandparenting is more frequent and the intensity of care provided is lower than in Korea.

Tables 10.1 and 10.2 show the results of an ANOVA of total time spent on daily activities in Korea and England. According to the analysis, childcaring Korean older adults spent less time on personal care, employment, other household related work, meeting friends,

Table 10.1: Time spent in daily activities: Korea

| Weekday | 2004 | | | | 2014 | | | |
|---|---|---|---|---|---|---|---|---|
| | Sum | Non-caring | Caring | F-value | Sum | Non-caring | Caring | F-value |
| Sleeping | 471.4 | 470.6 | 479.3 | 7.0 | 471.7 | 471.3 | 483.2 | 3.4 |
| | (92.1) | (92.4) | (88.6) | | (87.2) | (87.5) | (78.8) | |
| Eating | 98.2 | 98.4 | 96.3 | 3.0 | 122.2 | 122.2 | 122.2 | 0.0 |
| | (33.9) | (33.9) | (33.3) | | (43.3) | (43.3) | (44.7) | |
| Personal care | 72.7 | 73.4 | 64.9 | 14.2** | 80.8 | 81.5 | 62.6 | 24.7** |
| | (63.9) | (64.6) | (55.2) | | (51.2) | (51.2) | (47.2) | |
| Employment | 195.0 | 205.8 | 76.0 | 261.9** | 188.0 | 192.3 | 68.9 | 56.4** |
| | (229.4) | (232.1) | (152.6) | | (222.0) | (223.3) | (137.6) | |
| Study | 2.4 | 2.4 | 1.4 | 1.5 | 1.8 | 1.9 | 0.6 | 0.7 |
| | (24.5) | (25.1) | (15.2) | | (19.6) | (19.9) | (8.8) | |
| HH keeping | 112.0 | 109.6 | 138.0 | 45.2** | 108.0 | 106.4 | 150.9 | 28.9** |
| | (119.2) | (118.5) | (123.5) | | (111.4) | (110.7) | (122.2) | |
| Other HH related work | 8.7 | 8.8 | 7.5 | 1.6 | 7.8 | 7.9 | 5.8 | 1.5 |
| | (29.8) | (30.4) | (22.2) | | (23.8) | (23.9) | (18.2) | |
| Shopping | 10.0 | 9.8 | 12.0 | 6.2** | 13.1 | 12.9 | 17.5 | 5.2* |
| | (24.8) | (24.7) | (25.6) | | (27.3) | (27.1) | (31.7) | |
| Adult care | 6.1 | 6.0 | 7.2 | 1.0 | 9.1 | 9.3 | 4.9 | 2.2 |
| | (35.4) | (35.8) | (31.2) | | (39.5) | (39.9) | (22.9) | |
| Voluntary work and participation | 3.6 | 3.7 | 2.4 | 1.7 | 3.1 | 3.1 | 2.6 | 0.04 |
| | (28.5) | (28.8) | (24.5) | | (29.3) | (29.6) | (19.5) | |
| Religious activities | 15.6 | 15.6 | 15.3 | 0.03 | 16.5 | 16.7 | 11.0 | 2.0 |
| | (55.1) | (55.3) | (52.3) | | (54.7) | (55.1) | (40.4) | |

(continued)

275

**Table 10.1:** Time spent in daily activities: Korea (continued)

| Weekday | 2004 | | | | 2014 | | | |
|---|---|---|---|---|---|---|---|---|
| | Sum | Non-caring | Caring | F-value | Sum | Non-caring | Caring | F-value |
| Meeting friends | 63.2 | 63.8 | 56.9 | 6.0** | 47.3 | 47.6 | 38.9 | 4.3* |
| | (79.1) | (79.9) | (69.9) | | (56.4) | (56.8) | (46.1) | |
| Theater and cultural activities | 1.0 | 1.0 | 1.2 | 0.1 | 3.0 | 3.0 | 2.4 | 0.12 |
| | (13.6) | (13.6) | (14.2) | | (21.7) | (21.9) | (17.7) | |
| Leisure and outdoor | 7.7 | 7.8 | 5.8 | 2.1 | 10.9 | 11.1 | 6.1 | 2.1 |
| | (39.2) | (39.8) | (31.4) | | (46.3) | (46.9) | (28.2) | |
| Sports and physical activities | 29.2 | 29.0 | 32.3 | 3.5† | 38.7 | 38.7 | 39.5 | 0.03 |
| | (50.8) | (50.8) | (51.5) | | (57.6) | (57.7) | (56.0) | |
| Hobby | 39.7 | 40.2 | 33.5 | 9.5** | 12.3 | 12.5 | 6.6 | 4.5* |
| | (61.0) | (61.4) | (56.7) | | (37.6) | (38.0) | (22.8) | |
| Doing nothing | 25.3 | 25.7 | 21.0 | 10.9** | 14.4 | 14.6 | 10.4 | 5.3* |
| | (40.1) | (40.3) | (37.0) | | (24.2) | (24.3) | (22.3) | |
| Media | 173.8 | 173.8 | 174.4 | 0.02 | 170.3 | 169.7 | 188.2 | 3.9* |
| | (128.5) | (129.4) | (117.4) | | (126.2) | (126.5) | (118.6) | |
| Reading books | 10.9 | 11.0 | 10.0 | 0.8 | 8.3 | 8.4 | 6.8 | 0.6 |
| | (31.3) | (31.4) | (29.6) | | (27.7) | (27.8) | (25.0) | |
| Transportation | 87.7 | 88.8 | 74.9 | 23.0** | 89.7 | 90.5 | 66.0 | 18.0** |
| | (81.9) | (82.9) | (68.6) | | (77.6) | (78.1) | (59.3) | |
| Unclassified activities | 20.2 | 19.1 | 20.1 | 2.0 | 21.7 | 21.8 | 19.1 | 3.4† |
| | (21.5) | (20.5) | (21.4) | | (19.4) | (19.5) | (14.8) | |
| N | 10,504 | 9,634 | 870 | | 5,332 | 5,145 | 187 | |
| Active lifestyle | 115.6 | 116.3 | 108.6 | 3.7** | 111.3 | 111.8 | 96.3 | 4.2** |
| | (112.0) | (113.0) | (100.8) | | (101.9) | (102.4) | (88.3) | |

*Active lifestyle: time spent in activities including voluntary work and participation, meeting friends, theater and cultural activities, leisure and outdoor activities, sports and physical activities, hobby activities, reading books.

**Table 10.2:** Time spent in daily activities: UK

| Weekday | 2000 | | | | 2014 | | | |
|---|---|---|---|---|---|---|---|---|
| | Sum | Non-caring | Caring | F-value | Sum | Non-caring | Caring | F-value |
| Sleeping | 500.8 | 501.3 | 496.4 | 0.8 | 495.7 | 495.6 | 496.5 | 0.02 |
| | (96.0) | (96.9) | (85.9) | | (117.8) | (119.8) | (93.7) | |
| Eating | 104.9 | 105.4 | 99.4 | 3.0† | 101.8 | 102.0 | 99.8 | 0.3 |
| | (59.9) | (60.8) | (50.7) | | (67.9) | (68.5) | (61.2) | |
| Personal care | 47.8 | 48.3 | 42.8 | 6.6** | 60.6 | 61.0 | 57.1 | 1.2 |
| | (37.0) | (37.5) | (31.6) | | (60.3) | (62.0) | (37.7) | |
| Employment | 72.5 | 76.5 | 33.9 | 18.0** | 90.1 | 95.2 | 36.2 | 28.8** |
| | (173.2) | (178.1) | (106.4) | | (188.4) | (193.3) | (111.8) | |
| Study | 1.8 | 1.9 | 0.8 | 0.9 | 1.8 | 2.0 | 0.1 | 3.0† |
| | (20.6) | (21.4) | (10.6) | | (18.2) | (19.0) | (1.0) | |
| HH keeping | 138.0 | 136.4 | 154.1 | 6.9** | 122.0 | 119.1 | 153.0 | 28.8** |
| | (116.7) | (117.7) | (104.5) | | (106.6) | (106.2) | (106.1) | |
| HH maintain ie, gardening | 50.0 | 51.6 | 34.1 | 12.8** | 44.4 | 46.1 | 26.4 | 17.0** |
| | (84.6) | (86.6) | (59.2) | | (81.7) | (83.9) | (50.1) | |
| Shopping | 36.3 | 36.7 | 32.4 | 1.67 | 39.2 | 39.2 | 38.8 | 0.01 |
| | (58.0) | (59.0) | (47.4) | | (60.9) | (61.6) | (53.2) | |
| Adult care | 3.8 | 3.9 | 3.5 | 0.06 | 2.9 | 3.0 | 2.0 | 0.6 |
| | (26.6) | (26.7) | (25.2) | | (19.9) | (20.5) | (11.1) | |
| Voluntary work and participation | 5.1 | 5.4 | 3.0 | 1.3 | 5.7 | 6.0 | 2.7 | 2.0 |
| | (33.4) | (34.4) | (22.3) | | (39.5) | (41.0) | (17.5) | |
| Religious activities | 5.2 | 5.3 | 4.0 | 0.8 | 4.7 | 4.8 | 3.9 | 0.3 |
| | (25.5) | (25.7) | (23.7) | | (26.1) | (26.6) | (20.3) | |

(continued)

**Table 10.2:** Time spent in daily activities: the UK (continued)

| Weekday | 2000 | | | | 2014 | | | |
|---|---|---|---|---|---|---|---|---|
| | Sum | Non-caring | Caring | F-value | Sum | Non-caring | Caring | F-value |
| Meeting friends | 63.0 | 63.0 | 63.9 | 0.03 | 52.5 | 52.7 | 50.0 | 0.4 |
| | (84.5) | (85.1) | (78.3) | | (78.5) | (80.0) | (61.2) | |
| Theater and cultural activities | 1.8 | 1.9 | 0.9 | 0.8 | 3.5 | 3.6 | 2.1 | 1.2 |
| | (17.9) | (18.5) | (10.5) | | (23.7) | (24.3) | (16.5) | |
| Leisure and outdoor activities | 16.5 | 16.6 | 15.1 | 0.1 | 17.8 | 17.1 | 25.0 | 2.8† |
| | (74.1) | (75.2) | (62.7) | | (79.5) | (78.9) | (85.2) | |
| Sports and physical activities | 16.3 | 16.8 | 11.0 | 3.7† | 19.5 | 19.7 | 17.5 | 0.5 |
| | (52.5) | (53.9) | (36.0) | | (55.4) | (56.5) | (42.7) | |
| Hobby activities | 23.4 | 23.5 | 22.4 | 0.1 | 39.6 | 40.7 | 28.4 | 8.6** |
| | (54.1) | (54.6) | (48.9) | | (71.5) | (73.2) | (48.2) | |
| Doing nothing | 28.8 | 28.5 | 31.8 | 0.9 | 20.8 | 20.8 | 20.3 | 0.03 |
| | (60.9) | (60.1) | (68.3) | | (52.5) | (53.4) | (42.1) | |
| **Media** | 177.2 | 179.8 | 151.8 | 12.8** | 176.1 | 179.3 | 142.4 | 18.5** |
| | (135.2) | (136.3) | (120.5) | | (146.7) | (149.4) | (108.8) | |
| Reading books | 45.1 | 45.8 | 38.5 | 3.8† | 30.4 | 30.6 | 28.2 | 0.6 |
| | (64.7) | (65.9) | (50.4) | | (53.2) | (53.5) | (50.8) | |
| Transportation | 66.8 | 66.3 | 72.0 | 2.2 | 70.4 | 70.2 | 71.8 | 0.1 |
| | (65.6) | (65.8) | (63.6) | | (84.0) | (85.2) | (70.6) | |
| Unclassified activities | 28.2 | 28.2 | 27.7 | 0.02 | 35.9 | 36.2 | 32.5 | 0.4 |
| | (72.2) | (73.0) | (63.2) | | (104.8) | (107.7) | (66.3) | |
| N | 3,529 | 3,202 | 327 | | 3,706 | 3,387 | 319 | |
| | | (90.7) | (9.3) | | | (91.4) | (8.6) | |
| Active lifestyle | 147.9 | 149.5 | 132.4 | 4.57* | 129.3 | 125.4 | 129.7 | 0.3 |
| | (137.6) | (139.6) | (115.7) | | (137.4) | (139.0) | (119.7) | |

*Active lifestyle: Time spent in activities including voluntary work and participation, meeting friends, theater and cultural activities, leisure and outdoor activities, sports and physical activities, hobby activities, reading books.

resting, hobby activities and transportation (or travelling) than non-caregivers. The difference for personal care activity continued in 2014 and media usage was only significant in 2014. Child caregivers spent more time on household activity and engaging in passive leisure activity such as watching TV. Like English caregivers, the Korean caregivers spent more time on housekeeping activities in 2014 than in 2004. However, overall, Korea has more differences between caregivers and non-caregivers in social engagement.

Turning to English older adults who are caregivers, both men and women spent less time on personal care, employment, household maintenance (eg, gardening) and media usage than non-caregivers. The times spent on these activities were significantly different from each other at the 1 per cent level, and these differences for most activities were larger in 2014. Compared to before, in 2014 personal-care activity was non-significant while hobby activity was statistically significant. Child caregivers spent more time on household activities and the difference increased in 2014, despite the fact that both caregivers and non-caregivers spent less time on housekeeping that year. However, leisure activity and social participation activity did not show significant differences in 2014.

Grandparental childcare is often considered a gendered activity, with previous studies reporting that grandmothers are the more likely grandparent to be engaged in childcare (Gray, 2005; Taniguchi, 2006; Horsfall and Dempsey, 2015). On this basis, Figure 10.1 presents the weekday diaries for grandmothers who spend more than half an hour a day on childcare. The diary entries imply that the nature of grandparental childcare is quite different in England and Korea. British child caregivers seem to be the main caregivers during the daytime, while Korean grandmothers spend time on caregiving in the early morning and less time during the day. In Korea, the peak time was 8:00 a.m. to 9:00 a.m. and 5:00 p.m. to 8:00 p.m. in 2014. In England, the peak time was 3:00 p.m. to 4:00 p.m. in 2000 and 4:00 p.m. to 6:00 p.m. in 2014. This also indicates that female older adults in Korea start their day earlier and end later compared to British child caregivers. There is also a time change between 2004 to 2014: morning care work starts earlier and evening care work ends later in Korea. UK grandparents also experienced a shift in care time towards the evening, although their caring activities end much earlier than in Korea.

So what is the main activity during the daytime for caregivers in Korea? To answer, we compared the time diaries for housekeeping duties among female child caregivers with those of non-caregivers. As Figure 10.2 shows, there is a significant difference between Korean

**Figure 10.1:** Childcaring time diary of 55–70 year-olds (female, weekday)

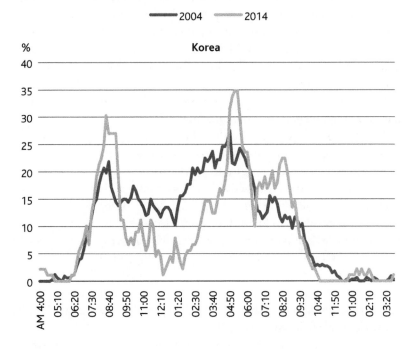

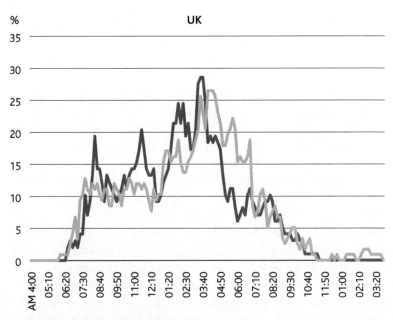

Note: England 2000 N=98, England 2014 N=117, Korea 2004 N=334, Korea 2014 N=89.
Source: Author's creation, based on the Time Use Survey

**Figure 10.2:** Housekeeping work time diary (female, weekday)

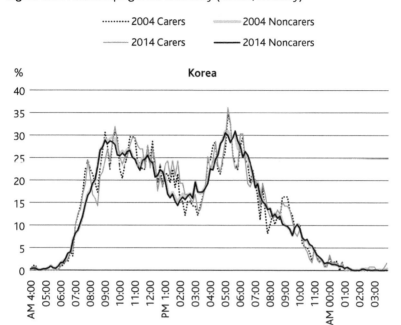

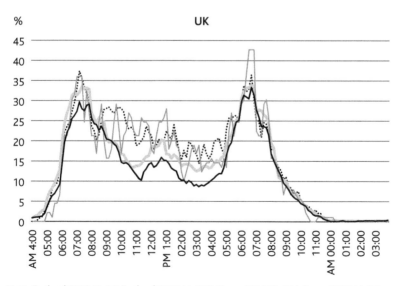

Note: England 2000 N=98, England 2014 N=117, Korea 2004 N=334, Korea 2014 N=89.
Source: Author's creation, based on the Time Use Survey

female older adults who provide childcare and those who do not. Childcaring female older adults spent more time on housekeeping chores compared to non-caregivers in both countries, with the difference being much greater in Korea. While studies have not suggested why this is the case for Korean child caregivers, Lee (2011) argues that grandparents often handle household chores in their children's home because of the long working hours common in the country.

## Evidence from KLoSA and ELSA

We investigated the longitudinal impact of grandparenting on active lifestyles among older adults by controlling other co-variates that may affect both the likelihoods of engaging in social as well as physical activities. Table 10.3 presents the statistics for the sample characteristics. For KLoSA, about 2.1 per cent of the pooled grandparent sample identified themselves as current caregivers for their grandchildren. Fifty-six per cent of respondents were female and 58 per cent reported having elementary school education or less, while 31 per cent had high-school education, and 11 per cent had post-secondary and higher education. The most prevalent social engagement activity was social group participation (63 per cent), followed by religious group participation (20 per cent). Participation in political or leisure groups was almost negligible. Less than 40 per cent reported exercising more than once a week.

With the ELSA data, about 2.5 per cent of our pooled grandparent sample identified themselves as current caregivers for their grandchildren, and 54 per cent of the respondents were female. Twenty-nine per cent reported having elementary school education or less, while 22 per cent had high-school education, and 41 per cent had post-secondary and higher education. The most prevalent social activity was leisure group participation (29 per cent), followed by religious group participation (18 per cent). The frequency of meeting friends was reported to be between once or twice a month and once or twice a week. More than 90 per cent reported exercising more than once a week.

Tables 10.4 and 10.5 show the results of grandparenting regressed on social group participation, frequency of meeting friends and doing regular exercise. In England, grandparents who take care of their grandchildren were not more or less likely than non-caregivers to participate in a social group, meet friends more frequently or do regular exercise. In Korea, grandparents providing childcare had lower

**Table 10.3:** Sample characteristics

| | Korea | | England | |
| --- | --- | --- | --- | --- |
| | Grandparenting | Non-grandparenting | Grandparenting | Non-grandparenting |
| Age | 63.64 (7.98) | 63.56 (5.67) | 67.24 (7.15) | 65.53 (5.22) |
| Gender (1=female) | 0.56 (0.50) | 0.83 (0.38) | 0.54 (0.52) | 0.74 (0.44) |
| Elementary edu.(=1) | 0.58 (0.49) | 0.67 (0.47) | 0.29 (0.45) | 0.25 (0.43) |
| Secondary edu. (=1) | 0.31 (0.46) | 0.24 (0.43) | 0.21 (0.41) | 0.22 (0.42) |
| Tertiary edu. (=1) | 0.11 (0.31) | 0.09 (0.29) | 0.41 (0.43) | 0.46 (0.50) |
| Having grandchildren (=1) | 0.79 (0.40) | 1.00 (0.00) | 0.69 (0.45) | 1.00 (0.04) |
| Household size | 2.74 (1.23) | 3.15 (1.57) | 1.96 (0.75) | 2.04 (0.75) |
| Marital status(=1) | 0.83 (0.38) | 0.80 (0.40) | 0.72 (0.45) | 0.79 (0.41) |
| Employed(=1) | 0.47 (0.50) | 0.18 (0.38) | 0.29 (0.45) | 0.23 (0.42) |
| HH income quantile | 3.12 (1.38) | 3.22 (1.32) | 3.02 (1.41) | 3.19 (1.32) |
| Having ADL problem (=1) | 0.08 (0.67) | 0.00 (0.00) | 0.28 (0.77) | 0.18 (0.58) |
| Having IADL problem (=1) | 0.31 (1.33) | 0.11 (0.74) | 0.15 (0.53) | 0.06 (0.29) |
| Cognitive ability | 8.55 (1.74) | 8.66 (1.47) | 9.50 (1.15) | 9.72 (0.67) |
| Self-reported health (5=very good) | 2.61 (0.93) | 2.52 (0.92) | 3.22 (1.03) | 3.39 (0.99) |
| Having depressive sym. (=1) | 0.83 (1.42) | 0.87 (1.46) | 0.94 (1.27) | 0.80 (1.11) |
| Participating in socialising group (=1) | 0.63 (0.48) | 0.55 (0.50) | 0.16 (0.37) | 0.17 (0.37) |
| Participating in political group (=1) | 0.00 (0.04) | 0.00 (0.00) | 0.11 (0.32) | 0.10 (0.30) |
| Participating in religious group (=1) | 0.20 (0.40) | 0.27 (0.45) | 0.18 (0.33) | 0.23 (0.42) |
| Participating in leisure group (=1) | 0.04 (0.21) | 0.07 (0.25) | 0.29 (0.45) | 0.38 (0.48) |
| Meeting friends (7=daily) | 4.80 (1.02) | 4.78 (0.96) | 4.48 (1.13) | 4.57 (1.10) |
| Doing regular exercise (=1) | 0.37 (0.48) | 0.39 (0.49) | 0.92 (0.25) | 0.99 (0.09) |
| N | 361 | 16,763 | 504 | 19,068 |

Source: Authors

**Table 10.4:** Fixed-effect logit regression: Korea

| | Social group participation | | | Frequency of meeting friends | | Doing regular exercise | | |
|---|---|---|---|---|---|---|---|---|
| | Coef | S.E. | OR | Coef. | S.E. | Coef | S.E. | OR |
| Grandparenting | -0.49* | 0.23 | 0.61 | -0.17** | 0.06 | -0.47* | 0.23 | 0.62 |
| Age | 0.08*** | 0.02 | 1.08 | -0.06*** | 0.00 | -0.11*** | 0.02 | 0.90 |
| Having grandchildren | 0.06 | 0.10 | 1.06 | -0.01 | 0.02 | -0.02 | 0.09 | 0.98 |
| Household size | 0.03 | 0.07 | 1.04 | -0.03** | 0.02 | -0.18** | 0.06 | 0.83 |
| Marital status | 0.19 | 0.25 | 1.21 | -0.18 | 0.06 | -0.71** | 0.26 | 0.49 |
| Employment | 0.24* | 0.11 | 1.27 | -0.03 | 0.03 | -0.77*** | 0.11 | 0.46 |
| Hh income2 | 0.27* | 0.12 | 1.31 | -0.04 | 0.03 | -0.18 | 0.12 | 0.83 |
| Hh income3 | 0.28* | 0.13 | 1.32 | -0.06 | 0.03 | -0.33* | 0.14 | 0.72 |
| Hh income4 | 0.27 | 0.15 | 1.31 | -0.08* | 0.04 | -0.36* | 0.15 | 0.70 |
| Hh income5 | 0.32 | 0.17 | 1.38 | -0.11 | 0.04 | -0.25 | 0.17 | 0.78 |
| Adl | -0.03 | 0.09 | 0.97 | -0.06 | 0.02 | -0.19 | 0.11 | 0.83 |
| Iadl | -0.08 | 0.04 | 0.92 | -0.02 | 0.01 | -0.12* | 0.05 | 0.89 |
| Cognitive ability | 0.05* | 0.02 | 1.05 | 0.00 | 0.01 | 0.05* | 0.02 | 1.05 |
| Self-reported health | 0.11* | 0.04 | 1.11 | 0.00 | 0.01 | 0.12** | 0.04 | 1.13 |
| Depressive sym. | 0.03 | 0.02 | 1.03 | -0.07*** | 0.01 | -0.05 | 0.02 | 0.95 |
| Constant | | | | 8.78 | 0.32 | | | |
| ML R2/Adj. R2 | 0.037 | | | 0.5246 | | 0.069 | | |
| Log-Lik | -2053.291 | | | | | -2086.514 | | |

*p<0.05, **p<0.01, ***p<0.001.

Notes:
Gender and education variable was omitted since it is a time-invariant variable.
OLS results follows exactly the logit regression results in terms of significance and the direction of the coefficient.

Source: Authors

**Table 10.5:** Fixed effect logit regression: England

| | Social group participation | | | Frequency of meeting friends | | Doing regular exercise | | |
| --- | --- | --- | --- | --- | --- | --- | --- | --- |
| | Coef | S.E. | OR | Coef. | S.E. | Coef | S.E. | OR |
| *Grandparenting* | -0.46 | 0.24 | 0.63 | 0.02 | 0.05 | 0.63 | 0.60 | 1.87 |
| *Age* | -0.01 | 0.02 | 0.99 | -0.01** | 0.00 | -0.02 | 0.02 | 0.98 |
| *Having grandchildren* | 0.23 | 0.24 | 1.26 | 0.07 | 0.05 | 0.10 | 0.35 | 1.10 |
| *Household size* | -0.01 | 0.12 | 0.99 | -0.03 | 0.02 | -0.06 | 0.13 | 0.94 |
| *Marital status* | -0.80* | 0.32 | 0.45 | -0.27*** | 0.06 | -0.28 | 0.33 | 0.75 |
| *Employment* | 0.12 | 0.15 | 1.13 | -0.07* | 0.03 | 0.00 | 0.23 | 1.00 |
| *Hh income2* | 0.15 | 0.13 | 1.17 | -0.01 | 0.03 | 0.25 | 0.15 | 1.28 |
| *Hh income3* | 0.17 | 0.15 | 1.18 | -0.04 | 0.03 | 0.08 | 0.17 | 1.08 |
| *Hh income4* | 0.35* | 0.16 | 1.42 | -0.03 | 0.03 | 0.17 | 0.19 | 1.18 |
| *Hh income5* | 0.18 | 0.18 | 1.20 | -0.05 | 0.04 | 0.10 | 0.24 | 1.10 |
| *Adl* | -0.02 | 0.08 | 0.98 | -0.02 | 0.02 | -0.25** | 0.07 | 0.78 |
| *Iadl* | -0.10 | 0.12 | 0.91 | -0.06* | 0.03 | -0.29** | 0.09 | 0.75 |
| *Cognitive ability* | 0.14** | 0.04 | 1.15 | 0.01 | 0.01 | 0.05 | 0.04 | 1.06 |
| *Self-reported health* | 0.03 | 0.06 | 1.03 | -0.01 | 0.01 | 0.23** | 0.07 | 1.26 |
| *Depressive sym.* | -0.04 | 0.04 | 0.96 | -0.01 | 0.01 | -0.06 | 0.05 | 0.94 |
| *Constant* | | | | 5.63*** | 0.30 | 0.63 | 0.60 | 1.87 |
| *ML R2/Adj. R2* | 0.025 | | | 0.5640 | | 0.086 | | |
| *Log-Lik* | -1403.122 | | | | | -796.666 | | |

*p<0.05, **p<0.01, ***p<0.001.

Notes:

Gender and education variable was omitted since it is a time-invariant variable.

OLS results follows exactly the logit regression results in terms of significance and the direction of the coefficient.

Source: Authors

odds of engagement in social groups, frequency of meeting friends and doing regular exercise than older adults providing no childcare. Results suggested that there was a significant negative effect of grandparenting on respondents' levels of social and physical activities, and that grandparenting is incompatible with an active ageing lifestyle in Korea.[1]

The control variables generally supported the findings of previous studies. Health variables supported the importance of health in the active ageing framework: lower physical limitation and higher cognitive abilities were positively associated with the active engagement relevant to all types of active ageing activities under consideration. However, some variables showed diverging patterns in Korea and England. Age was negatively related to the probability that older adults engage in social groups and frequency of meeting friends in England, but was positively related to social group participation in Korea. Household size was negatively associated with active lifestyle in Korea, while no similar impact was detected in England. Also, single men and women, compared to married respondents, were less likely to engage in social groups and less frequently met friends in England, but these associations were not found in Korea. Employed people were less likely to participate in socialising and regular exercise in Korea, neither of which was the case in England.

## Conclusion

Formal childcare programmes should introduce a certain degree of 'de-familisation', as defined by Lister (1994: 37) as 'the degree to which individuals can uphold a socially acceptable standard of living independently of family relations'. Using TUSs and longitudinal data, our analysis gave a nuanced explanation of the nature of the caregiving experience both with and without a formal childcare scheme.

Our time-use analysis and multivariate regression show that Korean childcaring grandparents do not necessarily enjoy more active lifestyles compared to their peers in England. Since grandparental care often take places when parents, particularly mothers, are involved in employment, it suggests that the broader labour market condition, ie, long working hours, should be considered as the key factor to understanding the pattern of grandparenting. The results of the present study do not argue that a universal childcare scheme does not contribute to de-familisation. We recognise the role of social services that supplement grandparents' abilities to manage their lives. But the finding of this study suggest that it is not a sufficient condition to develop a complementary relationship between grandparenting and active ageing. Many grandparents fill the gap between labour market time demand and public care time provisions in Korea. But if parents are able to spend more time caring for their children, the gap will consequently be reduced. Thus, to support the complementary relationship between two current goals of social investment strategy, this study suggests considering broader institutional conditions, such as working hours.

The present findings contribute to the existing literature in two main ways. First, to our knowledge, no previous study has formally examined the effect of caring by comparing the elderly populations of England and Korea. This study provides new insights in relation to this question. Second, this study contributes to the literature on the correlates of social engagement among older adults. Our results suggested that informal care may have a complex relationship with active ageing, depending on the broader institutional context of work–family balance.

From a policy perspective, this indicates that work–family balance is critical even for the active ageing of grandparents. In Korea, the new 52-hour working week was implemented in an attempt to reduce chronic overwork, and the legislation applies to companies with more than 300 employees, public institutions and government offices. Although there are many factors that augment or diminish the impact of the policy supporting work–life balance, including prevailing economic conditions and socio-cultural values, this study nevertheless supports the idea that reducing working hours an important institutional condition to support not only working mothers but also grandparents.

As with the right to request flexibility, there remains substantial scope to widen accessibility of such important leave entitlements, for example to all workers who care for a dependent child or adult. In mid-2014, England extended to the right to all workers who have had six months' tenure in their job, down from 12 months. This UK measure goes some way to extending the right to request flexibility to workers with more precarious work arrangements, such as those on casual or short-term contracts, many of whom are women and caregivers. The Korean right to request would be strengthened by expanding the eligibility criteria in the same manner.

## Note

[1]  Additional fixed effects of OLS regression conducted for both countries confirmed the results, but we do not report those in the chapter. We also implemented other

regression analyses for participation in political, leisure and religious groups; none of these were statistically significant in either country and thus were not reported in this chapter either.

## Reference

Arpino, B. and Bordone, V. (2014) 'Does grandparenting pay off? The effect of child care on grandparents' cognitive functioning', *Journal of Marriage and Family*, 76(2): 337–51.

Baker, L.A. and Silverstein, M. (2008) 'Depressive symptoms among grandparents raising grandchildren: the impact of participation in multiple roles', *Journal of Intergenerational Relationships*, 6(3): 285–304.

Bound, J., Jaeger, D.A. and Baker, R.M. (1995) 'Problems with instrumental variables estimation when the correlation between the instruments and the endogenous explanatory variable is weak', *Journal of the American statistical association*, 90(430): 443–50.

Bulanda, J.R. and Jendrek, M.P. (2014) 'Grandparenting roles and volunteer activity', *Journals of Gerontology Series B: Psychological Sciences and Social Sciences*, 71(1): 129–40.

Burr, J.A., Choi, N.G., Mutchler, J.E. and Caro, F.G. (2005) 'Caregiving and volunteering: are private and public helping behaviors linked?', *The Journals of Gerontology Series B: Psychological Sciences and Social Sciences*, 60(5): S247–56.

Butrica, B.A., Johnson, R.W. and Zedlewski, S.R. (2009) 'Volunteer dynamics of older Americans', *The Journals of Gerontology, Series B: Psychological Sciences and Social Sciences*, 64: 644–55.

Chamberlain, G. (1980) 'Analysis of covariance with qualitative data', *Review of Economic Studies*, 47(1): 225–38.

Chen, F. and Liu, G. (2011) 'The health implications of grandparents caring for grandchildren in China', *Journals of Gerontology Series B: Psychological Sciences and Social Sciences*, 67(1): 99–112.

Coall, D.A. and Hertwig, R. (2011) 'Grandparental investment: a relic of the past or a resource for the future?', *Psychological Science*, 20: 93–8.

Esping-Andersen, G., Gallie, D., Hemerijck, A. and Myles, J. (2002) *Why We Need a New Welfare State*, Oxford: Oxford University Press.

European Commission (2013) 'Social investment package: key facts and figures', Brussels: European Commission.

Fleckenstein, T. and Lee, S.C. (2017) 'Democratization, post-industrialization, and East Asian welfare capitalism: the politics of welfare state reform in Japan, South Korea, and Taiwan' *Journal of International and Comparative Social Policy*, 33(1): 36–54.

Gambaro, L., Stewart, K. and Waldfogel, J. (eds) (2014) *An Equal Start? Providing Quality Early Education and Care to Disadvantaged Children*, Bristol: Policy Press.

Giarrusso, R., Silverstein, M. and Feng, D. (2000) 'Psychological costs and benefits of raising grandchildren: evidence from a national survey of grandparents', in C.B. Cox (ed) *To Grandmother's House We Go and Stay: Perspectives on Custodial Grandparents*, New York: Springer, pp 71–90.

Gray, A. (2005) 'The changing availability of grandparents as carers and its implications for childcare policy in the UK', *Journal of Social Policy*, 34(4): 557–77.

Grundy, E.M., Albala, C., Allen, E., Dangour, A.D., Elbourne, D. and Uauy, R. (2012) 'Grandparenting and psychosocial health among older Chileans: A longitudinal analysis', *Aging & Mental Health*, 16(8): 1047–57.

Hank, K. and Buber, I. (2009) 'Grandparents caring for their grandchildren: findings from the 2004 Survey of Health, Ageing, and Retirement in Europe', *Journal of Family Issues*, 30(1): 53–73.

Hank, K. and Kreyenfeld, M. (2003) 'A multilevel analysis of child care and women's fertility decisions in Western Germany', *Journal of Marriage and Family*, 65(3): 584–96.

Hemerijck, A.C. (2007) *Towards Developmental Welfare Recalibration in Europe*, The Hague: Netherlands Scientific Council for Government Policy.

Horsfall, B. and Dempsey, D. (2015) 'Grandparents doing gender: experiences of grandmothers and grandfathers caring for grandchildren in Australia', *Journal of Sociology*, 51(4): 1070–84.

Igel, C. and Szydlik, M. (2011) 'Grandchild care and welfare state arrangements in Europe', *Journal of European Social Policy*, 21(3): 210–24.

Lewis, J., Campbell, M. and Huerta, C. (2008) 'Patterns of paid and unpaid work in Western Europe: gender, commodification, preferences and the implications for policy', *Journal of European Social Policy*, 18(1): 21–37.

Lister, R. (1994) '"She has other duties": women, citizenship and social security', in S. Baldwin and J. Falkingham (eds) *Social Security and Social Change: New Challenges to the Beveridge Model*, London: Harvester Wheatsheaf, pp 31–44.

Minkler, M. and Fuller-Thomson, E. (1999) 'The health of grandparents raising grandchildren: results of a national study', *American Journal of Public Health*, 89(9): 1384–9.

Pocock, B., Williams, P. and Skinner, N. (2012) 'Conceptualizing work, family and community: a socioecological systems model, taking account of power, time, space and life stage', *British Journal of Industrial Relations*, 50(3): 391–411.

Taniguchi, H. (2006) 'Men's and women's volunteering: gender differences in the effects of employment and family characteristics', *Nonprofit and Voluntary Sector Quarterly*, 35(1): 83–101.

Vandenbroucke, F. and Vleminck, K. (2011) 'Disappointing poverty trends: is the social investment state to blame? An exercise in soul-searching for policymakers', *Journal of European Social Policy*, 21(5): 450–71.

Vevers, S. (2004) 'Feeling the squeeze', *Nursery World*, 29, 10–11.

Waldrop, D.P. and Weber, J.A. (2001) 'From grandparent to caregiver: the stress and satisfaction of raising grandchildren', *Families in Society*, 82(5): 461–72.

Zaidi, A., Gasior, K., Hofmarcher, M.M., Lelkes, O., Marin, B., Rodrigues, R., Schmidt, A., Vanhuysse, P., and Zolyomi, E. (2013) 'Active Ageing Index 2013 concept, methodology and final results', Active Ageing Index (AAI) project, UNECE Grant No: ECE/GC/2012/003.

# 11

# The governance of social investment policies in comparative perspective: long-term care in England and South Korea

*Jooha Lee*

## Introduction

The welfare state is now confronted with a series of new changes in demographic, industrial and family structures that can be considered new social risks (Taylor-Gooby, 2004; Bonoli, 2007; Morel et al, 2012). The demographic shift, coupled with the transition towards a service economy, means that care services have, since the late 1990s, become a key social investment policy in industrialised societies in East Asia, as well as Western advanced industrial democracies. Nearly all Organisation for Economic Co-operation and Development (OECD) countries are experiencing significant ageing of their populations due to increasing life expectancy and declining fertility rates. According to a European Social Policy Network (ESPN) report (Bouget et al, 2015), long-term care is defined as a new social risk resulting from cumulative demographic, economic, and social factors. Consequently, there have been efforts to develop social policies, including long-term care services, which can effectively address new social risks.[1]

Faced with soaring demands for care services in an ageing population and the need to contain the cost of care provision, many Western welfare states have reformed their long-term care services (OECD, 2005; Newman et al, 2008; Pavolini and Ranci, 2008). However, the need for long-term care services is growing in other countries, including newly industrialised countries in East Asia, as the ageing population is increasing at a rate that far greater than in Western Europe (see Phillips and Chan, 2002). The search for effective long-term care policies is thus one of the most urgent and significant challenges in welfare regimes across Europe and Asia.

In line with the neoliberal view of social policy as costly and unproductive, long-term care is often portrayed as a cost. However, looking at long-term care from a social investment perspective involves moving away from an exclusive focus on costs, and towards an emphasis on social capital and social cohesion, which are essential to sustainable growth. Social investment strategies in the context of long-term care have social and economic returns, such as reducing disability and dependency in old age by improving older people's capacity for health promotion and independent living, and decreasing the 'hidden costs' of informal care – for example, the loss of tax contributions from family caregivers who are no longer able to work (European Social Network, 2013). In other words, long-term care policies within social investment can 'contribute to the most efficient use and allocation of labour resources over the life course in support of high levels of participation in the labour market, while enhancing and maintaining capacities and independent living of older people and simultaneously guaranteeing equity, well-being and quality of life' (Lopez, 2017: 7).

The recent debates on how to improve social care services highlight co-governance in the welfare mix – or 'care diamond' (Razavi, 2007) – and multi-level governance in the shape of a better balance between hierarchical decision-making and principles of decentralisation (Evers et al, 2005). The effective governance of social investment policies, including care services, relies not merely on the content of policy that embodies policy goals, principles and intended outputs (formal policy domain), but also on the mode of doing policy, such as the organisational arrangement and procedures for policy delivery (operational policy domain) (Carmel and Papadopoulos, 2003; Borghi and van Berkel, 2007). While the formal policy domain refers to the programmatic characteristics of social policies and services, the operational policy domain refers to issues regarding the organisation, administration, and delivery of policies and services.

The existing literature on social investment policies is concentrated primarily on the programmatic aspect of policy and its decision-making dimension, often ignoring or downplaying the operational policy domain where policy content is put into effect. Moreover, there has been relatively little comparative research into the governance of long-term care systems for the elderly. Therefore, this chapter features an investigation of a mode of governance in the operational policy domain between different welfare regimes, which has been rarely analysed in comparative welfare studies. Here, a mode of governance must be conceptualised in three dimensions: the vertical dimension, involving central–local (or inter-governmental) relations, and the two horizontal dimensions, operating at the centre (central–central), and the periphery (local–local) (Exworthy and Powell, 2004). On this basis, the chapter provides a comparison and contrast between England and Korea's approaches to the governance of long-term care for the elderly with a special focus on co-governance and coordination at the three dimensions.[2]

At first glance, the two selected countries appear to be quite different from each other in terms of both the general picture of socio-economic circumstances and the level of social policy development. However, as Tester argues, cross-national comparisons 'can be made between countries at different stages, for example of population aging, allowing lessons to be learned or predictions to be made' (1999: 140). More importantly, the two countries share similarities in governing long-term care, such as power-concentrated executive authority and the prominent welfare role of the private sector – regardless of some differences of funding systems of long-term care (the tax-based system in England and the social insurance system in Korea). To what extent does poor governance pose a risk to social investment and long-term care services? Particular attention will be paid to how legacies of governance in different welfare regimes characterise and differentiate the operational side of policy.

## Social investment and governance in the operational policy domain

Social investment as a policy paradigm in a post-industrial society is committed to addressing social risks within life-course dynamics in terms of public investment in early childhood care, education, reconciliation policies, lifelong learning and active ageing. It also involves moving from 'a focus on "repairing" the unforeseen damage caused by events to a focus on "preparing" individuals and families to address life chances and deal with disruptive events, preventing the damage they can cause' (Lopez, 2017: 6). The social investment approach applies to the whole life course, including older age and long-term care. The concept of social investment in the field of long-term care can be described as 'welfare expenditure and policies that generate equitable access to care to meet the needs of ageing populations, reduce current and future costs of care, improve quality of care and quality of life, increase capacities to participate in society and the economy, and promote sustainable and efficient resource allocation' (Ghibelli et al, 2017: 16).

Ensuring the quality of long-term care for the elderly should not only involve improvements in the goal and content of policy, but also in the governance and institutional frameworks that provide the context for care provisions. Given the nature of the care diamond, combined with the common phenomenon of service delivery fragmentation, successful long-term care policies are based on well-functioning networks and governance – or 'maximizing coordination in care provision' (Marczak et al, 2017). In a similar vein, it is essential for social investment goals to be achieved to effectively coordinate the efforts of the different private and public stakeholders of long-term care, and to align their objectives with social investment principles (Charbit, 2011; Ghibelli et al, 2017).

Although the term governance is not a single or coherent one and is founded on a variety of different interpretations, it refers to a new process of governing, characterised by self-organising and inter-organisational networks (Rhodes, 2007). Using the concept of governance as a framework, Carmel and Papadopoulos (2003) offered two distinct, but clearly related, domains in an analysis of social policy: (a) the formal policy domain, which is comprised of the content of policy, the legislation and regulations that embody policy goals, principles and intended outputs; and (b) the operational policy domain, comprised of the mode of doing policy, including the organisational arrangement and procedures for policy delivery. According to Borghi and van Berkel (2007), formal policy refers to the 'what' of policies, and operational policy concerns the 'how' of policies, namely the way in which policies are organised, administered and delivered. Furthermore, 'the distinction between formal and operational policy is not similar to that between social policy formation and social policy implementation: operational aspects of social policy are as much subject to policy formation (and implementation) as formal aspects' (Borghi and van Berkel, 2007: 84). In other words, the legislation of a law or the official adoption of a policy is not the end of the policy-making process: 'in the implementation stage policy *making* continues' (Hill and Hupe, 2002: 8).

There is a growing emphasis on the reforms of the operational policy domain, which are to an important degree inspired by principles of new governance (Carmel and Papadopoulos, 2003; Bode, 2006; Borghi and van Berkel, 2007; Newman et al, 2008; Allen et al, 2011). More attention should thus be given to the mode of governance underlying the operational aspects of social policy. In facilitating co-governance and negotiated coordination, the new modes of governance blur traditional dichotomies or boundaries between state and society, public and private, and local and global (Dent et al, 2007; Sørensen and Torfing, 2009). As Borghi and van Berkel (2007) point out, the focus of the operational policy domain is placed on the relationships between various levels of the state, relationships between the state, market and civil society in organising and delivering public services, divisions between purchasers and providers of services, and public–private partnerships in service delivery.

The mode of governance does not occur in a social vacuum but is located within a historically specific set of institutional arrangements. This contributes to explaining the differences in the nature and function of governance between countries (Rhodes, 2007; Sørensen and Torfing, 2009). The literature on policy transfer has also recently engaged with the role of institutional structures and historical legacies on shaping transfer in local contexts (Clavier, 2010; Stone, 2012). In this sense, the notion of formal versus operational policy domains needs to be incorporated into theoretical insights from historical institutionalism, as well as governance. Accordingly, a satisfactory analysis of governance in the operational policy domain cannot be conducted without taking the (path dependent) effect of historical legacies into account.

Here, historical legacies may refer to two dimensions: institutional legacies and policy legacies. Institutional legacies, in a narrow sense, denote the legacies of political and administrative institutions as the rules of the game. Institutional legacies can be construed to include what Pierson calls 'the structure of formal institutions', such as vertical and horizontal integration, and 'government capacities', such as administrative capacity, autonomous bureaucratic activity and revenue-generating capacity (see Pierson, 1994). Policy legacies denote the legacies of social policies or programmes, such as universal social provisions, social insurance schemes and cash transfers. Policy legacies can be related to Pierson's argument on 'policy feedback', which influence the prospects of policy change in four ways: interest-group activity, lock-in effects, policy learning and information effects (see Pierson, 1994). While the formal policy domain concerns policy legacies, the operational policy domain is more associated with institutional legacies.

Given that operational policy reform has been much less analysed than formal policy reform in the comparative literature, governance in the operational policy domain is placed at the centre of this analysis. This chapter focuses specifically on co-governance in the following dimensions: (a) the horizontal dimension at the central level (joined-up government at the centre); (b) the horizontal dimension at the local level (joined-up governance at the periphery); and (c) the vertical dimension between the central and local levels (Exworthy and Powell, 2004). Figure 11.1 provides an analytical framework based

**Figure 11.1:** Analytical framework for governance and social investment policies

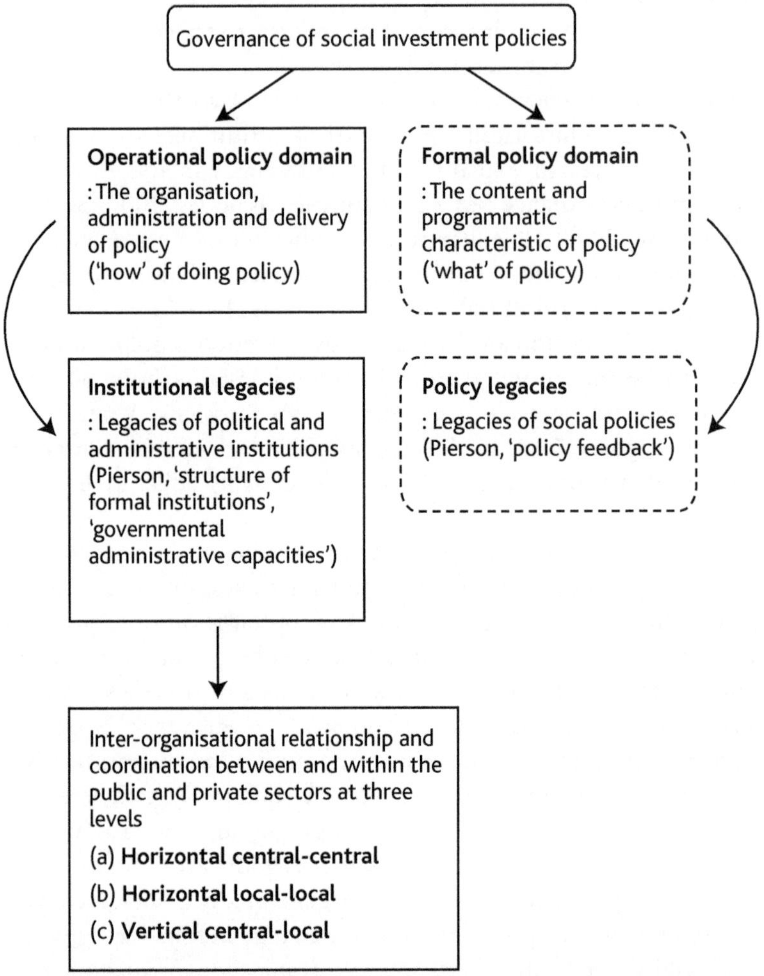

Note: This chapter does not explicitly and comprehensively deal with the formal policy domain together with policy legacies (the dotted-line boxes), as the operational policy domain (the full-line boxes) is the object of analysis.

Source: Lee et al (2016)

on the formal and operational policy domains, policy and institutional legacies, and the three levels of co-governance.

## Long-term care for the elderly in England and Korea

Social care services in England are funded by central and local taxation and user charges, while health services under the National Health Service (NHS) are financed mainly by central taxation. The public provision of social care is means-tested. The administration of social care services has historically been handled by local authorities, which are now 'responsible for assessing needs, setting eligibility criteria and arranging social services for their populations' (Comas-Herrera et al, 2006: 288). In particular, the central government handed over the responsibility of institutional and community long-term care services to the social service departments of local authorities under the NHS and Community Care Act of 1990. The two key features of the 1990 community care reforms were the shifts in the role of the local authority social service departments from that of a provider to that of an enabler or purchaser, and in the balance of care provisions from public funding to greater private funding through user charges, charitable spending and the family (Langan, 1998). Within this purchaser–provider split, local governments used their devolved budgets to purchase a majority of care services from an extensive market of private providers from both voluntary and commercial sectors.

With a the political era of New Labour after 1997, its 'Third Way' governance sought to overcome the fragmentation engendered by neoliberal reforms through public–private partnerships, and to transcend the dualism of state monopoly welfare versus private market provisions (Larsen et al, 2006; Newman et al, 2008). It should also be noted that state and local authorities have increasingly outsourced the care services previously delivered by the public sector; consequently, the private for-profit sector has grown in importance. For instance, three quarters of adult social care, such as residential care facilities and home care services, in England was run by for-profit providers in 2011 (Yeandle et al, 2012; see also Table 11.1). The subsequent Conservative Government, under David Cameron, did make some adjustments in the formal aspects of long-term care, but much less in its operational policy domain. In addition, New Labour stressed and pursued a policy of personalisation by expanding the use of direct payments and individual budgets, which could bring more choice and control over care services (Comas-Herrera et al, 2010; Brennan et al, 2012; Lewis and West, 2014). This personalisation agenda was then transferred to the Conservative-dominated Coalition Government led by Cameron (see DoH, 2010, 2012).

The most striking aspect of welfare development in East Asia, including Korea, is the fact that social policy was the handmaiden of economic policy. The 'economy first' developmental strategy, espoused by conservative political elites, engendered essential principles and features underlying the Korean welfare system, which can be captured by the notion of 'developmental welfare' (Chung, 2006; Ringen et al, 2011). The state in Korea, as a low social spender, has been less involved in providing social welfare than its Western counterparts. The provisions of social services have thus remained stagnant in terms of total expenditures on social services and the percentage of the labour forces engaged in the social service industry (Hong and Song, 2006; Park et al, 2013). Nevertheless, the Korean state did play a key welfare role as a regulator, using its regulatory power to force the private sector to provide certain types of social welfare.

Family welfare also negated much of the need for state support. Therefore, responsibility for providing personal social services, including care for the elderly, rested with families. However, family-based long-term care for the elderly has reached the limits of its supportive role due to the breakdown of traditional family structures, the loosening of community ties and an increasing level of female employment (Kim et al, 2010). As part of the efforts to cope with its unprecedented population ageing, Korea has recently recognised the necessity for state-provided care for older people and, like Germany and Japan, opted for mandatory long-term care insurance, instead of tax-based financing. This is attributable to legacies of developmental welfare. Given the state's role as a regulator combined with its low social spending, major social programs in Korea have depended on the social insurance principle, wherein a person has to contribute before claiming any benefits (Ringen et al, 2011). In addition, a new long-term care system could minimise administrative costs by making use of the existing administrative structure of the National Health Insurance (NHI) (Kwon, 2009). Subsequently, the Long-Term Care Insurance (LTCI) was launched in 2008. Its main financing comes from mandatory payroll contributions, and service providers are mostly private and operate on a fee-for-service basis (MoHW, 2010). Therefore, as is the case in England, the prominent role of the private sector in elderly care services seems common in Korea, albeit with different programmatic characteristics of long-term care for old people.

In both England and Korea, home and institutionalised care are provided exclusively by private for-profit and voluntary organisations. In 2010, private for-profit facilities in England were made up 73.3 per cent of institutionalised care and 73 per cent of home care, respectively, whereas the same statistics for Korea were 60.8 per cent and 78.7 per cent, respectively (see Tables 11.1 and 11.2). Therefore, in both countries, the government plays the role of the regulator rather than the provider of long-term care services. The major regulators at the centre include not only the Department of Health (DoH) in England and the Ministry of Health and Welfare (MoHW) in Korea, but also

**Table 11.1:** Long-term care facilities in England, March 2010 (percentage shown in brackets)

| | | | Ownership type | | | |
|---|---|---|---|---|---|---|
| | | NHS | Local authorities | Voluntary | Private for-profit | Other | Total |
| Service type | Institutionalised care | 167 (0.9) | 1,065 (5.8) | 3,545 (19.4) | 13,366 (73.3) | 91 (0.5) | 18,234 |
| | Home care | 42 (1.0) | 617 (11.0) | 765 (14.0) | 4,060 (73.0) | 42 (1.0) | 5,526 |
| | Total | 209 (0.9) | 1,682 (7.1) | 4,310 (18.1) | 17,426 (73.3) | 133 (0.6) | 23,760 |

Source: CQC (2010), Malley et al (2014)

**Table 11.2:** Long-term care facilities in Korea, December 2010 (percentage shown in brackets)

| | | Ownership type | | | | |
|---|---|---|---|---|---|---|
| | | Local authorities | Voluntary | Private for-profit | Other | Total |
| Service type | Institutionalised care | 105 (2.8) | 1,358 (36.2) | 2,281 (60.8) | 7 (0.2) | 3,751 |
| | Home care | 110 (1.0) | 2,227 (19.8) | 8,832 (78.7) | 59 (0.5) | 11,228 |
| | Total | 215 (1.4) | 3,585 (23.9) | 11,113 (74.2) | 66 (0.4) | 14,979 |

Source: National Health Insurance Corporation (2011)

a regulatory agency for healthcare – the Care Quality Commission (CQC) in England and the National Health Insurance Corporation (NHIC) in Korea. Both the central government and the local authorities play substantial roles in the management of long-term care in both countries.

However, the modes of the division of labour between the central regulatory agency and local authorities are different in the two countries. In England, the central CQC manages the registration and evaluation of long-term care facilities, while local authorities manage the registration and assessment of long-term care clients (Comas-Herrera et al, 2010). In Korea, the central NHIC manages the registration and assessment of clients, while local authorities manage the registration and inspection of long-term care facilities (Act on Long-Term Care Insurance for Senior Citizens, revised on August 13 2013, Articles 13, 14, 31, 32 and 61). In other words, the ways of dividing regulatory roles between the central and local regulatory authorities in the two countries are the opposite of each other.

## Governing long-term care in the operational policy domain

### Horizontal dimension at the central level

Radical and unilateral reform is more likely to be undertaken in the institutional arrangement of prevailing executive authority with centralisation of power than it is in governments with power-fragmented systems (Pierson, 1996; Bonoli, 2001). The British policy-making framework – the so-called Westminster model, characterised by a highly majoritarian system of government (Lijphart, 1999) – is capable of steering far-reaching reform with little consultation from the opposition and social partners. Nonetheless, in service-oriented policies, such as long-term care services, England employed an inclusive bottom-up approach, which 'invites external groups to public consultations or to participate actively in the design of policy' (Larsen et al, 2006: 631).

The policy-making framework of Korea is rooted in the concentration of power in the presidency and bureaucracy as institutional legacies of the developmental state. Two distinctive features of the organisational arrangements of the East Asian developmental state are bureaucratic autonomy insulated from various interests of social groups, and powerful economic bureaucracy as a pilot agency (Amsden, 1989; Chung, 2006). The strong state has effectively been engaged in dealing with civil society and voluntary organisations (Kim, 2008); thus, Korea has a weaker tradition of inclusive policy-making in favour of a negotiated approach to welfare reforms.

Like the traditional top-down Westminster model, the concentrated political authority implies that, in spite of increased political risk, the Korean state can implement radical reforms relatively swiftly. However, there are marked differences between England and Korea in the style of policy-making and implementation mechanism. In England, under New Labour, the service-oriented reforms 'tend be more inclusive, and in some areas stakeholders play a major role in the design of the new policies through taskforce groups or external commissions' (Larsen et al, 2006: 647). Furthermore, the Conservative-dominated Coalition Government also engaged in discussion with various internal and external groups, such as local authorities, the NHS, care users and their families, care providers, voluntary organisations, care workers, and communities. The government then published the white paper 'Caring for Our Future: Reforming Care and Support' in July 2012, which sets out the Coalition Government's key positions regarding social care reform (Gheera and Long, 2013; see also DoH, 2012).

The inclusive policy-making pattern in England is in contrast to the Korean case where societal forces, such as civil society organisations, have exerted a restricted role in the policy-making regarding the LTCI programme. In fact, there has been an increasing influence of civil society organisations in (social) policy-making since the democratisation of 1987, although state bureaucracy can command strong institutional resources afforded by historical legacies of the developmental state, such as bureaucratic autonomy (Ringen et al, 2011; Lee, 2014). Nonetheless, the process of designing and legislating the LTCI was driven by state elites, not pro-welfare civil groups (Lee and Cho, 2012).[3] Consequently, the LTCI was implemented according to the government's plan: the long-term care service is separated from the medical service (medical and nursing services are not necessary in all long-term care facilities); the long-term care system is based on a social insurance system with limited government subsidy (20 per cent of the long-term care insurance revenue); and care services for disabled persons are separated from the long-term care insurance (MoHW, 2009). The division between medical and long-term care services results in the separate development of medical institutions for older persons – 'elderly care hospitals' – outside the boundary of the LTCI. Elderly care hospitals are run separately from long-term care facilities without being integrated and coordinated with long-term care facilities, and medical services provided for 'patients' in these hospitals are not covered by the LTCI but by the NHI (Kim et al, 2013). In summary, the central governments in England and Korea feature strong power concentration, but the former has adopted a more inclusive style of governance at the central horizontal dimension than the latter.

### Horizontal dimension at the local level

Despite the fact that the UK is often depicted as a liberal market economy not in favour of non-market coordination (Hall and Soskice, 2001), it has relied on a partnership-based governance of welfare provisions. During the 1960s and 1970s, the British government embraced public–private partnerships within the social welfare sector. Voluntary organisations were already participating in the local governance of welfare; they were not mere transmission belts of social policies, but participants in the planning, delivery and supervision of social services (Bode, 2006). There was also the rise of strong local social service departments, which became the core of the welfare sector in the local-level implementation process after the 1970s.

New Labour then encouraged partnerships with the private sector in social services at the local level as a way of overcoming the fragmentation produced by the neoliberal strategies of marketisation (Evers et al, 2005). A broad range of service providers, including private for-profit and voluntary organisations, were heavily involved in the process of long-term care reform. Bringing local organisations into effective partnership arrangements can foster more successful use of resources and improve skill-sharing for different elements of the workforce (Local Government Association, 2005). The implementation of personalisation in adult social care has empowered voluntary sector organisations to play a larger role in enlarging the market, and offering support brokerage and planning services (Carr, 2012). However, it should also be noted that the development of private providers is related to shortages of publicly funded care for older people.

The active involvement of service users helps to formalise cooperative relations between public authorities and voluntary organisations at the local level (DoH, 2005). In order to induce the intensive participation of service users in the governance of social services, service agencies 'have engaged in evaluating their own policy and practice, and there has been a move towards creating a range of alternative forms of user participation' (such as consumer councils, panels and forums, and/or participation in agencies' governing structures) (Simmons and Birchall, 2005: 261). In its approach to modernising social care for the elderly, New Labour endeavoured to achieve effective, joined-up governance at the local level. However, the Coalition Government's public sector funding cuts damaged the capacity of local authorities, and voluntary and community organisations to expand user choice and control over care and support. Under the Coalition Government's deficit reduction programme and accompanying cuts to social services (HM Treasury, 2010), voluntary and community organisations are working with significantly reduced funds. This lead to swift decisions based mainly on cost rather than on social value or wider outcomes at the local level (see Carr, 2012). Given the privatisation and marketisation of long-term care, the lack of a long-term financial strategy is a pressing issue in England (Spasova et al, 2018).

Compared with England, Korea has little experience in delivering long-term care services in a unified way at the local governance level. Despite the fact that long-term care providers are predominantly private, there is lack of collaboration between social administrators and private organisations. Many assert that the number of public and non-profit long-term care facilities must be increased, as for-profit facilities have become overwhelmingly dominant (PSPD et al, 2009). In addition, there is a lack of participation of service users, which is crucial to ensure that limited resources are used to meet service users' priorities (see Kim, 2013).

Overall, Korea's welfare delivery system has been highly complicated and fragmented with a weak control tower at the central level (Lee, 2009, 2014). The delivery system for the LTCI is also fragmented between two organisations: local authorities and the NHIC. While local governments take charge of establishing and designating long-term care facilities, the NHIC is responsible for assessing eligibility, screening and rating applicants, collecting premiums, and conducting home visits (MoHW, 2010). The fragmentation of the responsibility might cause inefficiency in the governance of the LTCI. The NHIC is a highly centralised organisation that has limitations in delivering localised care services and building a partnership with a wide range of the private sector at the local level. Furthermore, the coordination between the NHI and the LTCI is 'a key to the continuum of care and the prevention of unmet need' (Kwon, 2009: 29). To this end, the Korean government needs to place a greater emphasis on reinforcing the public–private partnership and unified governance at the local level.

## Vertical dimension between the centre and local agencies

According to Exworthy and Powell (2004), the vertical dimension refers to the question of whether policy ownership should reside at the national or local levels, and whether it is important for all stakeholders to have a role in the partnership. In England, after the Thatcher government's reforms, the Department for Education and Employment and the Department of Social Security established service delivery divisions as executive agencies with their own chief executive officers and staff. The relationship between departments and agencies is then regulated in term of a series of quasi-contracts and agreements. Departmental executives can no longer demand direct control over programme decisions such as staffing, although they have various other devices for setting requirements that push agencies to follow central guidelines (DoH, 1998; Considine, 2000). The social services departments of local authorities have been responsible for running publicly funded social services, and have managed an assessment of care needs; therefore, eligibility criteria, budgetary arrangements and assessment procedures are determined locally (OECD, 2011).[4]

In the area of social services, managerialism has been developed through an existing professional hierarchy. Social workers have thus retained their monopoly over senior posts in social service departments, and overall responsibility for planning and funding has remained within the ambit of local governments. As Ackroyd et al (2007) argued, there has been a trend in delegating management responsibilities to middle- and junior-ranking professionals, and social service departments have devolved some budgetary authority to lower-level team leaders and care managers.

This is in marked contrast to Korea, where local (welfare) officials must adhere to the rules and guidelines of the central government. Local delivery agencies do not have budgetary autonomy, nor do they select their own officials. According to Kwon (2009), the role of local governments is very limited in the provision of long-term care, and empowering local governments is necessary to facilitate effective coordination between the LTCI and welfare services. The delivery system of social care for the elderly in Korea is fused with many ministries apart from the social bureaucracy. The Ministry of the Interior and Safety and the Ministry of Strategy and Finance deal with the main financial and legal links with local governments and agencies, but they have no substantial responsibility for social provisions. Local governments under the supervision of the Ministry of the Interior and Safety are responsible for the authentication and evaluation of long-term care facilities, whereas the MoHW determines policies for long-term care. Many intermediate managers in local governments and agencies are general administrative officials who have little expertise in welfare, and who tend to see social welfare work as an incidental or supplementary job to general administrative work (Lee, 2009, 2014; Chung, 2013). In this situation, there are strong demands for establishing an independent social welfare office – supervised directly by the MoHW – at the local level, or a so-called long-term care centre that aims to provide an integrated one-stop service (see PSPD et al, 2009; Chung, 2013; Kim, 2013).

Contrary to what most neoliberal reformists expected, the introduction of market-oriented mechanisms in the provision of long-term care in Western Europe 'has required a new regulatory set-up, which effectively guarantees competition and freedom of choice on the one hand, and reduces the risks of market failure on the other hand' (Pavolini and Ranci, 2008: 255). England has developed a professional regulatory agency for the assessment of health and social services, the CQC.[5] The purpose of the CQC is to ensure that people get better care by encouraging improvement across health and social care and stamping out bad practice; protecting the rights of service users, particularly the most vulnerable; and providing accessible and trustworthy information on the quality of care (see CQC, 2009, 2010). The CQC has since performed its role as an independent and integrated regulator responsible for assuring the safety and quality of care services. For instance, only 1 per cent of the total social care services inspected were found to be seriously deviating from the minimum standards in England (OECD, 2013).

The fragmented governance structure has prevented the long-term care system in Korea from having a single and independent regulatory agency, like the CQC in England. Although the NHIC is in charge of both the NHI and the LTCI, these two insurance schemes are run separately from each other. Moreover, the registration and inspection of long-term care facilities are at the discretion of local authorities, which are regulated by the Ministry of the Interior and Safety. Given that the structure of regulation remains fragmented, the Korean state needs to monitor the service quality of care providers, disseminate their information to users, and manage supply against demand (Kwon, 2009; Seok, 2010; Kim, 2013). Comprehensive and coordinated regulation for the quality of care is a critical issue, especially considering the predominance of private for-profit providers and the excessive competition among them.

## Conclusion

This chapter featured a discussion of the long-term care policies in England and Korea, highlighting the operational policy domain (more related to institutional legacies) that has been relatively less researched than the formal policy domain (more related to policy legacies). Table 11.3 summarises different modes of governance in the operational policy domain at the three levels: the horizontal central–central, the horizontal local–local and the vertical central–local.

Table 11.3: Governance in the operational policy domain between England and Korea

| | | England | Korea |
|---|---|---|---|
| Horizontal dimension | Central level | Power-concentrated and inclusive policy-making | Power-concentrated and exclusive policy-making |
| | Local level | Effective unified governance | Ineffective unified governance |
| Vertical dimension | | Strong local autonomy and independent regulatory management | Weak local autonomy and insufficient regulatory management |

Source: Lee et al (2016)

Compared with England, Korea has suffered more from insufficient co-governance in both the vertical and horizontal dimensions. In the governance of long-term care, England has a more coordinated system with strong local autonomy and a single regulatory agency, whereas Korea has a more fragmented system with weak local autonomy. These can be ascribed largely to institutional legacies; that is, exclusive policy-making authority and fragmented delivery mechanisms without autonomous field-level offices specialised in social welfare.

With a lack of substantial operational policy reforms, the shift that the formal policy domain has sought cannot be fully materialised in policy implementation. At this point, Korea can learn from the use of inter-organisational relationships and coordination between the public and private sectors, which characterise the operational aspects of social policy in England. The privatisation of service delivery and the introduction of market mechanisms are expected to reduce government responsibility and regulation. However, public organisations, such as central government or local authority social service departments in England, have still played a significant role in providing long-term care for the elderly. In order to solve the problems caused by neoliberal reforms, New Labour took a dual strategy by initially implementing more national regulation, and later an effort to personalise services by enhancing consumer choice in the social care market (Lewis and West, 2014). According to the ample research on the governance and finance of long-term care across European countries (Allen et al, 2011), England, together with Sweden and France, demonstrates a high level of government intervention in terms of service planning and long-term collaboration. Although a welfare mix in contemporary Europe has undergone a process of marketisation, the state – even in England, as a forerunner of quasi-market reforms – remains a key player in the context of a tendency towards greater co-governance and partnerships (Bode, 2006).

However, the English system is not immune to criticism. First, there have been severe shortages of publicly provided formal care due to a strong legacy and tendency towards the privatisation and marketisation of long-term care. This, in turn, involves 'a failure of public funding to keep pace with demographic trends; cuts in central government funding to local authorities; and short-term measures that increase local authorities' reliance on (inequitable) local sources of revenue' (Spasova et al, 2018: 35). Second, there is a linkage between market competition and reductions in the unit costs of care home services, possibly at the expense of service quality (Forder and Allan, 2014). Third, various long-term care facilities and funding sources are left under different authorities, including the DoH and local authorities, and the integration among them is not yet completed (Comas-Herrera et al, 2010). Finally, the significant level of local control and autonomy in the organisation and implementation of long-term care services has led to substantial geographical variations in coverage and care mix (Marczak et al, 2017; Fernández et al, 2018).

However, there have been continuous efforts to develop a participative and holistic coordination system in English governance, both between and at the central and local levels. In contrast, the Korean central government's strong hierarchical leadership in the construction of the LTCI has paradoxically created disintegrated domains outside of the LTCI, including elderly care hospitals funded separately by the NHI and local elderly care programs run autonomously by local authorities. Therefore, the English example, regardless of its own problems, can offer Korea lessons in how to find a way of making the centralised governance more participative and of coordinating the operation of the long-term care system. For instance, the 2015 Treasury Spending Review made an additional commitment to coordinating health and social care by specifying that local plans for full integration would be implemented by 2020; the Greater Manchester Combined Authority was granted full control of the integrated health and social care budget in 2016 (Marczak et al, 2017). Developing a framework for measuring quality is vital for social investment strategies, as well as long-term care services. In England, all formal care organisations must meet the 'Fundamental Standards' set out by the CQC, and the standards are positive from the social investment approach, as they focus on the quality of life outcomes for the individual (Fernández et al, 2018).[6] As a way of coordinating between medical and social care facilities for long-term care, the Korean government may consider setting up an independent agency in the MoHW to regulate both health and social care services. In addition, the MoHW may found a forum for discussing the operation of long-term care programmes attended by representatives of local authorities and civil society groups.

All in all, governance does not take place without government, and the state can bring substantial institutional capacity into play by developing strategic relationships with non-state actors (Kjær, 2004; Bell and Hindmoor, 2009; Lynn Jr., 2010). Given the overwhelming dominance of for-profit providers in social care services, the Korean state thus needs to enhance its welfare responsibility and steering capacity in governing the operational policy domain in order to ensure that essential quality and safety standards are met in terms of coordinated regulation. To get into the anatomy of social investment, it is not sufficient to examine the social investment principle within the formal policy domain; it is also necessary to observe how social investment policies are organised, administered and delivered. One may witness a meaningful change in policy intentions and contents in the formal aspects of social policy, but less so in their outputs and outcomes due to ineffective governance in the operational policy domain.

## Notes

[1]   This chapter is based on previous research by Lee, J., Chae, J.-H. and Lim, S.H. (2016) 'Governing a welfare mix: operation of long-term care policies in England and South Korea', *Korea Observer*, 47(1): 167–97.

[2]   Devolution of powers to England, Scotland, Wales and Northern Ireland affects a variety of policy areas, including the delivery of long-term care. Hence, there are different systems of long-term care in different parts of the UK, due to the devolution of social and health care. While Scotland has introduced free personal and nursing care, the other regions have introduced only free nursing care. According to an OECD report (2013), the majority of care service use and expenditure relates to England, considering that 83 per cent of the UK's elderly population resides in England.

[3]   The website of the People's Solidarity for Participatory Democracy (PSPD), one of the most influential and presentative civil organisations, provides a collection of pro-welfare civil groups' statements and papers, which clearly show that their ideas have not successfully been infused into the policy design of the LTCI.

[4]   Due to the harsh budget cuts and financial pressures after the global economic crisis of 2008, there has been an intensifying tension between the government and local authorities; 'local authorities could blame central government for funding cuts, while government may blame local authorities for spending money unwisely' (Glasby et al, 2013: 27).

[5]   Thatcher's Conservative government, which launched a series of neoliberal reforms, set up the Social Services Inspectorate for inspecting and assessing social services. The New Labour government renamed it as the Commission for Social Care Inspection (CSCI) in 2004. While bringing together into one body the social care components of different agencies, the CSCI combined inspection, review, performance and regulatory functions across the range of adult social care services in the public and independent sectors (CSCI, 2009). Moreover, in 2001, the government set up the Commission for Health Improvement and then in 2004 renamed it the Healthcare Commission (HC). In April 2009, as a way of joining up the regulation of health and social services, the New Labour government merged the CSCI and the HC, as well as the Mental Health Act Commission, into the CQC, which has been a major regulator of health care and adult social care.

[6]   The compatibility of the quality standards used in long-term care services with a social investment focus varies across countries. For example, the quality system ranges from having a lack of national quality standards in Italy, through prescriptive standards that are focused mainly on clinical care processes in Germany, to the use of outcomes indicators in England and Finland. As the quality systems in England and Finland are intended to include well-being and quality of life issues, they are better placed to support the social investment approach than in Germany (Fernández et al, 2018).

# References

Ackroyd, S., Kirkpatrick, I. and Walker, R.M. (2007) 'Public management reform in the UK and its consequences for professional organization', *Public Administration*, 85(1): 9–26.

Allen, K. et al (2011) 'Governance and financing of long-term care across Europe: overview report', Available from: http://interlinks. euro.centre.org/project/reports [Accessed 9 February 2015].

Amsden, A.H. (1989) *Asia's Next Giant: South Korea and Late Industrialization*, Oxford: Oxford University Press.

Bell, S. and Hindmoor, A. (2009) *Rethinking Governance: The Centrality of the State in Modern Society*, Cambridge: Cambridge University Press.

Bode, I. (2006) 'Disorganized welfare mixes: voluntary agencies and new governance regimes in Western Europe', *Journal of European Social Policy*, 16(4): 346–59.

Bonoli, G. (2001) 'Political institutions, veto points, and the process of welfare state adaptation', in P. Pierson (ed) *The New Politics of the Welfare State*, Oxford: Oxford University Press, pp 238–64.

Bonoli, G. (2007) 'Time matters postindustrialization, new social risks, and welfare state adaptation in advanced industrial democracies', *Comparative Political Studies*, 40(5): 495–520.

Borghi, V. and van Berkel, R. (2007) 'New modes of governance in Italy and the Netherlands: the case of activation policies', *Public Administration*, 85(1): 83–101.

Bouget, D., Frazer, H., Marlier, E., Sabato, S. and Vanhercke, B. (2015) *Social Investment in Europe: A Study of National Policies*, Brussels: European Commission.

Brennan, D., Cass, B., Himmelweit, S. and Szebehely, M. (2012) 'The marketization of care: rationales and consequences in Nordic and liberal care regimes', *Journal of European Social Policy*, 22(4): 377–91.

Carmel, E. and Papadopoulos, T. (2003) 'The new governance of social security in Britain', in J. Millar (ed) *Understanding Social Security*, Bristol: Policy Press, pp 31–52.

Carr, S. (2012) 'Personalisation and marketisation: implications for third sector provision of adult social care and support in England', paper presented at the 10th International Conference of the International Society for Third Sector Research, Siena, Italy, 10–13 July.

Charbit, C. (2011) 'Governance of public policies in decentralised contexts: the multi-level approach', OECD Regional Development Working Papers. Paris: OECD.

Chung, H.W. (2013) 'Jiyeogsahoe tonghabjeog bogjiseobiseuleul wihan jibangjachidanche bogjigineung ganghwa [Strengthening local government's welfare capacity for integrated welfare service delivery]', *Health and Welfare Policy Forum*, 195: 99–108.

Chung, M.-K. (2006) 'The Korean developmental welfare regime', *Shakai Seisaku Gakkai Shi*, 16: 149–71.

Clavier, C. (2010) 'Bottom–up policy convergence: a sociology of the reception of policy transfer in public health policies in Europe', *Journal of Comparative Policy Analysis*, 12(5): 451–66.

Comas-Herrera, A. et al (2006) 'Future long-term care expenditure in Germany, Spain, Italy and the United Kingdom', *Ageing and Society*, 26(2): 285–302.

Comas-Herrera, A., Wittenberg, R. and Pickard, L. (2010) 'The long road to universalism? Recent developments in the financing of long-term care in England', *Social Policy and Administration*, 44(4): 375–91.

CSCI (Commission for Social Care Inspection) (2009) *The State of Social Care in England 2007–08*, London: CSCI.

Considine, M. (2000) 'Contract regimes and reflexive governance', *Public Administration*, 78(3): 613–38.

CQC (Care Quality Commission) (2009) *Care Quality Commission Enforcement Policy*, London: CQC.

CQC (Care Quality Commission) (2010) *The State of Health Care and Adult Social Care in England: Key Themes and Quality of Services in 2009*, London: CQC.

Dent, M., van Gestel, N. and Teelken, C. (2007) 'Symposium on changing modes of governance in public sector organizations', *Public Administration*, 85(1): 1–8.

DoH (Department of Health) (1998) *Modernising Social Services*, London: DoH.

DoH (Department of Health) (2005) *Independence, Well-Being and Choice Services*, London: DoH.

DoH (Department of Health) (2010) *A Vision for Adult Social Care*, London: DoH.

DoH (Department of Health) (2012) *Caring for Our Future*, London: DoH.

European Social Network (2013) 'Long-term care & social investment: issues for social services', ESN discussion note, Available from: www.esn-eu.org [Accessed 9 February 2015].

Evers, A., Lewis, J. and Riedel, B. (2005) 'Developing child-care provision in England and Germany', *Journal of European Social Policy*, 15(3): 195–209.

Exworthy, M. and Powell, M. (2004) 'Big windows and little windows: implementation in the "congested state"', *Public Administration*, 82(2): 263–81.

Fernández, J.-L., Trigg, L., Reinhard, H.-J. and Micharikopoulos, D. (2018) 'European LTC models and compatibility with social investment approaches', Social Protection Innovative Investment in Long-Term Care (SPRINT) working paper D3.2, Brussels: SPRINT.

Forder, J. and Allan, S. (2014) 'The impact of competition on quality and prices in the English care homes market', *Journal of Health Economics*, 34, 73–83.

Gheera, M. and Long, R. (2013) *Social Care Reform: Funding Care for the Future*, London: House of Commons.

Ghibelli, P., Barbieri, D., Fernandez, J.L. and Knapp, M. (2017) 'The role of public and private actors in delivering and resourcing long-term care services', Social Protection Innovative Investment in Long-Term Care (SPRINT) working paper D2.3, Brussels: SPRINT.

Glasby, J., Miller, R. and Lynch, J. (2013) '"Turning the welfare state upside down"? Developing a new adult social care offer', Health Services Management Centre policy paper, Birmingham: University of Birmingham.

Hall, P.A. and Soskice, D. (eds) (2001) *Varieties of Capitalism*, Oxford: Oxford University Press.

Hill, M. and Hupe, P. (2002) *Implementing Public Policy*, London: Sage.

HM Treasury (2010) 'Spending review 2010', London: The Stationery Office.

Hong, K.-Z. and Song, H.-K. (2006) 'Continuity and change in the Korean welfare regime', *Journal of Social Policy*, 35(2): 247–65.

Kim, C.-W. (2013) 'Noinjanggiyoyangboheomjedo silhaengeseoui hangughyeong keeomaenijimeonteu doibe gwanhan gochal [A study on a model of prospective care management system aligning with current national long-term care insurance policy for elders]', *Health and Social Welfare Review*, 33(2): 219–42.

Kim, J. et al (2013) *Yoyangbyeongwongwa yoyangsiseolui yeoghaljeonglib bangan yeongu: Yeongyebanganeul jungsimeulo* [The Establishment of Roles of Elderly Care Hospitals and Nursing Home Facilities: Ways of Integration], Seoul: Korea Institute for Health and Social Affairs.

Kim, S.-H., Kim, D.H. and Kim, W.S. (2010) 'Long-term care needs of the elderly in Korean and elderly long-term care insurance', *Social Work in Public Health*, 25(2): 176–84.

Kim, T. (2008) 'The social construction of welfare control: a sociological review on state-voluntary sector links in Korea', *International Sociology*, 23(6): 819–44.

Kjær, A.M. (2004) *Governance*, Cambridge: Polity Press.

Kwon, S. (2009) 'The introduction of long-term care insurance in South Korea', *Eurohealth*, 15(1): 28–9.

Langan, M. (1998) 'The personal social services', in N. Ellison and C. Pierson (eds) *Development in British Social Policy*, Basingstoke: Macmillan, pp 160–72.

Larsen, T.P., Taylor-Gooby, P. and Kananen, J. (2006) 'New Labour's policy style: a mix of policy approaches', *Journal of Social Policy*, 35(4): 629–49.

Lee, J. (2009) 'Another dimension of welfare reform: the implementation of the Employment Insurance Programme in Korea', *International Journal of Social Welfare*, 18(3), 281–90.

Lee, J. (2014) 'What happens after the passage of reform initiatives? Two dimensions of social policy reform in Korea', *International Review of Administrative Sciences*, 80(1), 193–212.

Lee, J., Chae, J.-H. and Lim, S.H. (2016) 'Governing a welfare mix: operation of long-term care policies in England and South Korea', *Korea Observer*, 47(1): 167–97.

Lee, J.-S. and Cho, E.-Y. (2012) 'Noinjanggiyoyangboheombeobui jeongchaeggyeoljeonggwajeong bunseog [An analysis of policy making process of long term care insurance]', *Journal of Social Sciences*, 23(1): 2–33.

Lewis, J. and West, A. (2014) 'Re-shaping social care services for older people in England', *Journal of Social Policy*, 43(1): 1–18.

Lijphart, A. (1999) *Patterns of Democracy*, New Haven, CT: Yale University Press.

Local Government Association (2005) *The Future of Health and Adult Social Care: A Partnership Approach for Well-Being*, London: LGA.

Lopez, A. (2017) 'Conceptual report on long-term care', Social Protection Innovative Investment in Long-Term Care (SPRINT) working paper D2.1, Brussels: SPRINT.

Lynn Jr., L.E. (2010) 'Has governance eclipsed government?', in R.F. Durant (ed) *The Oxford Handbook of American Bureaucracy*, Oxford: Oxford University Press, pp 669–90.

Malley, J., Holder, J., Dodgson, R. and Booth, S. (2014) 'Regulating the quality and safety of long-term care in England', in V. Mor, T. Leone and A. Maresso (eds) *Regulating Long-Term Care Quality: An International Comparison*, Cambridge: Cambridge University Press, pp 180–210.

Marczak, J., Fernández, J.L. and Wittenberg, R. (2017) 'Quality and cost-effectiveness in long-term care and dependency prevention: the English policy landscape', CEQUA Network, Available from: www.cequa.org [Accessed 8 October 2019].

MoHW (Ministry of Health and Welfare) (2009) 'Press release: a public hearing on the long-term care pilot program for disabled persons', 29 May, Seoul: MoHW.

MoHW (Ministry of Health and Welfare) (2010) *2009 Health and Welfare White Paper*, Seoul: MoHW.

Morel, N., Palier, B., and Palme, J. (2012) *Towards a Social Investment Welfare State? Ideas, Policies and Challenges*, Bristol: Policy Press.

National Health Insurance Corporation (2011) *Long Term Care Insurance Statistical Yearbook 2011*, Seoul: National Health Insurance Corporation.

Newman, J., Glendinning, C. and Hughes, M. (2008) 'Beyond modernisation? social care and the transformation of welfare governance', *Journal of Social Policy*, 37(4): 531–57.

OECD (Organisation for Economic Co-operation and Development) (2005) 'Ensuring quality long-term care for older people', OECD policy brief, Paris: OECD.

OECD (Organisation for Economic Co-operation and Development) (2011) *Help Wanted? Providing and Paying for Long-Term Care*, Paris: OECD.

OECD (Organisation for Economic Co-operation and Development) (2013) *A Good Life in Old Age? Monitoring and Improving Quality in Long-Term Care*, Paris: OECD.

Park, S. et al (2013) *Sahoeseobiseu iljalichangchulbangan yeongu* [Job Creation in Social Service Activities], Seoul: Korea Institute for Health and Social Affairs.

Pavolini, E. and Ranci, C. (2008) 'Restructuring the welfare state: reforms in long-term care in Western European countries', *Journal of European Social Policy*, 18(3): 246–59.

PSPD (People's Solidarity for Participatory Democracy) et al (2009) 'Noinjanggiyoyangboheom 1nyeon pyeongga mich jedogaeseon yogu nodongsiminsahoedanche gijahoegyeon [A joint statement of labor and civil society organizations on the first-year implementation evaluation and improving demand of the long-term care insurance program]', Available from: http://www.peoplepower21.org/666784 [Accessed 19 April 2014].

Phillips, D.R. and Chan, A.C.M. (eds.) (2002) *Ageing and Long-Term Care: National Policies in the Asia-Pacific*, Singapore and Ottawa: Institute of Southeast Asian Studies and International Development Research Centre.

Pierson, P. (1994) *Dismantling the Welfare State?*, Cambridge: Cambridge University Press.

Pierson, P. (1996) 'The new politics of the welfare state', *World Politics*, 48(2): 143–79.

Razavi, S. (2007) *The Political and Social Economy of Care in a Development Context*, Geneva: United Nations Research Institute for Social Development.

Rhodes, R.A.W. (2007) 'Understanding governance: ten years on', *Organization Studies*, 28(8): 1243–64.

Ringen, S., Kwon, H-J., Yi, I., Kim, T. and Lee, J. (2011) *The Korean State and Social Policy*, New York: Oxford University Press.

Seok, J.E. (2010) 'Public long-term care insurance for the elderly in Korea', *Social Work in Public Health*, 25(2): 185–209.

Simmons, R. and Birchall, J. (2005) 'A joined-up approach to user participation in public services', *Social Policy and Administration*, 39(3): 260–83.

Sørensen, E. and Torfing, J. (2009) 'Making governance networks effective and democratic through metagovernance', *Public Administration*, 87(2): 234–58.

Spasova, S., Baeten, R., Coster, S., Ghailani, D., Peña-Casas, R. and Vanhercke, B. (2018) *Challenges in Long-Term Care in Europe: A Study of National Policies*, Brussels: European Commission.

Stone, D. (2012) 'Transfer and translation of policy', *Policy Studies*, 33(6): 483–99.

Taylor-Gooby, P.F. (2004) *New Risks, New Welfare: The Transformation of the European Welfare State*, Oxford: Oxford University Press.

Tester, S. (1999) 'Comparative approaches to long-term care for adults', in J. Clasen (ed) *Comparative Social Policy*, Oxford: Blackwell, pp 136–58.

Yeandle, S., Kröger, T. and Cass, B. (2012) 'Voice and choice for users and carers? Developments in patterns of care for older people in Australia, England and Finland', *Journal of European Social Policy*, 22(4): 432–45.

# 12

# Towards greater social investments and equality in Europe and East Asia: policies and politics

## Timo Fleckenstein and Soohyun Christine Lee

The various chapters of this book have shown that we can observe increased social investment efforts in both European and East Asian countries. In family policy particularly, governments have made considerable efforts to improve work–family reconciliation policy (including early childhood education and care provisions) with the objective of promoting women's employment, child development and increasing fertility rates. Unsurprisingly, the social investment literature draws heavily on the experience of family policy expansion across the Organisation for Economic Co-operation and Development (OECD) member countries. In addition to greater public social investments, we find intensified private social investments in the domain of education. Families' mobilisation of substantial resources for higher education is well documented, and student tuition has attracted much controversy in many OECD countries. Private tutoring (or shadow education) as private social investment has long enjoyed much prominence in East Asia, where it is a dominant feature of the lives of young learners. It has, however, received less attention that shadow education is on the rise in Europe too.

Besides the economic rationales that are typically associated with social investment strategies, policy-makers, especially on the political left, are also driven by the desire to improve equality of opportunities, which is thought to eventually translate into greater social equality, including greater gender equality. Most notably, childcare provisions promote women's employment participation and thereby increasing their economic independence, and early education provisions are widely assumed to benefit children from disadvantaged backgrounds the most. It is hoped this will close the achievement gap between children from different socio-economic backgrounds. However, as the literature on the Matthew effect suggests (Cantillon, 2011; Bonoli et al, 2017), the relationship between greater social investments and greater social equality is not necessarily straightforward, as publicly funded childcare provisions, for instance, are disproportionately taken up by middle-class families, and thus disproportionately promote the employment participation of middle-class women and the development of their children.

In Chapter 8, looking at employment outcomes of social investment policies in latecomer countries, Jaehyoung Park finds some empirical support for the Matthew effect, including evidence with regard to work–family reconciliation policy; and in Chapter 6, Ijin Hong and Jieun Lee present an institutional analysis showing how labour market regimes in the latecomer countries of Italy, Spain, Japan and South Korea undermine the effectiveness of work–family reconciliation policies and their objective of improving the economic activity rates of women. With a focus on reproductive work, Mi Young An's contribution to this book (Chapter 7) argues that improving work–family reconciliation policies has had limited effect on the gendered division of household work, which is largely driven by individual-level factors (such as education and gender-role ideology). Hence, it is suggested that work–family reconciliation policy has not contributed greatly towards gender equality at home. In other words, despite social investment efforts, social and gender equality have remained great concerns, and some might even argue social progress has been disappointing, though such assessments would need to consider that recent developments in social inequality might be better assessed against the backdrop of the financial crisis of 2008 and its long-lasting repercussions, rather than as outcomes of social investment policies. In any case, rather than calling these policies into question, the contributors in this book have advocated more careful policy design and complementary policy reform in order to achieve social investment policies' potential for social progress. In the second half of this chapter we review the findings of chapters of this book and their wide-ranging policy recommendations for social and economic progress.

In the first half of the chapter, though, we look at a different shortcoming of the social investment turn across the OECD world – the failure to invest in labour market outsiders. While work–family reconciliation and education policy, informed by social investment rationales, have received much attention from policy-makers (Morgan, 2013; Fleckenstein and Lee, 2014; Boling, 2015), active labour market policy promoting the employability of the unemployed and those at the margins of the labour market has been less prominent in social investment strategies. Instead, we find that labour market policy primarily pursues a trajectory of workforce activation. Labour market reform is dominated by retrenchment in unemployment protection with reducing benefit levels, shortening benefit duration and tightening eligibility criteria. Moreover, when not complying with expectations, the unemployed are typically exposed to a stricter sanction regime. At the same time, costly up-skilling has lost importance in labour market policy, where cost containment has become a major reform rationale, privileging negative incentive reinforcement in reforms across the different welfare regimes (Bengtsson et al, 2017; Fleckenstein and Lee, 2017b). In the light of skills shortages, one might argue that there is a very convincing case for investing in training as well, and a recent review of more than 200 labour market programme evaluations supports training as an effective social investment policy. While active labour market programmes do not appear to make much immediate difference, they produce more favourable results about two to three years after completion; this applies in particular to training programmes (Card et al, 2018). Obviously, the failure to support those at the periphery of the labour market has enormous implications for social equality and fairness in societies, and thus it requires scrutiny. In the growing dualisation literature, it is well documented that we have been observing a growing polarisation between fewer well-protected insiders and a growing number of outsiders at the margins of the labour market in increasingly precarious employment with poor social protection (Emmenegger et al, 2012; Rueda, 2014).

But what is driving the differences between investing in families and investing in the unemployed and labour market outsiders; or phrased differently, what are the political dynamics in the social investment turn we have witnessed? Not only comparing family and labour market policy but also comparing across countries within each policy domain allows us to analyse the roads and barriers towards greater social investments. And by including 'deviant' cases (cases that do not comply with the general trend in each of the policy domains), we are in a position to better capture the complexity of the political drivers in family policy and labour market reform. Rather than suggesting 'a politics of social investment', we argue that family and labour market policies and their very different outcomes are underpinned by very different political dynamics. Family policy expansion, it appears, is primarily driven by electoral competition with political parties of the left and right modernising their family policy portfolios in order to attract young voters and young women voters in particular, whereas labour market reform (that is retrenchment in unemployment protection and a decline in training) is underpinned by business turning away from the welfare compromise that had long informed their political strategies. In this new socio-political environment, political parties appear to make little difference in labour market policy.

## The politics of investing in families

In this section, we investigate the roads and barriers to investment in families by first analysing the politics of employment-oriented family policy expansion in Germany and South Korea, followed by the exploration of barriers that led to Japan returning to traditional family policy after some experimenting with progressive policy. In Germany, family policy has departed from the conservative path since the 1990s. As a strong male-breadwinner country, the provision of general family support was the main aim of German family policy, which was to facilitate a traditional, gendered division of paid work and unpaid care work. The support, in the form of generous subsidies through the tax system and child benefits paid to the family unit, was to ensure enough family income so that women could stay at home and be primary caregivers instead of engaging in paid employment (Ostner and Lewis, 1995; Korpi, 2000).

The predominant male-breadwinner model began to be modified after German unification, when childcare moderately expanded for children over 3 years of age, providing legal entitlement to part-time care only (Ostner, 1998). Then the centre-left government of social democrats and the green party (1998–2005) continued only limited family policy expansion. German social democrats continued to prioritise general family support, deviating from the Swedish model of employment-oriented family policy expansion under social-democratic leadership together with feminist agency (Mahon, 1997; Huber and Stephens, 2001). Child benefits were increased and the Christian-democratic flat-rate parental leave scheme remained largely untouched, although a right to part-time work for parents was introduced to promote part-time work. However, neither childcare expansion nor Swedish-style parental leave challenging the gendered division of labour was on the political agenda. Also, fierce opposition from employers limited the scope of reform (Bleses and Seeleib-Kaiser, 2004; Leitner et al, 2008). Nevertheless, in the run-up to the 2002 election, family policy gained some political salience in social democracy. In the face of significant electoral pressure, the instrumental value of family policy, not only its appeal to young voters (whose support for social democrats was dwindling) but also family policy investments as an economic rationale in the modernisation of the German welfare state, persuaded the previously sceptical chancellor to raise the status of family policy, and to commit the party to childcare expansion in the 2002 election manifesto. The re-elected government reiterated its commitment to childcare expansion, and planned to fund the expansion with savings from the integration of unemployment and social assistance (see below). However, the power of the chancellor in the party was weakened as the government's key agenda of modernising unemployment protection was proving unpopular. To restore his authority, he called a snap election only to lose the political gamble, and the social democrats became the junior partner in a coalition with the Christian democrats (Fleckenstein, 2011b; see also Chapter 2 in this book). In this so-called grand coalition of Christian and social democrats (2005–9), the former was in charge of the family ministry. Contrary to conventional wisdom that family policy modernisation would run out of steam under Christian democratic leadership, given its strong association with traditional family and gender values, Christian democrats continued on the modernisation path. The 1998 election defeat had become a turning point for the Christian democratic party to modernise its family policy platform. To reverse the electoral fortunes of the party, the then-secretary general, and later party leader and chancellor, Angela Merkel, led the modernisation, as the analysis of voting behaviour in the 1998 election presented a dim prospect for returning to power unless the party garnered much stronger support from young women voters. The unexpected 2002 election defeat further strengthened the call for the modernisation. In the grand coalition, not only did the new family minister continue with the expansion of childcare provisions initiated by social democrats, but also introduced a Swedish-style parental leave scheme including 'daddy months', which was initially proposed in the 2005 social democracy manifesto. Although significant resistance came from the conservative wing of Christian democracy and some parts of the Catholic church (Fleckenstein, 2011b), the family minister overcame intra-party opposition by skilfully building cross-class coalition with support from organised business (Fleckenstein and Seeleib-Kaiser, 2011).

South Korea, another example of a strong male-breadwinner country, has also seen family policy expansion driven by party competition. Confucian ideology, which was influential in East Asia just as conservative Catholic thinking was in Europe, emphasised the role of family in welfare provisions and viewed women as primary caregiver (Jones, 1993; Pascall and Sung, 2007). Traditional gendered division of labour went hand-in-hand with the developmental welfare strategy employed by the East Asian states. The provisions of unpaid care by women were vital to maximising investment in economic development (Lee, 2018). Thus in East Asia, public policies promoting work–family reconciliation were largely absent (Pascall and Sung, 2007). In Korea, maternity leave was paid but short, and only mothers were entitled to unpaid parental leave. Very limited public childcare was available only for low-income families as a measure of child poverty prevention. It was not before two centre-left governments (1998–2008), in line with power resources theory but without strong feminist agency, that employment-oriented family policy expanded. In particular, the second centre-left government introduced more progressive family policies, targeting young voters who were its core supporters. Middle-income families became eligible for childcare support for the first time, while parental leave became much more generous in terms of both benefit level and duration, although the benefit level remained modest by international standards (An and Peng, 2016; Lee, 2018). Two consecutive electoral defeats put conservatives under huge pressure to broaden their electoral base; and it was especially the somewhat unexpected second election victory of the centre-left that persuaded the political right of the imperative of winning young voters to reverse their electoral fortunes and of the instrumental value of family policy in appealing to these young voters. In the 2007 presidential election campaign, turning away from their previous commitment to Confucian family and gender ideals, conservatives made pledges of ambitious reform on a par with the centre-left party. When conservatives returned to power (2008–17), they continued with the expansion of employment-oriented family policy, demonstrating sustained effort to modernise the party and increase electoral appeal among young voters. Free childcare became universal, and parental leave improved as the flat-rate benefit turned into a more generous earnings-related one. With the U-turn of the conservatives on family policy, party competition over family policy emerged in pursuit of young voters. Moreover, as in Germany, family policy was presented as pro-natal policy to address the low-fertility 'crisis'. These developments allowed family policy to gain cross-party support. Nevertheless, employers had strongly objected to family policy reform at first, seeing little economic or human capital benefit in the reform. As family policy received broad political support they strategically consented to childcare expansion funded through general taxation to prevent a greater direct, financial burden on business (Fleckenstein and Lee, 2014, 2017a).

Unlike Germany and Korea, Japan is a deviant case that has not departed from the conservative path. Japan being a strong male-breadwinner country, it was common for women there to exit the labour market before childbirth and thus public policies supporting maternal employment were essentially absent. Yet, when centre-left forces came into power for the first time in the 1990s, ending almost 40 years of dominance by the conservative Liberal Democratic Party (LDP), Japan pioneered employment-oriented family policy in East Asia. In the aftermath of the so-called '1.57 fertility shock', the Japanese left led the launch of the Angel Plan (1994–9), pledging a considerable expansion of childcare services. This lends additional support for power resources theory in the East Asian context, although Japanese feminists, similar to their Korean counterparts, were rather weak (Schoppa, 2006). However, employment-oriented policy quickly lost its prominence when a subsequent conservative coalition government of LDP and Komeito (1998–2009) shifted their focus to general family support policy. At first, the government followed the childcare expansion of the centre-left by introducing the New Angel Plan (2000–4). Despite improvements brought about by the two Angel Plans (the enrolment rate of children under the age of 3 years increased from 10.1 per cent in 1995 to 24 per cent in 2010), chronic shortages of places in childcare facilities still remained, leaving many Japanese parents to use so-called baby hotels (private, unlicensed childcare services).

Instead, general family support policy was prioritised under the LDP-Komeito coalition government – child benefits were substantially expanded, both in terms of eligibility and generosity. The prioritisation of general family support over employment-oriented family support was a response to continued strong social conservatism in Japanese society. The wider public, including young voters, viewed childcare as a responsibility of the family, not the state. The lack of public appetite for state intervention in childcare strikes a contrast with Korea, where we find a much stronger support for it (Fleckenstein and Lee, 2017a). Hence, the LDP faced no electoral pressure to modernise their family policy platform beyond what was needed to address their initial concerns about low fertility. The prominence of general family support over employment support continued even when the left (the Democratic Party of Japan, DPJ) came back to power (2009–12). The DPJ government also prioritised the expansion of child benefits to underline its support for the family over childcare. Thus, in the face of strong social conservatism, Japan shifted its family policy focus to more traditional measures. Despite its legacy as a pioneer of progressive family policy in East Asia, the absence of pressing public demand for progressive policies provided

Japanese parties no electoral rationale for employment-oriented family policy. The fertility shock in Japan, like the low fertility crisis in Korea, became an important justification for family policy expansion. Indeed, policy experts in the ministerial bureaucracy pointed out not only that child benefits were inadequate measures for raising fertility but also that childcare was a more effective pro-natal policy (Boling, 2015). Notwithstanding these expert views, Japanese partisan policy-makers shifted their attention from childcare to financial support for families – underlining the electoral rationale shaped by persistent social conservatism (Fleckenstein and Lee, 2017a).

The politics of family policy reform in the three latecomer countries is evidently different to the politics that underpinned the expansion of (progressive) family policies in Nordic countries, which was firmly driven by the political left with feminist agency (for the power resources model including its feminist variant, see Korpi, 1983; Mahon, 1997; Huber and Stephens, 2001). Although it was left parties in all three countries that brought employment-oriented policies onto the political agenda, they failed to develop political momentum. The political left in Germany and Korea implemented rather modest family policy expansion, compared to the expansion pursued by the subsequent conservative governments; and the political left in Japan even returned to conservative general family support policies with the increase of child benefits, moving away from childcare expansion. It was thus the political right, driven by electoral calculations, that made a difference in the three latecomer countries. The political right in Germany and Korea consolidated the progressive family policy reform since electoral competition over young and women voters compelled it to adjust its very traditional family and gender models. By contrast, in Japan, the political right did not face meaningful and sustained electoral pressure for modernisation, given the persistence of traditional gender norms across Japanese society, including among young and women voters. In this electoral context, the left gave up on the family policy modernisation it had previously pioneered. In relation to cross-class coalitions, German employers supported employment-oriented family policies, just like their Swedish counterparts had done earlier (Swenson, 2002). The Korean case, with rather hostile employers, shows that a comprehensive family policy reform is possible in the absence of employer support. Instead, we identified party-political agency, seeking votes and political office (Strøm, 1990), as the driver of family policy reform – both the modernisation in Germany and Korean, and the return to traditional policies in Japan.

## The politics of investing in labour market outsiders

In this section, we investigate the roads and barriers to investment in the skills of the unemployed and those who are at the margins of the labour market. Unlike the electoral competition driving up enabling activation in family policy, labour market reform has been dominated by retrenchment that can be thought as an expression of 'condemning', with coercive activation pushing the unemployed into accepting any job rather than training efforts that invest in their employability to increase their chances of getting 'good jobs' (Clasen, 2000). We first examine the politics of labour market reform in Sweden and Germany before turning to the deviant case of Italy, where we found an unexpected rise of training investment in temporary agency workers.

Sweden is widely considered the prime example of social-democratic activation. In the event of unemployment, various active labour market policies (including extensive training programmes) were available as well as generous unemployment benefits. Swedish labour market policy was built on a broad cross-class coalition. In addition to social democracy and trade unions, the key architects of Nordic welfare capitalism (Korpi, 1983; Esping-Andersen, 1985), employers, driven by the shortage of skilled labour in post-war Sweden, supported a comprehensive welfare state, including investment in the unemployed. Employers saw the instrumental value of the welfare state in solving the labour shortage in the form of training programmes that upskill the unemployed and generous unemployment protection that promotes industry-specific skills formation (Swenson, 2002).

In the wake of a major recession in the early 1990s, Sweden responded to the mass unemployment, at first, with comprehensive active labour market policy measures, in accordance with its traditional model. Expenditure on active labour market policy reached a record high of 2.8 per cent of GDP and training expenditure reached 1 per cent of GDP. The recession and the huge amount of pressure it put on public finances, however, marked the beginning of paradigmatic reforms of the Swedish welfare state. Under a right-wing government (1991–4), a series of austerity measures were introduced, including the retrenchment of unemployment benefits and active labour market policy. Critically, the social democracy supported retrenchment, in principle, and moreover, when back in power in the mid-1990s, they continued the austerity path. We thus observe a decline in the programmatic differences between the political left and right since the 1990s (Anderson, 2001; Sjöberg, 2011). Unemployment protection in Sweden lost its hallmark of exceptional generosity, and training programmes also lost their prominence in labour market policy. Although during the Great Recession unemployment rose to levels that were very similar to those of the recession in the early 1990s, spending on training programmes was merely 0.1 per cent of GDP (Fleckenstein and Lee, 2017b). These changes signal that Sweden has departed from social-democratic activation towards workfare. It is clear that parties of different political persuasion have lost confidence in active labour market policy, and no longer consider it a worthwhile social investment in the unemployed (Lindvall, 2010). It is argued that Swedish employers' turn towards a Thatcherite political orientation and their proactive promotion of neoliberal reform in the welfare state is critical to understanding the policy turnaround. With employers withdrawing their support from the comprehensive Swedish welfare state, senior social-democratic policy-makers began to doubt the feasibility of the traditional Swedish model in a globalised world (Ryner, 2004). So, in the face of an increasingly 'aggressive neoliberal posture' of employers (Huber and Stephens, 2001: 241; see also Kinderman, 2017), the cross-class coalition that underpinned inclusive labour market and social protection policies collapsed; and we observe organised business claiming the driving seat in labour market policy. Retrenchment in social protection and the reluctance to invest in the unemployed suggest the unravelling of social solidarity in social-democratic Sweden (Fleckenstein and Lee, 2017b).

As for Germany, its traditional labour market policy was characterised as a welfare-without-work strategy, in which early retirement and temporary parking of the unemployed in cheap job-creation schemes rather than Swedish-style training programmes were widely used in times of rising unemployment. During the centre-right coalition government of Christian democrats and liberals (1982–98), early retirement schemes and unemployment insurance benefits were maintained, while unemployment and social assistance was reduced. This welfare-without-work strategy was largely supported by both organised labour and business, as they could externalise the costs of corporate restructuring, which often achieved substantial increases in labour productivity through publicly subsidised early retirement schemes (Manow and Seils, 2000; Thelen, 2000). A window of opportunity opened for a social-democratic turn in labour market policy, when the centre-left government was elected in 1998. Previously social democrats had heavily criticised workfare policies for assistance recipients. Moreover, in the light of the Third Way's emphasis on social investments (Giddens, 1998), social-democratic policy-makers and 'their' bureaucrats in the labour ministry were eager to depart from the workfare approach of the previous government. However, the ministry of finance, with support from the chancellery, demanded labour market reform be cost-neutral and thus blocked any ambitious proposals for social-democratic activation. The centre-left government found themselves stuck in neutral – they avoided further workfare and achieved modest improvements in the job placement regime, but failed to invest in training for the unemployed.

One reason for this failure was a stalemate between social-democratic traditionalists and modernisers. Another was, as in the Swedish case, the withdrawal of employers from the post-war cross-class compromise in social and labour market policy. It became clear during the 'Alliance for Jobs' concertation, the chancellor's priority agenda, that employers had neoliberal policy preferences that were largely unacceptable for social democrats and trade unions. Employers were sceptical about the benefits of generous unemployment protection, costly training programmes and job-creation schemes. Their active promotion of neoliberal stances had a huge impact on Christian democracy but also, again as in the case of Sweden, on social-democratic modernisers (Fleckenstein and Lee, 2017b; Kinderman, 2017). In 2002, it came to light that the federal employment office had manipulated placement statistics to lower unemployment rates. The placement scandal not only discredited labour market policy, but also shifted the balance between social-democratic traditionalists and modernisers, and trade unions and employers in favour of the latter. Seizing upon this opportunity, the chancellor established the Hartz Commission, with members hand-picked by himself, to develop proposals for labour market reform. Among 15 members, eight were appointed to represent business while only two represented trade unions. The recommendations of the Hartz Commission were strongly reflected in the chancellor's Agenda 2010, featuring substantial retrenchment of unemployment protection and labour market deregulation. Thus, not only did social democracy fail to pursue a social-democratic activation turn in labour market policy, it also intensified neoliberal workfare activation started by the centre-right government. Evidently, the influence of organised labour had dwindled, whereas business successfully put greater pressure on political parties that resulted in diminishing programmatic differences in labour market policy-making (Fleckenstein and Lee, 2017b; Fleckenstein, 2011a).

Turning to Italy, we observe a rise of training investment in temporary agency workers that is unexpected, especially considering that social welfare in Italy is widely seen as being geared towards labour market insiders. The Italian welfare state has been often described as a 'pension state' (Fargion, 2009), as old-age security is particularly generous (most notably for labour market insiders). In contrast, spending on labour market policy is modest with little provision of training to enhance the employability of labour market outsiders. Moreover, outsiders are typically not eligible for unemployment benefits, as they fail to meet the required level of social insurance contributions; and no other unemployment protection is available to them. Historically, the insider-oriented Italian welfare state was built by Christian democrats, with the support of trade unions. Italian organised labour adopted in principle the objective of standard employment for everybody, yet in practice they focused on insider-oriented policies, such as workplace issues, labour market regulation and old-age security for their members (Regini and Esping-Andersen, 1980; Ferrera, 1996; Jessoula et al, 2010). Despite their historical class identity (Hyman, 2001), trade unions failed to effectively represent labour market outsiders, who constituted a large part of the working class, but not of their membership. Hence, the industrial and public policy strategies of unions resembled insider–outsider theory (Rueda, 2005) rather than the class-analytical power resources model (Korpi, 1983; Stephens, 1979).

Since the late 1990s, a series of deregulation measures increased the dualism of the Italian labour market. In the face of rising irregular jobs, especially temporary agency work, and social inequality, unions accepted that their objective of standard employment for all was no longer feasible and revised their strategies accordingly. In the aftermath of the 1997 legislation that liberalised temporary agency work, all three confederal unions established special organisations for the representation of atypical workers, providing temporary agency workers full integration into organised labour with all statutory union rights. Examples of such improvements in the representation of agency workers are difficult to find in other European countries, where workplace representation of these workers is often compromised. The organisational inclusion led unions to call for a major policy initiative to invest in the skills of agency workers. In particular, during collective bargaining, unions demanded the creation of training funds for these workers jointly run by employers and unions. The initiative proved successful as, according to a European survey, more than one third of temporary agency workers received training. This impressive result put Italy at the top of the training league table by quite some margin with the Netherlands in second place. Less than one fifth of Dutch temporary agency workers participated in training; and in terms of training expenditure, they received around one third of the investment that went to their Italian counterparts (Durazzi, 2017; Durazzi et al, 2018).

With the emergence of investment into the skills of labour market outsiders, Italy presents a deviant case in labour market policy. Facing greater labour market dualisation and social polarisation, Italian unions shifted away from insider-oriented strategy towards a more inclusive approach. This change of union strategy was critical in the creation of a training fund for agency workers, a rather unexpected development from a laggard in public training policy. Contrary to increasing marginalisation experienced by unions in Germany and Sweden, Italian unions bucked the trend and, with innovations in industrial relations, successfully pushed employers into filling a vacuum in the Italian welfare state (see also Johnston et al, 2011). In addition to the unexpected mobilisation for training, unions launched a campaign for income protection for labour market outsiders. Joining forces with civil society organisations, unions formed the Alliance against Poverty, advocating means-tested, non-contributory income protection. Their campaign created considerable political pressure, and the government eventually legislated a 'social inclusion income' in 2017 to improve social protection for labour market outsiders. Thus, the Italian case suggests that, challenging insider–outsider theory, insider-focused trade unions have the capacity to develop a wider notion of social solidarity (Durazzi et al, 2018).

To conclude the labour market policy section, we examine the collapse of broad political support for unemployment protection and training in Sweden and Germany. In Sweden, employers' successful mobilisation for neoliberal policy was critical for labour market policy to shift away from social democratic activation towards workfare. In Germany, a similar neoliberal campaign of organised business prevented social democrats from making a social-democratic turn in labour market policy when in power. It does not come as too much of a surprise that the political right accommodated the preferences of organised business, but we would expect the political left to resist the pressure from business. However, defying conventional wisdom, social democrats in both Sweden and Germany responded to the pressure by moving towards the political centre – not only did they support retrenchment in unemployment protection, they also gave up on training as social investment in the employability of the unemployed. In other words, in the new socio-political environment in which employers do not support the long-held welfare compromise, political parties appear to make little difference to labour market policy. Therefore, the Swedish and German experiences show that the absence of effective union mobilisation and employer support poses a barrier to social investment for labour market outsiders. Conversely, the deviant experience of Italy suggests that compromise between trade unions and employers can pave a road to social investments for those at the margins of the labour market. Italian unions successfully persuaded employers, in the realm of industrial relations, to offer training for temporary agency workers. Although Italy is still a laggard in public training policy, the training initiative partially filled the vacuum for labour market outsiders.

Comparing the politics of family policy and labour market reform, we find differences in the politics underpinning the uneven social investment turn in the two policy domains. In family policy, political parties of both the political left and right display a capacity to respond to new social risks as expressed in the political attitudes of young voters in particular. The examples of Germany and Korea illustrate this, and equally the Japanese case shows that the absence of these underpinnings for electoral competition does not allow for a sustainable social investment turn in family policy. This argument appears to receive support from the study of Italy, where Blome (2016) has shown that the lack of more progressive gender role attitudes undermined the emergence of electoral competition as in Germany, for instance. While the persistence of the male-breadwinner model in Japan and Italy is somewhat disheartening from a gender equality point of view, it is refreshing that changes in societies can make a difference, as political parties still seem to respond to electoral pressure for social policy expansion even in difficult times. The story in labour market policy is different; here political parties appear to make little difference. Instead, we find business in the driving seat of labour market reform, making Sweden turn its back on social-democratic policies and preventing a social-democratic turn in Germany. However, the deviant case of Italy is encouraging, as it suggests that organised labour, when taking the mobilisation for labour market outsiders seriously, can still make a difference.

In the following section, we review and discuss more applied implications for social policy-making and policy substance developed in the contributions of this book project. For both aspects of social policy, the research of this volume yields important lessons with the potential to improve policy and the lived experience of people in Europe and East Asia, the two regions covered in the research here.

## Lessons for social investments and equality

On the issue of the capacity of political parties and political agency more generally, Samuel Mohun Himmelweit and Sung-Hee Lee, in Chapter 2, suggest some important lessons for social investment policy-making. With an empirical focus on work–family reconciliation policy, the authors argue that the different extent of social investment reform in the four latecomer countries of Germany, England, South Korea and Japan is intimately related to the ideational framing of social investments in the political discourse. They demonstrate that the ambiguity that is typically associated with social investments (Jenson, 2012) – often with a somewhat negative connotation – can be turned into an asset in policy-making. It is precisely the polysemic nature of social investments, they suggest, that can be exploited by political actors seeking to advance policy expansion. In both Germany and Korea, work–family reconciliation policy was explicitly framed as a critical reform agenda for the two countries' future prosperity, which was linked to multiple benefits associated with social investments (such as boosting female employment, providing business with skills, promoting gender equality, raising fertility and driving up educational attainment). This broad discourse of a wide range of benefits allowed different groups to pick an issue that was important to them from the social investment menu. Feminists, for instance, were keen to promote women's labour market participation and the greater gender equality that typically comes with it, while businesses could also show an interest in greater female employment, not for reasons of gender equality but to meet their skills needs. Conservatives might shudder at the thought of greater maternal employment and gender equality – policies that undermine the traditional, male-breadwinner family – but, in low-fertility contexts, they might be prepared to give up their opposition if it is believed that progressive policy can boost fertility, a key concern in conservative circles. In other words, the polysemic character of the social investment idea allows actors to interpret the idea and the benefits associated with social investment policy differently, which ultimately can enable social investments to become a coalition magnet (Béland and Cox, 2016) that can bring together a rather diverse range of actors.

Smart entrepreneurial actors, thus appear to have the capacity to facilitate the building of unlikely, cross-class coalitions by promoting a discourse that exploits the polysemic nature of an idea. The German case of work–family reconciliation shows that this allowed not only conservatives to join a progressive coalition, but also employers who had previously been rather sceptical when policy was predominantly framed in terms of gender equality. Policy-makers' proactive engagement with employers' association hence turned the business community, using Korpi's classification of agency (2006), from outspoken 'antagonists' into 'consenters' if not 'protagonists', as employers became one of successive German family ministers' most important allies. Having said this, there are limits to winning over hostile actors, and Korea is a case in point. Despite a broad political coalition and a comprehensive social investment turn, policy-makers failed to convince employers of the business case for work–family reconciliation policy. Admittedly, this did not prevent Korea from making bold social investment reforms – support across other political and social groups was strong enough to overcome political resistance from employers. However, employers continued to resist changes in the workplace, which seriously undermined the effectiveness of work–family reconciliation policy. For instance, in a survey, nearly one in three employers (28 per cent) conceded that they restricted their employees from taking up parental leave to which they were legally entitled (Song, 2019). This observation highlights the importance of policy implementation, for which broad support for policy is critical. If not, the rule-maker cannot necessarily expect that the rule-taker will comply – an issue also discussed in the institutionalist literature on change and the difficulties policy-makers might experience (Streeck and Thelen, 2005).

In this book, Jooha Lee's work on long-term care (Chapter 11) also highlights the importance of policy implementation, examining the case of long-term care. He argues that the social investment literature is preoccupied with what he calls the *formal* policy domain (that is essentially about the content of policy), while largely ignoring the *operational* policy domain (that is about organisational arrangements and procedures). With reference to social care, Lee shows that governance structures are critical for the effective delivery of policy and achieving desired outcomes. Especially in policy domains that involve a wide range of actors (such as central government, local authorities, voluntary organisations and private for-profit providers), a careful design of organisational arrangements and procedures is imperative. In England and Korea, for instance, non-state actors (especially the private for-profit sector) play a decisive role in service delivery. In fragmented systems, policy-makers might be tempted to pursue a top-down approach, as this could be thought to minimise transaction costs. However, such an approach, as the Korean case illustrates, might struggle with the rule-maker/rule-taker dilemma. Instead, Lee suggests a more inclusive governance approach where central government not only ascribes greater autonomy to local authorities but also service providers. For better inter-organisational relationships and more effective coordination, a case is made for the promotion of partnership and co-governance between the various actors in both policy-making and delivery, though with central government remaining a key player in service planning and long-term collaboration. Specifically, Lee argues that Korea can draw valuable lessons from the English experience about how to make rather centralised governance more participatory and coordinative in the operation of long-term care systems. As a starting point in Korea's journey, the Ministry of Health and Welfare might want to consider, as a vehicle for overcoming conflict between rule-makers and rule-takers, the establishment of a forum with representatives from different relevant groups to facilitate the discussion of the future operation of long-term care programmes, which needs to involve major institutional reform. Lee's chapter very much echoes the argument by Sabel et al that it is impossible to design social services in a simple top-down manner, as 'it is difficult to specify roles and responsibilities of members of integrated service teams ex-ante in detail without limiting the very autonomy that the actors at various levels in the reformed systems will need to respond to novel and changing circumstances' (2017: 141); and hence they make a case for bottom-up development of capacitating services, including the provision of spaces for experimentation and innovation.

As for the other end of the life course, Sonia Exley (Chapter 3) as well as Yun Young Kim and Young Jun Choi (Chapter 4) show the detrimental effect of excessive private social investments, specifically private tutoring. These investments might be viewed favourably, as they could be thought of as increasing the overall investment effort for greater educational progress and economic gains. However, drawing on the experience of the extreme case of Korea, a rather different picture emerges, as overly ambitious career aspirations have driven an over-investment in private education, which has critically contributed to skills mismatch in the Korean labour market (most notably, the lack of intermediate skills holding back the country's labour productivity). While one might understand why parents press for ever stronger educational credentials of their offspring so that they can secure good 'insider' jobs in large companies, this has locked small- and medium-sized companies into a low skills/low productivity equilibrium that has huge negative implications for the country's overall economic performance. In such a situation, from a macroeconomic point of view, financial resources are not allocated most efficiently (Fleckenstein and Lee, 2019).

Addressing the pathological equilibrium with over-investment in private tutoring, in Chapter 3 Exley shows the limited capacity of education reform to push back excessive shadow education. Korean policy-makers are well aware of the severe problem (not only the economic dimension but also in terms of child welfare issues), but successive reforms have failed to make a meaningful difference, as continued high spending on private tutoring suggests. In the chapter, it is demonstrated how the private tutoring industry has managed to adapt to changes in education. For instance, reforming university admission (such as reducing reliance on exams and putting a greater emphasis on personal statements) provided private tutors with new business opportunities (advising the writing of personal statements) rather than weakening the sector. The industry appears to display remarkable responsiveness to changes in their business environment, and it has managed to effectively exploit the anxieties of parents who feared they were not doing their best for their children. These anxieties have, ultimately, their roots in labour market dualisation and the lack of social protection. In the Korean winner-takes-all environment, success yields great returns, while failure comes at a high price in a polarised labour market with poor social protection for outsiders. Exley, for this reason, concludes that excessive private tutoring in Korea cannot sufficiently be dealt with in the domain of education policy, but that it requires more comprehensive reforms in the labour market and social protection that address the anxieties parents experience. In other words, employment regulation that takes on the dualism in Korea's labour market and welfare reforms that dramatically improve the inclusiveness of the country's current rather residual social protection regime are imperative (see also Fleckenstein et al, 2019a). Beyond East Asia, Exley's study also provides important lessons for policy-makers in European countries, where private tutoring is on the rise. In England and Wales, for instance, a recent report by the Sutton Trust shows that more than one quarter (27 per cent) of pupils between the ages of 11 and 16 received private tutoring, compared to less than one fifth (18 per cent) when the survey started in 2005. In London, we observe a dramatic development with four in ten young learners (41 per cent) receiving private tutoring. Unsurprisingly, the report confirms that children from affluent families are disproportionately receiving additional support to perform well in school, providing them a social advantage over their peers from weaker socio-economic backgrounds (Sutton Trust, 2019; see also Bray, 2020, for a European, cross-national perspective). Furthermore, we hasten to add, European countries face the challenges of dualisation and associated greater social polarisation of their societies. Policy-makers there are strongly advised to take early action on tackling the rise of shadow education to prevent, in Exley's words, 'sleep-walking' in the pathological equilibrium that is observed not only in Korea but also in other parts of East Asia.

While Exley's chapter presents a powerful institutional policy analysis of private tutoring in Korea, in Chapter 4, Yun Young Kim and Young Jun Choi engage in a quantitative analysis of Korean Education and Employment Panel (KEEP) data, showing how greater private tutoring translates into greater success in the labour market and corresponding higher income. From a social equality point of view, this is of course highly problematic, as high-income groups use their better resources for greater investment in private tutoring. This form of private social investment effectively becomes a mechanism for the reproduction of social advantage and disadvantage. Children from weak socio-economic backgrounds are held back, while privileged groups preserve their social and economic status. Using notions from the OECD, Kim and Choi show empirically that private tutoring creates 'sticky floors' and 'sticky ceilings' (cf. OECD, 2018). The authors argue that greater public investment is the only way to deal with the social inequalities private tutoring creates. In other words, more public education provision is the only medicine to cure Korea's education fever. This runs against some commentary in the Korean public debate, where greater public education expenditure is not considered a policy priority, as Korean youngsters not only achieve high educational attainment by international standards (see, for instance, OECD, 2019b) but also perform rather well in international student assessment (most notably, the OECD's PISA studies; OECD, 2019a); and it is difficult to deny that private tutoring contributed to these impressive performances. But the social costs Korean society incurs for this are high, making a strong case for the re-calibration of private and public investment for greater fairness.

Moving on from school-age education, Niccolo Durazzi's contribution on higher education (Chapter 5) illustrates the necessity of considering carefully a country's production regime in policy design, rather than assuming that there is a blueprint for modernising higher education. Across the OECD world, the sector faces considerable pressure to provide high skills that better meet labour market demands and equip individuals with skills that allow them to better cope with increasingly fast-changing workplaces. In policy debates, vertically differentiated higher education systems with strong competition between universities have received most attention as potential blueprints for higher education reform. This might be a suitable policy strategy for economies that rely greatly on dynamic services (as the UK case illustrates), but Durazzi shows, against much perceived wisdom, that horizontally differentiated higher education systems remain a viable if not desirable alternative to provide knowledge economies with high skills. The differentiation between traditional research universities and universities of applied sciences is compatible with both dynamic, high-end services and advanced manufacturing, as illustrated by the analysis of the Netherlands and Germany, respectively. Both countries expanded enrolment in universities of applied sciences to meet their high skills demands. By contrast, Korea, which has advanced manufacturing at the heart of its growth strategy (like Germany), embarked on a liberal policy trajectory of vertical differentiation and competition in higher education, which failed to provide the labour market with the high skills needed (especially STEM skills). This policy failure in Korea prompted top-down government intervention, with government seeking to make universities change their educational offerings. Durazzi suggests that this rather rigid approach, greatly relying on government skills forecasts, might not be responsive enough to fast-changing economies, and instead his research recommends decentralised cooperation as a 'more agile and effective' approach to coping with changing labour market needs. Notably, this call for more cooperation between different actors in higher education, rather than top-down intervention, is very similar to Jooha Lee's conclusion from the study of long-term care, calling further into question central governments' capacity to prescribe adequate policy reform in increasingly complex systems.

While Durazzi provides some critical lessons on skills formation in higher education, the research presented by Ga Woon Ban (Chapter 9), drawing on an econometric analysis of the OECD data from the Programme for International Assessment for Adult Competencies (PIAAC), considers the equally important issue of skills retention in the workplace. His analysis shows considerable cross-national difference in skill depreciation, and Ban warns that this suggests that countries need to take different, carefully designed policy approaches to preserve the skills of their working-age population. Essentially echoing Durazzi's finding in higher education, there is no one-size-fits-all solution that allows retention of achieved skills levels. In this research, Ban argues that the degree of skills use in the workplace is critical to human capital depreciation, providing strong support for the so-called use-it-or-lose-it hypothesis. Positive depreciation rates are found in most countries, implying that not only accumulating human capital, but also maintaining skills are important.

Three countries (the UK, Korea and Japan) provide interesting points of comparison. First, the UK and Korea have similar levels of human capital but they differ significantly in human capital depreciation rates. Korea has the highest rate whereas the UK has the lowest among OECD countries. Furthermore, Korea has the highest rate of depreciation for the employed, while the UK has a high depreciation rate for the unemployed. Second, Japan and Korea have a low level of skills use in the workplace and low ratio of skilled occupations, but their levels of the human capital depreciation rate are substantially different. While Korea has the highest depreciation rate for the employed, Japan exhibits a low level of the depreciation rate for the employed, and the lowest depreciation for the unemployed. These findings, Ban argues, call for tailored policy interventions. They suggest that countries should take different approaches to preserving human capital depending on their particular patterns of human capital depreciation. In countries where higher human capital depreciation rates are found among the employed (such as Korea), policy should promote higher skills use in the workplace to prevent the massive loss of human capital that low-skilled jobs facilitate. On the other hand, where the depreciation rate is high among the unemployed, policy should emphasise helping people find new, adequate jobs. Furthermore, Ban suggests that Japan's higher level of task discretion and cooperative culture in the workplace mitigates the adverse effects of hierarchical work culture, which would be expected to facilitate skills depreciation. By contrast, Korean workers have not only a low level of autonomy but also low task discretion by OECD standards. In this work culture, Korean workers rarely engage in problem-solving by themselves or in cooperative tasks. Moreover, both the level of learning at work and of job satisfaction are substantially lower in Korea. This shows that a low level of skills use in the workplace could be an important factor affecting depreciation of human capital; and public policy and industrial relations should promote organisational changes in workplaces that allow workers to make the best use of their skills, especially in countries like Korea, where high skill levels in the working-age population are compromised by poor employment practices. Ban's study also makes a strong argument that skills policy for the working-age population cannot be reduced to lifelong learning (as supply-side policy) but that workplaces are of pivotal importance too. In fact, the effectiveness of lifelong learning policy, as a social investment policy for the working-age population, could be expected to hugely depend on jobs that are ready to make good use of better skills. In other words, the demand side cannot be neglected in skills policy (see also Fleckenstein and Lee, 2018).

Looking at the success of work–family reconciliation policy as social investment with the view to promoting labour market flow, Ijin Hong and Jieun Lee (Chapter 6) show that the effectiveness of such policy strategies greatly relies on the labour market institutions and structures (such as workplace culture, the availability of part-time employment and labour market dualism). In other words, one cannot expect linear relationship between greater social investment and labour market flow (that is here, female employment participation in particular), and they demonstrate how labour market dualism in particular undermines the effectiveness of social investment reform. In their comparative analysis of latecomer countries (Korea, Japan, Italy and Spain), the Korean experience is particularly important, as it achieved the most comprehensive expansion of work–family reconciliation policy, but failed to produce a corresponding improvement in labour market flow (notably, employment participation of highly educated women). Hong and Lee suggest that work–family reconciliation policy needs to be complemented with labour market reform that addresses institutional deficiencies in the labour market which hold back women's employment. They show that Korean labour market structures are by no means prepared to support women's increasing desire to reconcile employment and family, most notably because of a workplace culture of very long hours and very poor availability of part-time jobs. Among the four countries analysed, Korea presents the worst gender equity culture. Also, the Korean labour market is characterised by strong dualism with many highly skilled employees working in jobs that do not utilise their skills, with women being over-represented in outsider and inadequate jobs. In this labour market environment, highly educated women, Hong and Lee argue, prefer disproportionately to become stay-at-home mothers rather than returning to the labour market after becoming a parent. This analysis suggests that effective work–family reconciliation policy requires a fundamental reform of the Korean labour market that addresses the widespread practices of gender discrimination.

In research for the Korean Deputy Prime Minister for Social Affairs (Fleckenstein et al, 2019a), we drew similar conclusions and recommended not only stricter labour market regulation for more women- and family-friendly employment practices, but also stricter enforcement of labour market regulation – an area where Korea is not performing well. It is also argued that greater gender equality is imperative not only for better utilising women's skills in the labour market, but also for boosting fertility. In research building on the work for the Korean government, we show that the country's ultra-low fertility is intimately linked with the dualisation of the labour market and social protection, and that the associated social insecurity is not only holding back families from growing larger but also driving increasing childlessness among young Koreans (Fleckenstein et al, 2019b). Hong's and Lee's examination of Japan provides additional support for the need of comprehensive labour market reform. Among the analysed countries, Japan presents the highest female employment participation, and it appears that access to part-time employment provides a bridge for mothers to return to the labour market. While this makes a case for part-time employment to facilitate flow, the Japanese case also indicates the limits of a part-time strategy, as Japanese women fail to escape from the periphery of the labour market. The heavily gendered structure of the labour market – with discriminatory practices in the workplace that are quite comparable to the Korean situation – pose an incredibly high barrier for women to enter well-protected and well-remunerated insider employment.

The importance of labour market institutions and structures in maximising the return from social investment is also demonstrated in Hyejin Choi's research (Chapter 10) on active ageing and grandparenting. Facilitating active ageing can be an important part of a more holistic social investment strategy that takes the life course seriously, and grandparenting can facilitate active ageing by providing meaningful social engagements. Obviously, grandparenting has the potential to be beneficial not only for grandparents but also their grandchildren and their parents. However, in countries where labour market practices make it difficult to reconcile work with caring responsibilities, grandparents can be under pressure to provide extensive childcare, and this can undermine active ageing and well-being. In her comparative analysis of England and Korea, Choi notes that Korean grandparents have to fill a considerable gap between long working hours and formal childcare provisions. Despite universal free childcare having been introduced in Korea, parents, due to their demanding work hours, often have to rely on grandparents to provide after-nursery/school care until late. Hence, Korean grandparents frequently face much longer and more intensive childcare and related responsibilities (including general housekeeping) than their English counterparts. Being exhausted and having little time to engage in other social and physical leisure activities, Korean caregiving grandparents do not enjoy a balanced, active lifestyle in old age compared to English grandparents. Choi, therefore, suggests that addressing institutional deficiencies in the labour market that hinder work–family reconciliation (notably, a widespread practice of very long working hours and the limited availability of part-time employment) is important for active ageing. For this reason, recent measures in Korea to promote shorter working hours are a step in the right direction, as shorter working hours are an important condition to support not only working parents but also grandparents. The maximum working hours allowed per week have been significantly reduced from 68 to 52, among which regular working hours must not exceed 40. However, only large firms and public institutions must comply with this legislation, leaving the majority of working parents who are employed in small and medium-sized workplaces unaffected. The expansion of the right to flexible working time for parents effectively doubled the length of flexible working one is entitled to from one to two years, but this remains insufficient especially given that for lower grades at primary school, the class hours end at lunchtime. Furthermore, as we observed in the case of parental leave, it is questionable to what extent employers will comply with this new legislation.

In England, a right to request flexible working time was extended to workers who have six months tenure in their job instead of 12 months previously. This change was thought to benefit workers with more precarious employment conditions, such as those on casual or short-term contracts, many of whom are women and caregivers. Nevertheless, it is still regarded as a weak measure as employers are not obliged to grant employees' requests for flexible working time. For a meaningful promotion of work–family balance, a stronger intervention, such as the German right to flexible working time, should be considered.

Greater public social investment – whether to tackle private tutoring, facilitate skills formation and retention, or boost women's labour market participation – raises distributional issues that need to be considered carefully, if social investments are pursued to promote greater equality. Cantillon and others (Cantillon, 2011; Bonoli et al, 2017) have warned that social investment policies might primarily benefit the middle classes, while benefit cuts for disadvantaged groups might pay for social investment innovation – with possibly considerable detrimental distributional outcomes. Jaehyoung Park, in his analysis of active labour market and work–family reconciliation policy (Chapter 8), finds some limited support for so-called Matthew effects of social investments. However, rather than arguing against social investment, he makes a case for carefully designed social investments in order to avoid regressive distributional outcomes. In training policy, for instance, specific targets for low-skilled people are proposed, acknowledging that street-level bureaucrats might favour participants with intermediate skills as they have much greater prospects of successful re-integration into the labour market after training. To facilitate low-income groups' use of childcare services, affordability is of great importance, and investment in childcare provisions should therefore prioritise those who struggle the most with the costs of childcare. From the English experience we know that considerable investment in childcare provisions can still leave significant childcare costs to parents. In addition to calling for careful social investment policy design, Park's chapter more generally reminds us of the critical importance of traditional social protection policies in attempts to reduce poverty and inequality – these were at the heart of social policy in industrial societies, and they remain imperative in increasingly knowledge-based economies. However, in today's labour markets, the greatest social progress might be expected when social protection and social investment policies are pursued hand-in-hand, and Park thus suggests welfare reform packages that combine adequate income support with social investment.

## Recalibrating social protection, investment and regulation

Welfare states in Europe and East Asia have been subject to comprehensive changes over the past 20 or so years, including massive changes in social protection and labour markets, as well as the rise of social investment policies. Retrenchment has undermined the redistributive capacity of welfare state, including those of coordinated welfare capitalism, which has previously produced more favourable distributive outcomes. However, the combination of cuts in social protection and labour market deregulation has left a rising number of increasingly vulnerable people at the margins of society and the labour market (Cantillon and Vandenbroucke, 2013; Fleckenstein and Lee, 2017b). In other words, social investment policies face the challenges of labour market dualisation and greater social inequality, and welfare reform striving for greater social investment cannot ignore these developments. Barbier (2017) points out that a neoliberal social investment strategy that fails to consider social protection, and indeed considers social investment as a replacement for social protection, cannot be expected to deliver greater social equality and the economic gains associated with the social investment; and Bonoli et al (2017) underline that a more equal distribution of incomes is imperative for social investment strategies delivering their promises. Certainly, the devil, as so often, is in the details, but the importance of social protection is certainly well recognised among key social investment advocates, with Esping-Andersen, for instance, arguing that 'minimization of poverty and income security is a precondition for an effective social investment strategy' (2002: 5). With a very similar impetus, Hemerijck (2017) highlights the key role of adequate income protection ('buffers' in his taxonomy) in social investment strategies – not only because of the wage replacement function of social protection but also the macroeconomic function of stabilising the business cycle in the Keynesian tradition. With reference to unemployment protection, for example, Hemerijck argues that generous unemployment benefits are critical to supporting the job search activities of the unemployed and thus their reintegration into the labour market. A very similar case for unemployment protection is made by Nolan (2013).

Nevertheless, the rise of inequality is not only the result of an increasing inadequacy of social protection but also due to far-reaching changes in labour markets; and it is difficult to ignore that these changes are, in part, the consequence of market deregulation across the OECD world, which allowed significant increases in precarious employment, as described in the dualisation literature. Critically, the dualisation of the labour market is often de-facto accompanied by a dualisation of social protection, as those at the margins of the labour market experience the greatest social protection gaps. In addition to buffers addressing these greater labour market risks, the issue of labour market regulation needs to be considered in order to push back precarious employment practices at the periphery of the labour market. Women, among others, are over-represented at the margins of the labour market, and for this reason, labour market regulation tackling precarious employment is also vital for greater gender equality. This is not to say that the solution is simply to return to previous employment regulation regimes; labour market dualisation and the rise in inequality create an imperative for an integrated welfare reform programme that not only balances social investment and social protection but also takes regulation seriously. Certainly, the capacity of social protection policies to correct rising inequality in the labour market is limited, providing the case for an increasingly multi-dimensional strategy for greater social equality. The research in this book, however, suggests that regulation needs to go beyond employment regulation tackling labour market dualisation, to include the regulation of working time in order to promote workplace practices that allow better work–family reconciliation (for instance, the right to flexible working). Admittedly, legislation does not necessarily change workplace cultures. So nominal rights in the workplace might be meaningless if parents do not feel sufficiently empowered to take advantage of them. Without downplaying the importance of public policy in changing workplace culture, dialogue with social partners (namely, employers and organised labour) can prove decisive in an effective implementation of rights for improving the lived experience of working people. Obviously, there are limits to social dialogue if one party fundamentally opposes changes in the workplace, but dialogue – especially in the 'shadow of hierarchy' with government being prepared to take unilateral action if needed (Visser and Hemerijck, 2000) – might prove more effective than conventionally expected.

In any multi-dimensional approach, the issue of public and private welfare needs to receive greater attention. In the domain of social protection, one observes an increasing awareness of the old and new divisions public and private social protection creates; and the dualisation literature has rightly emphasised the 'changing face of inequality' in post-industrial societies (Seeleib-Kaiser et al, 2012; Seeleib-Kaiser, 2008). In the social investment literature, however, private social investments have failed to receive sufficient attention, despite their possibly wide-ranging implications for social equality. In this book, Exley identified private tutoring for school-age children as a growth industry in a number of countries, with the capacity to reinforce existing inequalities in society. In other words, private tutoring is a rather potent mechanism for inheriting social advantage, as the chapter by Kim and Choi has shown empirically with reference to the Korean case. This might be seen to apply in particular in countries with vertically differentiated higher education systems with fierce competition for admission to leading universities, such as Korea and the United Kingdom. Although private tutoring is now gaining importance in the UK, traditionally fee-paying, private schools have been used by affluent social groups to preserve their social advantage. And unsurprisingly, the hugely disproportionate admission of students from private schools (so-called independent schools) at top universities like Oxford and Cambridge (Oxbridge) attracts much attention not only from policy-makers but also the wider public. This has translated into increasing pressure on universities from the Office for Students in England – the regulator and competition authority for the higher education sector – to not only widen participation among disadvantaged groups but also to close attainment gaps between different disadvantaged groups at university. The UK's Social Mobility Commission, working together with the Sutton Trust, has shown, for instance, the extent to which public and business life in the UK is dominated by elites from independent, fee-paying schools and Oxbridge (Sutton Trust and Social Mobility Commission, 2019), leaving little doubt that private social investments are critical in the reinforcement of social inequality in the UK.

Considering private social investments are virtually absent in the social investment debate, private investment activity should receive considerably more attention in future research – not only to improve our understanding of private social investments as mechanisms for the inheritance of social advantage but also as a mechanism that can undermine public social investment. Certainly, if greater social equality is strived for, private social investments cannot be ignored. Politically, this might present a more sensitive issue than one might expect. While affluent parents, for instance, might in principle resent the burden private tutoring or fee-paying schools put on family finances, it is less clear that they would be prepared to give up the social advantages their privileged financial positions allow them to buy. Hence, policy aiming at recalibrating the public and the private might face resistance from well-off families, including large parts of the middle class, which might also express some reservations about policy reform tackling observed Matthew effects. This could present a considerable challenge for political parties, and the study of family policy reform suggests that electoral considerations have been vital for parties to turn towards greater social investments. Further resistance might be expected when, more broadly, recalibrating social protection, investment and regulation. As already indicated, employers, for instance, can be expected to mobilise against greater regulation of the labour market, as business was the key driver for a more liberal trajectory in labour market reform. So, while social investment reform carries the potential for considerable economic and social progress, comprehensive reform strategies cannot be expected to be free from distributive conflicts.

This is where skilful political agency and coalition-building are important, and research presented in this book identified ideas as coalition magnets, a potentially powerful tool for the building of comprehensive political coalitions for ambitious welfare reform. Future research that improves our understanding of policy mixes that allow for greater social inclusion and economic progress might not only improve our understanding of the subject matter, but also inform political strategy. Critically, rather than focusing on one dimension (protection, investment or regulation), research programmes that shed insights into the interaction of different policy initiatives across the three dimensions might yield the greatest returns, and political–economic research informed by the notion of institutional complementarities – which are well recognised in the social investment literature – can be expected to be particularly insightful, as it takes institutional context and its importance for the viability and effectiveness of policy into account. Welfare states in both Europe and East Asia are very much in flux, facing challenges from old and new social risks in addition to considerable political pressures. Social investment policy is an important dimension in the search for new welfare state equilibria, and there can be little doubt that ambitious research programmes are vital to promote both policy and political learning for social and economic progress.

## References

An, M.Y. and Peng, I. (2016) 'Diverging paths? A comparative look at childcare policies in Japan, South Korea and Taiwan', *Social Policy & Administration*, 50(5): 540–58.

Anderson, K.M. (2001) 'The politics of retrenchment in a social democratic welfare state: reform of Swedish pensions and unemployment insurance', *Comparative Political Studies*, 34(9): 1063–91.

Barbier, J.-C. (2017) '"Social investment": With or against social protection?', in A. Hemerijck (ed) *The Uses of Social Investment*, Oxford: Oxford University Press, pp 51–8.

Béland, D. and Cox, R.H. (2016) 'Ideas as coalition magnets: coalition building, policy entrepreneurs, and power relations', *Journal of European Public Policy*, 23(3): 428–45.

Bengtsson, M., de la Porte, C. and Jacobsson, K. (2017) 'Labour market policy under conditions of permanent austerity: any sign of social investment?', *Social Policy & Administration*, 51(2): 367–88.

Bleses, P. and Seeleib-Kaiser, M. (2004) *The Dual Transformation of the German Welfare State*, Basingstoke: Palgrave Macmillan.

Blome, A. (2016) 'Normative beliefs, party competition, and work-family policy reforms in Germany and Italy', *Comparative Politics*, 48(4): 479–503.

Boling, P. (2015) *The Politics of Work-family Policies: Comparing Japan, France, Germany and the United States*, Cambridge: Cambridge University Press.

Bonoli, G., Cantillon, B. and Van Lancker, W. (2017) 'Social investment and the Matthew Effect: limits to a strategy', in A. Hemerijck (ed) *The Uses of Social Investment*, Oxford: Oxford University Press, pp 66–76.

Bray, M. (2020) 'Shadow education in Europe: Growing prevalence, underlying forces, and policy implications', *ECNU Review of Education*, Online First, Available from: https://doi.org/10.1177/2096531119890142 [Accessed 11 October 2020].

Cantillon, B. (2011) 'The paradox of the social investment state: growth, employment and poverty in the Lisbon era', *Journal of European Social Policy*, 21(5): 432–49.

Cantillon, B. and Vandenbroucke, F. (eds) (2013) *Reconciling Work and Poverty Reduction: How Successful Are European Welfare States?*, Oxford: Oxford University Press.

Card, D., Kluve, J. and Weber, A. (2018) 'What works? A meta analysis of recent active labor market program evaluations', *Journal of the European Economic Association*, 16(3): 894–931.

Clasen, J. (2000) 'Motives, means and opportunities: reforming unemployment compensation in the 1990s', *West European Politics*, 23(2): 89–112.

Durazzi, N. (2017) 'Inclusive unions in a dualized labour market? The challenge of organizing labour market policy and social protection for labour market outsiders', *Social Policy & Administration*, 51(2): 265–85.

Durazzi, N., Fleckenstein, T. and Lee, S.C. (2018) 'Social solidarity for all? Trade union strategies, labor market dualization, and the welfare state in Italy and South Korea', *Politics & Society*, 46(2): 205–33.

Emmenegger, P., Häusermann, S., Palier, B. and Seeleib-Kaiser, M. (eds) (2012) *The Age of Dualization: The Changing Face of Inequality in Deindustrializing Societies*, New York: Oxford University Press.

Esping-Andersen, G. (1985) *Politics against Markets: The Social Democratic Road to Power*, Princeton, NJ: Princeton University Press.

Esping-Andersen, G. (2002) 'Towards the good society, once again?', in G. Esping-Andersen, D. Gallie, A. Hemerijck and J. Myles (eds) *Why We Need a New Welfare State?*, Oxford: Oxford University Press, pp 1–25.

Fargion, V. (2009) 'Italy: still a pension state?', in P. Alcock and G. Craig (eds) *International Social Policy*, New York: Palgrave, pp 171–89.

Ferrera, M. (1996) 'The "Southern model" of welfare in social Europe', *Journal of European Social Policy*, 6(1): 17–37.

Fleckenstein, T. (2011a) *Institutions, Ideas and Learning in Welfare State Change: Labour Market Reforms in Germany*, Basingstoke: Palgrave Macmillan.

Fleckenstein, T. (2011b) 'The politics of ideas in welfare state transformation: Christian democracy and the reform of family policy in Germany', *Social Politics*, 18(4): 543–71.

Fleckenstein, T. and Lee, S.C. (2014) 'The politics of postindustrial social policy: family policy reforms in Britain, Germany, South Korea, and Sweden', *Comparative Political Studies*, 47(4): 601–30.

Fleckenstein, T. and Lee, S.C. (2017a) 'The politics of investing in families: comparing family policy expansion in Japan and South Korea', *Social Politics*, 24(1): 1–28.

Fleckenstein, T. and Lee, S.C. (2017b) 'The politics of labor reform in coordinated welfare capitalism: comparing Sweden, Germany, and South Korea', *World Politics*, 69(1): 144–83.

Fleckenstein, T. and Lee, S.C. (2018) 'Caught up in the past? Social inclusion, skills, and vocational education and training policy in England', *Journal of Education and Work*, 31(2): 109–24.

Fleckenstein, T. and Lee, S.C. (2019) 'The political economy of education and skills in South Korea: democratisation, liberalisation and education reform in comparative perspective', *The Pacific Review*, 32(2): 168–87.

Fleckenstein, T., Lee, S.C. and Ban, G. (2019a) 'Modernising the Korean welfare state, society and economy: the need for a new social contract for social and economic progress', in G. Ban (ed) *Developing an Agenda for Social Policy Reform*, Sejong: Korea Research Institute for Vocational Education and Training, pp 93–117.

Fleckenstein, T., Lee, S.C. and Mohun Himmelweit, S. (2019b) 'The political economy of ultra-low fertility and labour market dualization in South Korea', RC19 Annual Conference, Mannheim.

Fleckenstein, T. and Seeleib-Kaiser, M. (2011) 'Business, skills and the welfare state: the political economy of employment-oriented family policy in Britain and Germany', *Journal of European Social Policy*, 21(2): 136–49.

Giddens, A. (1998) *The Third Way: The Renewal of Social Democracy*, Cambridge: Polity Press.

Hemerijck, A. (2017) 'Social investment and its critics', in A. Hemerijck (ed) *The Uses of Social Investment*, Oxford: Oxford University Press, pp 3–39.

Huber, E. and Stephens, J.D. (2001) *Development and Crisis of the Welfare State: Parties and Policies in Global Markets*, Chicago: University of Chicago Press.

Hyman, R. (2001) *Understanding European Trade Unionism: Between Market, Class and Society*, London: Sage.

Jenson, J. (2012) 'Redesigning citizenship regimes after neoliberalism: moving towards social investment', in N. Morel, B. Palier and J. Palme (eds) *Towards a Social Investment Welfare State? Ideas, Policies and Challenges*, Bristol: Policy Press, pp 61–87.

Jessoula, M., Graziano, P.R. and Madama, I. (2010) '"Selective flexicurity" in segmented labour markets: the case of Italian "mid-siders"', *Journal of Social Policy*, 39(4): 561–83.

Johnston, A., Kornelakis, A. and d'Acri, C.R. (2011) 'Social partners and the welfare state: recalibration, privatization or collectivization of social risks?', *European Journal of Industrial Relations*, 17(4): 349–64.

Jones, C. (1993) 'The Pacific challenge: Confucian welfare states', in C. Jones (ed) *New Perspectives on the Welfare State in Europe*, London: Routledge, pp 198–217.

Kinderman, D. (2017) 'Challenging varieties of capitalism's account of business interests: neoliberal think-tanks, discourse as a power resource and employers' quest for liberalization in Germany and Sweden', *Socio-Economic Review*, 15(3): 587–613.

Korpi, W. (1983) *The Democratic Class Struggle*, London: Routledge and Kegan Paul.

Korpi, W. (2000) 'Faces of inequality: gender, class, and patterns of inequalities in different types of welfare states', *Social Politics*, 7(2): 127–91.

Korpi, W. (2006) 'Power resources and employer-centered approaches in explanations of welfare states and varieties of capitalism: protagonists, consenters, and antagonists', *World Politics*, 58(2): 167–206.

Lee, S.C. (2018) 'Democratization, political parties and Korean welfare politics: Korean family policy reforms in comparative perspective', *Government and Opposition*, 53(3): 518–41.

Leitner, S., Ostner, I. and Schmitt, C. (2008) 'Family policies in Germany', in I. Ostner and C. Schmitt (eds) *Family Policies in the Context of Family Change: The Nordic Countries in Comparative Perspective*, Wiesbaden: VS Verlag, pp 175–202.

Lindvall, J. (2010) *Mass Unemployment and the State*, Oxford: Oxford University Press.

Mahon, R. (1997) 'Child care in Canada and Sweden: policy and politics', *Social Politics*, 4(3): 382–418.

Manow, P. and Seils, E. (2000) 'Adjusting badly: the German welfare state', in F. W. Scharpf and V. A. Schmidt (eds) *Welfare and Work in the Open Economy*, vol. 2, Oxford and New York: Oxford University Press, pp 264–307.

Morgan, K.J. (2013) 'Path shifting of the welfare state: electoral competition and the expansion of work-family policies in Western Europe', *World Politics*, 65(1): 73–115.

Nolan, B. (2013) 'What use is "social investment"?', *Journal of European Social Policy*, 23(5): 459–68.

OECD (Organisation for Economic Co-operation and Development) (2018) *A Broken Social Elevator? How to Promote Social Mobility*, Paris: OECD.

OECD (Organisation for Economic Co-operation and Development) (2019a) 'Country note: Korea – PISA 2018 results', Paris: OECD.

OECD (Organisation for Economic Co-operation and Development) (2019b) *Education at a Glance 2019*, Paris: OECD.

Ostner, I. (1998) 'The politics of care policies in Germany', in J. Lewis (ed) *Gender, Social Care and Welfare State Restructuring in Europe*, Aldershot: Ashgate, pp 111–37.

Ostner, I. and Lewis, J. (1995) 'Gender and the evolution of European social policies', in S. Leibfried and P. Pierson (eds) *European Social Policy: Between Fragmentation and Integration*, Washington: Brookings, pp 159–93.

Pascall, G. and Sung, S. (2007) 'Gender and East Asian welfare states: from Confucianism to gender equality', conference paper presented at East Asian Social Policy Research Network.

Regini, M. and Esping-Andersen, G. (1980) 'Trade union strategies and social policy in Italy and Sweden', *West European Politics*, 3(1): 107–23.

Rueda, D. (2005) 'Insider-outsider politics in industrialized democracies: the challenge to social democratic parties', *American Political Science Review*, 99(1): 61–74.

Rueda, D. (2014) 'Dualization, crisis and the welfare state', *Socio-Economic Review*, 12(2): 381–407.

Ryner, J.M. (2004) 'Neo-liberalization of social democracy: the Swedish case', *Comparative European Politics*, 2(1): 97–119.

Sabel, C., Zeitlin, J. and Quack, S. (2017) 'Capacitating services and the bottom-up approach to social investment', in A. Hemerijck (ed) *The Uses of Social Investment*, Oxford: Oxford University Press, pp 140–9.

Schoppa, L.J. (2006) *Race for the Exits: The Unraveling of Japan's System of Social Protection*, Ithaca, NY: Cornell University Press.

Seeleib-Kaiser, M. (2008) 'Welfare state transformations in comparative perspective: shifting boundaries of "public" and "private" social policy?', in M. Seeleib-Kaiser (ed) *Welfare State Transformations: Comparative Perspectives*, Basingstoke: Palgrave Macmillan, pp 1–13.

Seeleib-Kaiser, M., Saunders, A. and Naczyk, M. (2012) 'Shifting the public-private mix: a new dualization of welfare?', in P. Emmenegger, S. Häusermann, B. Palier and M. Seeleib-Kaiser (eds) *The Age of Dualization: The Changing Face of Inequality in Deindustrializing Countries*, Oxford: Oxford University Press, pp 151–75.

Sjöberg, O. (2011) 'Sweden: ambivalent adjustment', in J. Clasen and D. Clegg (eds) *Regulating the Risks of Unemployment: National Adaptations to Post-industrial Labour Markets in Europe*, Oxford: Oxford University Press, pp 208–31.

Song, K.-s. (2019), 'Child care leave taken by fewer than may want it', 7 May, *Korea JoongAng Daily*, Available from https://koreajoongangdaily.joins.com/2019/05/07/economy/Child-care-leave-taken-by-fewer-than-may-want-it/3062779.html [Accessed 11 October 2020].

Stephens, J.D. (1979) *The Transition from Capitalism to Socialism*, London: Macmillan.

Streeck, W. and Thelen, K. (2005) 'Institutional change in advanced political economies', in W. Streeck and K. Thelen (eds) *Beyond Continuity: Institutional Change in Advanced Political Economies*, Oxford: Oxford University Press, pp 1–39.

Strøm, K. (1990) 'A behavioral theory of competitive political parties', *American Journal of Political Science*, 34(2): 565–98.

Sutton Trust (2019) 'Private tuition polling 2019', London: Sutton Trust.

Sutton Trust and Social Mobility Commission (2019) *Elitist Britain 2019: The Educational Background of Britain's Leading People*, London: Sutton Trust and Social Mobility Commission.

Swenson, P.A. (2002) *Capitalists against Markets: The Making of Labor Markets and Welfare States in the United States and Sweden*, Oxford: Oxford University Press.

Thelen, K. (2000) 'Why German employers cannot bring themselves to dismantle the German model', in T. Iversen, J. Pontusson and D. Soskice (eds) *Unions, Employers, and Central Banks: Wage Bargaining and Macro-economic Regimes in an Integrating Europe*, New York: Cambridge University Press, pp 138–72.

Visser, J. and Hemerijck, A. (2000) 'Die pragmatische Anpassung des niederl.ndischen Sozialstaates – ein Lehrstück? [The Pragmatic Adaptation of the Dutch Welfare State – a Best Practice?]', in S. Leibfried and U. Wagschal (eds) *Der Deutsche Sozialstaat. Bilanzen – Reformen – Perspektiven*, Frankfurt: Campus, pp 452–73.

# Index

Page numbers in *italics* refer to tables and figures; 'n' after
a page number indicates the endnote number.